The Communication Theory Reader

How are messages created, transmitted and received? Does our language act as a vehicle for thought or does it determine the nature of thought? Communication theory, the analysis of communication artefacts, has become an increasingly popular and important field of research. *The Communication Theory Reader* is designed to provide a clear introduction to communication studies.

The *Reader* presents the most important work which has shaped the field of communication studies and samples a range of theories from the disciplines of linguistics, semiotics, philosophy, literary theory, film theory and psychoanalysis. The articles are grouped in subject sections, with an editor's introduction, indications of further reading together with a glossary and comprehensive bibliography.

Essays by: Ien Ang, J. L. Austin, Roland Barthes, Émile Benveniste, Mikkel Borch-Jacobsen, Nick Browne, Steven Cohan, Jacques Derrida, Umberto Eco, Stanley Fish, M. A. K. Halliday, Stephen Heath, Wolfgang Iser, Roman Jakobson, Gunther Kress, Jacques Lacan, Theo van Leeuwen, Allan Luke, Jerry Palmer, Charles Sanders Peirce, Janice A. Radway, Ferdinand de Saussure, John Searle, Linda M. Shires, Brian Torode, V. N. Vološinov, Judith Williamson

Paul Cobley is Senior Lecturer in Communications at London Guildhall University.

The

Communication Theory

Reader

Edited by

PAUL COBLEY

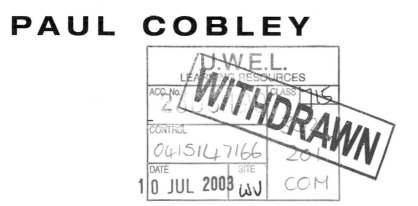

ROUTLEDGE

London and New York

First published 1996
by Routledge
11 New Fetter Lane, London EC4P 4EE

Simultaneously published in the USA and Canada
by Routledge
29 West 35th Street, New York, NY 10001

Typeset in Palatino by Florencetype Ltd, Stoodleigh, Devon

Printed and bound in Great Britain by
Biddles Ltd, Guildford and King's Lynn

British Library Cataloguing in Publication Data
A catalogue record for this book is available from the British Library

Library of Congress Cataloguing in Publication Data
The communication theory reader / [edited by] Paul Cobley.
     p.   cm.
   Includes bibliographical references and index.
   1. Communication–Philosophy.   I. Cobley, Paul, 1963–   .
   P90.C63357   1996
   302.2'01–dc20   96–17464
                                              CIP

ISBN   0–415–14716–6(hbk)
ISBN   0–415–14717–4(pbk)

Contents

PERSON, PROCESS AND PRACTICE

Part V   *THE INSCRIPTION OF THE AUDIENCE IN THE MESSAGE*

CINEMATIC INSCRIPTION

BODIES, SUBJECTS AND SOCIAL CONTEXT

Part VI   *READERS AND READING*

INTERPRETATION, IDEATION AND THE READING PROCESS

THE STUDY OF READERS' MEANINGS

Acknowledgements

Thanks are due to the following people who made this volume possible through their encouragement, advice and enthusiasm: Jerry Palmer; Chris Cudmore; Rebecca Barden; communication theory students past and present; Emily Elkington and my Mum and Dad.

Permission given by the following copyright holders and authors is gratefully acknowledged:

Ferdinand de Saussure, 'The object of linguistics' and 'Linguistic value' from *Course in General Linguistics* ed. by Charles Bally and Albert Sechehaye, trans. Wade Baskin (Glasgow: Fontana, 1974) pp. 7–47; pp. 111–127 © 1974 Peter Owen Ltd

Charles Sanders Peirce, 'A Guess at the Riddle' from *Collected Papers of Charles Sanders Peirce* ed. Charles Hartshorne, Paul Weiss and A. W. Burks (Cambridge, Mass.: Harvard University Press, 1931) paragraphs 365–367 and 269–372 © 1931, 1932, 1959, 1960 The President and Fellows of Harvard College

Émile Benveniste, 'The nature of the linguistic sign', 'The nature of pronouns' and 'Relationships of person in the verb' from *Problems in General Linguistics* trans. Mary Elizabeth Meek (Coral Gables: University of Miami Press, 1970) pp. 43–48; pp. 217–221; pp. 205–215 © 1970 University of Miami Press

V. N. Vološinov, 'Marxism and the philosophy of language' from *Marxism and the Philosophy of Language* trans. I. R. Titunik (New York: Seminar Press, 1973) pp. 58–61; 85–90; 99–106 © 1973

M. A. K. Halliday, 'Introduction to language as social semiotic' and 'Language as social semiotic' from *Language as Social Semiotic: The Social Interpretation of Language and Meaning* (London: Edward

Arnold, 1978) pp. 1–5; pp. 108–126 reprinted by permission of Hodder Headline © Edward Arnold

Steven Cohan and Linda M. Shires, 'Theorising language' from *Telling Stories: A Theoretical Analysis of Narrative Fiction* (London: Routledge, 1988) pp. 10–19 © 1988 Routledge

Roland Barthes, 'Denotation and connotation' from *Elements of Semiology* trans. Annette Lavers and Colin Smith pp. 89–94 (New York: Hill and Wang, 1973) pp. 89–94 © 1973 Farrar, Straus and Giroux Inc.

Roland Barthes, 'The photographic message' from *Image-Music-Text* ed. and trans. Stephen Heath (Glasgow: Fontana, 1977) pp. 15–31 reprinted by permission of HarperCollins © 1977 Fontana (an imprint of HarperCollins)

Umberto Eco, 'How culture conditions the colours we see' from Marshall Blonsky ed., *On Signs: A Semiotics Reader* (Oxford: Basil Blackwell, 1985) pp. 157–175 © 1985 Basil Blackwell

Gunther Kress and Theo van Leeuwen, 'Reading images' from *Reading Images: The Grammar of Visual Design* (London: Routledge, 1996) pp. 21–27 © 1996 Routledge

Jacques Lacan, 'The agency of the letter in the unconscious' from *Écrits: A Selection* trans. Alan Sheridan (London: Tavistock, 1977) pp. 146–154 reprinted by permission of Routledge © 1977 Tavistock Publications

Mikkel Borch-Jacobsen, 'Linguisteries' from *Lacan: The Absolute Master* trans. Douglas Brick (Stanford: Stanford University Press, 1991) pp. 169–182 reprinted by the permission of Stanford University Press © 1991 The Board and Trustees of the Leland Stanford Junior University

Jacques Derrida, 'Semiology and grammatology: interview with Julia Kristeva' from *Positions* trans. Alan Bass (Chicago: University of Chicago Press, 1981) pp. 17–36 © 1981 Chicago University Press

Brian Torode, 'Textuality, sexuality, economy' from David Silverman and Brian Torode eds, *The Material Word: Some Theories of Language and Its Limits* (London: Routledge and Kegan Paul, 1980) pp. 304–327 reprinted by permission of Routledge © 1980 Routledge and Kegan Paul

J. L. Austin, 'Performatives and constatives' from *How to do things with Words* 2nd edn. ed. J. O. Urmson and Marina Sbisa (Oxford: Oxford University Press, 1975) pp. 1–13 © 1975 Oxford University Press

John Searle, 'What is a speech act?' from M. Black ed., *Philosophy in America* (London and Ithaca: George, Allen and Unwin and Cornell University Press) pp. 221–239 reprinted by permission of Routledge © 1965 George, Allen and Unwin and Cornell University Press

Roman Jakobson, 'Shifters and verbal categories' from 'Shifters, verbal categories and the Russian verb' in Roman Jakobson, *Selected Writings* Vol 2 (The Hague: Mouton, 1971) pp. 13–146 reprinted by permission of the Roman Jakobson and Krystyna Pomorska-Jakobson Foundation Inc. © 1971 Roman Jakobson and Krystyna Pomorska-Jakobson Foundation Inc.

Gunther Kress, 'Social processes and linguistic change: time and history in language' from *Linguistic Processes in Sociocultural Practice* (Geelong: Deakin University, 1985) pp. 86–97 © 1985 Deakin University

Nick Browne, 'The spectator-in-the-text: the rhetoric of *Stagecoach*' from *Film Quarterly* 29 (2) pp. 26–26 by permission of the University of California Press and Nick Browne © 1985 The Regents of the University of California

Stephen Heath, 'Narrative space' from *Questions of Cinema* (London: Macmillan, 1981) pp. 51–54 © 1981 Macmillan Press Ltd

Allan Luke, 'The body literate: discourse and inscription in early literacy training' from *Linguistics and Education* 4 (1) 118–129 ©.

Judith Williamson, '. . . But I know what I like: the function of "art" in advertising' from *Consuming Passions: the Dynamics of Popular Culture* (London: Marion Boyars, 1986) pp. 67–74 © Marion Boyars, London, New York

Stanley Fish, 'Why no one's afraid of Wolfgang Iser' from *Diacritics* 11 (March) pp. 2–13 by permission of the Johns Hopkins University Press © 1981 Johns Hopkins University Press

Wolfgang Iser, 'Talk like whales: a reply to Stanley Fish' from *Diacritics* 11 (September) pp. 82–87 by permission of the Johns Hopkins University Press © 1981 Johns Hopkins University Press

Jerry Palmer, 'The act of reading and the reader' from *Potboilers: Methods, Concepts and Case Studies in Popular Fiction* (London: Routledge, 1991) pp. 24–30 © 1991 Routledge

Janice A. Radway, 'Reading the romance' from *Reading the Romance: Women, Patriarchy and Popular Literature* (Chapel Hill: University of North Carolina Press, 1984) pp. 50–51; 55–59; 59–63; 63–67; 210–211; 212 reprinted by permission of University of North Carolina

Press and Verso © 1984 University of North Carolina Press and 1987 Verso

Ien Ang, 'Dallas between reality and fiction' from *Watching Dallas: Soap Opera and the Melodramatic Imagination* (London: Methuen, 1985) pp. 24–34; 47–50 reprinted by permission of Routledge © 1985 Methuen

Special thanks to Gunther Kress and Nick Brown for providing otherwise unobtainable material.

Every effort has been made to trace copyright holders of material reproduced in this volume. Any rights not acknowledged here will be acknowledged in subsequent printings if notice is given to the publisher.

Notes and references in the extracts have been brought into conformity with the rest of this volume.

The gender bias that characterizes many of the extracts (for example, the use of 'he' and 'man' rather than 'he/she' and 'human') has not been altered.

1 **Paul Cobley**

Introduction

In spite of the increasing popularity and importance of the body of work known as 'communication theory', students seeking to become acquainted with it invariably find that the literature seems too vast or too complex to disentangle. This collection of readings is designed to provide easier access to what students of cultural studies, communications and media studies often refer to simply as 'theory', an exciting multidisciplinary area whose boundaries are ever evolving to embrace developments in linguistics, semiology, philosophy and literary theory. Within these boundaries lies a series of fundamental questions regarding communication; 'theory' asks the following: 'How are messages created?' 'How are messages transmitted?' 'How are messages constituted?' 'How are messages received?' 'Why is this the case?' 'Is it because of factors *outside* the message?' 'Or is it because of factors *inside* the message?'

In addressing these issues, the readings in this book are not far removed from the concerns of early mass communications researchers who developed (often unilinear) models for understanding the 'flow' of information (McQuail and Windahl 1993; cf. Beniger 1988). Both share a concern with the way in which 'senders', 'receivers' and 'something in between' are implicated in a process. More accurately, though, the uniting focus of the communication theory expounded in diverse ways by the writers included in this volume is the idea of 'Linguistic processes in socio-cultural practice', (the unwieldy but apt title of a book by Gunther Kress, see pp. 299–313). Linguistics provides the foundations and touchstone for communication theory, often demonstrating how the 'micro' is enshrined in the 'macro' and vice versa, and how language is the central institution of any society. Approaching communication by way of linguistic theory also raises the philosophical question of language's relation to other processes of mind: does language act as a vehicle for thought or does it actually determine the nature of thought?

Theories generated from different disciplines that concern themselves with these dilemmas have shaped communication theory's history in a complex way, prompting further common questions about how one body of work is relevant to another. 'What is the relation of semiology and linguistics?' is a frequent question (cf. Tobin 1990; Rauch 1978). Others include: 'What is the relation of semiology to semiotics?' 'Is structuralism simply semiology?' 'What is the difference between structuralism and post-structuralism?' 'Which comes first?' 'What is the role of the social world and human subjects in structuralism and post-structuralism?' 'What is required of a thoroughly social theory of communication?' To begin to answer these queries and to attempt to situate communication theory we must consider its tangled, unevenly developed and often bewildering international history.

SAUSSUREAN LINGUISTICS AND ITS INFLUENCE

The story of Ferdinand de Saussure and his influence on later generations of (mainly French-speaking) thinkers is probably the best known of those to be recounted here (see, for example, Culler 1976; Hawkes 1977; Merquior 1986; Sturrock 1979a, 1986). Saussure was born in 1857 and went to study at the University of Leipzig in 1876 where, two years later, he published his paper on the system of vowels in Indo-European languages. It was somewhat of a fluke that, in 1906, as a professor teaching Sanskrit at the University of Geneva, he was assigned to teach the course in general linguistics (1906–11) that would gain him reknown (Culler 1976 p. 15; Vickers 1993 p. 4). Saussure died in 1913; however, in 1916, his students published the *Course in General Linguistics,* compiled from the notes they made while attending Saussure's lectures. The editors point out in their introduction to this book that they are aware of their responsibility to the author who 'would not have authorized the publication of these pages' (Saussure 1974 p. xxxii).

The strange genesis of the book and the discrepancy between the historical Saussure and the author of the *Course* did not curtail the influence of some key components of the publication's argument. One clear example, the notion of the linguistic sign and its 'arbitrariness', would later be crucial for those applying Saussure's observations to artefacts outside language. Positing the sign as a dual entity composed of 'signifier' (material substance) and 'signified' (mental concept) allowed Saussure to argue that no *real, natural* link existed between the two but rather a conventional, unmotivated or arbitrary one (Saussure 1974 p. 67). In this way, language was to be thought of as a self-contained system of *differences* between signs (ibid. pp. 114–115) and therefore not bound to the world at large. Another important point for those who were to follow was that this system of differences could be conceived as language's social aspect. For Saussure the general phenomenon of language could be described with recourse to two terms in French: *parole* (individual acts of speech) and *langue* (the whole system of differences shared by a community in order to generate instances of *parole*) (ibid. p. 19; pp. 77–78). Saussure insisted that 'language is not complete in any speaker; it exists perfectly only within a collectivity' (see this volume p. 43); this was how the *Course* proposed that communication through language was a wholly social process.

Other features of the *Course* are also particularly evident in later attempts to recruit Saussure to a wide-ranging investigation of communication. Combination of linguistic units into larger communicative portions was envisaged by him in terms of 'syntagmatic' relations and 'associative' (or 'paradigmatic') relations. The former consist of linear connections, how words in a sentence, for example, are juxtaposed according to strict rules; the latter consist of the ways in which mental associative series allow for the substitution of one term for another (for example a word synonymous for another in a sentence) provided it complies with syntagmatic relations (pp. 124–127). The power of these rules was sufficient for Saussure to propose, in an oft quoted passage, 'a science that studies the life of signs within society', a science which he called 'semiology' (p. 16). This would also be 'synchronic' (p. 101–102) in its orientation: that is to say, it would look at the state of things, the rules governing items in a current system. Here, then, was a cue for introducing Saussurean principles outside the field of linguistics.

In Europe the *Course* did initially find prominence among linguists and its most celebrated explicators have been Louis Hjelmslev (1899–1965) from Denmark and Émile Benveniste (1902–76) from France. But the most far-reaching elevation of Saussurean principles into a quasi-science was effected in the 1950s by the French anthropologist, Claude Lévi-Strauss (b. 1908). Lévi-Strauss produced a huge body of work, much of it based on solid field research, but his writings on the nature of myth in particular demonstrate his debt to linguistics and his centrality as part of a movement in the human sciences, 'structuralism', which derives its name partly from the intellectual system he devised. The conclusions that Lévi-Strauss reached about Saussure – that 'language can be analyzed into things which are at the same time similar yet different' (Lévi-Strauss 1977 p. 209) – were initially prompted by his discovery of the linguistics of the Prague School, specifically that branch of language study known as phonology (the study of the binary principles that govern the organization of sounds in language). Having attended lectures given in New York in 1942–3 by the Russian born Prague linguist, Roman Jakobson (1896–1982), and consulted the work of the Russian phonologist, N. S. Troubetzkoy (1890–38), Lévi-Strauss 'discovered that anthropology of the nineteenth and even early twentieth century had been content [rather than form], as was the linguistics of the neo-grammarians' (1987 p. 139). His work from this time forward reveals how he reversed the priorities of what he saw as an outmoded discipline by adopting a resolutely *synchronic* approach to anthropological phenomena.

In his study of myth, Lévi-Strauss might be said to be searching through numerous examples of *parole* (individual myths) in order to reconstruct a universal *langue* (or master code). The most famous example of this is his 1955 interpretation of the Oedipus myth in which he treats it 'as an orchestra score would be if it were unwittingly considered as a unilinear series' (1977 p. 213). The method is systematic and is a typical example of his 'structuralist' approach:

Say, for instance, we were confronted with a sequence of the type: 1, 2, 4, 7, 8, 1, 3, 4, 6, 8, 1, 4, 5, 7, 8, 1, 2, 5, 7, 3, 4, 5, 6, 8 . . . the assignment being put to all the 1's together, all the 2's, the 3's, the result is a chart:

1	2		4			7	8
	2	3	4		6		8
1			4	5		7	8
1	2			5		7	
		3	4	5	6		8

(Lévi-Strauss 1977 p. 213)

He concludes that 'The kind of logic in mythical thought is as rigorous as modern science, and that the difference lies not in the quality of the intellectual process, but in the nature of things to which it is applied' (p. 230). The implication is that human thought is programmed by a pre-determined set of co-ordinates: a language.

Lévi-Strauss was not alone in proposing such formulae at this time. In a series of articles in the late 1950s and early 1960s, which culminated in the 1966 book, *Sémantique structurale*, A. J. Greimas (1917–1992) worked out a semiotic project influenced by Hjelmslev and Saussure. Considering myth and narrative, Greimas, in a fashion which, from a distance at least, seems akin to that of Lévi-Strauss, gave priority to structural relations between narrative entities rather than to their intrinsic qualities. Characters in myth, for example, exist as *actants*, strictly functions such as 'hero' and 'villain' (Schleifer 1987). Greimas also drew on the work of the Russian folk-lorist, Vladimir Propp (1895–1970). Propp's *The Morphology of the Folktale* originally appeared in Russian in 1928 and his work is often associated with the Russian Formalists (Jameson 1972 pp. 64–69; Hawkes 1977 pp. 67–69). The *Morphology* – appearing in translation, conveniently, in 1958 (see Dundes 1968) – characterized one hundred Russian folktales in terms of a small number of 'functions' or story actions (Propp 1968). Although Propp's work is by no means identical to that of Greimas and Lévi-Strauss – in fact, the latter wrote an incisive critique of Propp in 1961 (see Lévi-Strauss 1978) – it exudes a confidence in the ability to reduce complex components of culture to finite sets of structural rules.

Lévi-Strauss remained an unrepentant reductionist, revealing the *langue* behind copious examples of *parole*. Most criticisms of his structuralism involve misgivings regarding his reductive approach or, indeed, some scepticism over whether culture can actually be interrogated on a purely linguistic basis. Sperber argues that Lévi-Strauss was only one of many in the 1940s and 1950s who believed in and sought a unified science of communication based on semiology, cybernetics and information theory (Sperber 1979 p. 48). Almost contemporary with Lévi-Strauss, another French man likewise harboured a 'euphoric dream of scientificity' (quoted in Coward and Ellis 1977 p. 25).

In a series of essays written for French magazines between 1954 and 1956 Roland Barthes (1915–80) displayed his recently gained faith in a science of signs. *Mythologies* (1973; original French edition 1957) – the book in which these essays were collected, along with a further long and more technical essay entitled 'Myth Today' – reveals a debt to aspects of both the work of Saussure and Hjelmslev. The essays all focus on a feature of French life and media representation and seek to unveil the means by which *constructed* entities – the 'spectacle' of wrestling, the Hollywood-generated hairstyles of Romans in films, the allure of the striptease, etc. – pose as *natural* occurrences. As John Sturrock states, 'The bourgeoisie is the villain of *Mythologies*' (1979a p. 62) precisely because it is instrumental in the attempt to pass off as neutral those elements of culture which, when demystified (or *demythified*), are revealed as ideologically charged. Barthes clearly treats cultural artefacts as if they were bound in a self-perpetuating system which does not relate at all to the real world of social relations. In doing this, he re-enacts Saussure's argument regarding the 'arbitrary' relation of the sign's notation to the sign's concept. Coupled with this is the notion of the sign's ability to both denote and *connote*, the latter being the ability of the denotative sign to signify a general realm of systematic sign functioning, a master code of values and beliefs (see the sketchy comments of Hjelmslev 1961 pp. 114–125; original Danish edition 1943).

It would not be an exaggeration to say that Barthes' reputation as a penetrating analyst of popular cultural forms during this period rests on his application of these two arguments (see Barthes 1973 pp. 109–115; see also this volume pp. 129–33) demonstrated through a series of articles written in the early 1960s of which 'The Photographic Message' (see this volume pp. 134–47) and 'The Rhetoric of the Image' (see Barthes 1977) are the most famous. The problem that Barthes negotiates in both of these essays concerns the specific mode of visual (or analogic) signification and the way in which it might invoke second order connotative codes. For students these analyses, although gracefully articulated, can be very confusing. And with good reason; for Barthes insists on the internal, rule-bound nature of the signification in the photograph, explaining that the system which produces connotation is as governed by strict laws as that which allows denotation. At the same time, however, Barthes extends the realm of the analysis out beyond the components of the message itself, into the social world.

By cataloguing the items that appear in, for example, a pasta ad, and further listing the associations these engender, Barthes first maps the concept of denotation onto syntagmatic relations and, secondly, maps connotation onto paradigmatic relations. The schema which describes this mapping appears as Figure 1.1.

This seems like a very mechanical way of going about analysing the formation of meanings and Barthes is keen to point out that the process happens so quickly, particularly when we see a photograph, that it seems that it is not a process at all, as if connotation is *there* right from the start (1977 pp. 36–37). When theoretically interrogated, the denotative sign (made up of signified and signifier) is also a connotative signifier. That is to say, it is the material part of a whole connotative sign. The other part of the connotative sign is, of course, the connotative *signified* with which the connotative signifier must be inseparable if this schema is to be faithful to Saussure. However, the realm of the connotative signified ('myth' as Barthes calls it in his early work) is one which is *outside* the sign proper. Barthes initially attempts to systematize this realm and show that it is subject to convention but, as his work progresses, he begins to hint at the futility of such a project, writing that the realm's 'character is at once general, global and diffuse' (1990 p. 91).

How much of a message's meaning is determined from within and how much is determined from without? Barthes' attempt to answer this question by means of a science of signs was ill fated but, even so, should not be written off. His close analytic readings, informed by an implicit use of Saussure's notion of syntagmatic/paradigmatic interaction, have informed the practice of students of media, culture and communications to the present day. The perennial predicament of communications is thus evident as a turning point in Barthes' work. In a later book, *S/Z* (1973; translated

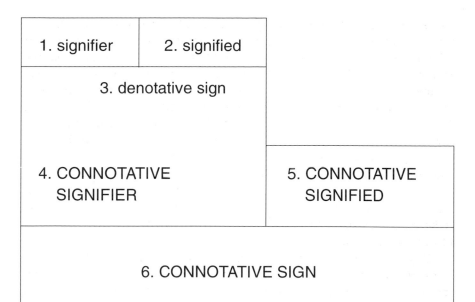

Figure 1.1

Source: adapted from Barthes (1973a p. 115 and 1973b p. 90)

1974) Barthes ponders the problem from a slightly different angle. Here he speaks in the opening pages of two kinds of texts, the *readerly* and the *writerly*, where the reader is respectively an idle *consumer* of the text or a diligent *producer* of it, almost rewriting what is presented (pp. 3–4). Barthes goes so far as to actively advocate the latter position but, curiously, the intense analysis which follows these comments and makes up the majority of the book produces an implicitly conflicting conclusion. *S/Z* dissects a Balzac short story, 'Sarrasine', dividing it up into very brief segments and by elaborating five codes through whose matrix the text passes. The result is to expose an abundancy of meanings, making a text which might have been billed as a 'simple realist narrative' into one which now threatens to be eminently 'writerly'. The importance of this for communication theory will become clearer shortly.

POST-STRUCTURALISM

Barthes' early work benefited, as we have observed, from the notion of the 'arbitrariness' of the sign. However, this Saussurean tenet had actually been laid to rest as early as 1939 (see this volume pp. 63–9) by the linguist Benveniste, who argued that the relations between the material substance of a sign and the mental concept attached to it were far from being arbitrary. In fact, the creation of a concept in the human mind which is prompted by sign material is rehearsed so often at an early age that it becomes an almost instantaneous process. Consequently the connection between a sign's materiality (signifier) and the concept it incites (signified) seems almost natural and should, more accurately, be stated as a *necessary* rather than an arbitrary relation. Benveniste's concern with the way in which signs work for the human subject points the way to further influential explorations of language and ultimately, it could be argued, to 'post-structuralism'. Although, as Easthope points out (1988 p. xxiii), the label 'post-structuralism' is not recognized in France in the same way as it is in the English-speaking academic world, the term is of use in designating a set of concerns with the role of the human subject in communication. Paradoxically, however, the questions that 'post-structuralism' asks about subjectivity in language were formulated by Benveniste in the 1940s, *before* the advent of Lévi-Strauss' structuralism.

In his essays on 'Subjectivity in language' and 'The nature of pronouns' (see this volume pp. 285–91) collected in the 1966 book *Problèmes de linguistique générale* (English translation 1971), Benveniste showed how linguistic categories not only allow human subjects to refer to themselves but actually create the parameters of human self-consciousness. He writes:

> 'Ego' is he who *says* 'ego'. That is where we see the foundation of 'subjectivity' which is determined by the linguistic status of 'person'.
>
> Consciousness of self is only possible if it is experienced by contrast. I use *I* only when I am speaking to someone who will be a *you* in my address.
>
> (Benveniste 1971 p. 225)

Because 'I' is a linguistic category – and therefore usable by the whole linguistic community – it cannot begin to represent the fullness of one human being's self-consciousness. It is only a word. However, as relations in the linguistic sign are *necessary*, it invariably feels natural to humans that the word does have this power to represent.

Structuralism tended to focus on isolated signs devoid of context, which meant that meaning was not necessarily viewed as a dynamic force, unfolding throughout the whole of a discourse, nor was it viewed as something that might change depending on the identity of the user or enunciator of that discourse. What Benveniste shows, conversely, is that a linguistic category such as 'I' relies wholly on the identity of the speaker for its meaning and that understanding an utterance (an instance of *parole*) also requires understanding how the many signs surrounding that utterance which make up a discourse (numerous instances of *parole*) may lend it a specific meaning. Where structuralism was content to describe how human subjects are caught up in the play of language, largely because the structure of culture was thought to be a product of the shape of the human mind, Benveniste paves the way for a vision of human subjectivity which itself is *created* by the institution of language. As Kaja Silverman insists, 'signification occurs only through discourse, . . . discourse requires a subject, and . . . the subject itself is an effect of discourse' (1983 p. vii). In post-structuralism, language, because it pre-exists the human being, therefore moulds and facilitates the expression of the mind's contents.

These ideas are especially significant for the French psychoanalyst, Jacques Lacan (1901–81). If language is the facilitator of the mind in social spaces (i.e. it allows us to talk about ourselves to others) the fact that we use the same signs tends to suggest that language somehow misses something, is unable to express the purely personal. For Lacan, this 'missing something' which is not accessible to language is the domain of the unconscious. In 1957 Lacan delivered a lecture at the Sorbonne entitled 'L'instance de la lettre dans l'inconscient ou la raison depuis Freud' (see this volume pp. 186–93), which incorporates a significant critique of Saussure, whilst also pursuing a series of related questions evident in Lacan's work since the completion of his Ph.D thesis in 1932 (see Benvenuto and Kennedy 1986 p. 107; Payne 1993 p. 74). In his published articles and conference papers before 1957, at a time when, internationally, psychoanalysis was entrenched in what were by now orthodox questions regarding therapy, Lacan had simultaneously insisted on a revaluation of Freud's early works along with an examination of the place of Saussurean linguistics in psychoanalytic investigation. Lacan's reorientation of Saussure was to be as startling as his reorientation of Freud.

Taking the fundamental constituent of the *Course in General Linguistics*, Saussure's map of the sign with 'signified' on top of 'signifier' enclosed by an ellipse, Lacan inverts it and opens it up. Although the language and breadth of thought Lacan employs make his argument seem very difficult, the crux of the matter is quite simple. He presents a picture of two identical doors distinguished only by the writing which appears above them (Figure 1.2).

Clearly, this is a version of Saussure's map (or algorithm) of the sign (Figure 1.3).

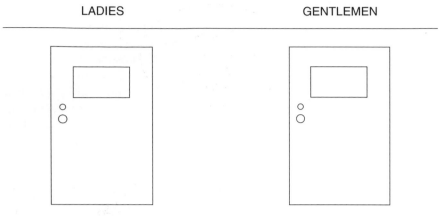

Figure 1.2

Source: Lacan 1977 (see this volume p. 190 and p. 200)

What is important here is that the priorities of Saussure are reversed by Lacan. The *signified* (or mental concept) of what lies behind each door is determined entirely by the *signifier* (or linguistic notation – 'Ladies', 'Gentlemen') that lies above the door. A whole cultural law – as Lacan puts it, the subjection of public life to the law of urinary segregation (see this volume p. 190) – is engendered by the existence and location of the two signifiers as well as their *difference* from one another. Whereas Saussure would have it that the mental concept pre-exists the word which simply becomes attached to the signified in an arbitrary way, Lacan seeks to demonstrate that the mental concept is *created* by the way in which language operates. So, in addition to inverting the priorities in the algorithm, Lacan also banishes the ellipse and reinforces the bar that separates signifier and signified to emphasize that there is an incessant possibility of the signified sliding under the signifier. The signifier is therefore responsible for the birth of subjectivity; however, it does not give birth to the human as a whole. There remains in the human a complex domain of desires – the unconscious – ruled by an order which is totally different from that of the social institution, language.

The implications of Lacan's inversion of the Saussurean algorithm for communication theory may not seem immediately clear. However, this aspect of Lacan's work – and it is only a small one at that – became very influential in film theory circles, particularly in the 1970s in Britain (see this volume pp. 13–18; 352–5). The Sorbonne lecture in which Lacan revolutionized Saussure took place, as has been noted, in 1957, the year that

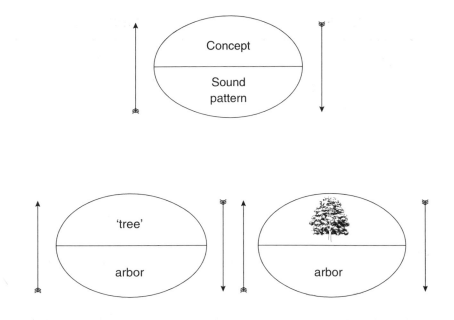

Figure 1.3

Source: Saussure (1974 p. 114)

Barthes' heavily structuralist opus, *Mythologies*, first appeared. While British theorists in the early 1970s grappled with structuralist methodologies based, often, on recent French translations of texts by Lévi-Strauss, Barthes and others, it is curious to consider that what might be called the post-structuralist age proper was inaugurated by the publication in 1967 of three books by the Algerian-born French philosopher, Jacques Derrida (b. 1930). Throughout his career, Derrida has maintained good public relations and commanded attention by both the depth of his knowledge and his pro-claimed assault on virtually the whole Western philosophical tradition since Plato. It can be argued that the well-spring of this assault is the intellectual milieu in which he found himself in France in the 1960s. His famous paper at the 'Languages of Criticism and the Sciences of Man Conference' in Baltimore during 1966 consisted of a lengthy critique of Lévi-Strauss' struc-turalism, kicking off in the process the highly influential 'method' of 'decon-struction' with which Derrida is problematically associated in North America (see Macksey and Donato 1972; Norris 1982); similarly, central to *Of Grammatology* is a detailed critical consideration of Saussure's pronounce-ments on writing (Derrida 1976 pp. 27–73; original French edition 1967).

It is Derrida's comments on the Saussurean tradition which have been particularly fruitful for communication theory. Employing a method which has proved extremely useful in his investigations of Western philosophy Derrida 'reads on the margins' of Saussure: he alights on that part of the *Course in General Linguistics* which has generally been neglected by structuralists in favour of the aspects of the book which by the 1960s were considered commonplace in French intellectual circles. The section of the *Course* in question is that on 'Graphic representation of language' (Saussure 1974 pp. 23–31) which contains some of Saussure's more outrageous assertions. Derrida puts these under scrutiny and demonstrates that Saussure's implication is that there exists a hierarchy of social world, representation of this world by speech, and representation of speech by writing: in short, Saussure holds that writing is an impoverished form of speech. Yet, if Saussure was to be consistent about the 'arbitrariness' of the sign, then he should surely say that the written *and* the verbal signifier are *both* conventionally linked to a signified. Derrida takes Saussure to task for his inconsistency and insists on taking to its logical limit the Saussurean notion of signification by means of a sign's difference from another sign. If the means by which linguistic elements signify is by difference from each other then surely all signs, including written ones, function according to this principle; indeed, writing is preeminently embroiled in difference by virtue of the distinctions of notation that are required in order to identify discrete letters (see Derrida 1976 pp. 50–51; Norris 1987 pp. 87–94).

Derrida pursues the idea of difference further, using it to illustrate some general principles of signification that Saussure failed to elaborate. Chief among these is the idea of the unfolding of meaning through syntagmatic relations which is not dissimilar to the way in which, for Silverman and Benveniste, signification occurs through discourse. For Derrida, however, something special takes place in the unfolding of a syntagm (instance of *parole* or discourse). Take a sentence such as 'The cat sat on the mat': clearly, the 'mat' by the time one reaches it in the syntagm is one that is occupied by a cat and is conceived accordingly. But what Derrida also implies is that while 'the cat' might be envisaged as a standing one when first encountered, by the end of the syntagm it has been retroactively constructed as not only sitting but also in contact with a 'mat'. The sitting and the mat are built into the conception of the cat from the start. So, two Derridean terms are relevant here: 'trace' and '*différance*'. The sign 'cat' carries the 'trace' of those signs that are built into it in order for signification to take place (in this case, 'sat' and 'mat'). In addition, the sign 'cat' *differs* from other signs in the syntagm and this, in a Saussurean fashion, imputes to it a value or meaning; yet the more comprehensive version of the meaning of 'cat' can begin to be grasped only if its present meaning is *deferred* until 'sat' and 'mat' appear in the syntagm. Thus Derrida coins the new term, *différance*, which describes this process and is pronounced identically to the French word for 'difference' but is *written*, ironically, in a distinct way. Treating this term in Derridean mode, then, one would say that it carries not only the 'trace' of Saussure's 'difference' but also the extra trace of 'deferring' (Derrida 1982 pp. 14–15).

Much of what has made 'deconstruction' controversial, especially among literary theorists in the United States, stems from these propositions of Derrida (see Ellis 1989 pp. 18–66). For not only does Derrida propose that *différance* takes place in the simplest kind of examples such as the one given above but also that it ranges across all texts. Moreover, the act of deferral experienced in signification, both backward through the past and forward through the future, is, according to Derrida (1982 p. 13) potentially endless. This should be a cause for some panic as it implies that meaning can never be established definitively. However, the discrepancy between potential phenomena and what actually happens in communication is one that is recognized by Derrida and which will become evident (see this volume pp. 209–24). If there is one salient feature of Derrida's teaching that should not be neglected when reading other works of communication theory it is the arguments by which he creates an awareness of the multiplicity of texts, their constant flux and their capacity for polysemy.

AN EPISODE FROM BRITISH POST-STRUCTURALISM

Although it might be possible to say that Lacan's influence on British theory in the 1970s and 1980s almost eclipsed that of Derrida (cf. Easthope 1988 p. xii) the character of British post-structuralism, as distinct from the French variety, is defined by the existing intellectual landscape in Britain. Structuralism in France arose out of an education system and a set of political values much different from those of the Anglo-Saxon world. An oft noted factor in the difference between the British and French sensibilities is that philosophy is taught at secondary school level in France; in addition, philosophical problems are posed against a backdrop of the continental tradition of thought: Hegel, Schopenhauer, phenomenology and hermeneutics rather than the empirical tradition associated with British thinking. This philosophical bent was enhanced in France from the 1940s to the 1960s by the fact that the cradle of structuralist and post-structuralist thought was the elitist Grandes Ecoles, especially the Ecole Normale Supérieure (roughly equivalent to Oxford and Cambridge in Britain) which tolerated new movements in a fashion unknown to British academia. In Britain during the 1970s and 1980s the most productive work in theory was carried out in polytechnics (now called 'new universities' and not to be confused with the French Polytechnique), thus spreading continental ideas to a broader audience but bypassing the acceptance of mainstream British intellectual culture. The two most celebrated occasions when British elitist academia was confronted by the spectre of modern contintental thought concerned the ejection of Colin MacCabe from Cambridge in 1981 (for teaching 'structuralism') and the opposition to Derrida who was offered an honorary doctorate at Cambridge in 1992 (see Simpson 1990; O'Leary 1992). It is also worth mentioning that theoretical ideas developed freely in France at a time when the question of the relevance of degree courses to the job market was one which was not really taken seriously; conversely, through the late 1970s and early 1980s in Britain, theoretical competence began to take on an increasingly vocational guise in spite of some of the misgivings of its pedagogues (see, for instance, Donald 1990).

Another factor in the promotion of theoretical ideas where Britain differs from France is the latter's indulgence of the intellectual as celebrity. It was precisely Jean-Paul Sartre's celebrity as the dominant Leftist post-war thinker in France which provided the yardstick and *bête noire* for the generation of ambitious academics that followed him. Sartre's domination of the post-war intellectual scene in France, it could be argued, meant that his brand of humanist Marxism gave birth to the anti-humanism (where the subject is merely the bearer of the structure of society, rather than an agent) of Althusser, Foucault, Lévi-Strauss, Derrida and Lacan. But it is also the capacity of Sartre and his successors for creating (media) movements around such matters as existentialism, structuralism and post-structuralism that is perplexing to the Anglo-Saxon mind and which is often refracted in its transmission across the Channel. While Baudrillard makes pronouncements about the Gulf War in the *Guardian*, who in Britain pays attention to the celebrity philosophers feted in France during the 1980s and early 1990s, Rightist thinkers such as Alain de Benoist and Henri-Bernard Lévy? Manifestly, theory has had a special context in France, mainly because of the special place that intellectuals and Left-wing ideas hold in French life. The intensity of the student revolt of May 1968 in Paris, for example, in itself offers a stark contrast with Britain, but it was also seen in France as an opportunity for theorists to transcend those rigid structures of French education which gave rise to the unrest. This opportunity was not uniformly seized (although an apocryphal story has it that the student leader, Daniel Cohn-Bendit, wanted by the French police, was smuggled to safety in the boot of a car driven across the Franco-German border by Jacques Lacan).

The high-point of Left-wing activism in Britain took place, as Easthope describes (1988 pp. 1–3), six years later than in France, with the miners' strike, power cuts and the three-day week, culminating in the collapse of the Conservative government in the early months of 1974. It is against this backdrop of industrial unrest and, in intellectual circles, the temporary coalition of a humanist, culturalist tradition in British Marxism and an anti-humanist, structuralist version of Marxism borrowed from Althusser, that British post-structuralism begins to find its niche (p. 3). The central figure for new work on communication in the 1970s was Jacques Lacan. Far more than Derrida's *oeuvre*, a version of Lacan made headway in British theorizing, particularly in the study of film. The key component of the version of Lacan that dominated the writing of contributors to the journal, *Screen*, in the 1970s and early 1980s was the notion of the semiological *production* of the subject. In fact, this was where Lacan had the edge over Derrida in Britain: human subjectivity in Derrida's early writings featured in an implicit way and his comments in this area seemed, to many, to bear too much resemblance to that of the structuralists (see Dews 1987 pp. 91–101). It must be added, though, that Derrida's later work contains some eminently sensible remarks on the way in which human subjectivity has been a historical concept caught up in the play of *différance* (see Derrida 1991). Nevertheless, Lacan made a more suitable ideological ally for British Marxism in the 1970s and, as David Macey puts it, '*Screen*'s approach to Lacan [was] from the outset strikingly instrumental' (1988 p. 16).

The project of *Screen* in the 1970s, which has been assessed on numerous occasions (Britton 1979; Easthope 1982; McDonnell and Robins 1980) was built on a fusion of Althusserian Marxism, a feminism unhindered by questions of class and a blinkered version of psychoanalysis (diluted Lacan). One might say that the chief aim of *Screen* was to explore the way in which the human subject, constituted partly by the state apparatuses of capitalism which provided him or her with a place in the relations of production, is made even more suitable for the purposes of capitalism by being constructed at an early age through the patriarchal family and, continually, by such items of ideology as film, which places the subject in yet more relations which invariably serve the requirements of the capitalist system. In a sense, the *Screen* theorists were pursuing the argument from Lacan that signification, specifically the signifier, is responsible for producing subjectivity. To this end, film was frequently discussed in terms of its communication – and provision – of a position to be occupied by the spectator in viewing the film. At the moment of viewing, numerous essays argue, the subject not only engages with the narrative and the organization of shots in the film, but also is *sewn into* the very fabric of the movie, helping to reproduce a subjectivity which, if not subservient to ruling ideology, is, at least for a time, complicit with it. Although this may sound like a sophisticated conspiracy theory it actually produced a number of sincere attempts to analyse the processes by which capitalism – in the sphere of ideology as opposed to the sphere of coercion (police forces, the law, etc.) – sought to maintain itself.

In a much-hyped essay, Laura Mulvey (1975) describes how the very act of looking is split between active/male and passive/female, a troublesome coupling which she exacerbates by asserting that the act of viewing as it is constructed in mainstream film sets the woman up as spectacle. The spectator of a film, she argues, watches in order to simultaneously replay the act of looking in early childhood which the child uses to situate him/(her)self in relation to others and to satisfy his/(her) voyeuristic impulses, usually on a representation of woman. Viewing is therefore to be construed as a masculine, patriarchal act and the way to break with this kind of tyranny, Mulvey suggests at the end of her essay, is through 'radical' film (cf. Dyer 1979 pp. 58–59; de Lauretis 1984 pp. 37–69; Doane 1987 pp. 6–10; L. Williams 1984; and Jay 1994). This *Screen* shibboleth, 'radical' cinema, is also to be understood as an invocation of the German playwright, Bertholt Brecht (1898–1956) whose writings on theatre revolve around 'naturalist' drama which tries to pass off its contents as 'realistic', and 'epic' theatre, which draws attention to itself, and basically announces its contents as 'only a play' (see Brecht 1964). In a series of articles for *Screen*, culminating in the book, *Questions of Cinema* (1981), Stephen Heath promotes the second kind of representation favoured by Brecht while analysing the former. Heath restates the division between the human being and language as outlined by Benveniste (see this volume p. 8) and notes also how the signifier 'creates' the subject in Lacanian terms; he then argues that the division between the human and language entails that the human being is constantly trying to engage with language (to enact subjectivity, to carve out a place in the world), and the subject tries to 'perform' this in numerous ways, one of which is through viewing films. What 'narrative' ('mainstream') film does is to allow this 'performance', but only within limits; the way in which a narrative film might round-off and resolve a narrative, with a happy ending for instance, effectively makes cinema spectators forget that there is a division between their desires and the world of representation which allows the articulation of those desires (Heath 1981 pp. 117–19; see also this volume pp. 352–5).

These arguments, derived from the publications of both Benveniste and Lacan, are crucial to the *Screen* writers. For them, there is something very distinctive about the way 'mainstream' films are organized which reconciles spectators to their place in the capitalist system. This, they feel, can really be challenged only by a 'radical' practice of film which is not unlike the kind of theatre advocated by Brecht. The task of providing a means of referring to these arguments without becoming overburdened by jargon was carried out by Colin MacCabe. In two articles in particular (1974, 1977) and a book (1978), MacCabe demonstrates how certain texts can serve to disrupt subject positions and others serve only to maintain them. He argues (1974) that the nineteenth-century novel provides a model for a kind of text (literary, cinematic or televisual) which, through the erection of an internal hierarchy, purports to be able to accurately narrate the real. MacCabe calls this model 'the classic realist text'. An example of the hierarchy in the 'classic realist text' concerns inverted commas: those words which are presented inside inverted commas consist of dialogue, characters' speech, and are therefore to be treated as secondary items; of primary importance are the words outside inverted commas, the narrative prose. As a rule, narrative prose is able to state 'truths' about the world and control or contextualize what goes on in characters' speech. In audio-visual presentations the same things occur: characters may talk, but the way scenes in a narrative which contain those characters is arranged both controls and contextualizes what the characters utter. Films as well as novels of this kind purport to present, in an unbiased fashion, 'what is there' in the world; but, as MacCabe argues, what they efface is the fact that, at all times, they are perspectival, narrated from a point of view. Even a realist film with a strong anti-capitalist slant cannot be considered as revolutionary because, for MacCabe, it will still partake of those old methods of revealing 'what is there' and expecting spectators to take action on the basis of some depicted injustice; what is required, instead, is a thoroughgoing change to modes of representation, a change to the way we see.

In the same way as subjects believe themselves to be capable of expressing desires through language, the 'classic realist text' believes that it can express the truth of the world. The 'classic realist text' therefore embarks on an act of collusion with subjects to cover up the fact that there is a gap between human beings and they who posit themselves in language. MacCabe's is a useful and digestible way of thinking about different kinds of texts and the various modes by which they might invite an audience to read them; there is a also a clear overlap with the work of Heath and his observations on 'performance'. The main problem with the conception of the 'classic realist text', however, is that it underestimates 'realism'. If one were to compare MacCabe's arguments to those of Barthes in *S/Z* then there can be little doubt that the *readerly* corresponds to 'classic realism' and the *writerly* can be mapped onto the 'radical' or 'revolutionary' text. As has been noted (see p. 7), Barthes' conclusions in *S/Z* tended to imply the richness of interpretation to be culled from the scrutiny of a realist text. Marshalling these same arguments against MacCabe, David Lodge (1981) insists that 'realist' fiction is as much an instance of representation as *any* kind of writing; therefore, *every* text, by virtue of its own divorce from the world that it represents, re-enacts the split between language and reality: as Wolfgang Iser has stated succinctly, 'no rendering can *be* that which it renders' (1989 p. 251).

Without being overly reductive, the *Screen* project can be characterized as an attempt, once more, to answer the question of where meaning is to be found in communication, with the added goal of describing how certain kinds of communication *constitute* the reader. Not surprisingly, these questions were also posed elsewhere by different means.

SPEECH-ACT THEORY AND READER-RESPONSE

One of the most influential strands in contemporary American thought in the 1970s and 1980s actually evolved from the writings of an English philosopher, J. L. Austin (1911–60). His most famous work, *How to Do Things with Words*, was published in 1965, although the lectures on which it was based were given at Harvard in 1955 and Austin remarks in the preface that these were derived from ideas formulated in 1939 (Austin 1980 p. vi). Those ideas are built on some premises which are actually quite simple to comprehend and are stated with such economy and eloquence by Austin (see this volume pp. 255–62) that it is unnecessary to rehearse them at any length here. The general point that it is crucial to understand is that Austin looks not at how a language is composed but what it *does*. Whereas Saussure sought to produce a synchronic 'cross-section' of language's rules (*langue*) Austin focuses on the way instances of *parole* or 'speech-acts' (a) describe; (b) perform; (c) produce some kind of response. He calls these *locutions* (or 'constative' statements), *illocutions* (or 'performative' statements) and *perlocutions*, respectively.

The distinctions between the first two (see this volume pp. 255–7) are of paramount importance for two reasons. The first is that Austin's ultimate conclusion is that all statements are largely 'performative' (or illocutionary in their orientation). The second is that the character of all statements, what they *do*, is totally determined by a set of conventions about who speaks, in what situation, with what authority, in what institution and so on. In their own way, they also force the investigation of utterances outside the formal structure of the communication, and into an analysis of situation. To take a very simple example: a traditional advertisement may describe a product (a locution), whilst simultaneously exhorting the receiver of the advertisement to buy the product (an illocution), which leads to the receiver registering the existence of the product – or even, eventually buying it (both of which are perlocutions). In order to understand the role of each player in the total act of communication one has to consult the necessary rules governing how the advertisement is transmitted, in what capacity, through which medium, etc.

One instructive means of situating speech-act theory is to consider the Derrida/Searle debate. John Searle has occupied a leading position in American philosophy since the publication of his influential 1969 book, *Speech Acts* and as one of the original Faculty Leaders of the University of California, Berkeley Free Speech Movement he is also well-known as a commentator on the student unrest of the 1960s, particularly through his book, *The Campus War* (1971). By the time that his critiques of speech-act theory were written Derrida had himself already become an established figure in American literary theory circles. Derrida occupied a number of visiting posts at Yale, Cornell and the University of California at Irvine from the 1970s to mid-1980s. Moreover a group of elder literary theorists, much influenced by Derrida's writings and the 'method' derived from them, 'deconstruction', formed a school at Yale. (The most prominent of these were Harold Bloom, Geoffrey Hartman, Paul de Man and J. Hillis Miller.) Yale was significant because it had also been the home of a dominant literary theory in the 1950s, the 'New Criticism' which, like 'deconstruction', was concerned not with the subjectivities of authors and readers but with the text as the locus of meaning. It is within this frame – disagreements over the role of text, context and subjectivity in communication – that Derrida was to publish two articles highly critical of speech-act theory (in Derrida 1982 [originally 1977]; 1977), to which John Searle replied (1977; 1983b). Ironically, a reading of the articles in the debate reveals that Derrida, in his attack on Austin, has more affinities with him than, perhaps, Searle does.

In 'Signature Event Context', Derrida once more invokes the concept of 'writing' as an exception to the established rules of communication, rules which make commentators treat writing like a second-class citizen. Writing consists of marks on paper which do not require the *presence* of the sender and receiver of the message in order for them to work. The traditional face-to-face interaction which props up the usual understanding of the communication process is, Derrida implies, a sham; communication theorists all too often, by privileging face-to-face interaction, seem to suggest that the straightforward communication of consciousnesses is possible. For Derrida, writing is a typical form of signification because it is traversed by *différance* rather than by the *presence* of sender and receiver; the only thing that is atypical about it is that the absence of sender and receiver in writing is more obvious to the casual observer (1982 p. 315). The other thing about writing that is important for Derrida is its *iterability*: writing can be repeated and contain signification even in the absence of its addressee, or even if

it was a secret code created between two people, both of whom subsequently died taking their secret to the grave (pp. 315–316). What iterability entails is that, even if there seems to be no meaning – or perhaps
limited meaning – within an artefact, that is not to say that meaning which
is not *present* (easily available) simply is not there. Applying this to speech-
act theory, Derrida writes,

> Could a performative statement succeed if its formulation did not repeat
> a 'coded' or iterable statement, in other words if the expressions I use
> to open a meeting, launch a ship or marriage were not identifiable as
> *conforming* to an iterable model, and therefore if they were not
> identifiable in this way as 'citation'?
>
> (Derrida 1982 p. 326)

What Derrida is saying, then, is that performative statements – and
remember that Austin concludes that all statements tend to be performatives, if only covertly – are bound by rules that are contextual through and
through. Unlike Derrida, Austin does not pay attention to how a text's
internal mechanisms – iterability, *différance* – do the work of encoding. For
Austin, the rules enshrined in an event (for example a marriage) are a
midwife to the performative statement's effectiveness; for Derrida, difference, *différance* and iterability, in a sense, precede the event and create
the possibility of the performative being successful.

In the opening salvo of the Derrida–Searle debate, Derrida concerns
himself with Austin; but his main adversary, by implication, is Searle. Derrida
frequently refers to the 'intentionality' to be witnessed in speech-act theory
but Austin's intentionality (if this is what it is) is much different from that
of Searle, and the latter, in his reply to Derrida, actively distances himself
from Austin in this respect (Searle 1977 p. 204). In Austin's work, all the
rules which govern speech acts are conventional and circumstantial, they
are outside the composition of the utterance itself whilst also making up
its vital component; they are apersonal and not the 'intention' of an individual speaker. Searle, on the other hand, while schematizing and advancing
the analysis of these rules in *Speech Acts*, later abandons Austin in favour
of an understanding of acts of speech which incorporates 'intentionality'
(the title of his 1983a book). For Searle, the illocutionary force of a statement derives not from the convention and *collective* pressure acting on it
as Austin had argued, but from the will of an individual speaker. On this
question, then, Derrida and Searle diverge; on the question of the imper-
sonality of the means by which signification is arrived at Derrida and Austin,
despite their differences, converge.

It is precisely these predicaments that have been at issue in reader-
response theory since the mid-1960s. Does meaning reside in the text,

context/convention or the individual user of the text? A range of theorists, mainly from literary theory backgrounds, have introduced a number of perspectives on the role of the reader in commmunications. These have included Norman Holland (ego psychology), Umberto Eco (semiotics), Georges Poulet (phenomenology) and others (see Suleiman and Crosman 1980; Tompkins 1980). One literary theorist of reader-response who has explicitly employed speech-act theory is the American, Stanley Fish. In his essay, 'How to Do Things with Austin and Searle', Fish analyses *Coriolanus* as a 'speech-act play' and comes up with conclusions about readership which are thoroughly Austinian. The first is that statements cannot be set apart by means of categories such as 'truth' and 'fiction', the second is that meaning is located in the force of 'speech-act communities' (Fish 1980 p. 244). When Coriolanus responds to his banishment from Rome with a defiant 'I banish you' the discrepancy in illocutionary force in both performatives of banishment is striking. 'Rome' embodies the power of the state, a community. Coriolanus seems to be very sincere in his wish to banish Rome (i.e. his intentionality) but the truth of his statement is neither here or there unless it is backed by the force of convention.

This, essentially, is how Fish's model of reader-response works. The meanings of communications at a given moment are not simply available within the confines of a text. Meanings are, instead, imputed to that text by the work of an 'interpretive community' of readers (see Fish 1980). This, of course, is not the only way of conceiving text–reader interaction; in a famous quarrel with Fish, published in *Diacritics* in 1981 (see this volume pp. 407–34), Wolfgang Iser insists on the existence and powers of mechanisms intrinsic to texts. Working through the problem of 'intentionality' (specifically, in this case, what the *author* provides in a text for a *reader*) Iser is at pains to point out that the reader's contribution to the generation of textual meaning is guided by what is 'given' in a text. The reader Is, In fact, 'implied' in the text (see Iser 1974, 1978). The *most damaging* criticisms one could make of Fish's notion of 'interpretive community' – and which Fish accepts – are that it is not dynamic enough (he does not show how its internal relations might change over time) and it is not informed by an analysis of differential social relations. In short, Fish's theory would benefit from some empirical back-up. In this respect, various investigations of non-literary communication were to transform the field of reader-response theory in the 1980s.

Ethnographic studies such as David Morley's *The* Nationwide *Audience* (1980) sought to gauge the response of real readers to samples of media output, a goal central to a plethora of works published through the 1980s in the field of media and cultural studies (see, for example, Seiter *et al.* 1989; Liebes and Katz 1993; Lull 1990, etc.). Morley's study was quite explicit about its methodology in that *The* Nationwide *Audience* consisted of an analysis of the responses to the sample of media, but was also supplemented by *Everyday Television:* Nationwide (1978) by Brunsdon and Morley, which consisted of a semiotic analysis (without reference to audience response) of the programme in question. In several guises this methodology – a textual analysis coupled with an analysis of readers' responses – was used in discussions of television in particular. Ang's *Watching Dallas* (1984), a study of the famous soap opera's fans, and Radway's *Reading the Romance* (1984), a study of an 'interpretive community' of romance readers, both implement this method. What such a strategy tends to imply, straightaway, is that they have a particular take on the text–reader interaction: for such studies, readers are conceived as an entity whose response is in some measure guided by the text which pre-exists them. For researchers such as Liebes and Katz (1993), however, the text is not to be considered as an independent entity; instead, it is the sum of readings which the respondents give to a text which constitutes its meaning (see Palmer, this volume pp. 438–47). Most notably, though, what Radway, Morley and Liebes and Katz show is that the readings made by ethnographic subjects manifest evidence of the subjects' social background: age, gender, occupation, ethnicity, class, etc.

Audience study reasons that the meanings of a fictional text such as a soap opera are constructed with reference to the pre-existing values, attitudes and experiences of the reader. This raises an important question: what if everyday language is similarly constructed by the social world?

A SOCIAL THEORY OF LANGUAGE

In their own fashion, all the major communication theories discussed above have either promoted themselves as socially informed or have tried to come to terms with incorporating the social world. More often than not, the recurring impasse is a result of the desire to build a system for understanding communication and the difficulty of accounting for the diversity of possible experiences and imperatives acting upon users of communication. This was a problem that was recognized and cogently formulated not recently but in 1929 by the Soviet theorist Valentin Vološinov. The reasons that Vološinov's observations were not able to enter debates at the inauguration of structuralism, post-structuralism and speech-act theory are a further fascinating example of the uneven development of communication theory. Vološinov (1895–1936), who had written a number of articles since 1922, published two books in the Soviet Union: in 1926, *Freudianism: A Critical Sketch* (1987) and, in 1929, *Marxism and the Philosophy of*

Language (1973). Both remained virtually unknown for three decades except for the enthusiasm about the latter which was generated by Roman Jakobson in his communications to the Prague Linguistic Circle in the 1930s (Titunik 1987 p. xv). At about the time that Vološinov was rediscovered in the Soviet Union, coinciding with the renaissance of Soviet semiotics (see Lucid 1988) and leading to the translation into English of *Marxism and the Philosophy of Language* (1973) a number of sources began to argue that the author of Vološinov's works was none other than Mikhail Bakhtin (1895–1975) (see Todorov 1984 pp. 6–13).

Bakhtin (sometimes transliterated as 'Baxtin') was the author of numerous works through the 1920s and 1930s although less in the post-war period. A 1941 postgraduate thesis on Rabelais which he converted into a book was eventually published in the Soviet Union in 1965 and, after its translation into English in 1968, became his best known work in the West (Bakhtin 1984). Since then, there have been a steady flow of translations and discoveries of the depth and breadth of Bakhtin's work. The problems of authorship – which result, mainly, from the lack of documentary evidence from the 1930s – as well as the political repression under Stalin (Vološinov died in unknown circumstances; Bakhtin was exiled to Kazakhstan until 1934 for unknown reasons), was responsible for the delay in Vološinov's ideas gaining ground in the West. Arguably, Vološinov's formulations about language have reached a wider audience since he 'became' Bakhtin, whose star has been in the ascendant throughout the 1980s. The debate about authorship, however, rages on (see Perlina 1983; Clark and Holquist 1984; Titunik 1985; Morson and Emerson 1989).

What is influential in Vološinov's *Marxism and the Philosophy of Language*, and what is also found in Bakhtin, is a 'dialogic' theory of the word. Rather than building a self-contained but socially owned system which is bracketed off from the world, as in Saussure's *Course*, Vološinov proceeds from an understanding of the linguistic sign as totally shot through with the social world from the outset. In fact, he devotes a considerable amount of time to criticizing 'individualistic subjectivism' in the philosophy of language for simply studying words/utterances without the social dimension, and 'abstract objectivism' as represented by Saussure, for imagining that the social world exists only in the shared system *langue*. For Vološinov, actual utterances (*parole*) must be understood in terms of the role played by a speaker and listener: 'A word is a bridge thrown between myself and another. . . . A word is a territory shared by both addresser and addressee, between the speaker and his [or her] interlocutor' (see this volume p. 74). All words are built to be received, even if the identity of the receiver is unclear or the receiver is not present; what is important is that speaker and listener are bound in a social relationship which derives from both the

utterance and the wider set of social relationships in which the verbal interaction takes place.

Whereas Saussure sees instances of *parole* as being generated by a
set of differences (in *langue*), Vološinov sees them as products of social
situations. For Saussure, then, the production of utterances is ruled by
purely formal laws while for Vološinov it is ruled by the multifarious nature
of 'ideology'. 'Ideology' is to be understood here, as Vološinov makes clear
at the beginning of *Marxism and the Philosophy of Language*, as both a
part of reality and a reflection and refraction of a wider reality by means
of signs (1973 p. 9). Ideology is not to be understood as consciousness
but as a sign system like that which makes up utterances; moreover, it fills
the territory that is engendered by a verbal interaction. This, Vološinov
argues, is because speakers and listeners are not concerned with the form
of language, nor do they utter or hear 'words' as such; rather, they say
and hear 'what is true or false, good or bad, important or unimportant,
pleasant or unpleasant, and so on' (p. 70). It is for this reason that any
analysis of language must take into account the '*common spatial purview*
of the interlocutors', 'the interlocutors' *common knowledge and understanding of the situation*' and 'their *common evaluation* of that situation'
(see the essay, 'Discourse in life and discourse in art' included in Vološinov
1987). When two people are in a room and the single word 'Well' passes
between them, what does it mean? For a sociolinguistic theory such as
Vološinov's, performative rules or a system of differences are insufficient
for explaining what is going on (ibid. p. 99).

Vološinov's concerns, in many ways, foreshadow those of linguistic
theory since the late 1960s. In 1968, Joshua Fishman wrote of the possibility of a sociology of language in which there would exist a view of society
as being broader than language (Fishman 1968 p. 6). He was referring to
a number of contemporary researchers that included William Labov, Dell
H. Hymes, Basil Bernstein, John J. Gumperz and M. A. K. Halliday (b. 1925).
Like Vološinov, they explore the ways in which situations of speaking and
the wider social framework are responsible for language as a cultural
phenomenon. For instance, in an argument that is now well known,
Bernstein has posited the existence of 'elaborated' and 'restricted' codes
in the speech of school-age children, the former being the language of
formal situations such as school and the latter being a home-orientated
discourse. The wider implications of this separation lie in Bernstein's finding
that, while middle-class children can usually employ both modes in expression, working-class children invariably have access only to the 'restricted'
code (see Bernstein 1971). Similarly, Labov found that supposedly 'verbally
deprived' urban black children, when removed from the research interview
situation to one which resembled a party with friends, demonstrated not

only an unpredicted loquacity but also a seemingly smoother transmission of thought into speech (Labov 1972 pp. 184–191).

It is in this area that the work of Halliday has contributed so much to the understanding of communications. Through his work in the 1960s and 1970s in Britain and then in Australia, where he was located in the 1980s with similarly minded theorists of considerable stature (Gunther Kress, Terry Threadgold, Theo van Leeuwen), Halliday has pursued a complex but sociologically informed model of language. In general, what sets Halliday apart from those linguists who are concerned with how a *langue* (or grammar) generates speech acts, is his insistence on the social restraints and imperatives that mould that *langue* into a specific potential. For Halliday, *langue* is not an objective system, nor should it be considered as entirely separate from speech acts; instead, it is suffused with the logic of speaker–listener interaction, utterance situations and the wider world of social relations. 'The social context is therefore not so much an external condition on the learning of meanings as a generator of the meanings that are learnt' (see Halliday 1975 p. 140). It is easy to see how this might have implications for at least one of the theories discussed above.

Where reader-response theorists and audience ethnographers examine text–reader interactions within fairly limited contexts, Halliday has sought to investigate the wider process of children's language development in order to determine the ways in which humans are engaged in 'learning how to mean' and how this is responsible for the creation and recognition of specific genres of text. Some reader-response theory – Morley's in particular (1986) – has analysed situation and also what Halliday frequently calls, the 'social semiotic', a more general set of relationships in the world of which a given situation (for instance, the domestic environment) is only one. But the matrix of relations which constitute language as Halliday describes it is multifaceted and dynamic; in an account which implicitly extends the famous model of communication put forward by Jakobson (1960; for a summary, see Hawkes 1977 pp. 82–87) and which maps the territory which Vološinov argues exists between speaker and listener, Halliday represents the 'sociolinguistic order' as 'neither an ideal order nor a reality that has no order at all; it is a human artefact having some of the properties of both' (see this volume pp. 359–83). In addition to listing and analysing the features of the communication process, Halliday also provides the impetus for further interrogations of texts. His idea of the child as an active partic- ipant in the production of a system of meaning (rather than the passive recipient of grammatical rules) has been used by Gunther Kress (b. 1940) to demonstrate the way in which changes in sociocultural practices are effected without obliterating existing systems (see this volume pp. 299–313). Moreover, the specific situational variables which, under the heading of *ideational*, *interpersonal* and *textual* functions, Halliday (see this volume pp. 364–6 and Halliday 1985) shows to be operating in a linguistic text can also be identified in the way readers are implicated in visual 'grammar' (see Kress and van Leeuwen, this volume pp. 172–80).

Halliday's is probably one of the most thoroughly social theories of language and it has inspired an array of sociologically informed investigations into communication (see, for instance, Hodge 1988; Hodge and Kress 1988; Kress and van Leeuwen 1992a, 1992b; Thibault 1989; Fairclough 1989 pp. 109–139; 1992 pp. 137–168). Halliday's work has also fundamentally re-aligned the relationship between signs and the social world.

PEIRCE, SEMIOTICS AND THE FUTURE OF COMMUNICATION THEORY

It should be clear by now that communication theory has been concerned with the process of a sender transmitting a message to a receiver, with theorists homing in on either the message, the receiver, the sender or complex combinations of these, plus the troublesome intrusion of the social world, as the locus of meaning. It can be no coincidence, then, that the disciplines of media studies, communications and cultural studies have grown out of the investigation of 'literature' (see Easthope 1991; During 1993); traditionally, literary criticism has employed a model of production and reception of its object based on the illusion of heroic authors in their garrets, beavering away alone to create a masterpiece which is then unproblematically transmitted to readers who will then (ideally) lavish the same attention on the artefact in isolation. In fact, such a tradition of theorizing literary production and consumption lives on in the review sections of Sunday newspapers. Contemporary communication is, of course, far more complicated than this.

One tradition in communication theory which has remained largely aloof from the literary model is the school of semiotics (or *semeiotic*) influenced by the American philosopher, Peirce. Charles Sanders Peirce (pronounced 'Purse') is the earliest of the figures so far considered, having lived from 1839 to 1914 and conducted much of his work in the final years of the nineteenth century. Although he never held an academic post for any length of time and spent a celebrated period working for the Coast and Geodetic Survey of the United States (see Brent 1993), Peirce maintained a prodigious output, writing not only on philosophy, logic and mathematics primarily but also, seemingly, on everything else as well. For a number of reasons, however, Peirce's work has not been recruited to the European cause of literary analysis. One is Peirce's original basis in philosophy and science (although this is not a good enough reason *per se*). Another is that Peirce studies have been located largely in philosophy and linguistics in the United States with notable exceptions such as the work of the Italian semiotician, Umberto Eco (b. 1932); Peirce's leading living exponent in America, Thomas A. Sebeok (b. 1920) has, on the other hand, been concerned with signs in biology and elsewhere other than literature (see Sebeok 1972). This last reason also bears on the usage of the term 'semiotics' as opposed to 'semiology': the latter is Saussure's term and should, strictly, be associated with the European tradition although, possibly because of Eco's influence, 'semiotics' is frequently used to refer to any theoretical interest in signs on either side of the Atlantic (see Cobley forthcoming).

A third reason for the failure of Peircean semiotics to significantly pene-trate the kind of literary critical analysis that paved the way for cultural and communication studies is the reductionist manner in which Peirce has been introduced into such areas. Because the writings of Peirce are so disparate and range over many years, many developments and many revisions, it is difficult to pin down a basic core of ideas. The result has been that influ-ential commentators have attempted to graft onto structuralism and post-structuralism those theories of signification from Peirce which seem most conducive to the European project. For example, Jonathan Culler (1975 p. 16; 1981 pp. 22–25) and John Fiske (1991 p. 46), among others, perpetuate the notion that Peirce proposed three types of signs: 'icon', 'index' and symbol'. As 'symbol' was closest to Saussure's version of the linguistic sign this became a supplement to existing literary theory while the term 'icon' creeps into analyses of analogic communication (a well-known example is Wollen 1972 pp. 120 ff). This may all seem very convenient from the point of view of many European theorists but Peirce's work amounts to much more than a mere supplement to 'semiology'.

What it is essential to know about Peirce's *semeiotic* is that it is pred-icated on the basis of his classification of phenomena. Peirce identified three categories of phenomena which he labelled Firstness, Secondness and Thirdness. The realm of Firstness is difficult to conceive but is usually understood in terms of 'feeling'; Firstness has no relations, it is not to be thought of in opposition to another thing and it is merely a 'possibility'. It is like a musical note or a vague taste or a sense of a colour. Secondness is the realm of brute facts which arise from a relationship. It is the sense that arises when, in the process of closing a door, it is found that the door is stuck as the result of an object being in its way. The relation between pushing the door and its failure to close is an example of what makes up the realm of Secondness. Thirdness, on the other hand, is the realm of general laws. The law that heavy objects in front of pushed doors can prevent the door's closure is an example of Thirdness. In this manner,

Firstness is associated with the 'possible', Secondness is associated with the 'brutally factual' and Thirdness is associated with the 'virtual' (Pharies 1985 pp. 10–12).

This is the framework in which, for Peirce, signs function. These signs are, similarly, a trichotomy consisting of a Sign (or, as it is sometimes called, 'Representamen', which is not unlike Saussure's signifier); an Object (that which it refers to – either in the mind or in the world); and, the most difficult of the three, an Interpretant. Each of these corresponds to one of the three categories of phenomena: so, the Sign/Representamen is Firstness, the Object is Secondness and the Interpretant is Thirdness.

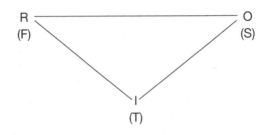

R = Sign/Representamen
O = Object
I = Interpretant
(F) = Firstness
(S) = Secondness
(T) = Thirdness

The Interpretant is that which the sign produces, its 'significate effect' (Zeman 1973 p. 25): it is usually another sign and is usually – but not always – located in the mind. An interpretant's most important role is in the contribution to a further triad in which it becomes the Sign, with a subsequent Object and another Interpretant which, in turn, fulfils the same role (potentially *ad infinitum*). This is the process of semiosis, the continual production of meaning through one sign triad leading to another by means of the invocation of new interpretants (see K. B. Jensen 1995 pp. 221–223). Gallie (1952 p. 120) gives a preliminary example of this process by stating that an individual, A, might point at the floor whereupon companion, B, would interpret by looking in that direction, to be followed by C who asks 'What are you looking at?' One original sign from A therefore gives rise to two further signs from B and C which have taken a component (the Interpretant) from the signs that precede them. Attentive readers will recognize some affinities here with Derrida's concept of *différance*, one sign giving way to another continuously. The main distinction between Derrida and Peirce, however, is that the latter is clear in his conviction that the process of signification takes place primarily in the mind.

The parameters within which any sign operates are created by a 'sort of idea' or what Peirce calls a 'ground' (Zeman 1973 p. 26). The 'ground' is the set of properties which engender its own specific kind of signification and, without being identical to any of them, the 'ground' is not dissimilar from grammar, Saussure's *langue* and Austin's contextual conventions. It is what imputes character to a particular kind of sign. The ground is at work in the three kinds of signs (icon, index, symbol) which are often cited by European semiologists; but this needs to be extended. Peirce actually embarked on a lifelong project (unfinished) to bring all signs into a typology and, late in life, estimated that there might be as many as 59, 049 different sign types to be considered (Pharies 1985 p. 32). These are generated by the three categories of phenomena (Firstness, Secondness, Thirdness) in relation to the three levels of the sign triad (which represent the sign form of Firstness, Secondness and Thirdness); as Sheriff demonstrates, these are best represented in the form of a table (Figure 1.4, p. 31).

The three columns (across the top of the table) refer to the three categories of phenomena that have been discussed (p. 27). The three horizontal rows (labelled at the left side of the table) refer to the sign triad at the level of form (Firstness = Sign/Representamen; Secondness = Object; Thirdness = Interpretant). As the two axes interact different kinds of signs are produced.

The first row – the level of the Sign/Representamen produces three fundamental kinds of sign: one which is considered only in relation to itself, a mere quality – Qualisign; one which is considered in relation to an existing thing or fact – a Sinsign; and one which is considered in relation to a general law – a Legisign.

The second row – the level of the Object produces three more kinds of signs: one which shares some character (resemblance) with its Object – an Icon; one which has an actual physical connection with its Object – an Index; and a sign which is related to its Object only by convention or habit – a Symbol.

The third row – the level of the Interpretant produces three higher grade signs: one which is related to its Interpretant as a possibility or concept – a Rheme; one which relates to its Interpretant as a fact – a Dicent sign; and one which relates to its Interpretant as reasoning or logic – an Argument.

One can see how this relatively simple schema might be able to generate a sufficient number of combinatory sign types (for example, 'rhematic symbol') that even Peirce might not manage to analyse completely in a lifetime. However, it is certainly worth noting that there is a considerable difference here from the structuralist and post-structuralist projects. Peirce's semeiotic threatens to address a whole universe of signs rather than the fairly limited domain of communicative functions where Saussure has been put to work. In fact, the increased attention given to Peirce's work in the 1980s and 1990s often looks as though it might upset the whole applecart of post-structuralism. Sheriff extends the table (Figure 1.4) taking all the combinations that Peirce argues is the result, and builds them into ten classifications such as Rhematic Index, Dicent Symbol and so on. Only three of the ten are what could be termed Symbols, or signs that function as a consequence of their own conventional properties in the fashion of the Saussurean linguistic sign. While much of the Saussurean tradition bases social existence and communication on exactly such signs, then, it is only operating within a small part of semiosis in general. Moreover, Sheriff argues, the Saussurean tradition forgets what Peirce's semiotics makes central: that signification – even literary signification – is not wholly Symbolic (or Thirdness) but makes reference to Firstness:

> Without denying that we cannot escape from language, from Thirdness, Peirce shows us that Thirdness (linguistic, symbolic signs) can symbolically represent Firstness. According to his theory of signs, literary art is language (Rhematic Symbol) used to show, picture, symbolize the quality of immediate consciousness that can never be immediate to consciousness.
>
> (Sheriff 1989 p. 89)

For Sheriff, this is not a naive pre-structuralist version of reference, largely because it remains sceptical about a direct confrontation with Firstness; it also entails the work of the 'ground' in determining the function of signs and the role of the reader in generating a chain of interpretants in successive awarenesses (p. 84).

Peirce's semiotics, then, 'without making him sound like Pollyanna' (Sheriff 1989 p. 89), appears to offer a new perspective on how communication might be thought to refer to the real world. It also opens up an undiscovered country, populated with diverse indigenous signs, which it is the task of communication theory to explore.

Theory has ever expanding horizons and a busy future ahead. There are positive reasons for this as well as some slightly negative ones. The negatives first. Communication theory has, necessarily, attempted to be a broad church, incorporating insights from a number of disciplines. We have really been able to take only a cursory glance at theory's breadth in this brief history and we have been forced to bypass a host of fecund schools including

Phenomenological or formal categories	Ontological or material categories		
	Firstness	Secondness	Thirdness
Firstness	A sign is:	a 'mere quality' QUALISIGN	an 'actual existent' SINSIGN	a 'general law' LEGISIGN
Secondness	A sign *relates* to its object in having:	'some character in itself' ICON	'some existential relation to that object' INDEX	'some relation to the interpretant' SYMBOL
Thirdness	A sign's interpretant *represents* it (sign) as a sign of:	'possibility' RHEME	'fact' DICENT SIGN	'reason' ARGUMENT

Figure 1.4

Source: Sheriff (1989 p. 67)

the Russian Formalists (see Ehrlich 1990), the Prague School of Linguistics (see Galan 1985), the school of Soviet Semiotics (see Lucid 1988) and the work of Julia Kristeva (see Moi 1985). As a consequence of its diversity, communication theory has not always been able to represent the fullness of its fellow subject areas and this has contributed to its uneven development. As we have seen, Lacan gave his famous seminar on 'L'instance de la lettre' in 1957, coinciding with the publication that year of Barthes' *Mythologies* and its much different approach to theory. But, in addition, 1957 was the year that one massively influential book on linguistics was published followed by another that was to totally transform the field: these were, respectively, Jakobson and Halle's *Fundamentals of Language* and Chomsky's *Syntactic Structures*. The latter, despite its enormity in the world of language study, has had relatively little impact on communication theory. The same might be said of other zones within disciplines: why has there been so much Lacanian theory and so little based on the British school of psychoanalysis? Why has there been so much written on Derrida's influence on communications, media and cultural studies and so little on the work of other contemporary philosophers such as Richard Rorty?

There are numerous answers to these questions including the fact that some areas of companion disciplines are simply more amenable for appropriation than others. However, there are signs that theoretical pluralism has made advances since the 1980s (for example, on British psychoanalysis as applied to communications artefacts see Richards 1994 and Silverstone 1994; on Rorty and mass communication see K. B. Jensen 1995). The negative side of being a hybrid discipline also presents, therefore, an immense opportunity. For students it sometimes seems a Sisyphean task to inculcate one body of theory only to find that it is the subject of a critique by another, or to find that concepts from one discipline are tantalizingly close to another without being precisely congruent. But the pluralism that this entails is both productive and absolutely necessary. One of the key features of social formations in late modernity is the phenomenon of globalization, in which the media act as an 'honest broker' in negotiating our orientation to the global and the local. But those media are plural, having many forms of ownership, technology and a seemingly limitless array of messages and audiences which differentially decode those messages. If it is possible to argue that there are five main types of global cultural flow – ethnoscapes, mediascapes, technoscapes, finanscapes, ideoscapes (Appadurai 1990 p. 296) – then it is equally feasible to argue that there are a plethora of messages, communication strategies, technologies, audiences and decoding techniques for each audience.

At the present juncture, then, communication needs all the theorization it can get.

Part I

Signification

Part 1

Theories of the sign

EDITOR'S INTRODUCTION

It is customary to refer to Saussure and Peirce as the founding fathers of semiology/semiotics. As the following extracts from their work show, they were both active in different areas utilizing totally different methodologies. Nevertheless, Saussure and Peirce share a concern with signification. The extract from Saussure's *Course in General Linguistics* addresses this question in a very general way, asking what might be the object of linguistics. Within the space of a page Saussure lays out his terms: without, at this stage, explicitly naming them, he mentions that signs are made up of (1) 'signifiers' and (2) 'signifieds', that the general phenomenon of language consists of (3) *parole* and *langue*, and that (4) there is the possibility of both a 'diachronic' and a 'synchronic' approach to language.

These ideas are, of course, central to an understanding of Saussurean linguistics and the semiology to which it gives birth; but there are also some general arguments in this extract that it is necessary to register. When Saussure posits a 'speaking-circuit', he sets up a fundamental understanding of communication as a transmission of consciousness from one point to another. This is not an uncommon understanding of the act of communication but it is one that Jacques Derrida criticizes at some length (see this volume pp. 19–20; 209–24). Against this psychologistic understanding of speech it is evident that Saussure is striving to counterpose *parole* to a concept of language as a *social* institution. From this results the possibility of a science '*that studies the life of signs within society*'.

Peirce's semeiotic, on the other hand, is a doctrine of signs that is embedded in a general theory which takes in logic, philosophy and mathematics. Fundamental to any appreciation of Peirce is an acquaintance with his three categories of phenomena. The first lengthy exposition of these appears in Peirce's 1867 essay, 'On a New List of Categories', which also contains fledgling versions of his classifications of sign types. The extract in this section is taken from the notes Peirce made in 1890 for a book and it sets out in digestible summary form the highly complicated work in this area that had consumed him for the preceding twenty-three years. As Peirce states in 'A Guess at the Riddle', various numbers have had their champions in the past; he, however, finds himself in favour of '3' and the chapter consists of a series of trichotomies which make up Peirce's phenomenology.

It is easy to begin to imagine that the recurrence of the number 3 is either contrived or unrealistically neat but Peirce presents his arguments with force and it is clear that he has himself contemplated this possibility. What is probably the most important part of the essay in relation to Saussure's work is Peirce's insistence on the triad as the fundamental structure of relations between phenomena. If we compare Peirce's comments on the correlates involved in A presenting to B a gift C as analogous to semieotic relations, the gulf between this and the Saussurean dyadic version of the sign is palpable. Like all metaphysics, Peirce's consideration of signification concentrates on the basics; but the style in which 'A Guess at the Riddle' is written hints at a myriad of possibilities.

There can be no doubt that it is worth taking these seminal graspings for a theory of signification seriously. This is partly because they enable one to follow the closely reasoned arguments of semiotics, structuralism and post-structuralism; but, also, because Peirce and Saussure make such fundamental observations that they enable us to survey the benefits of any general theory of signification.

Further reading: Culler 1976 pp. 18–28; Holdcroft 1991 pp. 4–68; Weber 1976; Harris 1987; Belsey 1980 pp. 37–55; K. B. Jensen 1995 pp. 20–25; Colapietro 1989; Hoopes 1991; Sheriff 1994; Eco 1976 pp. 58–72.

2 Ferdinand de Saussure

The object of linguistics

1 DEFINITION OF LANGUAGE

What is both the integral and concrete object of linguistics? The question is especially difficult; later we shall see why; here I wish merely to point up the difficulty.

Other sciences work with objects that are given in advance and that can then be considered from different viewpoints; but not linguistics. Someone pronounces the French word *nu* 'bare': a superficial observer would be tempted to call the word a concrete linguistic object; but a more careful examination would reveal successively three or four quite different things, depending on whether the word is considered as a sound, as the expression of an idea, as the equivalent of Latin *nudum*, etc. Far from it being the object that antedates the viewpoint, it would seem that it is the viewpoint that creates the object; besides, nothing tells us in advance that one way of considering the fact in question takes precedence over the others or is in any way superior to them.

Moreover, regardless of the viewpoint that we adopt, the linguistic phenomenon always has two related sides, each deriving its values from the other. For example:

1 Articulated syllables are acoustical impressions perceived by the ear, but the sounds would not exist without the vocal organs; an *n*, for example, exists only by virtue of the relation between the two sides. We simply cannot reduce language to sound or detach sound from oral articulation; reciprocally, we cannot define the movements of the vocal organs without taking into account the acoustical impression (see Saussure 1974 pp. 38ff.).

2 But suppose that sound were a simple thing: would it constitute speech? No, it is only the instrument of thought; by itself, it has no existence. At this point a new and redoubtable relationship arises: a sound, a complex acoustical-vocal unit, combines in turn with an idea to form a complex physiological-psychological unit.

3 Speech has both an individual and a social side, and we cannot conceive of one without the other. Besides:

4 Speech always implies both an established system and an evolution; at every moment it is an existing institution and a product of the past. To distinguish between the system and its history, between what it is and what it was, seems very simple at first glance; actually the two things are so closely related that we can scarcely keep them apart. Would we simplify the question by studying the linguistic phenomenon in its earliest stages – if we began, for example, by studying the speech of children? No, for in dealing with speech, it is completely misleading to assume that the problem of early characteristics differs from the problem of permanent characteristics. We are left inside the vicious circle.

From whatever direction we approach the question, nowhere do we find the integral object of linguistics. Everywhere we are confronted with a dilemma: if we fix our attention on only one side of each problem, we run the risk of failing to perceive the dualities pointed out above; on the other hand, if we study speech from several viewpoints simultaneously, the object of linguistics appears to us as a confused mass of heterogeneous and unrelated things. Either procedure opens the door to several sciences – psychology, anthropology, normative grammar, philology, etc. – which are distinct from linguistics, but which might claim speech, in view of the faulty method of linguistics, as one of their objects.

As I see it there is only one solution to all the foregoing difficulties: *from the very outset we must put both feet on the ground of language and use language as the norm of all other manifestations of speech.* Actually, among so many dualities, language alone seems to lend itself to independent definition and provide a fulcrum that satisfies the mind.

But what is language [*langue*]? It is not to be confused with human speech [*langage*], of which it is only a definite part, though certainly an essential one. It is both a social product of the faculty of speech and a collection of necessary conventions that have been adopted by a social body to permit individuals to exercise that faculty. Taken as a whole, speech is many-sided and heterogeneous; straddling several areas simultaneously – physical, physiological, and psychological – it belongs both to the individual and to society; we cannot put it into any category of human facts, for we cannot discover its unity.

Language, on the contrary, is a self-contained whole and a principle of classification. As soon as we give language first place among the facts of speech, we introduce a natural order into a mass that lends itself to no other classification.

One might object to that principle of classification on the ground that since the use of speech is based on a natural faculty whereas language is something acquired and conventional, language should not take first place but should be subordinated to the natural instinct.

That objection is easily refuted.

First, no one has proved that speech, as it manifests itself when we speak (*parole*), is entirely natural, i.e. that our vocal apparatus was designed for speaking just as our legs were designed for walking. Linguists are far from agreement on this point. For instance Whitney, to whom language is one of several social institutions, thinks that we use the vocal apparatus as the instrument of language purely through luck, for the sake of convenience: men might just as well have chosen gestures and used visual symbols instead of acoustical symbols. Doubtless his thesis is too dogmatic; language is not similar in all respects to other social institutions (see Saussure 1974 pp. 73–76); moreover, Whitney goes too far in saying that our choice happened to fall on the vocal organs; the choice was more or less imposed by nature. But on the essential point the American linguist is right; language is a convention, and the nature of the sign that is agreed upon does not matter. The question of the vocal apparatus obviously takes a secondary place in the problem of speech.

One definition of *articulated speech* might confirm that conclusion. In Latin, *articulus* means a member, part, or subdivision of a sequence; applied to speech, articulation designates either the subdivision of a spoken chain into syllables or the subdivision of the chain of meanings into significant units; *gegliederte Sprache* is used in the second sense in German. Using the second definition, we can say that what is natural to mankind is not oral speech but the faculty of constructing a language, i.e. a system of distinct signs corresponding to distinct ideas.

Broca discovered that the faculty of speech is localized in the third left frontal convolution; his discovery has been used to substantiate the attribution of a natural quality to speech. But we know that the same part of the brain is the center of *everything* that has to do with speech, including writing. The preceding statements, together with observations that have been made in different cases of aphasia resulting from lesion of the centers of localization, seem to indicate: (1) that the various disorders of oral speech are bound up in a hundred ways with those of written speech; and (2) that what is lost in all cases of aphasia or agraphia is less the faculty of producing a given sound or writing a given sign than the ability to evoke by means of an instrument, regardless of what it is, the signs of a regular system of speech. The obvious implication is that beyond the functioning of the various organs there exists a more general faculty which governs signs and which would be the linguistic faculty proper. And this brings us to the same conclusion as above.

To give language first place in the study of speech, we can advance a final argument: the faculty of articulating words – whether it is natural or not – is exercised only with the help of the instrument created by a collectivity and provided for its use; therefore, to say that language gives unity to speech is not fanciful.

2 PLACE OF LANGUAGE IN THE FACTS OF SPEECH

In order to separate from the whole of speech the part that belongs to language, we must examine the individual act from which the speaking-circuit can be reconstructed. The act requires the presence of at least two persons; that is the minimum number necessary to complete the circuit. Suppose that two people, A and B, are conversing with each other (Figure 2.1).

Suppose that the opening of the circuit is in A's brain, where mental facts (concepts [signifieds]) are associated with representations of the linguistic sounds (sound-images [signifiers]) that are used for their expression. A given concept unlocks a corresponding sound-image in the brain; this purely *psychological* phenomenon is followed in turn by a *physiological* process: the brain transmits an impulse corresponding to the image to the organs used in producing sounds. Then the sound waves travel from the mouth of A to the ear of B:

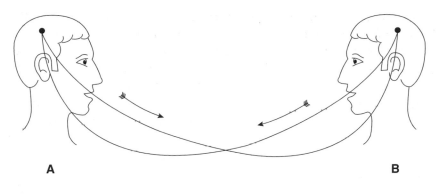

A   B

Figure 2.1

a purely *physical* process. Next, the circuit continues in B, but the order is reversed: from the ear to the brain, the physiological transmission of the sound-image; in the brain, the psychological association of the image with the corresponding concept. If B then speaks, the new act will follow – from his brain to A's – exactly the same course as the first act and pass through the same successive phases, which I shall diagram as Figure 2.2.

The preceding analysis does not purport to be complete. We might also single out the pure acoustical sensation, the identification of that sensation with the latent sound-image, the muscular image of phonation, etc. I have included only the elements thought to be essential, but the drawing brings out at a glance the distinction between the physical (sound waves), physiological (phonation and

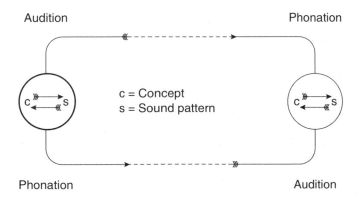

Figure 2.2

audition), and psychological parts (word-images and concepts). Indeed, we should not fail to note that the word-image stands apart from the sound itself and that it is just as psychological as the concept which is associated with it.

The circuit that I have outlined can be further divided into:

(a) an outer part that includes the vibrations of the sounds which travel from the mouth to the ear, and an inner part that includes everything else;
(b) a psychological and a nonpsychological part, the second including the physiological productions of the vocal organs as well as the physical facts that are outside the individual;
(c) an active and a passive part: everything that goes from the associative center of the speaker to the ear of the listener is active, and everything that goes from the ear of the listener to his associative center is passive;
(d) finally, everything that is active in the psychological part of the circuit is executive ($c \rightarrow s$), and everything that is passive is receptive ($s \rightarrow c$).

We should also add the associative and co-ordinating faculty that we find as soon as we leave isolated signs; this faculty plays the dominant role in the organization of language as a system (see Saussure 1974 pp. 122 ff.).

But to understand clearly the role of the associative and co-ordinating faculty, we must leave the individual act, which is only the embryo of speech, and approach the social fact.

Among all the individuals that are linked together by speech, some sort of average will be set up: all will reproduce – not exactly of course, but approximately – the same signs united with the same concepts.

How does the social crystallization of language come about? Which parts of the circuit are involved? For all parts probably do not participate equally in it.

The nonpsychological part can be rejected from the outset. When we hear people speaking a language that we do not know, we perceive the sounds but remain outside the social fact because we do not understand them.

Neither is the psychological part of the circuit wholly responsible: the executive side is missing, for execution is never carried out by the collectivity. Execution is always individual, and the individual is always its master: I shall call the executive side *speaking* [*parole*].

Through the functioning of the receptive and co-ordinating faculties, impressions that are perceptibly the same for all are made on the minds of speakers. How can that social product be pictured in such a way that language will stand apart from everything else? If we could embrace the sum of word-images stored in the minds of all individuals, we could identify the social bond that constitutes language. It is a storehouse filled by the members of a given community through their active use of speaking, a grammatical system that has a potential existence in each brain, or, more specifically, in the brains of a group of individuals. For language is not complete in any speaker; it exists perfectly only within a collectivity.

In separating language from speaking we are at the same time separating: (1) what is social from what is individual; and (2) what is essential from what is accessory and more or less accidental.

Language is not a function of the speaker; it is a product that is passively assimilated by the individual. It never requires premeditation, and reflection enters in only for the purpose of classification, which we shall take up later (Saussure 1974 pp. 122ff.).

Speaking, on the contrary, is an individual act. It is wilful and intellectual. Within the act, we should distinguish between: (1) the combinations by which the speaker uses the language code for expressing his own thought; and (2) the psychophysical mechanism that allows him to exteriorize those combinations.

Note that I have defined things rather than words; these definitions are not endangered by certain ambiguous words that do not have identical meanings in different languages. For instance, German *Sprache* means both 'language' and 'speech'; *Rede* almost corresponds to 'speaking' but adds the special connotation of 'discourse'. Latin *sermo* designates both 'speech' and 'speaking' while *lingua* means 'language', etc. No word corresponds exactly to any of the notions specified above; that is why all definitions of words are made in vain; starting from words in defining things is a bad procedure.

To summarize, these are the characteristics of language:

1 Language is a well-defined object in the heterogeneous mass of speech facts. It can be localized in the limited segment of the speaking-circuit where an auditory image becomes associated with a concept. It is the social side of speech, outside the individual who can never create nor modify it by himself; it exists only by virtue of a sort of contract signed by the members of a community.

Moreover, the individual must always serve an apprenticeship in order to learn the functioning of language; a child assimilates it only gradually. It is such a distinct thing that a man deprived of the use of speaking retains it provided that he understands the vocal signs that he hears.

2 Language, unlike speaking, is something that we can study separately. Although we no longer speak dead languages, we are certainly capable of assimilating their linguistic systems. We can dispense with the other elements of speech; indeed, the science of language is possible only if the other elements are excluded.

3 Whereas speech is heterogeneous, language, as defined, is homogeneous. It is a system of signs in which the only essential thing is the union of meanings and sound-images, and in which both parts of the sign are psychological.

4 Language is concrete, no less so than speaking; and this is a help in our study of it. Linguistic signs, though basically psychological, are not abstractions; associations which bear the stamp of collective approval – and which added together constitute language – are realities that have their seat in the brain. Besides, linguistic signs are tangible; it is possible to reduce them to conventional written symbols, whereas it would be impossible to provide detailed photographs of acts of speaking [*actes de parole*]; the pronunciation of even the smallest word represents an infinite number of muscular movements that could be identified and put into graphic form only with great difficulty. In language, on the contrary, there is only the sound-image, and the latter can be translated into a fixed visual image. For if we disregard the vast number of movements necessary for the realization of sound-images in speaking, we see that each sound-image is nothing more than the sum of a limited number of elements or phonemes that can in turn be called up by a corresponding number of written symbols (see Saussure 1974 pp. 61 ff.). The very possibility of putting the things that relate to language into graphic form allows dictionaries and grammars to represent it accurately, for language is a storehouse of sound-images, and writing is the tangible form of those images.

3 PLACE OF LANGUAGE IN HUMAN FACTS: SEMIOLOGY

The foregoing characteristics of language reveal an even more important characteristic. Language, once its boundaries have been marked off within the speech data, can be classified among human phenomena, whereas speech cannot.

We have just seen that language is a social institution; but several features set it apart from other political, legal, etc. institutions. We must call in a new type of facts in order to illuminate the special nature of language.

Language is a system of signs that express ideas, and is therefore comparable to a system of writing, the alphabet of deaf-mutes, symbolic rites, polite formulas, military signals, etc. But it is the most important of all these systems.

A science that studies the life of signs within society is conceivable; it would be part of social psychology and consequently of general psychology; I shall call it *semiology*[1] (from Greek *sēmeîon* 'sign'). Semiology would show what constitutes signs, what laws govern them. Since the science does not yet exist, no one can say what it would be; but it has a right to existence, a place staked out in advance. Linguistics is only a part of the general science of semiology; the laws discovered by semiology will be applicable to linguistics, and the latter will circumscribe a well-defined area within the mass of anthropological facts.

To determine the exact place of semiology is the task of the psychologist.[2] The task of the linguist is to find out what makes language a special system within the mass of semiological data. This issue will be taken up again later; here I wish merely to call attention to one thing: if I have succeeded in assigning linguistics a place among the sciences, it is because I have related it to semiology.

Why has semiology not yet been recognized as an independent science with its own object like all the other sciences? Linguists have been going around in circles: language, better than anything else, offers a basis for understanding the semiological problem; but language must, to put it correctly, be studied in connection with something else, from other viewpoints.

There is first of all the superficial notion of the general public: people see nothing more than a name-giving system in language (see Saussure 1974 p. 65), thereby prohibiting any research into its true nature.

Then there is the viewpoint of the psychologist, who studies the sign-mechanism in the individual; this is the easiest method, but it does not lead beyond individual execution and does not reach the sign, which is social.

Or even when signs are studied from a social viewpoint, only the traits that attach language to the other social institutions – those that are more or less voluntary – are emphasized; as a result, the goal is by-passed and the specific characteristics of semiological systems in general and of language in particular are completely ignored. For the distinguishing characteristic of the sign – but the one that is least apparent at first sight – is that in some way it always eludes the individual or social will.

In short, the characteristic that distinguishes semiological systems from all other institutions shows up clearly only in language where it manifests itself in the things which are studied least, and the necessity or specific value of a semiological science is therefore not clearly recognized. But to me the language problem is mainly semiological, and all developments derive their significance from that important fact. If we are to discover the true nature of language we must learn what it has in common with all other semiological systems; linguistic forces that seem very important at first glance (e.g., the role of the vocal apparatus) will receive only secondary consideration if they serve only to set language apart from the other systems. This procedure will do more than to clarify the linguistic problem. By studying rites, customs, etc. as signs, I believe that we shall throw new light on the facts and point up the need for including them in a science of semiology and explaining them by its laws.

NOTES

1 *Semiology* should not be confused with *semantics*, which studies changes in meaning, and which Saussure did not treat methodically; the fundamental principle of semantics is formulated in Saussure 1974 p. 75 [Ed.].
2 Cf. A. Naville, *Classification des Sciences* (2nd ed.), p. 104 [Ed.] The scope of semiology (or semiotics) is treated in Morris (1946) [Tr.].
(Note: the editors of Saussure (1974) are Charles Bally and Albert Sèchehaye with Albert Reidlinger; the translator is Wade Baskin. Baskin renders *langue* as 'language', *langage* as 'all human speech' and *parole* as 'speaking'; see this volume p. 3 – P.C.)

3 Charles Sanders Peirce

A guess at the riddle

1 TRICHOTOMY

355 Perhaps I might begin by noticing how different numbers have found their champions. Two was extolled by Peter Ramus, Four by Pythagoras, Five by Sir Thomas Browne, and so on. For my part, I am a determined foe of no innocent number; I respect and esteem them all in their several ways; but I am forced to confess to a leaning to the number Three in philosophy. In fact, I make so much use of threefold divisions in my speculations, that it seems best to commence by making a slight preliminary study of the conceptions upon which all such divisions must rest. I mean no more than the ideas of first, second, third – ideas so broad that they may be looked upon rather as moods or tones of thought, than as definite notions, but which have great significance for all that. Viewed as numerals, to be applied to what objects we like, they are indeed thin skeletons of thought, if not mere words. If we only wanted to make enumerations, it would be out of place to ask for the significations of the numbers we should have to use; but then the distinctions of philosophy are supposed to attempt something far more than that; they are intended to go down to the very essence of things, and if we are to make one single threefold philosophical distinction, it behooves us to ask beforehand what are the kinds of objects that are first, second, and third, not as being so counted, but in their own true characters. That there are such ideas of the really first, second, and third, we shall presently find reason to admit.

356 The first is that whose being is simply in itself, not referring to anything nor lying behind anything. The second is that which is what it is by force of something to which it is second. The third is that which is what it is owing to things between which it mediates and which it brings into relation to each other.

357 The idea of the absolutely first must be entirely separated from all conception of or reference to anything else; for what involves a second is itself a second to that second. The first must therefore be present and immediate, so as not to be second to a representation. It must be fresh and new, for if old it is second to its former state. It must be initiative, original, spontaneous, and free; otherwise it is second to a determining cause. It is also something vivid and conscious; so only it avoids being the object of some sensation. It precedes all synthesis and all differentiation; it has no unity and no parts. It cannot be articulately thought: assert it, and it has already lost its characteristic innocence; for assertion always implies a denial of something else. Stop to think of it, and it has flown! What the world was to Adam on the day he opened his eyes to it, before he had drawn any distinctions, or had become conscious of his own existence – that is first, present, immediate, fresh, new, initiative, original, spontaneous, free, vivid, conscious, and evanescent. Only, remember that every description of it must be false to it.

358 Just as the first is not absolutely first if thought along with a second, so likewise to think the second in its perfection we must banish every third. The second is therefore the absolute last. But we need not, and must not, banish the idea of the first from the second; on the contrary, the second is precisely that which cannot be without the first. It meets us in such facts as another, relation, compulsion, effect, dependence, independence, negation, occurrence, reality, result. A thing cannot be other, negative, or independent, without a first to or of which it shall be other, negative, or independent. Still, this is not a very deep kind of secondness; for the first might in these cases be destroyed yet leave the real character of the second absolutely unchanged. When the second suffers some change from the action of the first, and is dependent upon it, the secondness is more genuine. But the dependence must not go so far that the second is a mere accident or incident of the first; otherwise the secondness again degenerates. The genuine second suffers and yet resists, like dead matter, whose existence consists in its inertia. Note, too, that for the second to have the finality that we have seen belongs to it, it must be determined by the first immovably, and thenceforth be fixed; so that unalterable fixity becomes one of its attributes. We find secondness in occurrence, because an occurrence is something whose existence consists in our knocking up against it. A hard fact is of the same sort; that is to say, it is something which is there, and which I

cannot think away, but am forced to acknowledge as an object of second beside myself, the subject or number one, and which forms material for the exercise of my will. The idea of second must be reckoned as an easy one to comprehend. That of first is so tender that you cannot touch it without spoiling it; but that of second is eminently hard and tangible. It is very familiar, too; it is forced upon us daily; it is the main lesson of life. In youth, the world is fresh and we seem free; but limitation, conflict, constraint, and secondness generally, make up the teaching of experience. With what firstness

> The scarfed bark puts from her native bay;

with what secondness

> doth she return,
> with overweathered ribs and ragged sails.

But familiar as the notion is, and compelled as we are to acknowledge it at every turn, still we never can realize it; we never can be immediately conscious of finiteness, or of anything but a divine freedom that in its own original firstness knows no bounds.

359 First and second, agent and patient, yes and no, are categories which enable us roughly to describe the facts of experience, and they satisfy the mind for a very long time. But at last they are found to be inadequate, and the third is the conception which is then called for. The third is that which bridges over the chasm between the absolute first and last, and brings them into relationship. We are told that every science has its qualitative and its quantitative stage; now its qualitative stage is when dual distinctions – whether a given subject has a given predicate or not – suffice; the quantitative stage comes when, no longer content with such rough distinctions, we require to insert a possible halfway between every two possible conditions of the subject in regard to its possession of the quality indicated by the predicate. Ancient mechanics recognized forces as causes which produced motions as their immediate effects, looking no further than the essentially dual relation of cause and effect. That was why it could make no progress with dynamics. The work of Galileo and his successors lay in showing that forces are accelerations by which [a] state of velocity is gradually brought about. The words 'cause' and 'effect' still linger, but the old conceptions have been dropped from mechanical philosophy; for the fact now known is that

in certain relative positions bodies undergo certain accelerations. Now an acceleration, instead of being like a velocity a relation between two successive positions, is a relation between three; so that the new doctrine has consisted in the suitable introduction of the conception of threeness. On this idea, the whole of modern physics is built. The superiority of modern geometry, too, has certainly been due to nothing so much as to the bridging over of the innumerable distinct cases with which the ancient science was encumbered; and we may go so far as to say that all the great steps in the method of science in every department have consisted in bringing into relation cases previously discrete.

360 We can easily recognize the man whose thought is mainly in the dual stage by his unmeasured use of language. In former days, when he was natural, everything with him was unmitigated, absolute, ineffable, utter, matchless, supreme, unqualified, root and branch; but now that it is the fashion to be depreciatory, he is just as plainly marked by the ridiculous inadequacy of his expressions. The principle of contradiction is a shibboleth for such minds; to disprove a proposition they will always try to prove there lurks a contradiction in it, notwithstanding that it may be as clear and comprehensible as the day. Remark for your amusement the grand unconcern with which mathematics, since the invention of the calculus, has pursued its way, caring no more for the peppering of contradiction-mongers than an ironclad for an American fort.

361 We have seen that it is the immediate consciousness that is preëminently first, the external dead thing that is preëminently second. In like manner, it is evidently the representation mediating between these two that is preëminently third. Other examples, however, should not be neglected. The first is agent, the second patient, the third is the action by which the former influences the latter. Between the beginning as first, and the end as last, comes the process which leads from first to last.

362 According to the mathematicians, when we measure along a line, were our yardstick replaced by a yard marked off on an infinitely long rigid bar, then in all the shiftings of it which we make for the purpose of applying it to successive portions of the line to be measured, two points on that bar would remain fixed and unmoved. To that pair of points, the mathematicians accord the title of the absolute; they are the points that are at an infinite distance one way and the other as measured by that yard. These points are either really

distinct, coincident, or imaginary (in which case there is but a finite distance completely round the line), according to the relation of the mode of measurement to the nature of the line upon which the measurement is made. These two points are the absolute first and the absolute last or second, while every measurable point on the line is of the nature of a third. We have seen that the conception of the absolute first eludes every attempt to grasp it; and so in another sense does that of the absolute second; but there is no absolute third, for the third is of its own nature relative, and this is what we are always thinking, even when we aim at the first or second. The starting-point of the universe, God the Creator, is the Absolute First; the terminus of the universe, God completely revealed, is the Absolute Second; every state of the universe at a measurable point of time is the third. If you think the measurable is all there is, and deny it any definite tendency whence or whither, then you are considering the pair of points that makes the absolute to be imaginary and are an Epicurean. If you hold that there is a definite drift to the course of nature as a whole, but yet believe its absolute end is nothing but the Nirvana from which it set out, you make the two points of the absolute to be coincident, and are a pessimist. But if your creed is that the whole universe is approaching in the infinitely distant future a state having a general character different from that toward which we look back in the infinitely distant past, you make the absolute to consist in two distinct real points and are an evolutionist.[1] This is one of the matters concerning which a man can only learn from his own reflections, but I believe that if my suggestions are followed out, the reader will grant that one, two, three, are more than mere count-words like 'eeny, meeny, miny, mo', but carry vast, though vague, ideas.

363 But it will be asked, why stop at three? Why not go on to find a new conception in four, five, and so on indefinitely? The reason is that while it is impossible to form a genuine three by any modification of the pair, without introducing something of a different nature from the unit and the pair, four, five, and every higher number can be formed by mere complications of threes. To make this clear, I will first show it in an example. The fact that A presents B with a gift C, is a triple relation, and as such cannot possibly be resolved into any combination of dual relations. Indeed, the very idea of a combination involves that of thirdness, for a combination is something which is what it is owing to the parts which it brings into mutual relationship.

But we may waive that consideration, and still we cannot build up the fact that A presents C to B by any aggregate of dual relations between A and B, B and C, and C and A. A may enrich B, B may receive C, and A may part with C, and yet A need not necessarily give C to B. For that, it would be necessary that these three dual relations should not only coexist, but be welded into one fact. Thus we see that a triad cannot be analyzed into dyads. But now I will show by an example that a four can be analyzed into threes. Take the quadruple fact that A sells C to B for the price D. This is a compound of two facts: first, that A makes with C a certain trans- action, which we may name E; and second, that this transaction E is a sale of B for the price D. Each of these two facts is a triple fact, and their combination makes up [as] genuine [a] quadruple fact as can be found. The explanation of this striking difference is not far to seek. A dual relative term, such as 'lover' or 'servant', is a sort of blank form, where there are two places left blank. I mean that in building a sentence round 'lover', as the principal word of the pred- icate, we are at liberty to make anything we see fit the subject, and then, besides that, anything we please the object of the action of loving. But a triple relative term such as 'giver' has two correlates, and is thus a blank form with three places left blank. Consequently, we can take two of these triple relatives and fill up one blank place in each with the same letter, X, which has only the force of a pronoun or identifying index, and then the two taken together will form a whole having four blank places; and from that we can go on in a similar way to any higher number. But when we attempt to imitate this proceeding with dual relatives, and combine two of them by means of an X, we find we only have two blank places in the combi- nation, just as we had in either of the relatives taken by itself. A road with only three-way forkings may have any number of termini, but no number of straight roads put end on end will give more than two termini. Thus any number, however, large, can be built out of triads; and consequently no idea can be involved in such a number, radically different from the idea of three. I do not mean to deny that the higher numbers may present interesting special configurations from which notions may be derived of more or less general applicability; but these cannot rise to the height of philosophical categories so fundamental as those that have been considered.

364 The argument of this book has been developed in the mind of the author, substantially as it is presented, as a following out of these

three conceptions, in a sort of game of 'follow-my-leader' from one field of thought into another. Their importance was originally brought home to me in the study of logic, where they play so remarkable a part that I was led to look for them in psychology. Finding them there again, I could not help asking myself whether they did not enter into the physiology of the nervous system. By drawing a little on hypothesis, I succeeded in detecting them there; and then the question naturally came how they would appear in the theory of protoplasm in general. Here I seemed to break into an interesting avenue of reflections giving instructive *aperçus* both into the nature of protoplasm and into the conceptions themselves; though it was not till later that I mapped out my thoughts on the subject as they are presented in Section 4.[2] I had no difficulty in following the lead into the domain of natural selection; and once arrived at that point, I was irresistibly carried on to speculations concerning physics. One bold saltus landed me in a garden of fruitful and beautiful suggestions, the exploration of which long prevented my looking further. As soon, however, as I was induced to look further, and to examine the application of the three ideas to the deepest problems of the soul, nature and God, I saw at once that they must carry me far into the heart of those primeval mysteries. That is the way the book has grown in my mind: it is also the order in which I have written it; and only this first chapter is more or less an afterthought, since at an earlier stage of my studies I should have looked upon the matter here set down as too vague to have any value. I should have discerned in it too strong a resemblance to many a crack-brained book that I had laughed over. A deeper study has taught me that even out of the mouths of babes and sucklings strength may be brought forth, and that weak metaphysical trash has sometimes contained the germs of conceptions capable of growing up into important and positive doctrines.

365 Thus, the whole book being nothing but a continual exemplification of the triad of ideas, we need linger no longer upon this preliminary exposition of them. There is, however, one feature of them upon which it is quite indispensable to dwell. It is that there are two distinct grades of Secondness and three grades of Thirdness. There is a close analogy to this in geometry. Conic sections are either the curves usually so called, or they are pairs of straight lines. A pair of straight lines is called a degenerate conic. So plane cubic curves are either the genuine curves of the third order, or they are conics paired with straight lines, or they consist of three straight lines; so

that there are the two orders of degenerate cubics. Nearly in this same way, besides genuine Secondness, there is a degenerate sort which does not exist as such, but is only so conceived. The medieval logicians (following a hint of Aristotle) distinguished between real relations and relations of reason. A real relation subsists in virtue of a fact which would be totally impossible were either of the related objects destroyed; while a relation of reason subsists in virtue of two facts, one only of which would disappear on the annihilation of either of the relates. Such are all resemblances: for any two objects in nature resemble each other, and indeed in themselves just as much as any other two; it is only with reference to our senses and needs that one resemblance counts for more than another. Rumford and Franklin resembled each other by virtues of being both Americans; but either would have been just as much an American if the other had never lived. On the other hand, the fact that Cain killed Abel cannot be stated as a mere aggregate of two facts, one concerning Cain and the other concerning Abel. Resemblances are not the only relations of reason, though they have that character in an eminent degree. Contrasts and comparisons are of the same sort. Resemblance is an identity of characters; and this is the same as to say that the mind gathers the resembling ideas together into one conception. Other relations of reason arise from ideas being connected by the mind in other ways; they consist in the relation between two parts of one complex concept, or, as we may say, in the relation of a complex concept to itself, in respect to two of its parts. This brings us to consider a sort of degenerate Secondness that does not fulfill the definition of a relation of reason. Identity is the relation that everything bears to itself: Lucullus dines with Lucullus. Again, we speak of allurements and motives in the language of forces, as though a man suffered compulsion from within. So with the voice of conscience: and we observe our own feelings by a reflective sense. An echo is my own voice coming back to answer itself. So also, we speak of the abstract quality of a thing as if it were some second thing that the first thing possesses. But the relations of reason and these self-relations are alike in this, that they arise from the mind setting one part of a notion into relation to another. All degenerate seconds may be conveniently termed internal, in contrast to external seconds, which are constituted by external fact, and are true actions of one thing upon another.

366 Among thirds, there are two degrees of degeneracy. The first is where there is in the fact itself no Thirdness or mediation, but

where there is true duality; the second degree is where there is not even true Secondness in the fact itself. Consider, first, the thirds degenerate in the first degree. A pin fastens two things together by sticking through one and also through the other: either might be annihilated, and the pin would continue to stick through the one which remained. A mixture brings its ingredients together by containing each. We may term these accidental thirds. 'How did I slay thy son?' asked the merchant, and the jinnee replied, 'When thou threwest away the date-stone, it smote my son, who was passing at the time, on the breast, and he died forthright.' Here there were two independent facts, first that the merchant threw away the date-stone, and second that the date-stone struck and killed the jinnee's son. Had it been aimed at him, the case would have been different; for then there would have been a relation of aiming which would have connected together the aimer, the thing aimed, and the object aimed at, in one fact. What monstrous injustice and inhumanity on the part of that jinnee to hold that poor merchant responsible for such an accident! I remember how I wept at it, as I lay in my father's arms as he first told me the story. It is certainly just that a man, even though he had no evil intention, should be held responsible for the immediate effects of his actions; but not for such as might result from them in a sporadic case here and there, but only for such as might have been guarded against by a reasonable rule of prudence. Nature herself often supplies the place of the intention of a rational agent in making a Thirdness genuine and not merely accidental; as when a spark, as third, falling into a barrel of gunpowder, as first, causes an explosion, as second. But how does nature do this? By virtue of an intelligible law according to which she acts. If two forces are combined according to the parallelogram of forces, their resultant is a real third. Yet any force may, by the parallelogram of forces, be mathematically resolved into the sum of two others, in an infinity of different ways. Such components, however, are mere creations of the mind. What is the difference? As far as one isolated event goes, there is none; the real forces are no more present in the resultant than any components that the mathematician may imagine. But what makes the real forces really there is the general law of nature which calls for them, and not for any other components of the resultant. Thus, intelligibility, or reason objectified, is what makes Thirdness genuine.

367 We now come to thirds degenerate in the second degree. The dramatist Marlowe had something of the character of diction in

which Shakespeare and Bacon agree. This is a trivial example; but the mode of relation is important. In natural history, intermediate types serve to bring out the resemblance between forms whose similarity might otherwise escape attention, or not be duly appreciated. In portraiture, photographs mediate between the original and the likeness. In science, a diagram or analogue of the observed fact leads on to a further analogy. The relations of reason which go to the formation of such a triple relation need not be all resemblances. Washington was eminently free from the faults in which most great soldiers resemble one another. A centaur is a mixture of a man and a horse. Philadelphia lies between New York and Washington. Such thirds may be called intermediate thirds or thirds of comparison.

2 THE TRIAD IN REASONING[3]

369 Kant, the King of modern thought, it was who first remarked the frequency in logical analytics of *trichotomics* or threefold distinctions. It really is so; I have tried hard and long to persuade myself that it is only fanciful, but the facts will not countenance that way of disposing of the phenomenon. Take any ordinary syllogism:

> All men are mortal,
> Elijah was a man;
> Therefore, Elijah was mortal.

There are here three propositions, namely, two premisses and a conclusion; there are also three terms, *man*, *mortal*, and *Elijah*. If we transpose one of the premisses with the conclusion, denying both, we obtain what are called the indirect figures of syllogism; for example

> All men are mortal,
> But Elijah was not mortal;
> Therefore, Elijah was not a man.

> Elijah was not mortal,
> But Elijah was a man;
> Therefore, some men are not mortal.

Thus, there are three figures of ordinary syllogism. It is true there are other modes of inference which do not come under any of these heads; but that does not annul the fact that we have here a trichotomy. Indeed, if we examine by itself what is by some logicians called the fourth figure, we find that it also has three varieties related to one another as the three figures of ordinary syllogism. There is an entirely different way of conceiving the relations of the figures of syllogism; namely, by means of the conversion of propositions. But from that point of view also, the same classes are preserved. DeMorgan has added a large number of new syllogistic moods which do not find places in this classification.[4] The reasoning in these is of a peculiar character and introduces the principle of dilemma. Still, regarding these dilemmatic reasonings by themselves, they fall into three classes in a precisely similar manner. Again, I have shown that the probable and approximate inferences of science must be classified on the very same principles,[5] being either Deductions, Inductions, or Hypotheses. Other examples of threes in logic are statements of what is actual, what is possible, and what is necessary; the three kinds of forms, Names,[6] Propositions, and Inferences;[7] affirmative, negative, and uncertain answers to a question. One very important triad is this: it has been found that there are three kinds of signs which are all indispensable in all reasoning; the first is the diagrammatic sign or *icon*, which exhibits a similarity or analogy to the subject of discourse; the second is the *index*, which like a pronoun demonstrative or relative, forces the attention to the particular object intended without describing it; the third [or symbol] is the general name or description which signifies its object by means of an association of ideas or habitual connection between the name and the character signified.

370 But there is one triad in particular which throws a strong light on the nature of all the others. Namely, we find it necessary to recognize in logic three kinds of characters, three kinds of facts. First there are *singular* characters which are predicable of single objects, as when we say that anything is white, large, etc. Secondly, there are dual characters which appertain to pairs of objects; these are implied by all relative terms as 'lover', similar', other', etc. Thirdly, there are plural characters, which can all be reduced to triple characters but not to dual characters. Thus, we cannot express the fact that A is a benefactor of B by any descriptions of A and B separately; we must introduce a relative term. This is requisite, not merely in English, but in every language which might be invented. This is true even of such a fact as A is taller than B. If we say 'A is tall, But B is short', the conjugation 'but' has relative force, and if we omit this word the

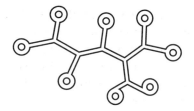

Figure 3.1

mere collocation of the two sentences is a relative or dual mode of signifying. . . .

371 Let us now consider a triple character, say that A gives B to C. This is not a mere congeries of dual characters. It is not enough to say that A parts with C, and that B receives C. A synthesis of these two facts must be made to bring them into a single fact; we must express that C, in being parted with by A, is received by B. If, on the other hand, we take a quadruple fact, it is easy to express as a compound of two triple facts. . . . We are here able to express the synthesis of the two facts into one, because a triple character involves the conception of synthesis. Analysis involves the same relations as synthesis; so that we may explain the fact that all plural facts can be reduced to triple facts in this way. A road with a fork in it is the analogue of a triple fact, because it brings three termini into relation with one another. A dual fact is like a road without a fork; it only connects two termini. Now, no combination of roads without forks can have more than two termini; but any number of termini can be connected by roads which nowhere have a knot of more than three ways. See Figure 3.1, where I have drawn the termini as self-returning roads, in order to introduce nothing beyond the road itself. Thus, the three essential elements of a network of roads are *road about a terminus, roadway-connection*, and *branching*; and in like manner, the three fundamental categories of fact are, fact about an object, fact about two objects (relation), fact about several objects (synthetic fact).

372 We have seen that the mere coexistence of two singular facts constitutes a degenerate form of dual fact; and in like manner there are two orders of degeneracy in plural facts, for either they may consist in a mere synthesis of facts of which the highest is dual, or they may consist in a mere synthesis of singular facts. This explains

why there should be three classes of *signs*; for there is a triple connection of *sign, thing signified, cognition produced in the mind*. There may be a mere relation of reason between the sign and the thing signified; in that case the sign is an *icon*. Or there may be a direct physical connection; in that case, the sign is an *index*. Or there may be a relation which consists in the fact that the mind associates the sign with its object; in that case the sign is a *name* [or *symbol*].[8] Now consider the difference between a logical *term*, a *proposition*, and an *inference*. A term is a mere general description, and as neither *icon* nor *index* possesses generality, it must be a name; and it is nothing more. A proposition is also a general description, but it differs from a term in that it purports to be in a real relation to the fact, to be really determined by it; thus, a proposition can only be formed of the conjunction of a name and an index. An inference, too, contains a general description.

NOTES

1 The last view is essentially that of Christian theology, too. The theologians hold the physical universe to be finite, but considering that universe which they will admit to have existed from all time, it would appear to be in a different condition in the end from what it was in the beginning, the whole spiritual creation having been accomplished, and abiding.

2 [See 'The Triad in Philosophy'. Scholars use a shorthand notation to refer to the *Collected Papers of Charles Sanders Peirce* (1931–58). This consists of the volume number followed by a colon and then a second number denoting the paragraph. Hence 'The Triad in Psychology' can be referenced as (1: 374–384) P.C.].

3 From 'One, Two, Three: Fundamental Categories of Thought and of Nature', c. 1885. This paper does not seem to form part of 'A Guess at the Riddle', but is here inserted to take the place of the unwritten section 2 of the original work [Edited by C. Hartshorne and P. Weiss].

4 *Formal Logic*, ch. 8. See also Peirce 1931 ch. 2. 568.

5 See Peirce 1931 vol. 2, bk III, chs 2 and 5.

6 Or Terms, but see 372.

7 Or Arguments.

8 Cf. 369.

The sign in use

EDITOR'S INTRODUCTION

What Benveniste says about the 'arbitrariness' of relations in the sign is crucial for communication theory. Saussure had insisted that the connection between a signifier and a signified was not a 'natural' one; rather it was based on convention or habit. Benveniste sympathetically summarizes this but mentions that Saussure seems to have omitted from his signifier/signified dyad a third term, the thing in the world to which the sign refers. This is a salient omission because, as Benveniste argues, the arbitrary relation is one which exists between the *whole sign* and the *object* in the real world that it refers to. Relations between the signifier and signified are not arbitrary at all for language users; in fact, the sound and the concept seem to be as one in the human mind. This essay is characteristic of Benveniste's take on linguistics: his extensions of Saussure are always conducted in an effort to apprehend *the user's* feelings in language. In this, he is not alone.

Even though it was published in 1929, Vološinov's critique of Saussure is still probably the most incisive one that we possess. The first part of the extract reprinted below is dedicated to a discussion of the Geneva school (Saussure and his students, Bally and Sèchehaye) as representative of 'abstract objectivism'. Saussure's *Course* is 'abstract' because it does not take as its main focus concrete utterances, opting, instead, for 'form' (*langue*, the non-concrete system of differences) as the basis of language study. It is 'objectivist' because it promotes the idea that this form rules concrete utterances and is the common denominator of all meaning among all people.

Against this, Vološinov describes his own understanding of language in which the uttered word is a 'two-sided act'. No longer is utterance (*parole*) to be considered as determined by an abstract system; instead, in its 'addressivity' or 'dialogism', the utterance is always a socially situated phenomenon. This observation, although at first reading it seems inconsequential, has significant ramifications. It shifts the focus of language study to the social environment in which utterance takes place; it also entertains the notion of language as ever open to change, adjustment and inflection. Hence Vološinov's theory embodies precisely the 'diachrony' which Saussure felt it necessary to exclude from his general linguistics.

Vološinov also introduces 'theme' and 'accent' in the extract, concepts which indicate the material fashion in which meaning is different each time an utterance occurs because the situation is different on every occasion. The term 'meaning' is quite a problematic one for both Vološinov *and* Saussure: the latter insists on 'value' rather than 'meaning' as the distinguishing attribute possessed by a sign in a system of differences; likewise, Vološinov denies the possibility that a sign can have 'meaning' on its own. But whereas Saussure locates 'value' in the interaction of signs (see this volume pp. 99–114), Vološinov finds that 'meaning' is only part of a 'theme' which resides in the whole interaction *between speakers*. Moreover, 'meaning' is subject to the specific socially orientated intonation of utterances that Vološinov names 'accent'.

There can be little doubt that communication as Vološinov sees it is a 'linguistic process in socio-cultural practice'. In this respect it is useful to compare his comments on 'I' and 'we' with those of Benveniste, below (see this volume pp. 320–30). Halliday's understanding of language as a 'social semiotic' is far closer to Vološinov than it is to Saussure. Where Halliday has the edge on his Russian predecessor, however, is that he has been a tireless modern researcher into the child's acquisition of language. The passage that follows contains a very succinct summary of Halliday's position following years of sociolinguistic exploration. Writing in the 1970s, Halliday finds himself in an intellectual position comparable to that of Vološinov in 1929: on the one side is a linguistics which is heavily systematic, based on the study of the generative processes embodied in grammar; on the other is a semantics which considers every utterance as new and individual. Halliday indicates the need for a linguistics which accounts for the means by which the learning of the semantic system (learning how to denote) is bound up with learning *about* the world denoted.

All three of these readings, then, provide perspectives on communication in which the user's experience of the social institution of language is the directing principle in the ensuing theoretical framework. It will be useful to bear such perspectives in mind when reading subsequent parts of this volume.

Further reading: Harland 1987 pp. 77–80; Vološinov 1987; Dentith 1995 or Morris 1994; Holquist 1990 pp. 44–49; Pearce 1994 pp. 27–79; Halliday 1976 pp. 3–31; Hodge and Kress 1988 pp. 83–91; Threadgold 1987.

4 Émile Benveniste

The nature of the linguistic sign

The idea of the linguistic sign, which is today asserted or implied in most works of general linguistics, came from Ferdinand de Saussure. And it was as an obvious truth, not yet explicit but nevertheless undeniable in fact, that Saussure taught that the nature of the sign is *arbitrary*. The formula immediately commanded attention. Every utterance concerning the essence of language or the modalities of discourse begins with a statement of the arbitrary character of the linguistic sign. The principle is of such significance that any thinking bearing upon any part of linguistics whatsoever necessarily encounters it. That it is cited everywhere and always granted as obvious are two good reasons for seeking at least to understand the sense in which Saussure took it and the nature of the proofs which show it.

In the *Cours de linguistique générale*,[1] this definition is explained in very simple statements. One calls *sign* 'the total resultant of the association of signifier [= sound image] and what is signified [= concept]'. . . . 'The idea of 'sister' is not linked by any inner relationship to the succession of sounds s-ö-r which serves as its signifier in French; that it could be represented equally by just any other sequence is proved by differences among languages and by the very existence of different languages: the signified 'ox' has as its signifier b-ö-f on one side of the order and o-k-s (Ochs) on the other' (p. 102 [pp. 67–8]). This ought to establish that 'The bond between the signifier and the signified is arbitrary', or, more simply, that 'the linguistic sign is arbitrary', [p. 67]. By 'arbitrary', the author means that 'it is *unmotivated*, i.e., arbitrary in that it actually has no natural connection with the signified' (p. 103 [p. 69]). This characteristic ought then to explain the very fact by which it is verified: namely, that expressions of a given notion vary in time and space and in consequence have no necessary relationship with it.

We do not contemplate discussing this conclusion in the name of other principles or by starting with different definitions. The question is whether it is consistent and whether, having accepted the bipartite nature of the sign (and we do accept it), it follows that the sign should be characterized as arbitrary. It has just been seen that Saussure took the linguistic sign to be made up of a signifier and signified. Now – and this is essential – he meant by 'signified', the *concept*. He declared in so many words (p. 100 [p. 66]) that the 'linguistic sign unites, not a thing and a name, but a concept and a sound image'. But immediately afterward he stated that the nature of the sign is arbitrary because it 'actually has no natural connection with the signified' [p. 69]. It is clear that the argument is falsified by an unconscious and surreptitious recourse to a third term which was not included in the initial definition. This third term is the thing itself, the reality. Even though Saussure said that the idea of 'sister' is not connected to the signifier *s-ö-r*, he was not thinking any the less of the *reality* of the notion. When he spoke of the difference between *b-ö-f* and *o-k-s*, he was referring in spite of himself to the fact that these two terms applied to the same *reality*. Here, then, is the *thing*, expressly excluded at first from the definition of the sign, now creeping into it by detour, and permanently installing a contradiction there. For if one states in principle – and with reason – that language is *form*, not *substance* (p. 163 [p. 113]) it is necessary to admit – and Saussure asserted it plainly – that linguistics is exclusively a science of forms. Even more imperative is the necessity for leaving the 'substance', *sister* or *ox*, outside the realm of the sign. Now it is only if one thinks of the animal *ox* in its concrete and 'substantial' particularity, that one is justified in considering 'arbitrary' the relationship between *böf* on the one hand and *oks* on the other to the same reality. There is thus a contradiction between the way in which Saussure defined the linguistic sign and the fundamental nature which he attributed to it.

Such an anomaly in Saussure's close reasoning does not seem to me to be imputable to a relaxation of his critical attention. I would see instead a distinctive trait of the historical and relativist thought of the end of the nineteenth century, an inclination often met within the philosophical reflection of comparative thought. Different people react differently to the same phenomenon. The infinite diversity of attitudes and judgments leads to the consideration that apparently nothing is necessary. From the universal dissimilarity, a universal contingency is inferred. The Saussurian concept is in some measure dependent on this system of thought. To decide that the linguistic sign is arbitrary because the same animal is called *bœuf* in one country and *Ochs* elsewhere, is equivalent to saying that the notion of mourning is arbitrary because in Europe it is symbolized by black, in China by white. Arbitrary, yes, but only under the impassive regard of Sirius or for the person who limits himself to observing from the outside the bond established between an objective reality and human behaviour and condemns himself thus to seeing nothing in it but contingency. Certainly with respect to a same reality, all the denominations have equal value; that they exist is thus the proof that none of them can claim that the denomination in itself is absolute. This is true. It is only too true and thus not very instructive. The real problem is far more profound. It consists in discerning the inner structure of the phenomenon of which only the outward appearance is perceived, and in describing its relationship with the ensemble of manifestations on which it depends.

And so it is for the linguistic sign. One of the components of the sign, the sound image, makes up the signifier; the other, the concept, is the signified. Between the signifier and signified, the connection is not arbitrary; on the contrary, it is *necessary*. The concept (the 'signified') *bœuf* is perforce identical in my consciousness with the sound sequence (the 'signifier') *böf*. How could it be otherwise? The mind does not contain empty forms, concepts without names. Saussure himself said:

> Psychologically our thought – apart from its expression in words – is only a shapeless and indistinct mass. Philosophers and linguists have always agreed in recognizing that without the help of signs we would be unable to make a clear-cut, consistent distinction between two ideas. Without language, thought is a vague, uncharted nebula. There are no preexisting ideas, and nothing is distinct before the appearance of language.
>
> (p. 161 [pp. 111–112])

Conversely, the mind accepts only a sound form that incorporates a representation identifiable for it; if it does not, it rejects it as unknown or foreign. The signifier and the signified, the mental representation and the sound image, are thus in reality the two aspects of a single notion and together make up the ensemble as the embodier and the embodiment. The signifier is the phonic translation of a concept;

the signified is the mental counterpart of the signifier. This consub-stantiality of the signifier and the signified assures the structural unity of the linguistic sign. Here again we appeal to Saussure himself for what he said of language:

> Language can also be compared with a sheet of paper: thought is the front and the sound the back; one cannot cut the front without cutting the back at the same time; likewise in language, one can neither divide sound from thought nor thought from sound; the division could be accomplished only abstractedly, and the result would be either pure psychology or pure phonology.
>
> (p. 163 [p. 113])

What Saussure says here about language holds above all for the linguistic sign in which the primary characteristics of language are incontestably fixed.

One now sees the zone of the 'arbitrary', and one can set limits to it. What is arbitrary is that one certain sign and no other is applied to a certain element of reality, and not to any other. In this sense, and only in this sense, is it permissible to speak of contingency, and even in so doing we would seek less to solve the problem than to point it out and then to take leave of it temporarily. For the problem is none other than the famous φύσει or θέσει? and can only be resolved by decree. It is indeed the metaphysical problem of the agreement between the mind and the world transposed into linguistic terms, a problem which the linguist will perhaps one day be able to attach with results but which he will do better to put aside for the moment. To establish the relationship as arbitrary is for the linguist a way of defending himself against this question and also against the solution which the speaker brings instinctively to it. For the speaker there is a complete equivalence between language and reality. The sign overlies and commands reality; even better, it *is* that reality (*nomen/omen*, speech taboos, the magic power of the word, etc.). As a matter of fact, the point of view of the speaker and of the linguist are so different in this regard that the assertion of the linguist as to the arbitrariness of designations does not refute the contrary feeling of the speaker. But, whatever the case may be, the nature of the linguistic sign is not at all involved if one defines it as Saussure did, since the essence of this definition is precisely to consider only the relationship of the signifier and the signified. The domain of the arbitrary is thus left outside the extension of the linguistic sign.

It is thus rather pointless to defend the principle of the 'arbitrariness of the sign' against the objection which could be raised from onomatopoeia and expressive words (Saussure, pp. 103–104 [pp. 69–70]). Not only because their range of use is relatively limited and because expressivity is an essentially transitory, subjective, and often secondary effect, but especially because, here again, whatever the reality is that ls depicted by the onomatopoeia or the expressive word, the allusion to that reality in most cases is not immediate and is only admitted by a symbolic convention analogous to the convention that sanctions the ordinary signs of the system. We thus get back to the definition and the characteristics which are valid for all signs. The arbitrary does not exist here either, except with respect to the phenomenon or to the *material* object, and does not interfere with the actual composition of the sign.

Some of the conclusions which Saussure drew from the principle here discussed and which had wide effect should now be briefly considered. For instance, he demonstrated admirably that one can speak at the same time of the mutability and immutability of the sign; mutability, because since it is arbitrary it is always open to change, and immutability, because being arbitrary it cannot be challenged in the name of a rational norm. 'Language is radically powerless to defend itself against the forces which from one moment to the next are shifting the relationship between the signified and the signifier. This is one of the consequences of the arbitrary nature of the sign' (p. 112 [p. 75]). The merit of this analysis is in no way diminished, but on the contrary is reinforced, if one states more precisely the relationship to which it in fact applies. It is not between the signifier and the signified that the relationship is modified and at the same time remains immutable; it is between the sign and the object; that is in other terms, the objective *motivation* of the designation, submitted, as such, to the action of various historical factors. What Saussure demonstrated remains true, but true of the *signification*, not the sign.

Another problem, no less important, which the definition of the sign concerns directly, is that of *value*, in which Saussure thought to find a confirmation of his views: '. . . the choice of a given slice of sound to name a given idea is completely arbitrary. If this were not true, the notion of value would be compromised, for it would include an externally imposed element. But actually values remain entirely relative, and that is why the bond between the sound and the idea is radically arbitrary' (p. 163 [p. 113]). It is worth the trouble to take up in succession the several parts of this argument. The choice that invokes a certain sound slice for a certain idea is not at all arbitrary; this sound slice would not exist without the corresponding idea and vice versa. In reality, Saussure was always thinking of the representation of the *real object* (although he spoke of the 'idea') and of the evidently unnecessary and unmotivated character of the bond which united the sign to the *thing* signified. The proof of this confusion lies in the following sentence in which I have underlined the characteristic part: 'If this were not true, the notion of value would be compromised *since it would include an externally imposed element.*' It is indeed an 'externally imposed element', that is, the *objective* reality which this argument takes as a pole of reference. But if one considers the sign in itself and insofar as it is the carrier of value, the arbitrary is necessarily eliminated. For – the last proposition is the one which most clearly includes its own refutation – it is quite true that values remain entirely 'relative' but the question is how and with respect to what. Let us state this at once: value is an element of the sign; if the sign taken in itself is not arbitrary, as we think to have shown, it follows that the 'relative' character of the value cannot depend on the 'arbitrary' nature of the sign. Since it is necessary to leave out of account the conformity of the sign to reality, all the more should one consider the value as an attribute only of the *form*, not of the substance. From then on, to say that the values are 'relative' means that they are relative *to each other*. Now, is that not precisely the proof of their *necessity*? We deal no longer here with the isolated sign but with language as a system of signs, and no one has conceived of and described the systematic economy of language as forcefully as Saussure. Whoever says system says arrangement or conformity of parts in a structure which transcends and explains its elements. Everything is so *necessary* in it that modifications of the whole and of details reciprocally condition one another. The relativity of values is the best proof that they depend closely upon one another in the synchrony of a system which is always being threatened, always being restored. The point is that all values are values of opposition and are defined only by their difference. Opposed to each other, they maintain themselves in a mutual relationship of necessity. An opposition is, owing to the force of circumstances, subtended by necessity, as it is necessity which gives shape to the opposition. If language is something other than a fortuitous conglomeration of erratic notions and sounds uttered at random, it is because necessity is inherent in its structure as in all structure.

It emerges, then, that the role of contingency inherent in language affects denomination insofar as denomination is a phonic symbol of reality and affects it in its relationship with reality. But the sign, the primordial element in the linguistic system, includes a signifier and a signified whose bond has to be recognized as *necessary*, these two components being consubstantially the same. *The absolute character of the linguistic sign* thus understood commands in its turn the dialectical *necessity* of values of constant opposition, and forms the structural principle of language. It is perhaps the best evidence of the fruitfulness of a doctrine that it can engender a contradiction which promotes it. In restoring the true nature of the sign in the internal conditioning of the system, we go beyond Saussure himself to affirm the rigor of Saussure's thought.

NOTE

1 Cited here from the first edition, Lausanne-Paris (1916). The page numbers in square brackets refer to the translation (1974).

V. N. Vološinov

Toward a Marxist philosophy of language

TWO TRENDS IN PHILOSOPHY OF LANGUAGE

Abstract objectivism finds its most striking expression at the present time in the so-called Geneva school of Ferdinand de Saussure. Its representatives, particularly Charles Bally, are among the most prominent linguists of modern times. The ideas of this second trend all have been endowed with amazing clarity and precision by Ferdinand de Saussure. His formulations of the basic concepts of linguistics can well be accounted classics of their kind. Moreover, Saussure undauntedly carried his ideas out to their conclusions, providing all the basic lines of abstract objectivism with exceptionally clear-cut and rigorous definition.

In Russia, the Saussure school is as popular and influential as the Vossler school is not. It can be claimed that the majority of Russian thinkers in linguistics are under the determinative influence of Saussure and his disciples, Bally and Sèchehaye.[1]

In view of the fundamental importance of Saussure's views for the whole second trend and for Russian linguistic thought in particular, we shall consider those views in some detail. Here as elsewhere, to be sure, we shall confine ourselves to basic philosophical-linguistic positions only.[2]

Saussure's point of departure is a distinction among three aspects of language: *language-speech* (langage), *language as a system of forms* (langue) and *the individual speech act – the utterance* (parole). Language (in the sense of *langue*: a system of forms) and utterance (*parole*) are constituents of language-speech (*langage*), and the latter is understood to mean the sum total of all the phenomena – physical, physiological, and psychological – involved in the realization of verbal activity.

Language-speech (*langage*), according to Saussure, cannot be the object of study for linguistics. In and of itself, it lacks unity and validity as an autonomous entity; it is a heterogeneous composite. Its contradictory composition makes it difficult to handle. Precise definition of linguistic fact would be an impossibility on its grounds. Language-speech cannot be the point of departure for linguistic analysis.

What, then, does Saussure propose should be chosen as the correct methodological procedure for the identification of the specific object of linguistics? We shall let him speak for himself:

> In our opinion, there can be but one solution to all these [i.e., difficulties entailed in taking *langage* as the point of departure for analysis–V.V.]: *we must first and foremost take our stand on the grounds of language* (langue) *and accept it as the norm for all other manifestations of speech* (langage). Indeed, amidst so many dualities, language alone appears susceptible to autonomous definition, and it alone can provide the mind a satisfactory base of operations.
>
> (Saussure 1922 p. 24)

And in what does Saussure see the fundamental difference between speech (*langage*) and language (*langue*)?

> Taken in its totality, speech is manifold and anomalous. Astride several domains at once – the physical, the physiological, the psychological, it pertains, also, both to the domain of the individual and to the domain of society. It resists classification under any of the categories of human facts because there is no knowing how to elicit its unity.
>
> Language, on the contrary, is a self-contained whole and a principle of classification. Once we give it first place among the facts of speech, we introduce a natural order into an assemblage that is amenable to no other classification.
>
> (Saussure 1922 p. 25)

Thus, Saussure's contention is that language as a system of normatively identical forms must be taken as the point of departure and that all manifestations of speech must be illuminated from the angle of these stable and autonomous forms.

husband, and so on) or not. There can be no such thing as an abstract addressee, a man unto himself, so to speak. With such a person, we would indeed have no language in common, literally and figuratively. Even though we sometimes have pretensions to experiencing and saying things *urbi et orbi*, actually, of course, we envision this 'world at large' through the prism of the concrete social milieu surrounding us. In the majority of cases, we presuppose a certain typical and stabilized *social purview* toward which the ideological creativity of our own social group and time is oriented, i.e., we assume as our addressee a contemporary of our literature, our science, our moral and legal codes.

Each person's inner world and thought has its stabilized *social audience* that comprises the environment in which reasons, motives, values and so on are fashioned. The more cultured a person, the more closely his inner audience will approximate the normal audience of ideological creativity; but, in any case, specific class and specific era are limits that the ideal of addressee cannot go beyond.

Orientation of the word toward the addressee has an extremely high significance. In point of fact, *word is a two-sided act*. It is determined equally by *whose* word it is and *for whom* it is meant. As word, it is precisely *the product of the reciprocal relationship between speaker and listener, addresser and addressee*. Each and every word expresses the 'one' in relation to the 'other'. I give myself verbal shape from another's point of view, ultimately, from the point of view of the community to which I belong. A word is a bridge thrown between myself and another. If one end of the bridge depends on me, then the other depends on my addressee. A word is territory shared by both addresser and addressee, by the speaker and his interlocutor.

But what does being the speaker mean? Even if a word is not entirely his, constituting, as it were, the border zone between himself and his addressee – still, it does in part belong to him.

There is one instance of the situation wherein the speaker is the undoubted possessor of the word and to which, in this instance, he has full rights. This instance is the physiological act of implementing the word. But insofar as the act is taken in purely physiological terms, the category of possession does not apply.

If, instead, of the physiological act of implementing sound, we take the implementation of word as sign, then the question of proprietorship becomes extremely complicated. Aside from the fact that word as sign is a borrowing on the speaker's part from the social stock of available signs, the very individual manipulation of this social sign in a concrete utterance is wholly determined by social relations. The stylistic individualization of an utterance that the Vosslerites speak about represents a reflection of social interrelationships that constitute the atmosphere in which an utterance is formed. *The immediate social situation and the broader social milieu wholly determine – and determine from within, so to speak – the structure of an utterance.*

Indeed, take whatever kind of utterance we will, even the kind of utterance that is not a referential message (communication in the narrow sense) but the verbal expression of some need – for instance, hunger – we may be certain that it is socially oriented in its entirety. Above all, it is determined immediately and directly by the participants of the speech event, both explicit and implicit participants, in connection with a specific situation. That situation shapes the utterance, dictating that it sound one way and not another – like a demand or request, insistence on one's rights or a plea for mercy, in a style flowery or plain, in a confident or hesitant manner, and so on.

The immediate social situation and its immediate social participants determine the 'occasional' form and style of an utterance. The deeper layers of its structure are determined by more sustained and more basic social connections with which the speaker is in contact.

Even if were to take an utterance still in process of generation 'in the soul', it would not change the essence of the matter, since the structure of experience is just as social as is the structure of its outward objectification. The degree to which an experience is perceptible, distinct, and formulated is directly proportional to the degree to which it is socially oriented.

In fact, not even the simplest, dimmest apprehension of a feeling – say, the feeling of hunger not outwardly expressed– can dispense with some kind of ideological form. Any apprehension, after all, must have inner speech, inner intonation and the rudiments of inner style; one can apprehend one's hunger apologetically, irritably, angrily, indignantly, etc. We have indicated, of course, only the grosser, more egregious directions that inner intonation may take; actually, there is an extremely subtle and complex set of possibilities for intoning an experience. Outward expression in most cases only continues and makes more distinct the direction already taken by inner speech and the intonation already embedded in it.

Which way the intoning of the inner sensation of hunger will go depends upon the hungry person's general social standing as well as upon the immediate circumstances of the experience. These are, after all, the circumstances that determine in what evaluative contexts, within what social purview, the experience of hunger will be apprehended. The immediate social context will determine possible addressees, friends or foes, toward whom the consciousness and the experience of hunger will be oriented: whether it will involve dissatisfaction with cruel Nature, with oneself, with society, with a specific group within society, with a specific person, and so on. Of course, various degrees of perceptibility, distinctiveness, and differentiation in the social orientation of an experience are possible; but without some kind of evaluative social orientation there is no experience. Even the cry of a nursing infant is 'oriented' toward its mother. There is the possibility that the experience of hunger may take on political coloring, in which case its structure will be determined along the lines of a potential political appeal or a reason for political agitation. It may be apprehended as a form of protest, and so on.

With regard to the potential (and sometimes even distinctly sensed) addressee, a distinction can be made between two poles, two extremes between which an experience can be apprehended and ideologically structured, tending now toward the one, now toward the other. Let us label these two extremes the '*I-experience*' and the '*we-experience*'.

The 'I-experience' actually tends toward extermination: the nearer it approaches its extreme limit, the more it loses its ideological structuredness and, hence, its apprehensible quality, reverting to the physiological reaction of the animal. In its course toward this extreme, the experience relinquishes all its potentialities, all outcroppings of social orientation, and, therefore, also loses its verbal delineation. Single experiences or whole groups of experiences can approach this extreme, relinquishing, in so doing, their ideological clarity and structuredness and testifying to the inability of the consciousness to strike social roots.

The 'we-experience' is not by any means a nebulous herd experience; it is differentiated. Moreover, ideological differentiation, the growth of consciousness, is in direct proportion to the firmness and reliability of the social orientation. The stronger, the more organized, the more differentiated the collective in which an individual orients himself, the more vivid and complex his inner world will be.

The 'we-experience' allows of different degrees and different types of ideological structuring.

Let us suppose a case where hunger is apprehended by one of a disparate set of hungry persons whose hunger is a matter of chance (the man down on his luck, the beggar, or the like). The experience of such a declassé loner will be colored in some specific way and will gravitate toward certain particular ideological forms with a range potentially quite broad: humility, shame, enviousness, and other evaluative tones will color his experience. The ideological forms along the lines of which the experience would develop would be either the individualistic protest of a vagabond or repentant, mystical resignation.

Let us now suppose a case in which the hungry person belongs to a collective where hunger is not haphazard and does bear a collective character – but the collective of these hungry people is not itself tightly bound together by material ties, each of its members experiencing hunger on his own. This is the situation most peasants are in. Hunger is experience 'at large', but under conditions of material disparateness, in the absence of a unifying economic coalition, each person suffers hunger in the small, enclosed world of his own individual economy. Such a collective lacks the unitary material frame necessary for united action. A resigned but unashamed and undemeaning apprehension of one's hunger will be the rule under such conditions – 'everyone bears it, you must bear it, too'. Here grounds are furnished for the development of the philosophical and religious systems of the nonresistor or fatalist type (early Christianity, Tolstoyanism).

A completely different experience of hunger applies to a member of an objectively and materially aligned and united collective (a regiment of soldiers; workers in their association within the walls of a factory; hired hands on a large-scale, capitalist farm; finally, a whole class once it has matured to the point of 'class unto itself'). The experience of hunger this time will be marked predominantly by overtones of active and self-confident protest with no basis for humble and submissive intonation. These are the most favorable grounds for an experience to achieve ideological clarity and structuredness.

All these types of expression, each with its basic intonations, come rife with corresponding terms and corresponding forms of possible utterances. The social situation in all cases determines which term, which metaphor, and which form may develop in an utterance expressing hunger out of the particular intonational bearings of the experience.

A special kind of character marks the individualistic *self-experience*. It does not belong to the 'I-experience' in the strict sense of the term as defined above. The individualistic experience is fully differentiated and structured. Individualism is a special ideological form and the 'we-experience' of the bourgeois class (there is also an analogous type of individualistic self-experience for the feudal aristocratic class). The individualistic type of experience derives from a steadfast and confident social orientation. Individualistic confidence in oneself, one's sense of personal value, is drawn not from within, not from the depths of one's personality, but from the outside world. It is the ideological interpretation of one's social recognizance and tenability by rights, and of the objective security and tenability provided by the whole social order, of one's individual livelihood. The structure of the conscious, individual personality is just as social a structure as is the collective type of experience. It is a particular kind of interpretation, projected into the individual soul, of a complex and sustained socioeconomic situation. But there resides in this type of individualistic 'we-experience', and also in the very order to which it corresponds, an inner contradiction that sooner or later will demolish its ideological structuredness.

An analogous structure is presented in solitary self-experience ('the ability and strength to stand alone in one's rectitude'), a type cultivated by Romain Rolland and, to some extent, by Tolstoj. The price involved in this solitude also depends upon 'we'. It is a variant of the 'we-experience' characteristic of the modern-day West European intelligentsia. Tolstoj's remarks about there being different kinds of thinking – 'for oneself' and 'for the public' – merely juxtapose two different conceptions of 'public'. Tolstoj's 'for oneself' actually signifies only another social conception of addressee peculiar to himself. There is no such thing as thinking outside orientation toward possible expression and, hence, outside the social orientation of that expression and of the thinking involved.

Thus the personality of the speaker, taken from within, so to speak, turns out to be wholly a product of social interrelations. Not only its outward expression but also its inner experience are social territory. Consequently, the whole route between inner experience (the 'expressible') and its outward objectification (the 'utterance') lies entirely across social territory. When an experience reaches the stage of actualization in a full-fledged utterance, its social orientation acquires added complexity by focusing on the immediate social circumstances of discourse and, above all, upon actual addressees.

THEME AND MEANING IN LANGUAGE

The problem of meaning is one of the most difficult problems of linguistics. Efforts toward solving this problem have revealed the one-sided monologism of linguistic science in particularly strong relief. The theory of passive understanding precludes any possibility of engaging the most fundamental and crucial features of meaning in language.

The scope of the present study compels us to limit ourselves to a very brief and perfunctory examination of this issue. We shall attempt only to map out the main lines of its productive treatment.

A definite and unitary meaning, a unitary significance, is a property belonging to any utterance *as a whole*. Let us call the significance of a whole utterance its *theme*. The theme must be unitary, otherwise we would have no basis for talking about any one utterance. The theme of an utterance itself is individual and unreproducible, just as the utterance itself is individual and unreproducible. The theme is the expression of the concrete, historical situation that engendered the utterance. The utterance 'What time is it?' has a different meaning each time it is used, and hence, in accordance with out terminology, has a different theme, depending on the concrete historical situation ('historical' here in microscopic dimensions) during which it is enunciated and of which, in essence, it is a part.

It follows, then, that the theme of an utterance is determined not only by the linguistic forms that comprise it – words, morphological and syntactic structures, sounds, and intonation – but also by extraverbal factors of the situation. Should we miss these situational factors, we would be as little able to understand an utterance as if we were to miss its most important words. The theme of an utterance is concrete – as concrete as the historical instant to which the utterance belongs. *Only an utterance taken in its full, concrete scope as an historical phenomenon possesses a theme.* That is what is meant by the theme of an utterance.

However, if we were to restrict ourselves to the historical unreproducibility and unitariness of each concrete utterance and its theme, we would be poor dialecticians. Together with theme or, rather, within the theme, there is also the *meaning* that belongs to an utterance. By meaning, as distinguished from theme, we understand all those aspects of the utterance that are *reproducible* and *self-identical* in all instances of repetition. Of course, these aspects are abstract:

they have no concrete, autonomous existence in an artificially isolated form, but, at the same time, they do constitute an essential and inseparable part of the utterance. The theme of an utterance is, in essence, indivisible. The meaning of an utterance, on the contrary, does break down into a set of meanings belonging to each of the various linguistic elements of which the utterance consists. The unreproducible theme of the utterance 'What time is it?' taken in its indissoluble connection with the concrete historical situation, cannot be divided into elements. The meaning of the utterance 'What time is it?' – a meaning that, of course, remains the same in all historical instances of its enunciation – is made up of the meanings of the words, forms of morphological and syntactic union, interrogative intonations, etc., that form the construction of the utterance.

Theme is a complex, dynamic system of signs that attempts to be adequate to a given instant of generative process. Theme is reaction by the consciousness in its generative process to the generative process of existence. Meaning is *the technical apparatus for the implementation of theme.* Of course, no absolute, mechanistic boundary can be drawn between theme and meaning. There is no theme without meaning and no meaning without theme. Moreover, it is even impossible to convey the meaning of a particular word (say, in the course of teaching another person a foreign language) without have made it an element of theme, i.e., without having constructed an 'example' utterance. On the other hand, a theme must base itself on some kind of fixity of meaning; otherwise it loses its connection with what came before and what comes after – it altogether loses its significance.

The study of the languages of prehistoric peoples and modern semantic paleontology have reached a conclusion about the so-called 'complex-ness' of prehistoric thinking. Prehistoric man used one word to denote a wide variety of phenomena that, from our point of view, are in no way related to one another. What is more, the same word could be used to denote diametrically opposite notions – top and bottom, earth and sky, good and bad, and so on. Declares Marr:

> Suffice it to say that contemporary paleontological studies of language has given us the possibility of reaching through its investigations, back to an age when a tribe had only one word at its disposal for usage in all the meanings of which mankind was aware.
>
> (Marr 1926 p. 278)

'But was such an all-meaning word in fact a word?' we might be asked. Yes, precisely a word. If, on the contrary, a certain sound complex had only one single, inert, and invariable meaning, then such a complex would not be a word, not a sign, but only a signal. *Multiplicity of meanings is the constitutive feature of word.* As regards the all-meaning word of which Marr speaks, we can say the following: *such a word, in essence, has virtually no meaning; it is all theme.* Its meaning is *inseparable from the concrete situation of its implementation.* This meaning is different each time, just as the situation is different each time. Thus the theme, in this case, subsumed meaning under itself and dissolved it before meaning had any chance to consolidate and congeal. But as language developed further, as its stock of sound complexes expanded, meaning began to congeal along lines that were basic and most frequent in the life of the community for the thematic application of this or that word.

Theme, as we have said, is an attribute of a whole utterance only; it can belong to a separate word only inasmuch as that word operates in the capacity of a whole utterance. So, for instance, Marr's all-meaning word always operates in the capacity of a whole (and has no fixed meanings precisely for that reason). Meaning, on the other hand, belongs to an element or aggregate of elements in their relation to the whole. Of course, if we entirely disregard this relation to the whole (i.e., to the utterance), we shall entirely forfeit meaning. That is the reason why a sharp boundary between theme and meaning cannot be drawn.

The most accurate way of formulating the interrelationship between theme and meaning is in the following terms. Theme is the *upper, actual limit of linguistic significance*; in essence, only theme means something definite. Meaning is the *lower limit* of linguistic significance. Meaning, in essence, means nothing; it only possesses potentiality – the possibility of having a meaning within a concrete theme. Investigation of the meaning of one or another linguistic element can proceed, in terms of our definition, in one of two directions: either in the direction of the upper limit, toward theme, in which case it would be investigation of the contextual meaning of a given word within the conditions of a concrete utterance; or investigation can aim toward the lower limit, the limit of meaning, in which case it would be investigation of the meaning of a word in the system of language or, in other words, investigation of a dictionary word.

A distinction between theme and meaning and a proper under-standing of their interrelationship are vital steps in constructing a genuine science of meanings. Total failure to comprehend their importance has persisted to the present day. Such discriminations as those between a word's *usual* and *occasional* meanings, between its central and lateral meanings, between its denotation and connotation, etc., are fundamentally unsatisfactory. The basic tendency underlying all such discriminations – the tendency to ascribe greater value to the central, usual aspect of meaning, presupposing that that aspect really does exist and is stable – is completely fallacious. Moreover, it would leave theme unaccounted for, since theme, of course, can by no means be reduced to the status of the occasional or lateral meaning of words.

The distinction between theme and meaning acquires particular clarity in connection with the *problem of understanding*, which we shall now briefly touch upon.

We have already had occasion to speak of the philological type of passive understanding, which excludes response in advance. Any genuine kind of understanding will be active and will constitute the germ of a response. Only active understanding can grasp theme – a generative process can be grasped only with the aid of another generative process.

To understand another person's utterance means to orient oneself with respect to it, to find the proper place for it in the corresponding context. For each word of the utterance that we are in process of understanding, we, as it were, lay down a set of our own answering words. The greater their number and weight, the deeper and more substantial our understanding will be.

Thus each of the distinguishable significative elements of an utterance and the entire utterance as a whole entity are translated in our minds into another, active, and responsive, context. *Any true understanding is dialogic in nature.* Understanding is to utterance as one line of a dialogue is to the next. Understanding strives to match the speaker's word with a *counter word*. Only in understanding a word in a foreign tongue is the attempt made to match it with the 'same' word in one's own language.

Therefore, there is no reason for saying that meaning belongs to a word as such. In essence, meaning belongs to a word in its position between speakers; that is, meaning is realized only in the process of active, responsive understanding. Meaning does not reside in the word or in the soul of the speaker or in the soul of the listener. Meaning is the *effect of interaction between speaker and listener produced via the material of a particular sound complex*. It is like an electric spark that occurs only when two different terminals are hooked together. Those who ignore theme (which is accessible only to active, responsive understanding) and who, in attempting to define the meaning of a word, approach its lower, stable, self-identical limit, want, in effect, to turn on a light bulb after having switched off the current. Only the current of verbal intercourse endows a word with the light of meaning.

Let us now move on to one of the most important problems in the science of meanings, the problem of the *interrelationship between meaning and evaluation*.

Any word used in actual speech possesses not only theme and meaning in the referential, or content, sense of these words, but also value judgment: i.e., all referential contents produced in living speech are said or written in conjunction with a specific *evaluative accent*. There is no such thing as word without evaluative accent.

What is the nature of this accent, and how does it relate to the referential side of meaning?

The most obvious, but, at the same time, the most superficial aspect of social value judgement incorporated in the word is that which is conveyed with the help of *expressive intonation*. In most cases, intonation is determined by the immediate situation and often by its most ephemeral circumstances. To be sure, intonation of a more substantial kind is also possible. Here is a classic instance of such a use of intonation in real-life speech. Dostoevskij, in *Dairy of a Writer*, relates the following story.

> One Sunday night, already getting on to the small hours, I chanced to find myself walking alongside a band of six tipsy artisans for a dozen paces or so, and there and then I became convinced that all thoughts, all feelings, and even whole trains of reasoning could be expressed merely by using a certain noun, a noun, moreover, of utmost simplicity in itself [Dostoevskij has in mind here a certain widely used obscenity.–V.V.]. Here is what happened. First, one of these fellows voices this noun shrilly and emphatically by way of expressing his utterly disdainful denial of some point that had been in general contention just prior. A second fellow repeats this very same noun in response to the first fellow, but now in an altogether different tone and sense – to wit,

in the sense that he fully doubted the veracity of the first fellow's denial. A third fellow waxes indignant at the first one, sharply and heatedly sallying into the conversation and shouting at him that very same noun, but now in a pejorative, abusive sense. The second fellow, indignant at the third for being offensive, himself sallies back in and cuts the latter short to the effect: 'What the hell do you think you're doing, butting in like that?! Me and Fil'ka were having a nice quiet talk and just like that you come along and start cussing him out!' And in fact, this whole train of thought he conveyed by emitting just that very same time-honored word, that same extremely laconic designation of a certain item, and nothing more, save only that he also raised his hand and grabbed the second fellow by the shoulder. Thereupon, all of a sudden a fourth fellow, the youngest in the crowd, who had remained silent all this while, apparently having just struck upon the solution to the problem that had originally occasioned the dispute, in a tone of rapture, with one arm half-raised, shouts – What do you think: 'Eureka!' 'I found it, I found it!'? No, nothing at all like 'Eureka', nothing like 'I found it'. He merely repeats that very same unprintable noun, just that one single word, just that one word alone, but with rapture, with a squeal of ecstasy, and apparently somewhat excessively so, because the sixth fellow, a surly character and the oldest in the bunch, didn't think it seemly and in a trice stops the young fellow's rapture cold by turning on him and repeating in a gruff and expostulatory bass – yes, that very same noun whose usage is forbidden in the company of ladies, which, however, in this case clearly and precisely denoted: 'What the hell are you shouting for, you'll burst a blood vessel!' And so, without having uttered one other word, they repeated just this one, but obviously beloved, little word of theirs six times in a row, one after the other, and they understood one another perfectly.

(Dostoevskij 1906 pp. 274–275)

All six 'speech performances' by the artisans are different, despite the fact that they all consisted of one and the same word. That word, in this instance, was essentially only a vehicle for intonation. The conversation was conducted in intonations expressing the value judgments of the speakers. These value judgments and their corresponding intonations were wholly determined by the immediate social situation of the talk and therefore did not require any referential support. In living speech, intonation often does have a meaning quite independent of the semantic composition of speech. Intonational material pent up inside us often does find an outlet in linguistic constructions completely inappropriate to the particular kind of intonation involved. In such a case, intonation does not impinge upon the intellectual, concrete, referential significance of the construction. We have a habit of expressing our feelings by imparting expressive and meaningful intonation to some word that crops up in our mind by chance, often a vacuous interjection or adverb. Almost everybody has his favourite interjection or adverb or sometimes even a semantically full-fledged word that he customarily uses for purely intonational resolution of certain trivial (and sometimes not so trivial) situations and moods that occur in the ordinary business of life. There are certain expressions like 'so-so', 'yes-yes', 'now-now', 'well-well' and so on that commonly serve as 'safety valves' of that sort. The doubling usual in such expressions is symptomatic; i.e., it represents an artificial prolongation of the sound image for the purpose of allowing the pent up intonation to expire fully. Any one such favorite little expression may, of course, be pronounced in an enormous variety of intonations in keeping with the wide diversity of situations and moods that occur in life.

In all these instances, theme, which is a property of each utterance, (each of the utterances of the six artisans had a theme proper to it), is implemented entirely and exclusively by the power of expressive intonation without the aid of word meaning or grammatical coordination. This sort of value judgment and its corresponding intonation cannot exceed the narrow confines of the immediate situation and the small, intimate social world in which it occurs. Linguistic evaluation of this sort may rightly be called an accompaniment, an accessory phenomenon, to meaning in language.

However, not all linguistic value judgments are like that. We may take any utterance whatsoever, say, an utterance that encompasses the broadest possible semantic spectrum and assumes the widest possible social audience, and we shall still see that, in it, an enormous importance belongs to evaluation. Naturally, value judgement in this case will not allow of even minimally adequate expression by intonation, but it will be the determinative factor in the choice and deployment of the basic elements that bear the meaning of the utterance. No utterance can be put together without value judgment. Every utterance is above all an *evaluative orientation*. Therefore, each element in a living utterance not only has a meaning but also has a value. Only the abstract element, perceived within the system of language and not within the structure of an utterance, appears devoid of value judgment. Focusing their attention on the abstract system of language is what led most linguists to divorce evaluation from meaning and to consider evaluation an accessory factor of meaning, the expression of a speaker's individual attitude toward the subject matter of his discourse.

In Russian scholarship, G. Špett has spoken of evaluation as the *connotation* of a word. Characteristically, he operates with a strict division between referential denotation and evaluative connotation, locating this division in various spheres of reality. This sort of disjuncture between referential meaning and evaluation is totally inadmissible. It stems from failure to note the more profound functions of evaluation in speech. Referential meaning is molded by evaluation; it is evaluation, after all, which determines that a particular referential meaning may enter the purview of speakers – both the immediate purview and the broader social purview of the particular social group. Furthermore, with respect to changes of meaning, it is precisely evaluation that plays the creative role. A change in meaning is, essentially, always a *reevaluation*: the transposition of some particular word from one evaluative context to another. The separation of word meaning from evaluation inevitably deprives meaning of its place in the living social process (where meaning is always permeated with value judgment), to its being ontologized and transformed into ideal Being divorced from the historical process of Becoming.

Precisely in order to understand the historical process of generation of theme and of the meanings implementing theme, it is essential to take social evaluation into account. The generative process of signification in language is always associated with the generation of the evaluative purview of a particular social group, and the generation of an evaluative purview – in the sense of the totality of all those things that have meaning and importance for the particular group – is entirely determined by expansion of the economic basis. As the economic basis expands, it promotes an actual expansion in the scope of existence which is accessible, comprehensible, and vital to man. The prehistoric herdsman was virtually interested in nothing, and virtually nothing had any bearing on him. Man at the end of the epoch of capitalism is directly concerned about everything, his interests reaching the remotest corners of the earth and even the most distant stars. This expansion of evaluative purview comes about dialectically. New aspects of existence, once they are drawn into the sphere of social interest, once they make contact with the human world and human emotion, do not coexist peacefully with other elements of existence previously drawn in, but engage them in a struggle, reevaluate them, and bring about a change in their position within the unity of the evaluative purview. This dialectical generative process is reflected in the generation of semantic properties in language. A new significance emanates from an old one, and does so with its help, but this happens so that the new significance can enter into contradiction with the old one and restructure it.

The outcome is a constant struggle of accents in each semantic sector of existence. There is nothing in the structure of signification that could be said to transcend the generative process, to be independent of the dialectical expansion of social purview. Society in process of generation expands its perception of the generative process of existence. There is nothing in this that could be said to be absolutely fixed. And that is how it happens that meaning – an abstract, self-identical element – is subsumed under theme and torn apart by theme's living contradictions so as to return in the shape of a new meaning with a fixity and self-identity only for the while, just as it had before.

NOTES

1   R. Šor's (1926) *Jazyk i obščestvo* [Language and Society] (Moscow) is entrenched in the spirit of the Geneva School. She also functions as an ardent apologist of Saussure's basic ideas in her article, 'Krizis sovremennoj lingvistiki'. The linguist V. V. Vinogradov may be regarded a follower of the Geneva School. Two schools of Russian linguistics, the Förtunatov school and the so-called Kazan' school (Kruševskij and Baudouin de Courtenay), both of them vivid expressions of linguistic formalism, fit entirely within the framework we have mapped out as that of the second trend of thought in philosophy of language.
2   Saussure's basic theoretical work, published after his death by his students, is *Cours de linguistique générale* (1916). We shall be quoting from the second edition of 1922. Puzzlingly enough, Saussure's book, for all its influence, has not yet been translated into Russian. A brief summary of Saussure's views can be found in the above-cited article by R. Šor and in an article by Peterson, 'Obščaja lingvistika' [General Linguistics], *pečat' i Revoljucija*, 6, 1923.
3   Saussure does, it is true, allow the possibility of a special linguistics of utterance ('linguistique de la parole'), but he remains silent on just what sort of linguistics that would be. Here is what he says on this point:

> Il faut choisir entre deux routes qu'il est impossible de prendre en même temps; elles doivent être suivies séparément. On peut à la rigueur conserver le nom de linguistique celle dont la langue est l'unique object.
>
> (Saussure 1922 p. 39)

6 M. A. K. Halliday

'Introduction', Language as social semiotic: the social interpretation of language and meaning

'Language is a social fact', in the frequently-quoted words of Saussure; and to recognize this is, in Saussure's view, a necessary step towards identifying 'language' as the true object of linguistics. Others before him had stressed the social character of language; for example Sweet, who wrote in 1888, 'Language originates spontaneously in the individual, for the imitative and symbolic instinct is inherent in all intelligent beings, whether men or animals; but, like that of poetry and the arts, its development is social'.

Observations such as these can be, and on occasion are, taken as the springboard for a display of exegetical acrobatics which leaves the original writer's intention far behind. In reality, such statements always have a context; they are part of a particular chain of reasoning or interpretative scheme. Saussure is concerned, at this point in his discussion, with the special character of linguistics in relation to other sciences; Sweet is explaining the origin and evolution of dialectal variation in language. It is only at the risk of distortion that we isolate such remarks from their context and fix them in a frame on the wall.

The formulation 'language as social semiotic' says very little by itself; it could mean almost anything, or nothing at all. It belongs to a particular conceptual framework, and is intended to suggest a particular interpretation of language within that framework. This certainly encompasses the view that language is a social fact, though probably not quite in the Saussurean sense, which Firth glossed as 'the language of the community, a function of *la masse parlante*, stored and residing in the *conscience collective.*'

Language arises in the life of the individual through an ongoing exchange of meanings with significant others. A child creates, first his child tongue, then his mother tongue, in interaction with that little coterie of people who constitute his meaning group. In this sense, language is a product of the social process.

A child learning language is at the same time learning other things through language – building up a picture of the reality that is bound around him and inside him. In this process, which is also a social process, the construal of reality is inseparable from the construal of the semantic system in which the reality is encoded. In this sense, language is a shared meaning potential, at once both a part of experience and an intersubjective interpretation of experience.

There are two fundamental aspects to the social reality that is encoded in language: to paraphrase Lévi-Strauss, it is both 'good to think' and 'good to eat'. Language expresses and symbolizes this dual aspect in its semantic system, which is organized around the twin motifs of reflection and action – language as a means of reflecting on things, and language as a means of acting on things. The former is the 'ideational' component of meaning; the latter is the 'interpersonal' – one can act *symbolically* only on persons, not on objects.

A Social reality (or a 'culture') is itself an edifice of meanings – a semiotic construct. In this perspective, language is one of the semiotic systems that constitute a culture; one that is distinctive in that it also serves as an encoding system for many (though not all) of the others.

This in summary terms is what is intended by the formulation 'language as social semiotic'. It means interpreting language within a sociocultural context, in which the culture itself is interpreted in semiotic terms – as an information system, if that terminology is preferred.

At the most concrete level, this means that we take account of the elementary fact that people talk to each other. Language does not consist of sentences; it consists of text, or discourse – the exchange of meanings in interpersonal contexts of one kind or another. The contexts in which meanings are exchanged are not devoid of social value; a context of speech is itself a semiotic construct, having a form (deriving from the culture) that enables the participants to predict features of the prevailing register – and hence to understand one another as they go along.

But they do more than understand each other, in the sense of exchanging information and goods-and-services through the dynamic interplay of speech roles. By their everyday acts of meaning, people act out the social structure, affirming their own statuses and roles, and establishing and transmitting the shared systems of value and knowledge. In recent years our understanding of these processes has been advanced most of all by Bernstein and Labov, two original thinkers whose ideas, though often presented as conflicting, are in fact strikingly complementary, the one starting from social structure and the other from linguistic structure. Bernstein has shown how the semiotic systems of the culture become differentially accessible to different social groups; Labov has shown how variation in the linguistic system is functional in expressing variation in social status and roles.

Putting these two perspectives together, we begin to see a little way into the rather elusive relation between language and social structure. Variation in language is in a quite direct sense the expression of fundamental attributes of the social system; dialect variation expresses the diversity of social *structures* (social hierarchies of all kinds), while register variation expresses the diversity of social *processes*. And since the two are interconnected – what we do is affected by who we are: in other words, the division of labour is *social* – dialects become entangled with registers. The registers a person has access to are a function of his place in the social structure; and a switch of register may entail a switch of dialect.

This is how we try to account for the emergence of standard dialects, the correlation of dialects and registers, and the whole complex ideology of language attitudes and value judgements. But these imply more than the simple notion that language 'expresses' social structure and the social system. It would be nearer the point to say that language *actively symbolizes* the social system, representing metaphorically in its patterns of variation the variation that characterizes human cultures. This is what enables people to play with variation in language, using it to create meanings of a social kind: to participate in all forms of verbal context and verbal display, and in the elaborate rhetoric of ordinary daily conversation. It is this same twofold function of the linguistic system, its function both as expression of and as metaphor for social processes, that lies behind the dynamics of the interrelation of language and social context; which ensures that, in the microencounters of everyday life where meanings are exchanged, language not only serves to facilitate and support other modes of social action that constitute its environment, but also actively creates an environment of its own, so making possible all the imaginative modes of meaning, from backyard gossip to narrative fiction and epic poetry. The context plays a part in determining what we say; and what we say plays a part in determining the context. As we learn how to mean, we learn to predict each from the other.

The significance of all this for linguistics is that these considerations help to explain the nature of the linguistic system. We shall not come to understand the nature of language if we pursue only the kinds of question about language that are formulated by linguists. For linguists, language is object – linguistics is defined, as Saussure and his contemporaries so often felt the need to affirm, by the fact that it has language as its object of study; whereas for others, language is an instrument, a means of illuminating questions about something else. This is a valid and important distinction. But it is a distinction of goals, not one of scope. In the walled gardens in which the disciplines have been sheltered since the early years of this century, each has claimed the right to determine not only what questions it is asking but also what it will take into account in answering them; and in linguistics, this leads to the construction of elegant self-contained systems that are of only limited application to any real issues – since the objects themselves have no such boundary walls. We have to take account of the questions that are raised by others; not simply out of a sense of the social accountability of the discipline (though that would be reason enough), but also out of sheer self-interest – we shall better understand language as an object if we interpret it in the light of the findings and seekings of those for whom language is an instrument, a means towards inquiries of a quite different kind.

In these essays, the attempt is made to look into language from the outside; and specifically, to interpret linguistic processes from the standpoint of the social order. This is in some contrast to the recently prevailing mode, in which the angle of reasoning has been from the language outwards, and the main concern was with the individual mind. For much of the past twenty years linguistics has been dominated by an individualist ideology, having as one of its articles of faith the astonishing dictum, first enunciated by Katz and Fodor in a treatise on semantics which explicitly banished all reference to the social context of language, that 'nearly every sentence uttered is uttered for the first time'. Only in a very special kind of social context could such a claim be taken seriously – that of a highly intellectual and individual conception of language in which the object of study was the idealized sentence of an equally idealized speaker. Even with the breakthrough to a 'sociolinguistic' perspective, it has proved difficult to break away from the ideal individual in whose mind all social knowledge is stored.

The 'grammar' of this kind of linguistics is a set of rules; and the conceptual framework is drawn from logic, whence is derived a model of language in which the organizing concept is that of structure. Since the structural functions are defined by logical relations (e.g. subject and predicate), the linguistic relations are seen as formal relations between classes (e.g. noun and verb). It was Chomsky's immense achievement to show how natural language can be reduced to a formal system; and as long as the twofold idealization of speaker and sentence is maintained intact, language can be represented not only as rules but even as ordered rules. But when social man comes into the picture, the ordering disappears and even the concept of rules is seen to be threatened.

In real life, most sentences that are uttered are not uttered for the first time. A great deal of discourse is more or less routinized; we tell the same stories and express the same opinions over and over again. We do, of course, create new sentences; we also create new clauses, and phrases, and words – the image of language as 'old words in new sentences' is a very superficial and simplistic one. But it really does not matter whether we do this or not; what matters is that we all the time exchange meanings, and the exchange of meanings is a creative process in which language is one symbolic resource – perhaps the principal one we have, but still one among others. When we come to interpret language in this perspective, the conceptual framework is likely to be drawn from rhetoric rather than from logic, and the grammar is likely to be a grammar of choices rather than of rules. The structure of sentences and other units is explained by derivation from their functions – which is doubtless how the structures evolved in the first place. Language is as it is because of the functions it has evolved to serve in people's lives; it is to be expected that linguistic structures could be understood in functional terms. But in order to understand them in this way we have to proceed form the outside inwards, interpreting language by reference to its place in the social process. This is not the same thing as taking an isolated sentence and planting it out in some hothouse that we call a social context. It involves the difficult task of focusing attention simultaneously on the actual and the potential, interpreting both discourse and the linguistic system that lies behind it in terms of the infinitely complex network of meaning potential that is what we call the culture.

Part II

'Meaning': linguistic and visual

Linguistic 'meaning'

EDITOR'S INTRODUCTION

The thrust of the readings in Part II is to move the analysis of signification beyond the individual sign and on to the scrutiny of more complex inter-actions of significatory material. Since the writings of Barthes and Lévi-Strauss in the 1950s, a great deal of work in communication theory has been dedicated to exposing the operation of connotative processes. *Mythologies* is, of course, the most famous example of this. Barthes' method essentially consisted of treating combinations of signs in a way that is faithful to the Saussurean understanding of individual signs. In the extract from Saussure's *Course* (pp. 99–114), the conception of language as a self-contained system is extended by the positing of *syntagmatic* relations of sign combination, *paradigmatic* relations of sign association, and the pro-duction through these of a system in which the sign has 'value' in relation to other signs rather than an intrinsic 'meaning' or 'identity'. According to the Saussurean tradition, it is from here that connotation is be generated.

It would be difficult to find a statement of the consequences of paradigmatic/syntagmatic interaction as concise or as informative as that of Cohan and Shires (reprinted on pp. 115–25). Using a number of small examples, including *Alice's Adventures in Wonderland*, they show the myriad of permutations involved in creating meaning, from the correct ordering of syntagms to the different signifieds of items in paradigm sets. Their exposition is sufficiently clear to require no summary here. However, there are two things to look out for beyond their commentary on Saussure: the first is the way that Cohan and Shires point out that connotation is associated not only with the action of paradigmatic signifieds, but also in the syntagmatic play of *discourse* (instances of *parole*); the second thing, related to the first, concerns their argument about the *far-reaching* conno-tative potential of syntagms. This is where Cohan and Shires foreshadow the (theoretically) 'infinite' semiosis of Derrida and Peirce.

Further reading: Holdcroft 1991 pp. 98–104; Hjelmslev 1961 pp. 114–127; K. Silverman 1983 pp. 25–32; Coward and Ellis 1977 pp. 28–33; Harland 1987 pp. 52–64; Kress and van Leeuwen 1992a; K.B. Jensen 1995 pp. 3–13.

7 Ferdinand de Saussure

Linguistic value

LINGUISTIC VALUE

1 Language as organized thought coupled with sound

To prove that language is only a system of pure values, it is enough to consider the two elements involved in its functioning: ideas and sounds.

Psychologically our thought – apart from its expression in words – is only a shapeless and indistinct mass. Philosophers and linguists have always agreed in recognizing that without the help of signs we would be unable to make a clear-cut, consistent distinction between two ideas. Without language, thought is a vague, uncharted nebula. There are no pre-existing ideas, and nothing is distinct before the appearance of language.

Against the floating realm of thought, would sounds by themselves yield predelimited entities? No more so than ideas. Phonic substance is neither more fixed nor more rigid than thought; it is not a mold into which thought must of necessity fit but a plastic substance divided in turn into distinct parts to furnish the signifiers needed by thought. The linguistic fact can therefore be pictured in its totality – i.e. language – as a series of contiguous subdivisions marked off on both the indefinite plane of jumbled ideas (*A*) and the equally vague plane of sounds (*B*). Figure 7.1 gives a rough idea of it.

The characteristic role of language with respect to thought is not to create a material phonic means for expressing ideas but to serve as a link between thought and sound, under conditions that of necessity bring about the reciprocal delimitations of units. Thought, chaotic by nature, has to become ordered in the process of its decomposition.

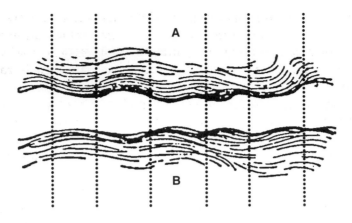

Figure 7.1

Neither are thoughts given material form nor are sounds transformed into mental entities; the somewhat mysterious fact is rather that 'thought-sound' implies division, and that language works out its units while taking shape between two shapeless masses. Visualize the air in contact with a sheet of water; if the atmospheric pressure changes, the surface of the water will be broken up into a series of divisions, waves; the waves resemble the union or coupling of thought with phonic substance.

Language might be called the domain of articulations, using the word as it was defined earlier (Saussure 1974 p. 10). Each linguistic term is a member, an *articulus* in which an idea is fixed in a sound and a sound becomes the sign of an idea.

Language can also be compared with a sheet of paper: thought is the front and the sound the back; one cannot cut the front without cutting the back at the same time; likewise in language, one can neither divide sound from thought nor thought from sound; the division could be accomplished only abstractedly, and the result would be either pure psychology or pure phonology.

Linguistics then works in the borderland where the elements of sound and thought combine; *their combination produces a form, not a substance.*

These views give a better understanding of what was said before (see Saussure 1974 pp. 67 ff.) about the arbitrariness of signs. Not only are the two domains that are linked by the linguistic fact shapeless and confused, but the choice of a given slice of sound to name a given idea is completely arbitrary. If this were not true, the notion of value would be compromised, for it would include an externally imposed element. But actually values remain entirely relative, and that is why the bond between the sound and the idea is radically arbitrary.

The arbitrary nature of the sign explains in turn why the social fact alone can create a linguistic system. The community is necessary if values that owe their existence solely to usage and general acceptance are to be set up; by himself the individual is incapable of fixing a single value.

In addition, the idea of value, as defined, shows that to consider a term as simply the union of a certain sound with a certain concept is grossly misleading. To define it in this way would isolate the term from its system; it would mean assuming that one can start from the terms and construct the system by adding them together when, on the contrary, it is from the interdependent whole that one must start and through analysis obtain its elements.

To develop this thesis, we shall study value successively from the viewpoint of the signified or concept (Section 2), the signifier (Section 3), and the complete sign (Section 4).

Being unable to seize the concrete entities or units of language directly, we shall work with words. While the word does not conform exactly to the definition of the linguistic unit (see Saussure 1974 p. 105), it at least bears a rough resemblance to the unit and has the advantage of being concrete; consequently, we shall use words as specimens equivalent to real terms in a synchronic system, and the principles that we evolve with respect to words will be valid for entities in general.

2 Linguistic value from a conceptual viewpoint

When we speak of the value of a word, we generally think first of its property of standing for an idea, and this is in fact one side of linguistic value. But if this is true, how does *value* differ from *signification*? Might the two words by synonyms? I think not, although it is easy to confuse them since the confusion results not so much from their similarity as from the subtlety of the distinction that they mark.

From a conceptual viewpoint, value is doubtless one element in signification, and it is difficult to see how signification can be

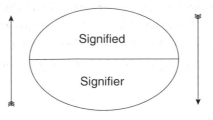

Figure 7.2

dependent upon value and still be distinct from it. But we must clear up the issue or risk reducing language to a simple naming-process (see Saussure 1974 p. 65).

Let us first take signification as it is generally understood (see Saussure 1974 p. 67). As the arrows in the Figure 7.2 show, it is only the counterpart of the sound-image. Everything that occurs concerns only the sound-image and the concept when we look upon the word as independent and self-contained.

But here is the paradox: on the one hand the concept seems to be the counterpart of the sound-image, and on the other hand the sign itself is in turn the counterpart of the other signs of language.

Language is a system of interdependent terms in which the value of each term results solely from the simultaneous presence of the others, as in Figure 7.3.

How, then, can value be confused with signification, i.e. the counterpart of the sound-image? It seems impossible to liken the relations represented here by horizontal arrows to those represented in Figure 7.2 by vertical arrows. Putting it another way – and again taking up the example of the sheet of paper that is cut in two (see p. 100) – it is clear that the observable relation between the different pieces A, B, C, D, etc. is distinct from the relation between the front and back of the same piece as in A/A', B/B', etc.

Figure 7.3

To resolve the issue, let us observe from the outset that even outside language all values are apparently governed by the same paradoxical principle. They are always composed:

1 of a *dissimilar* thing that can be *exchanged* for the thing of which the value is to be determined; and
2 of *similar* things that can be *compared* with the thing of which the value is to be determined.

Both factors are necessary for the existence of a value. To determine what a five-franc piece is worth one must therefore know: (1) that it can be exchanged for a fixed quantity of a different thing, e.g. bread; and (2) that it can be compared with a similar value of the same system, e.g. a one-franc piece, or with coins of another system (a dollar, etc.). In the same way a word can be exchanged for something dissimilar, an idea; besides, it can be compared with something of the same nature, another word. Its value is therefore not fixed so long as one simply states that it can be 'exchanged' for a given concept, i.e. that it has this or that signification: one must also compare it with similar values, with other words that stand in opposition to it. Its content is really fixed only by the concurrence of everything that exists outside it. Being part of a system, it is endowed not only with a signification but also and especially with a value, and this is something quite different.

A few examples will show clearly that this is true. Modern French *mouton* can have the same signification as English *sheep* but not the same value, and this for several reasons, particularly because in speaking of a piece of meat ready to be served on the table, English uses *mutton* and not *sheep*. The difference in value between *sheep* and *mouton* is due to the fact that *sheep* has beside it a second term while the French word does not.

Within the same language, all words used to express related ideas limit each other reciprocally; synonyms like French *redouter* 'dread', *craindre* 'fear', and *avoir peur* 'be afraid' have value only through their opposition: if *redouter* did not exist, all its content would go to its competitors. Conversely, some words are enriched through contact with others: e.g. the new element introduced in *décrépit* (un vieillard *décrépit*, see Saussure 1974 p. 83) results from the co-existence of *décrépi* (un mur *décrépi*). The value of just any term is accordingly determined by its environment; it is impossible to fix even the value of the word signifying 'sun' without first considering its surroundings: in some languages it is not possible to say 'sit in the *sun*'.

Everything said about words applies to any term of language, e.g. to grammatical entities. The value of a French plural does not coincide with that of a Sanskrit plural even though their signification is usually identical; Sanskrit has three numbers instead of two (*my eyes, my ears, my arms, my legs*, etc. are dual);[1] it would be wrong to attribute the same value to the plural in Sanskrit and in French; its value clearly depends on what is outside and around it.

If words stood for pre-existing concepts, they would all have exact equivalents in meaning from one language to the next; but this is not true. French uses *louer* (*une maison*) 'let (a house)' indifferently to mean both 'pay for' and 'receive payment for', whereas German uses two words, *mieten* and *vermieten*; there is obviously no exact correspondence of values. The German verbs *schätzen* and *urteilen* share a number of significations, but that correspondence does not hold at several points.

Inflection offers some particularly striking examples. Distinctions of time, which are so familiar to us, are unknown in certain languages. Hebrew does not recognize even the fundamental distinctions between the past, present, and future. Proto-Germanic has no special form for the future; to say that the future is expressed by the present is wrong, for the value of the present is not the same in Germanic as in languages that have a future along with the present. The Slavic languages regularly single out two aspects of the verb: the perfective represents action as a point, complete in its totality; the imperfective represents it as taking place, and on the line of time. The categories are difficult for a Frenchman to understand, for they are unknown in French; if they were predetermined, this would not be true. Instead of pre-existing ideas then, we find in all the foregoing examples *values* emanating from the system. When they are said to correspond to concepts, it is understood that the concepts are purely differential and defined not by their positive content but negatively by their relations with the other terms of the system. Their most precise characteristic is in being what the others are not.

Now the real interpretation of the diagram of the signal becomes apparent. Thus Figure 7.4 means that in French the concept 'to judge' is linked to the sound-image *juger*; in short, it symbolizes signification. But it is quite clear that initially the concept is nothing, that is only a value determined by its relations with other similar values,

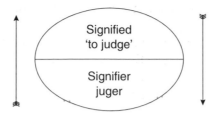

Figure 7.4

and that without them the signification would not exist. If I state simply that a word signifies something when I have in mind the associating of a sound-image with a concept, I am making a statement that may suggest what actually happens, but by no means am I expressing the linguistic fact in its essence and fullness.

3 Linguistic value from a material viewpoint

The conceptual side of value is made up solely of relations and differences with respect to the other terms of language, and the same can be said of its material side. The important thing in the word is not the sound alone but the phonic differences that make it possible to distinguish this word from all others, for differences carry signification.

This may seem surprising, but how indeed could the reverse be possible? Since one vocal image is no better suited than the next for what it is commissioned to express, it is evident, even *a priori*, that a segment of language can never in the final analysis be based on anything except its noncoincidence with the rest. *Arbitrary* and *differential* are two correlative qualities.

The alteration of linguistic signs clearly illustrates this. It is precisely because the terms *a* and *b* as such are radically incapable of reaching the level of consciousness – one is always conscious of only the *a/b* difference – that each term is free to change according to laws that are unrelated to its signifying function. No positive sign characterizes the genitive plural in Czech *žen* (see Saussure 1974 p. 86); still the two forms *žena*: *žen* function as well as the earlier forms *žena*: *ženb*; *žen* has value only because it is different.

Here is another example that shows even more clearly the systematic role of phonic differences: in Greek, *éphēn* is an imperfect and *éstēn* an aorist although both words are formed in the same way; the first belongs to the system of the present indicative of *phēmí* 'I say', whereas there is no present *stēmi*; now it is precisely the relation *phēmí*: *éphēn* that corresponds to the relation between the present and the imperfect (cf. *déiknūmi*: *edéiknūn*, etc.). Signs function, then, not through their intrinsic value but through their relative position.

In addition, it is impossible for sound alone, a material element, to belong to language. It is only a secondary thing, substance to be put to use. All our conventional values have the characteristic of not being confused with the tangible element which supports them. For instance, it is not the metal in a piece of money that fixes its value. A coin normally worth five francs may contain less than half its worth of silver. Its value will vary according to the amount stamped upon it and according to its use inside or outside a political boundary. This is even more true of the linguistic signifier, which is not phonic but incorporeal – constituted not by its material substance but by the differences that separate its sound-image from all others.

The foregoing principle is so basic that it applies to all the material elements of language, including phonemes. Every language forms its words on the basis of a system of sonorous elements, each element being a clearly delimited unit and one of a fixed number of units. Phonemes are above all else opposing, relative, and negative entities.

Proof of this is the latitude that speakers have between points of convergence in the pronunciation of distinct sounds. In French, for instance, general use of a dorsal *r* does not prevent many speakers from using a tongue-tip trill; language is not in the least disturbed by it; language requires only that the sound be different and not, as one might imagine, that it have an invariable quality. I can even pronounce the French *r* like German *ch* in *Bach*, *doch*, etc., but in German I could not use *r* instead of *ch*, for German gives recognition to both elements and must keep them apart. Similarly, in Russian there is no latitude for *t* in the direction of *t'* (palatalized *t*), for the result would be the confusing of two sounds differentiated by the language (cf. *govorit'* 'speak' and *goverit* 'he speaks'), but more freedom may be taken with respect to *th* (aspirated *t*) since this sound does not figure in the Russian system of phonemes.

Since an identical state of affairs is observable in writing, another system of signs, we shall use writing to draw some comparisons that will clarify the whole issue. In fact:

1 The signs used in writing are arbitrary; there is no connection, for example, between the letter *t* and the sound that it designates.
2 The value of letters is purely negative and differential. The same person can write *t*, for instance, in different ways:

The only requirement is that the sign for *t* not be confused in his script with the signs used for *l*, *d*, etc.
3 Values in writing function only through reciprocal opposition within a fixed system that consists of a set number of letters. This third characteristic, though not identical to the second, is closely related to it, for both depend on the first. Since the graphic sign is arbitrary, its form matters little or rather matters only within the limitations imposed by the system.
4 The means by which the sign is produced is completely unimportant, for it does not affect the system (this also follows from characteristic 1). Whether I make the letters in white or black, raised or engraved, with pen or chisel – all this is of no importance with respect to their signification.

4 The sign considered in its totality

Everything that has been said up to this point boils down to this: in language [*langue*] there are only differences. Even more important: a difference generally implies positive terms between which the difference is set up; but in language there are only differences *without positive terms*. Whether we take the signified or the signifier, language has neither ideas nor sounds that existed before the linguistic system, but only conceptual and phonic differences that have issued from the system. The idea or phonic substance that a sign contains is of less importance than the other signs that surround it. Proof of this is that the value of a term may be modified without either its meaning or its sound being affected, solely because a neighbouring term has been modified (see p. 103).

But the statement that everything in language is negative is true only if the signified and the signifier are considered separately; when we consider the sign in its totality, we have something that is positive in its own class. A linguistic system is a series of differences of sound combined with a series of differences of ideas; but the pairing of a certain number of acoustical signs with as many cuts made from the mass of thought engenders a system of values; and this system serves as the effective link between the phonic and psychological elements within each sign. Although both the signified and the signifier are purely differential and negative when considered separately, their combination is a positive fact; it is even the sole type of facts that language has, for maintaining the parallelism between the two classes of differences is the distinctive function of the linguistic institution.

Certain diachronic facts are typical in this respect. Take the countless instances where alteration of the signifier occasions a conceptual change and where it is obvious that the sum of the ideas distinguished corresponds in principle to the sum of the distinctive signs. When two words are confused through phonetic alteration (e.g. French *décrépit* from *dĕcrepitus* and *décrépi* from *crispus*), the ideas that they express will also tend to become confused if only they have something in common. Or a word my have different forms (cf. *chaise* 'chair' and *chaire* 'desk'). Any nascent difference will tend invariably to become significant but without always succeeding or being successful on the first trial. Conversely, any conceptual difference perceived by the mind seeks to find expression through a distinct signifier, and two ideas that are no longer distinct in the mind tend to merge into the same signifier.

When we compare signs – positive terms – with each other, we can no longer speak of difference; the expression would not be fitting, for it applies only to the comparing of two sound-images, e.g. *father* and *mother*, or two ideas, e.g. the idea 'father' and the idea 'mother'; two signs, each having a signified and signifier, are not different but only distinct. Between them there is only *opposition*. The entire mechanism of language, with which we shall be concerned later, is based on oppositions of this kind and on the phonic and conceptual differences that they imply.

What is true of value is true also of the unit (see Saussure 1974 pp. 110 ff.). A unit is a segment of the spoken chain that corresponds to a certain concept; both are by nature purely differential.

Applied to units, the principle of differentiation can be stated in this way: *the characteristics of the unit blend with the unit itself.* In language, as in any semiological system, whatever distinguishes one sign from the others constitutes it. Difference makes character just as it makes value and the unit.

Another rather paradoxical consequence of the same principle is this: in the last analysis what is commonly referred to as a 'grammatical fact' fits the definition of the unit, for it always expresses an opposition of terms; it differs only in that the opposition is particularly significant (e.g. the formation of German plurals of the type *Nacht: Nächte*). Each term present in the grammatical fact (the singular without umlaut or final *e* in opposition to the plural with umlaut and *-e*) consists of the interplay of a number of oppositions within the system. When isolated, neither *Nacht* nor *Nächte* is anything: thus everything is opposition. Putting it another way, the *Nacht:Nächte* relation can be expressed by an algebraic formula a/b in which a and b are not simple terms but result from a set of relations. Language, in a manner of speaking, is a type of algebra consisting solely of complex terms. Some of its oppositions are more significant than others; but units and grammatical facts are only different names for designating diverse aspects of the same general fact: the functioning of linguistic oppositions. This statement is so true that we might very well approach the problem of units by starting from grammatical facts. Taking an opposition like *Nacht:Nächte*, we might ask what are the units involved in it. Are they only the two words, the whole series of similar words, *a* and *ä*, or all singulars and plurals, etc.?

Units and grammatical facts would not be confused if linguistic signs were made up of something besides differences. But language being what it is, we shall find nothing simple in it regardless of our approach; everywhere and always there is the same complex equilibrium of terms that mutually condition each other. Putting it another way, *language [langue] is a form and not a substance* (see p. 100). This truth could not be overstressed, for all the mistakes in our terminology, all our incorrect ways of naming things that pertain to language, stem from the involuntary supposition that the linguistic phenomenon must have substance.

SYNTAGMATIC AND ASSOCIATIVE RELATIONS

1 Definitions

In a language-stage everything is based on relations. How do they function?

Relations and differences between linguistic terms fall into two distinct groups, each of which generates a certain class of values. The opposition between the two classes gives a better understanding of the nature of each class. They correspond to two forms of our mental activity, both indispensable to the life of language.

In discourse, on the one hand, words acquire relations based on the linear nature of language because they are chained together. This rules out the possibility of pronouncing two elements simultaneously (see Saussure 1974 p. 70). The elements are arranged in sequence on the chain of speaking. Combination supported by linearity are *syntagms*.[2] The syntagm is always composed of two or more consecutive units (e.g. French *re-lire* 're-read', *contre tous* 'against everyone', *la vie humaine* 'human life', *Dieu est bon* 'God is good', *s'il fait beau temps, nous sortirons* 'if the weather is nice, we'll go out', etc.). In the syntagm a term acquires its value only because it stands in opposition to everything that precedes or follows it, or to both.

Outside discourse, on the other hand, words acquire relations of a different kind. Those that have something in common are associated in the memory, resulting in groups marked by diverse relations. For instance, the French word *enseignement* 'teaching' will unconsciously call to mind a host of other words (*enseigner* 'teach', *renseigner* 'acquaint', etc.; or *armement* 'armament', *changement* 'amendment', etc.; or *éducation* 'education', *apprentissage* 'apprenticeship', etc.). All those words are related in some way.

We see that the co-ordinations formed outside discourse differ strikingly from those formed inside discourse. Those formed outside discourse are not supported by linearity. Their seat is in the brain; they are a part of the inner storehouse that makes up the language of each speaker. They are *associative relations*.

The syntagmatic relation is *in praesentia*. It is based on two or more terms that occur in an effective series. Against this, the associative relation unites terms *in absentia* in a potential mnemonic series.

From the associative and syntagmatic viewpoint a linguistic unit is like a fixed part of a building, e.g. a column. On the one hand, the column has a certain relation to the architrave that it supports; the arrangement of the two units in space suggests the syntagmatic relation. On the other hand, if the column is Doric, it suggests a mental comparison of this style with others (Ionic, Corinthian, etc.) although none of these elements is present in space: the relation is associative.

Each of the two classes of co-ordination calls for some specific remarks.

2 Syntagmatic relations

The examples on page 110 have already indicated that the notion of syntagm applies not only to words but to groups of words, to complex units of all lengths and types (compounds, derivatives, phrases, whole sentences).

It is not enough to consider the relation that ties together the different parts of syntagms (e.g. French *contre* 'against' and *tous* 'everyone' in *contre tous*, *contre* and *maître* 'master' in *contremaître* 'foreman'),[3] one must also bear in mind the relation that links the whole to its parts (e.g. *contre tous* in opposition on the one hand to *contre* and on the other *tous*, or *contremaître* in opposition to *contre* and *maître*).

An objection might be raised at this point. The sentence is the ideal type of syntagm. But it belongs to speaking, not to language (see Saussure 1974 p. 14). Does it not follow that the syntagm belongs to speaking? I do not think so. Speaking is characterized by freedom of combinations; one must therefore ask whether or not all syntagms are equally free.

It is obvious from the first that many expressions belong to language. These are the pat phrases in which any change is prohibited by usage, even if we can single out their meaningful elements (cf. *à quoi bon?* 'what's the use?' *allons donc!* 'nonsense!'). The same is true, though to a lesser degree, of expressions like *prendre la mouche* 'take offense easily',[4] *forcer la main à quelqu'un* 'force someone's hand', *rompre une lance* 'break a lance',[5] or even *avoir mal (à la tête, etc.)* 'have (a headache, etc.),' *à force de (soins, etc.)* 'by dint of (care, etc.),' *que vous en semble?* 'how do you feel about it?' *pas n'est besoin de . . .* 'there's no need for . . .', etc., which are characterized by peculiarities of signification or syntax. These idiomatic twists cannot be improvised; they are furnished by tradition. There are also words which, while lending themselves perfectly to analysis, are characterized by some morphological anomaly that is kept solely by dint of usage (*cf.* difficulté 'difficulty' beside *facilité* 'facility', etc., and *mourrai* '[I] shall die' beside *dormirai* '[I] shall sleep').[6]

There are further proofs. To language rather than to speaking belong the syntagmatic types that are built upon regular forms. Indeed, since there is nothing abstract in language, the types exist only if language has registered a sufficient number of specimens. When a word like *indécorable* arises in speaking (see Saussure 1974 pp. 167 ff.), its appearance supposes a fixed type, and this type is in turn possible only through remembrance of a sufficient number of similar words belonging to language (*impardonable* 'unpardonable', *intolérable* 'intolerable', *infatigable* 'indefatigable', etc.). Exactly the same is true of sentences and groups of words built upon regular patterns. Combinations like *la terre tourne* 'the world turns', *que vous dit-il?* 'what does he say to you?' etc. correspond to general types that are in turn supported in the language by concrete remembrances.

But we must realize that in the syntagm there is no clear-cut boundary between the language fact, which is a sign of collective usage, and the fact that belongs to speaking and depends on individual freedom. In a great number of instances it is hard to class a combination of units because both forces have combined in producing it, and they have combined in indeterminable proportions.

3 Associative relations

Mental association creates other groups besides those based on the comparing of terms that have something in common; through its grasp of the nature of the relations that bind the terms together, the mind creates as many associative series as there are diverse relations. For instance, in *enseignement* 'teaching', *enseigner* 'teach', *enseignons* '(we) teach', etc., one element, the radical, is common to every term; the same word may occur in a different series formed around another common element, the suffix (cf. *enseignement, armament, changement*, etc.); or the association may spring from the analogy of the concepts signified (*enseignement, instruction, apprentissage, éducation*, etc.); or again, simply from the similarity of the sound-images (e.g. *enseignement* and *justement* 'precisely').[7] Thus there is at times a double

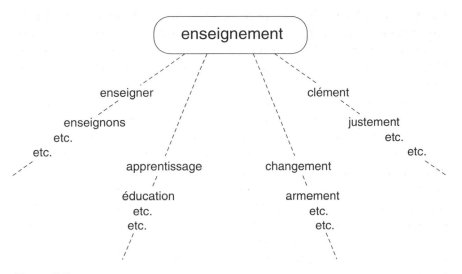

Figure 7.5

similarity of meaning and form, at times similarity only of form or of meaning. A word can always evoke everything that can be associated with it in one way or another.

Whereas a syntagm immediately suggests an order of succession and a fixed number of elements, terms in an associative family occur neither in fixed numbers nor in a definite order. If we associate *painful, delightful, frightful,* etc. we are unable to predict the number of words that the memory will suggest or the order in which they will appear. A particular word is like the center of a constellation; it is the point of convergence of an indefinite number of co-ordinated terms (see Figure 7.5).

But of the two characteristics of the associative series – indeterminate order and indefinite number – only the first can always be verified; the second may fail to meet the test. This happens in the case of inflectional paradigms, which are typical of associative groupings. Latin *dominus, dominī, dominō,* etc. is obviously an associative group formed around a common element, the noun theme *domin-*, but the series[8] is not definite as in the case of *enseignement, changement,* etc.; the number of cases is definite. Against this, the words have no fixed order of succession, and it is by a purely arbitrary act that the grammarian groups them in one way rather than in another; in the mind of speakers the nominative case is by no means the first one in the declension, and the order in which terms are called depends on circumstances.

NOTES

1 The use of the comparative form for two and the superlative for more than two in English (e.g. *may the* better *boxer win*: *the* best *boxer in the world*) is probably a remnant of the old distinctive between the dual and the plural number. [Wade Baskin: Tr.]

2 It is scarcely necessary to point out that the study of *syntagms* is not to be confused with syntax. Syntax is only one part of the study of syntagms (see Saussure 1974 pp. 134 ff.) [Charles Bally and Albert Sèchehaye with Albert Reidlinger: Eds]

3 Cf. English *head* and *waiter* in *headwaiter*. [Tr.]

4 Literally 'take the fly.' Cf. English *take the bull by the horns*. [Tr.]

5 Cf. English *bury the hatchet*. [Tr.]

6 The anomaly of the double *r* in the future forms of certain verbs in French may be compared to irregular plurals like *oxen* in English. [Tr.]

7 The last case is rare and can be classed as abnormal, for the mind naturally discards associations that becloud the intelligibility of discourse. But its existence is proved by a lower category of puns based on the ridiculous confusions that can result from pure and simple homonomy like the French statement: 'Les musiciens produisent les *sons* ["sounds, bran"] et les graine-tiers les vendent' 'musicians produce *sons* and seedsmen sell them.' [Cf. Shakespeare's 'Not on thy *sole*, but on thy *soul*.' (Tr.)] This is distinct from the case where an association, while fortuitous, is supported by a compar-ison of ideas (cf. French *ergot* 'spur': *ergoter* 'wrangle'; German *blau* 'blue': *durchbluaen* 'thrash soundly'); the point is that one member of the pair has a new interpretation. Folk etymologies like these are of interest in the study of semantic evolution, but from the synchronic viewpoint they are in the same category as *enseigner*: *enseignement*. [Eds]

8 Cf. English *education* and the corresponding associative series: *educate, educates*, etc.; *internship, training*, etc.; *vocation, devotion*, etc.; and *lotion, fashion*, etc. [Tr.]

which constitutes the sign, one has to recognize that the signified is not the same as the *referent*, the object in reality. The signified of 'cat' is a conceptualization of the animal, a mental construction. The feline animal does not appear in the sign – it is not there to be petted or to purr (which is why it must be signified).

That the signified is not the same as the referent is even more obvious when we use language to formulate ideas. Saussure concluded:

> Concepts are purely differential and defined not by their positive content but negatively by their relations with the other terms of the system. Their most precise characteristic is in being what the others are not . . . Signs function, then, not through their intrinsic value but through their relative position.
>
> (Saussure 1974 pp. 117–118)

For instance, when the King of Hearts decides that there is no difference between important and unimportant evidence, the sign *important* does not refer to anything outside of language but is actually a category of value constructed by language. You cannot find a material referent of the sign *important*, though you can indeed cite things you consider important. In doing that, however, you are still relating one sign to another, referring to other meanings produced in language, and participating in the system of comparison and contrast – of *differentiation* – that language makes possible. 'In language,' Saussure maintained as the fundamental axiom of semiotics, 'there are only differences' (Saussure 1974 p. 120).

The differential field of a language system, Saussure went on to show, regulates the arbitrary relation of signifier and signified in terms of: *similarity*, the function of one sign when vertically compared to other signs; and *placement*, the position of one sign when horizontally combined with others. In learning a second language, for example, one studies much more than vocabulary, the system's repertoire of signs. Among other conventions of the language system, one has to learn verb conjugations – *I am, you are, it is*, and so forth – which establish patterns of subject–verb agreement. Actual use of English never reproduces this set of conjugations so schematically. Rather, the conjugations of a verb outlines its possible relations with a subject, which the language system makes available to its users. Such knowledge is necessary for recognizing the grammatical structure of a given utterance (*The cat is outside*, say) as a statement, a meaningful arrangement of signs and not a random combination. The statement *The cat is outside* organizes familiar signs – *cat*, *outside*, *is*, *the* – into a familiar pattern of subject–verb agreement, one which differs from other possible patterns of subject–verb agreement made available by the system, such as *I am outside* or *You are outside*.

Verb conjugations establish just one of the many *paradigms* which comprise a language system. 'Those [signs] that have something in common are associated in the memory, resulting in groups marked by diverse relations; (Saussure 1974 p. 123). Paradigms are the sets of relationships, on the level of either the signifier or the signified, between a sign and all the other elements in the system. The motor-vehicle code outlines the paradigms of the driving system, just as the rules of chess outline the paradigms of the game, just as grammar books outline some of the paradigms of English. In addition to grammar, other common paradigms of English include rhymes (such as 'fig' and 'pig'), homonyms (words that sound the same, such as 'tale' and 'story'), and antonyms (words that mean the opposite, such as 'growl' and 'purr'). Each of these paradigms locates a sign within the language system by structuring a relation of similarity, on the level of signifier or signified, and this similarity helps to mark out the sign's identifiable difference from other signs. *Tale*, for instance, has the same phonetic signifier as *tail* but not the same signified; conversely, it has the same signified as *story* but not the same signifier. *Tale* is a distinct sign for this reason.

Saussure described paradigmatic associations as an effort of memory. His explanation does not fully consider how paradigms regulate the use of signs by enclosing them in a system. The paradigms of a language maintain its operation as a system by keeping its conventions stable and continually recognizable to users of the language – so stable and recognizable, in fact, that one is rarely conscious of the elaborate grid of similarity and difference which this system of paradigmatic marking constructs for language use. Phonetics, syntax, and semantics comprise major sets of paradigmatic relationships that classify groups of similar signs (nouns versus verbs, questions versus statements, animals versus fruits), and that differentiate one individual sign from another. A phonetic paradigm of the English language distinguishes the signifier 'cat' from 'bat' and from 'dat', for example, by marking out the similarity in sound ('at') and the difference ('*k*at' as opposed to '*b*at' and '*d*at') which one needs in order to pronounce the word 'cat'. Similarly, a syntactic paradigm determines the function of the signifier 'c-a-t' as a noun and not a verb in a sentence such as *The cat is outside*, and a semantic paradigm distinguishes this signifier from those of other animals ('b-a-t' and 'd-o-g') and from other signifiers of feline creatures ('k-i-t-t-e-n' and 'p-u-s-s' and even 'W-h-i-s-k-e-r-s').

Semantic paradigms differentiate meaning on the level of the signified. To understand the meaning of *cat* is to recognize that it signifies something different from the concept of canine or rodent, and something different from the youthfulness signified by *kitten* as well. All the same, *cat* can signify many different things. It signifies either a class or small, tame feline animals (house pet) or large, wild ones (lion). It also signifies qualities associated with cats, such as stealthy movement, resilience, aloofness, and, in slang, a gossipy or promiscuous person. For that matter, to Alice *cat* signifies 'pet', whereas to the mouse it signifies 'enemy'! The many possible signifieds of *cat* suggest how easily language instigates a relay of signification to establish a network of interrelated signs that can, paradigmatically, substitute for each other: the signified of one sign (*cat*) easily becomes the signifier of another signified (pet, enemy, gossip, and so forth). This is essentially how connotation works, by relating a signifier to a variety of signifieds according to the semantic paradigms of the language system.

How does a language structure meaning to differentiate one signified from others in order to give a sign its precise meaning? In addition to paradigms, language also constructs a meaning through *syntagms*, which position one sign along a chain of signs, as in a sentence. 'In the syntagm a term acquires its value only because it stands in opposition to everything that precedes or follows it, or to both' (Saussure 1974 p. 123). Specific articulations of the system – the discourses we speak, hear, read, and write – consist of signs set in syntagmatic relation to each other. A sign thus acquires its specific meaning in part because of its paradigmatic location in the language system but in part because of its syntagmatic location in discourse too.

Whereas paradigms organize the vertical relations of similarity between one sign and others at the systematic level of language competence, syntagms organize the horizontal relations of contiguity between one sign and others at the discursive level of language performance. For example, the paradigms of chess determine a particular value for each playing piece, that the queen, say, is more significant than a pawn. But, in an actual game of chess, each piece also acquires its value according to its syntagmatic position on the board – what square it is on at any given time during the game, what pieces are next to it, what other pieces have been captured by the opponent, and so forth. As a sign of fashion, hair length functions in much the same way. Fashion operates according to a paradigm of conformity, a set of norms that determines what is in vogue and what is not. In the fifties and early sixties, long hair on men was considered unfashionable – anti-establishment, in fact – but only in comparison to short hair, which was the norm. In the late sixties and early seventies, however, the signs of fashion were reversed: long hair became a sign of fashion and, hence, the norm, whereas short hair signified old-fashioned, even reactionary in political and social values. In either case, what short or long hair signified as a sign of fashion depended on the length of a man's hair in syntagmatic relation to the way in which other men wore their hair at the same time.

A verbal language like English relies on the syntagmatic arrangement of signs in even more intricate ways. Earlier we noted that *The cat is outside* is a meaningful statement because of its underlying paradigmatic structure. That statement is also meaningful because of the syntagmatic location of *The cat* in the particular sequence of words that make up the sentence. Moving *The cat* to the right of the verb *is* would change the syntagmatic structure to produce a question: *Is the cat outside?* Either sequence depends upon the exact order of words for its identity as a statement or a question, so its meaning is determined syntagmatically as well as paradigmatically.

Similarly, recall Alice's inability to tell the difference between the two questions 'Do cats eat bats?' and 'Do bats eat cats?' These two questions are indeed paradigmatically reversible insofar as each has the same underlying structure of auxiliary verb + subject + main verb + object. However, they are *not* syntagmatically reversible. In each version of her question, *cats* appears in a different syntagmatic relation to *bats*, so it signifies differently. In the first version *cats* is the subject, the agent of the action *eat*, while in the second version *cats* is the object, the goal or destination of that action.

Syntagms are most apparent in determining the identity of a sentence structure according to the actual sequential relation of its parts, but they also organize every aspect of discourse, from phrases of conversation to complete books. Syntagms place signs in a contiguous relation to each other, and these relations form the basis of complex meanings. When a noun is modified by an adjective (*black cat*), or a verb by an adverb (*purrs loudly*), the placement of one sign in relation to another syntagmatically determines a signified that neither word could bear singly. Likewise, relative and dependent clauses, participial phrases, parenthetical interjections, coordinate and subordinate sentence structures, and forms of figurative language arrange signs in a syntagmatic sequence. In each case, while paradigms make the underlying structure of the sequence possible, the value of a single sign is determined by the signs that surround it.

Although our examples so far may suggest otherwise, signs do not have to be directly adjacent to each other to be placed in syntagmatic relation. A pronoun, for instance, is a signifier which simply points elsewhere in the discourse for its signified, to a noun in close proximity that can serve as the pronoun's antecedent. When Alice uses 'it' as a substitution for 'time' in her conversation with the Mad Hatter, the pronoun *it* establishes a syntagmatic relation with the noun *time*. Alice and the Hatter each use the word 'time' to refer to something difference because the *words* they use keep pointing to other signifiers of time within two mutually exclusive syntagms, each producing a different meaning for time.

We have concentrated on the systematic structure of language, and have used as examples of non-verbal systems well-regulated languages such as driving. In doing so we have been following the parameters set forth by Saussure's theory of language. 'Language', he claimed, 'is a self-contained whole' (Saussure 1974 p. 9), 'speech less speaking' (ibid. p. 77). To define his object of study, he distinguished between a *synchronic* analysis of language as a static, timeless system, and a *diachronic* analysis more concerned with changes to the system that occur in speech over time. The primary importance of Saussure's synchronic model to contemporary studies of the sign lies in (1) his separation of the signifier and the signified; (2) his concentration on the differential basis of meaning; (3) and his analysis of the structural relations between signs. There are radical implications of this theory for thinking about the language of narrative, and we shall be returning to and building upon these three key points throughout.

But we must also acknowledge that Saussure's model has limitations for a full understanding of signs as cultural units of meaning. Saussure minimized discourse as a factor in the production and dissemination of signs. Signs mean something to and for someone, and they do so not in the abstract but in a discourse. All of our examples have illustrated both how language means systematically, and how language means only as it gets used. The tea party in particular shows what happens to the meaning of signs by virtue of their location in a particular instance of language use. Scholars who have critiqued Saussure's emphasis on a synchronically closed system of language agree that 'meaning can belong only to a sign', but they also point out that 'the sign cannot be separated from the social situation without relinquishing its nature as sign' (Vološinov 1973 pp. 28, 37).[2]

It is tempting to conclude from Saussure's model that language is an unchanging, universal system governed by unalterable rules but, in actual practice, those rules do not always apply. For just as a driver might have to stop, even though the light is green, in order to avoid hitting a pedestrian, so too a writer might split an infinitive, rearranging the conventionally 'correct' syntagmatic sequence of words, in order to forcefully make a point. A language system does not prescribe right and wrong uses for discourse so much as it establishes possible conditions of signification. In sum, a sign system does not 'exist' materially as language in the way that discourse does. The system is merely an abstraction, a paradigmatic reconstruction of the principles governing actual language use and, thus, marking out possibilities of meaning for discourse.

The pairing of system/discourse, furthermore, is not hierarchical; discourse is not simply the concrete realization of a master system. Since discourse is the domain of actual language use, it stabilizes and conserves the system in which it operates, but it also continually revises the system to allow for new conditions by which meanings are produced. Revisions of grammar (such as the growing legitimacy of split infinitives), of spelling and punctuation (the different British and American styles), of pronunciation (regional dialects), of vocabulary (computer terminology), and of new ways of thinking about language and literature (the ideas informing this book), these are all changes in the language system of English that first occurred in discourse. Originating in usage, an alteration of the system becomes standardized – producing a genuine historical change of the system's paradigms – once users of the language consistently reproduce the alteration.

In the light of what we are saying about linguistic changes, it is also important to realize that neither a language system nor its discourse is ever singular, universal, and timeless. On the contrary, both are plural, cultural, and historical. We have spoken repeatedly of the language of driving as if the same system operates everywhere around the world in the same way, but that is far from the case. In California, for example, pedestrians have the right of way at intersections, so drivers routinely stop for anyone at a crosswalk; there, too, pedestrians can expect to be ticketed if they walk against a red light or cross in the middle of a street, and this practice encourages them to cross only at the marked intersections that give them the right of way. In New York, on the other hand, drivers do not automatically stop for pedestrians who step off the pavement, even at an intersection with a crosswalk; and pedestrians also routinely take the right of way, crossing against red lights when there is no oncoming traffic. While following the same system in many respects, the discourses of driving in these two states differ enough in practice to challenge and revise the competence of strangers.

What we are saying applies even more to a verbal language like English. As Alice's adventures demonstrate, while English may appear to be the same language to all its users, in practice just the opposite is true. Different English-speaking cultures use the language differently, as we have already indicated, so there are, in fact, many English languages, each regulated by a different version of the system and each further modified because of its interaction with other, non-verbal, cultural sign systems.

Moreover, in any given culture and historical time, individual speakers and writers of any one English language produce many different types of discourse. Spoken discourse, for example, varies according to the social situation: whether addressing friends, parents, teachers, strangers, clerks. Likewise, writing a letter, or a report, or a job application, or a civil service exam, or a literature paper depends upon one's ability as a user of English to produce a variety of discourses. In addition, writing can often turn out to be discursively plural, or heterogenic, even within the same piece of prose: when combining description, for instance, with exposition, or with argumentation. Each of these modes of writing comprises a different type of discourse, and combinations result in an even greater variety. Legal, medical, scientific, scholarly, business, technological, bureaucratic, and literary writing also use English differently, in that they follow different conventions of organization, style, documentation, vocabulary, and so constitute different discourses too. Using English, then, requires one's participation in a communal sign system which is historically specific, culturally located, and discursively varied. A sign system enables the production of meaning, but, in practice, discourse is where meanings actually get produced.

Saussure's attention to system (*langue*) over discourse (*parole*) – to language as 'speech less speaking' – prevented him from considering that, while signs are regulated by a system, they are produced in and, more importantly, transformed by discourse. The limitations of Saussure's analysis have therefore required an extension of his theory in order to bring out its most radical implication: that in discourse a sign has the potential to *disrupt* as well as *facilitate* the passage of meaning because the relation of signifier to signified is unstable. While Saussure recognized the arbitrary and conventional features of the sign, he still treated a signifier as merely an expression of a signified. He did not fully consider the extent to which a signifier like the green light at Tipperary Hill in Syracuse produces a signified ('Irish') which functions as another signifier (of Ireland's historical political relation to Britain) in a relay of signification. A sign is thus not always bound by a system, as Saussure would have it, for a signifier can transgress the system.

Every use of language always positions a speaker (or writer, or listener, or reader) along a chain of signs. A sign, according to Charles S. Peirce, 'addresses somebody, that is, creates in the mind of that person an equivalent sign, or perhaps a more developed sign' (Peirce 1955: 99). The contemporary French philosopher Jacques Derrida puts this issue more extremely, perhaps, but very directly: 'From the moment that there is meaning there are nothing but signs. *We think only in signs*' (Derrida 1976 p. 50).

Saussure did not acknowledge the complete dependency of meaning on signs. His privileging of speech over writing as the epitome of language use (*parole*) makes this clear. Despite what he explained about the sign, he still treated writing as a mere transcription of speech. 'Language and writing', he stated, 'are two distinct systems of signs; the second exists for the sole purpose of representing the first' (Saussure 1974 p. 23). Language, in this view, is constituted prior to rather than in writing, which simply performs the function of phonetic notation. As a result, Saussure attributed to the written sign a transparency of expression which he denied to the spoken sign. But elsewhere in the *Course in General Linguistics* Saussure also compared language to writing as 'a system of signs that express ideas' (Saussure 1974 p. 16). This kind of contradiction, Derrida argues in a very complex but important analysis, exposes the troubling status of writing in Saussure's theory of the sign.[3]

Far from transcribing speech, Derrida maintains, writing inscribes the absence which speech conceals or traces over, 'the absence of the signatory, to say nothing of the absence of the referent. Writing is the name of these two absences' (Derrida 1976 pp. 40–41). Writing signifies the difference from speech, the absence of an extra-linguistic ground, of a 'transcendental signified which . . . would place a reassuring end to the reference from sign to sign' (ibid. p. 49). In writing, 'there is not a single signified that escapes, even if recaptured, the play of signifying references that constitute language. The advent of writing is the advent of this play' (ibid. p. 7). Although discourse is in no way limited to writing, writing typifies how discourse presents us with a situation calling for interpretation, for stabilizing the play of signification. Unlike speech, writing foregrounds the constitution of discourse as a chain of references, not from sign to meaning, but from sign to sign.

Narrative, we said in opening this chapter, cannot be considered apart from language. The post-Saussurean theory of language as a system and discourse, as structure and play, therefore demands a revision of traditional notions about narrative. To start with, this theory calls for rigorous attention to narrative as a set of signs. It requires a method of textual analysis responsive to both the structuring operation of a sign system and the instability of signs in discourse.

NOTES

1 For further discussion of 'fiction' and 'non-fiction' as functional categories of language use, see Smith (1978).
2 Two more recent critiques of Saussure, each discussing Vološinov's argument as a point of contrast are R. Williams (1977) and Bennett (1979). See also Macdonell (1986) for a useful introduction to contemporary post-Saussurean arguments about language practices which move beyond Saussure's emphasis on language as a single closed system while still retaining the concepts of system and sign.
3 Derrida's critique of Saussure clearly does not reject the semiotic project; rather, as Christopher Norris points out, Derrida pushes Saussure's conclusions as far as they can go in order to analyse how they radically undermine the traditional premise of an extra-linguistic referentiality which supports the project (see Norris 1982 pp. 24–32).

Visual 'meaning'

EDITOR'S INTRODUCTION

Borrowing from Hjelmslev (1961), Barthes (1990) sets out his connotative system in *Elements of Semiology* (see this volume pp. 129–33). He sees the conjunction of the signifier and signified as the first stage in signification. When that conjunction is taken as the signified (or 'content') of a signifying order it assumes the role of a 'metalanguage'. When that conjunction is taken as the signifier (or 'expression') of a signifying order it assumes the role of *connotation*. This latter order requires that the signifier be inseparable from a signified. As described and diagrammatized by Barthes, it all seems like a neat system; moreover, there can be no denying that second-order meanings such as connotation have a vital role to play in communication. But what needs to be asked about Barthes' schema is where the 'connotative' signified comes from and whether, in experience, connotation can be separated from denotation.

These comments about Barthes may seem excessively negative; however, as we shall see, Barthes' applications of his connotative theory, though faulty, are quite productive in what they tell us about the analysis of communication. In 'The Photographic Message', Barthes grapples with the enormity of meaning. He describes the pure denotative function of photographs as, seemingly, '*a message without a code*'; in other words, it appears that one does not have to learn a special language in order to recognize what is depicted in a photo. The 'analogical plenitude' of photographs is so overwhelming that, for Barthes, it is almost pointless to try to stick on a connotative code such as a written or spoken commentary. Such codes simply cannot match analogic representation (text under photographs is sometimes sucked in or invalidated by the photo) and the only way in which connotation can really be effected is through 'trick effects', 'pose', 'objects', 'photogenia', 'aestheticism' and 'syntax'.

Barthes' effectively uncovers the 'constructedness' of a cultural item that poses as the ideal of representation and his postulates regarding the historical/ideological nature of connotation deserve to be taken seriously. In addition, he does not reduce the connotative and denotative processes to easy categories: where Fiske (1991 p. 86, ironically, summarizing Barthes) pronounces 'denotation' to be 'what is photographed' and 'connotation' to be 'how it is photographed', Barthes is acutely aware that 'connotative' trappings can be manifest on either side of the camera. What one needs to ask about Barthes' essay, however, is whether it is possible to identify pure denotation, a perfect analogon, a message without a code or interpretation. (Stanley Fish has something to say about this in this volume pp. 407–26). In addition, Barthes sees 'culture' as a *langue* (or master code) and the text accompanying a photograph as this code's parasite on denotation. Eco describes a similar transaction, but his understanding of the relationship of 'culture' and the visual is considerably different.

In an entertaining but powerfully argued essay (this volume pp. 148–71), Eco demonstrates how the human capacity to recognize a massive number of colours is restricted by a relatively small range of cultural imperatives. Unlike Barthes, Eco holds that a visual phenomenon (colour) is experienced in a manner determined by a descriptive non-visual code. Our powers of description of colours provide the parameters for our actual recognition of their distinctions. Furthermore, the limited range of cultural uses to which we can put colours are largely responsible for the way in which we discriminate between them. 'Culture' here is not so much a global and diffuse phenomenon but something predicated on first principles. For Eco, then, the logic and restrictions of verbal language are sufficiently strong to overcome the plenitude of the visual.

Such a position is not that far from the Hallidayan perspective on 'visual literacy' of Kress and van Leeuwen. The latter insist that, far from being 'messages without codes' or 'perfect analogons', pictures are always highly structured. Clearly, they argue, there is a difference between those highly representational pictures and those stylized and idealized ones (e.g. trees which resemble lollipops) that might appear in children's books. In addition, visual representation of the most simple kind is not without its own mode of address, offering positions for 'interactive' and 'represented' participants. What distinguishes the approach of Kress and van Leeuwen from Barthes and from Eco is that, while appropriating the terms of linguistics for their analysis, Kress and van Leeuwen stress that visual representation possesses an autonomous language.

The problem that Kress and van Leeuwen confront as pioneers in their variety of visual analysis should, to an extent, be evident in the readings that precede them. Barthes largely overlooks the syntagmatic production of meaning (although he moves in this direction when commenting on 'pose' and 'objects') and Eco restricts his analysis to visual components which are, in a sense, not yet coded into messages. It might be argued, then, that we can only really get to grips with the idea of a visual *representation* if we avoid overvaluing its putative power as analogon and consider the combinations which impute it with meaning.

Further reading   Harland 1993 pp. 3–12; Hartley 1988 pp. 20–37; J. Palmer 1990 pp. 51–69; Stam *et al.* 1992 pp. 28–68; Metz 1974; Eco 1986; Hodge 1988; Kress and van Leeuwen 1992b; Kress 1994 pp. 194–237.

9 Roland Barthes

Denotation and connotation

STAGGERED SYSTEMS

It will be remembered that any system of significations comprises a plane of expression (E) and a plane of content (C) and that the signification coincides with the relation (R) of the two planes: ERC. Let us now suppose that such a system ERC becomes in its turn a mere element of a second system, which thus is more extensive than the first: we then deal with two systems of significations which are imbricated but are out of joint with each other, or staggered. But this derivation can occur in two entirely different ways dependent upon the point of insertion of the first system into the second, and therefore it can result in two opposite sets.

In the first case, *the first system (ERC) becomes the plane of expression, or signifier, of the second system*:

2   E   R   C

1   E R C

or else: (ERC) RC. This is the case which Hjelmslev calls *connotative semiotics*; the first system is then the plane of *denotation* and the second system (wider than the first) the plane of *connotation*. We shall therefore say that *a connoted system is a system whose plane of expression is itself constituted by a signifying system*: the common cases of connotation will of course consist of complex systems of which language forms the first system (this is, for instance, the case with literature).

In the second (opposite) case of derivation, *the first system (ERC)
becomes, not the plane of expression, as in connotation, but the plane of
content, or signified, of the second system =*

2   E   R   C

1   E R C

or else: ER (ERC). This is the case with all *metalanguages: a metalanguage is a system whose plane of content is itself constituted by a signifying
system; or else, it is a semiotics which treats of a semiotics.*

Such are the two ways of amplification of double systems
(Figure 9.1).

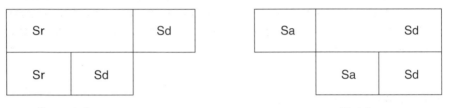

Connotation   Metalanguage

Figure 9.1

Connotative phenomena have not yet been systematically studied
(a few indications will be found in Hjelmslev's *Prolegomena*). Yet the
future probably belongs to a linguistics of connotation, for society
continually develops, from the first system which human language
supplies to it, second-order significant systems, and this elaboration,
now proclaimed and now disguised, is very close to a real historical
anthropology. Connotation, being itself a system, comprises signifiers, signifieds, and the process which unites the former to the latter
(signification), and it is the inventory of these three elements which
one should undertake in the first place for each system.

The signifiers of connotation, which we shall call *connotators*, are
made up of *signs* (signifiers and signifieds united) of the denoted
system. Naturally, several denoted signs can be grouped together to
form a single connotator – provided the latter has a single signified
of connotation; in other words, the units of the connoted system do
not necessarily have the same size as those of the denoted system:
large fragments of the denoted discourse can constitute a single unit

of the connoted system (this is the case, for instance, with the tone of a text, which is made up of numerous words, but which nevertheless refers to a single signified). Whatever the manner in which it 'caps' the denoted message, connotation does not exhaust it: there always remains 'something denoted' (otherwise the discourse would not be possible) and the connotators are always in the last analysis discontinuous and scattered signs, naturalized by the denoted language which carries them.

As for the signified of connotation, its character is at once general, global and diffuse; it is, if you like, a fragment of ideology: the sum of the messages in French refers, for instance, to the signified 'French'; a book can refer to the signified 'Literature'. These signifieds have a very close communication with culture, knowledge, history, and it is through them, so to speak, that the environmental world invades the system. We might say that *ideology* is the *form* (in Hjelmslev's sense of the word) of the signifieds of connotation, while *rhetoric* is the form of the connotators.

METALANGUAGE

In connotative semiotics, the signifiers of the second system are constituted by the signs of the first; this is reversed in metalanguage: there the signifieds of the second system are constituted by the signs of the first. Hjelmslev has made the notion of metalanguage explicit in the following way: it being understood that an *operation* is a *description* founded on the empirical principle, that is to say non-contradictory (coherent), exhaustive and simple, scientific semiotics, or metalanguage, is an operation, whereas connotative semiotics is not. It is evident that semiology, for instance, is a metalanguage, since as a second-order system it takes over a first language (or language-object) which is the system under scrutiny; and this system-object is *signified* through the metalanguage of semiology. The notion of meta-language must not be confined to scientific languages; when ordinary language, *in its denoted state*, takes over a system of signifying objects, it becomes an 'operation', that is, a metalanguage. This is the case, for instance, with the fashion magazine which 'speaks' the significations of garments, just as one speaks a language; this, however, is only ideally speaking, for magazines do not usually exhibit a purely denoted discourse, so that eventually we deal here with a complex ensemble, where language, at its denoted level, is a metalanguage, but where this metalanguage is in its turn caught up in a process of connotation (Figure 9.2).

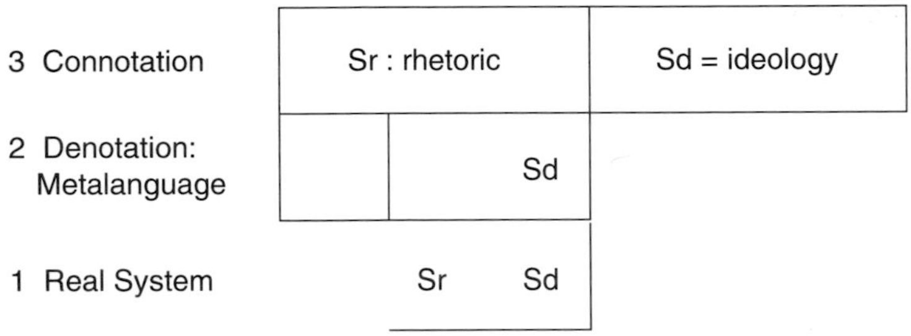

3 Connotation	Sr : rhetoric		Sd = ideology
2 Denotation: Metalanguage		Sd	
1 Real System	Sr	Sd	

Figure 9.2

CONNOTATION AND METALANGUAGE

Nothing in principle prevents a metalanguage from becoming in its turn the language-object of a new metalanguage; this would, for example, be the case with semiology if it were to be 'spoken' by another science. If one agreed to define the social sciences as coherent, exhaustive and simple languages (Hjelmslev's empirical principle), that is as *operations*, each new science would then appear as a new language which would have as its object the metalanguage which precedes it, while being directed towards the reality-object which is at the root of these 'descriptions'; the history of the social sciences would thus be, in a sense, a diachrony of metalanguages, and each science, including of course semiology, would contain the seeds of its own death, in the shape of the language destined to speak it. This relativity, which is an inherent part of the general system of metalanguages, allows us to qualify the image which we might at first form, of a semiologist over-confident in the face of connotation; the whole of a semiological analysis usually requires, in addition to the studied system and the (denoted) language which in most cases takes it over, a system of connotation and the metalanguage of the analysis which is applied to it. We might say that society, which holds the plane of connotation, speaks the signifiers of the system considered, while the semiologist speaks its signifieds; he therefore seems to have the objective function of decipherer (his language is an operation) in relation to the world which naturalizes or conceals the signs of the first system under the signifiers of the second; but his objectivity is made provisional by the very history which renews metalanguages.

10 Roland Barthes

The photographic message

The press photograph is a message. Considered overall this message is formed by a source of emission, a channel of transmission and a point of reception. The source of emission is the staff of the newspaper, the group of technicians certain of whom take the photo, some of whom choose, compose and treat it, while others, finally, give it a title, a caption and a commentary. The point of reception is the public which reads the paper. As for the channel of transmission, this is the newspaper itself, or, more precisely, a complex of concurrent messages with the photograph as centre and surrounds constituted by the text, the title, the caption, the lay-out and, in a more abstract but no less 'informative' way, by the very name of the paper (this name represents a knowledge that can heavily orientate the reading of the message strictly speaking: a photograph can change its meaning as it passes from the very conservative *L'Aurore* to the communist *L'Humanité*). These observations are not without their importance for it can readily be seen that in the case of the press photograph the three traditional parts of the message do not call for the same method of investigation. The emission and the reception of the message both lie within the field of a sociology: it is a matter of studying human groups, of defining motives and attitudes, and of trying to link the behaviour of these groups to the social totality of which they are a part. For the message itself, however, the method is inevitably different: whatever the origin and the destination of the message, the photograph is not simply a product or a channel but also an object endowed with a structural autonomy. Without in any way intending to divorce this object from its use, it is necessary to provide for a specific method prior to sociological analysis and which can only be the immanent analysis of the unique structure that a photograph constitutes.

Naturally, even from the perspective of a purely immanent analysis, the structure of the photograph is not an isolated structure; it is in communication with at least one other structure, namely the text – title, caption or article – accompanying every press photograph. The totality of the information is thus carried by two different structures (one of which is linguistic). These two structures are co-operative but, since their units are heterogeneous, necessarily remain separate from one another: here (in the text) the substance of the message is made up of words; there (in the photograph) of lines, surfaces, shades. Moreover, the two structures of the message each occupy their own defined spaces, these being contiguous but not 'homogenized', as they are for example in the rebus which fuses words and images in a single line of reading. Hence, although a press photograph is never without a written commentary, the analysis must first of all bear on each separate structure; it is only when the study of each structure has been exhausted that it will be possible to understand that manner in which they complement one another. Of the two structures, one is already familiar, that of language (but not, it is true, that of the 'literature' formed by the language-use of the newspaper; an enormous amount of work is still to be done in this connection), while almost nothing is known about the other, that of the photograph. What follows will be limited to the definition of the initial difficulties in providing a structural analysis of the photographic message.

THE PHOTOGRAPHIC PARADOX

What is the content of the photographic message? What does the photograph transmit? By definition, the scene itself, the literal reality. From the object to its image there is of course a reduction – in proportion, perspective, colour – but at no time is this reduction a *transformation* (in the mathematical sense of that term). In order to move from the reality to its photograph it is in no way necessary to divide up this reality into units and to constitute these units as signs, substantially different from the object they communicate; there is no necessity to set up a relay, that is to say a code, between the object and its image. Certainly the image is not the reality but at least it is its perfect *analogon* and it is exactly this analogical perfection which, to common sense, defines the photograph. Thus can be seen the special status of the photographic image: *it is a message without a code*; from which proposition an important corollary must immediately be drawn; the photographic message is a continuous message.

Are there other messages without a code? At first sight, yes: precisely the whole range of analogical reproductions of reality – drawings, paintings, cinema, theatre. In fact, however, each of those messages develops in an immediate and obvious way a supplementary message, in addition to the analogical content itself (scene, object, landscape), which is what is commonly called the *style* of the reproduction; second meaning, whose signifier is a certain 'treatment' of the image (result of the action of the creator) and whose signified, whether aesthetic or ideological, refers to a certain 'culture' of the society receiving the message. In short, all these 'initiative' arts comprise two messages: a *denoted* message, which is the *analogon* itself, and a *connoted* message, which is the manner in which the society to a certain extent communicates what it thinks of it. This duality of messages is evident in all reproductions other than photographic ones: there is no drawing, no matter how exact, whose very exactitude is not turned into a style (the style of 'verism'); no filmed scene whose objectivity is not finally read as the very sign of objectivity. Here again, the study of these connoted messages has still to be carried out (in particular it has to be decided whether what is called a work of art can be reduced to a system of significations); one can only anticipate that for all these imitative arts – when common – the code of the connoted system is very likely constituted either by a universal symbolic order or by a period rhetoric, in short by a stock of stereotypes (schemes, colours, graphisms, gestures, expressions, arrangements of elements).

When we come to the photograph, however, we find in principle nothing of the kind, at any rate as regards the press photograph (which is never an 'artistic' photograph). The photograph professing to be a mechanical analogue of reality, its first-order message in some sort completely fills its substance and leaves no place for the development of a second-order message. Of all the structures of information,[1] the photograph appears as the only one that is exclusively constituted and occupied by a 'denoted' message, a message which totally exhausts its mode of existence. In front of a photograph, the feeling of 'denotation', or, if one prefers, of analogical plenitude, is so great that the description of a photograph is literally impossible; *to describe* consists precisely in joining to the denoted message a relay or second-order message derived from a code which is that of language and constituting in relation to the photographic analogue, however much care one takes to be exact, a connotation: to describe is thus not simply to be imprecise or incomplete, it is to change structures, to signify something different to what is shown.[2]

This purely 'denotative' status of the photograph, the perfection and plenitude of its analogy, in short its 'objectivity', has every chance of being mythical (these are the characteristics that common sense attributes to the photograph). In actual fact, there is a strong probability (and this will be a working hypothesis) that the photographic message too – at least in the press – is connoted. Connotation is not necessarily immediately graspable at the level of the message itself (it is, one could say, at once invisible and active, clear and implicit) but it can already be inferred from certain phenomena which occur at the levels of the production and reception of the message: on the one hand, the press photograph is an object that has been worked on, chosen, composed, constructed, treated according to professional, aesthetic or ideological norms which are so many factors of connotation; while on the other, this same photograph is not only perceived, received, it is *read*, connected more or less consciously by the public that consumes it to a traditional stock of signs. Since every sign supposes a code, it is this code (of connotation) that one should try to establish. The photographic paradox can then be seen as the co-existence of two messages, the one without a code (the photographic analogue), the other with a code (the 'art', or the treatment, or the 'writing', or the rhetoric, of the photograph); structurally, the paradox is clearly not the collusion of a denoted message and a connoted message (which is the – probably inevitable – status of all the forms of mass communication), it is that here the connoted (or coded) message develops on the basis of a message *without a code*. This structural paradox coincides with an ethical paradox; when one wants to be 'neutral', 'objective', one strives to copy reality meticulously, as though the analogical were a factor of resistance against the investment of values (such at least is the definition of aesthetic 'realism'); how then can the photograph be at once 'objective' and 'invested', natural and cultural? It is through an understanding of the mode of imbrication of denoted and connoted messages that it may one day be possible to reply to that question. In order to undertake this work, however, it must be remembered that since the denoted message in the photograph is absolutely analogical, which is to say *continuous*, outside of any recourse to a code, there is no need to look for the signifying units of the first-order message; the connoted message on the contrary does comprise a plane of expression and a plane of content, thus necessitating a veritable decipherment. Such a decipherment would as yet be premature, for in order to isolate the signifying units and the signified themes (or values) one would have to carry out (perhaps using tests) directed readings, artificially varying certain elements of a photograph to see if the variations of forms led to variations in meaning. What can at least be done now is to forecast the main planes of analysis of photographic connotation.

CONNOTATION PROCEDURES

Connotation, the imposition of second meaning on the photographic message proper, is realized at the different levels of the production of the photograph (choice, technical treatment, framing, lay-out) and represents, finally, a coding of the photographic analogue. It is thus possible to separate out various connotation procedures, bearing in mind however that these procedures are in no way units of signification such as a subsequent analysis of a semantic kind may one day manage to define; they are not strictly speaking part of the photographic structure. The procedures in question are familiar and no more will be attempted here than to translate them into structural terms. To be fully exact, the first three (trick effects, pose, objects) should be distinguished from the last three (photogenia, aestheticism, syntax), since in the former the connotation is produced by a modification of the reality itself, of, that is, the denoted message (such preparation is obviously not peculiar to the photograph). If they are nevertheless included amongst the connotation procedures, it is because they too benefit from the prestige of the denotation: the photograph allows the photographer to *conceal elusively* the preparation to which he subjects the scene to be recorded. Yet the fact still remains that there is no certainty from the point of view of a subsequent structural analysis that it will be possible to take into account the material they provide.

1 Trick effects

A photograph given wide circulation in the American press in 1951 is reported to have cost Senator Millard Tydings his seat; it showed the Senator in conversation with the Communist leader Earl Browder. In fact, the photograph had been faked, created by the artificial bringing together of the two faces. The methodological interest of trick effects is that they intervene without warning in the plane of denotation; they utilize the special credibility of the photograph – this, as was seen, being simply its exceptional power of denotation – in order to pass off as merely denoted a message which is in reality heavily connoted; in no other treatment does connotation assume so completely the 'objective' mask of denotation. Naturally, signification is only possible to the extent that there is a stock of signs, the beginnings of a code. The signifier here is the conversational attitude of the two figures and it will be noted that this attitude becomes a sign only for a certain society, only given certain values. What makes the speakers' attitude the sign of a reprehensible familiarity is the tetchy anti-Communism of the American electorate; which is to say that the code of connotation is neither artificial (as in a true language) nor natural, but historical.

2 Pose

Consider a press photograph of President Kennedy widely distributed at the time of the 1960 election: a half-length profile shot, eyes looking upwards, hands joined together. Here it is the very pose of the subject which prepares the reading of the signifieds of connotation: youthfulness, spirituality, purity. The photograph clearly only signifies because of the existence of a store of stereotyped attitudes which form ready-made elements of signification (eyes raised heavenwards, hands clasped). A 'historical grammar' of iconographic connotation ought thus to look for its material in painting, theatre, associations of ideas, stock metaphors, etc., that is to say, precisely in 'culture'. As has been said, pose is not a specifically photographic procedure but it is difficult not to mention it insofar as it derives its effect from the analogical principle at the basis of the photograph. The message in the present instance is not 'the pose' but 'Kennedy praying': the reader receives as a simple denotation what is in actual fact a double structure – denoted-connoted.

3 Objects

Special importance must be accorded to what could be called the posing of objects, where the meaning comes from the objects photographed (either because these objects have, if the photographer had the time, been artificially arranged in front of the camera or because the person responsible for lay-out chooses a photograph of this or that object). The interest lies in the fact that the objects are accepted inducers of associations of ideas (book-case = intellectual) or, in a more obscure way, are veritable symbols (the door of the gas-chamber for Chessman's execution with its reference to the funeral gates of ancient mythologies). Such objects constitute excellent elements of signification: on the one hand they are discontinuous and complete in themselves, a physical qualification for a sign, while on the other they refer to clear, familiar signifieds. They are thus the elements of a veritable lexicon, stable to a degree which allows them to be readily constituted into syntax. Here, for example, is a 'composition' of objects: a window opening on to vineyards and tiled roofs; in front of the window a photograph album, a magnifying glass, a vase of flowers. Consequently, we are in the country, south of the Loire (vines and tiles), in a bourgeois house (flowers on the table) whose owner, advanced in years (the magnifying glass), is reliving his memories (the photograph album) – François Mauriac in Malagar (photo in *Paris-Match*). The connotation somehow 'emerges' from all the signifying units which are nevertheless 'captured' as though the scene were immediate and spontaneous, that is to say, without signification. The text renders the connotation explicit, developing the theme of Mauriac's ties with the land. Objects no longer perhaps possess a *power*, but they certainly possess meanings.

4 Photogenia

The theory of photogenia has already been developed (by Edgar Morin in *Le Cinéma ou l'homme imaginaire*) and this is not the place to take up again the subject of the general signification of that procedure; it will suffice to define photogenia in terms of informational structure. In photogenia the connoted message is the image itself, 'embellished' (which is to say in general sublimated) by techniques of lighting, exposure and printing. An inventory needs to be made of these techniques, but only insofar as each of them has a corresponding signified of connotation sufficiently constant to allow its incorporation in a cultural lexicon of technical 'effects' (as for instance the 'blurring of movement' or 'flowingness' launched by Dr Steinert and his team to signify space-time). Such an inventory would be an excellent opportunity for distinguishing aesthetic effects from signifying effects – unless perhaps it be recognized that in photography, contrary to the intentions of exhibition photographers, there is never *art* but always *meaning*; which precisely would at last provide an exact criterion for the opposition between good painting, even if strongly representational, and photography.

5 Aestheticism

For if one can talk of aestheticism in photography, it is seemingly in an ambiguous fashion: when photography turns painting, composition or visual substance treated with deliberation in its very material 'texture', it is either so as to signify itself as 'art' (which was the case with the 'pictorialism' of the beginning of the century) or to impose a generally more subtle and complex signified than would be possible with other connotation procedures. Thus Cartier-Bresson constructed Cardinal Pacelli's reception by the faithful of Lisieux like a painting by an early master. The resulting photograph, however, is in no way a painting: on the other hand, its display of aestheticism refers (damagingly) to the very idea of a painting (which is contrary to any true painting); while on the other, the composition signifies in a declared manner a certain ecstatic spirituality translated precisely in terms of an objective spectacle. One can see here the difference between photograph and painting: in a picture by a Primitive, 'spirituality' is not a signified but, as it were, the very being of the image. Certainly there may be coded elements in some paintings, rhetorical figures, period symbols, but no signifying unit refers to spirituality, which is a mode of being and not the object of a structured message.

6 Syntax

We have already considered a discursive reading of object-signs within a single photograph. Naturally, several photographs can come together to form a sequence (this is commonly the case in illustrated magazines); the signifier of connotation is then no longer to be found at the level of any one of the fragments of the sequence but at that – what the linguists would call the suprasegmental level – of the concatenation. Consider for example four snaps of a presidential shoot at Rambouillet: in each, the illustrious sportsman (Vincent Auriol) is pointing his rifle in some unlikely direction, to the great peril of the keepers who run away or fling themselves to the ground. The sequence (and the sequence alone) offers an effect of comedy which emerges, according to a familiar procedure, from the repetition and variation of the attitudes. It can be noted in this connection that the single photograph, contrary to the drawing, is very rarely (that is, only with much difficulty) comic; the comic requires movement, which is to say repetition (easy in film) or typification (possible in drawing), both these 'connotations' being prohibited to the photograph.

TEXT AND IMAGE

Such are the main connotation procedures of the photographic image (once again, it is a question of techniques, not of units). To these may invariably be added the text which accompanies the press photograph. Three remarks should be made in this context.

Firstly, the text constitutes a parasitic message designed to connote the image, to 'quicken' it with one or more second-order signifieds. In other words, and this is an important historical reversal, the image no longer *illustrates* the words; it is now the words which, structurally, are parasitic on the image. The reversal is at a cost: in the traditional modes of illustration the image functioned as an episodic return to denotation from a principal message (the text) which was experienced as connoted since, precisely, it needed an illustration; in the relationship that now holds, it is not the image which comes to elucidate or 'realize' the text, but the latter which comes to sublimate, patheticize or rationalize the image. As however this operation is carried out accessorily, the new informational totality appears to be chiefly founded on an objective (denoted) message in relation to which the text is only a kind of secondary vibration, almost without consequence. Formerly, the image illustrated the text (made it clearer); today, the text loads the image, burdening it with a culture, a moral, an imagination. Formerly, there was reduction from text to image; today, there is amplification from the one to the other. The connotation is now experienced only as the natural resonance of the fundamental denotation constituted by the photographic analogy and we are thus confronted with a typical process of naturalization of the cultural.

Secondly, the effect of connotation probably differs according to the way in which the text is presented. The closer the text to the image, the less it seems to connote it; caught as it were in the iconographic message, the verbal message seems to share in its objectivity, the connotation of language is 'innocented' through the photograph's denotation. It is true that there is never a real incorporation since the substances of the two structures (graphic and iconic) are irreducible, but there are most likely degrees of amalgamation. The caption probably has a less obvious effect of connotation than the headline or accompanying article: headline and article are palpably separate from the image, the former by its emphasis, the latter by its distance; the first because it breaks, the other because it distances the content of the image. The caption, on the contrary, by its very disposition, by its average measure of reading, appears to duplicate the image, that is, to be included in its denotation.

It is impossible however (and this will be the final remark here concerning the text) that the words 'duplicate' the image; in the movement from one structure to the other second signifieds are inevitably developed. What is the relationship of these signifieds of connotation to the image? To all appearances, it is one of making explicit, of providing a stress; the text most often simply amplifying a set of connotations already given in the photograph. Sometimes, however, the text produces (invents) an entirely new signified which is retroactively projected into the image, so much so as to appear denoted there. *'They were near to death, their faces prove it'*, reads the headline to a photograph showing Elizabeth and Philip leaving a plane – but at the moment of the photograph the two still knew nothing of the accident they had just escaped. Sometimes too, the text can even contradict the image so as to produce a compensatory connotation. An analysis by G. Gerbner (*The Social Anatomy of the Romance Confession Cover-girl*) demonstrated that in certain romance magazines the verbal message of the headlines, gloomy and anguished, on the cover always accompanied the image of a radiant covergirl; here the two messages enter into a compromise, the connotation having a regulating function, preserving the irrational movement of projection-identification.

PHOTOGRAPHIC INSIGNIFICANCE

We saw that the code of connotation was in all likelihood neither 'natural' nor 'artificial' but historical, or, if it be preferred, 'cultural'. Its signs are gestures, attitudes, expressions, colours or effects, endowed with certain meanings by virtue of the practice of a certain society: the link between signifier and signified remains if not unmotivated, at least entirely historical. Hence it is wrong to say that modern man projects into reading photographs feelings and values which are characterial or 'eternal' (infra- or trans-historical), unless it be firmly specified that *signification* is always developed by a given society and history. Signification, in short, is the dialectical movement which resolves the contradiction between cultural and natural man.

Thanks to its code of connotation the reading of the photograph is thus always historical; it depends on the reader's 'knowledge' just as though it were a matter of a real language [*langue*], intelligible only if one has learned the signs. All things considered, the photographic 'language' ['*langage*'] is not unlike certain ideographic languages which mix analogical and specifying units, the difference being that the ideogram is experienced as a sign whereas the photographic 'copy' is taken as the pure and simple denotation of reality. To find this code of connotation would thus be to isolate, invetoriate and structure all the 'historical' elements of the photograph, all the parts of the photographic surface which derive their very discontinuity from a certain knowledge on the reader's part, or, if one prefers, from the reader's cultural situation.

This task will perhaps take us a very long way indeed. Nothing tells us that the photograph contains 'neutral' parts, or at least it may be that complete insignificance in the photograph is quite exceptional. To resolve the problem, we would first of all need to elucidate fully the mechanisms of reading (in the physical, and no longer the semantic, sense of the term), of the perception of the photograph. But on this point we know very little. How do we read a photograph? What do we perceive? In what order, according to what progression? If, as is suggested by certain hypotheses of Bruner and

Piaget, there is no perception without immediate categorization, then the photograph is verbalized in the very moment it is perceived; better, it is only perceived verbalized (if there is a delay in verbalization, there is disorder in perception, questioning, anguish for the subject, traumatism, following G. Cohen-Séat's hypothesis with regard to filmic perception). From this point of view, the image – grasped immediately by an inner metalanguage, language itself – in actual fact has no denoted state, is immersed for its very social existence in at least an initial layer of connotation, that of the categories of language. We know that every language takes up a position with regard to things, that it connotes reality, if only in dividing it up; the connotations of the photograph would thus coincide, *grosso modo*, with the overall connotative planes of language.

In addition to 'perceptive' connotation, hypothetical but possible, one then encounters other, more particular, modes of connotation, and firstly a 'cognitive' connotation whose signifiers are picked out, localized, in certain parts of the analogon. Faced with such and such a townscape, I *know* that this is a North African country because on the left I can see a sign in Arabic script, in the centre a man wearing a gandoura, and so on. Here the reading closely depends on my culture, on my knowledge of the world, and it is probable that a good press photograph (and they are all good, being selected) makes ready play with the supposed knowledge of its readers, those prints being chosen which comprise the greatest possible quantity of information of this kind in such a way as to render the reading fully satisfying. If one photographs Agadir in ruins, it is better to have a few signs of 'Arabness' at one's disposal, even though 'Arabness' has nothing to do with the disaster itself; connotation drawn from knowledge is always a reassuring force – man likes signs and likes them clear.

Perceptive connotation, cognitive connotation; there remains the problem of ideological (in the very wide sense of the term) or ethical connotation, that which introduces reasons or values into the reading of the image. This is a strong connotation requiring a highly elaborated signifier of a readily syntactical order: conjunction of people (as was seen in the discussion of trick effects), development of attitudes, constellation of objects. A son has just been born to the Shah of Iran and in a photograph we have: royalty (cot worshipped by a crowd of servants gathering round), wealth (several nursemaids), hygiene (white coats, cot covered in Plexiglas), the nevertheless human condition of kings (the baby is crying) – all the elements, that is, of the myth of princely birth as it is consumed today. In this instance the values are apolitical and their lexicon is abundant and clear. It is possible (but this is only a hypothesis) that political connotation is generally entrusted to the text, insofar as political choices are always, as it were, in bad faith: for a particular photograph I can give a right-wing reading or a left-wing reading (see in this connection an IFOP survey published by *Les Temps modernes* in 1955). Denotation, or the appearance of denotation, is powerless to alter political opinions: no photograph has ever convinced or refuted anyone (but the photograph can 'confirm') insofar as political consciousness is perhaps non-existent outside the *logos*: politics is what allows *all* languages.

These few remarks sketch a kind of differential table of photographic connotations, showing, if nothing else, that connotation extends a long way. Is this to say that a pure denotation, a *this-side of language*, is impossible? If such a denotation exists, it is perhaps not at the level of what ordinary language calls the insignificant, the neutral, the objective, but, on the contrary, at the level of absolutely traumatic images. The trauma is a suspension of language, a blocking of meaning. Certainly situations which are normally traumatic can be seized in a process of photographic signification but then precisely they are indicated via a rhetorical code which distances, sublimates and pacifies them. Truly traumatic photographs are rare, for in photography the trauma is wholly dependent on the certainty that the scene 'really' happened: *the photographer had to be there* (the mythical definition of denotation). Assuming this (which, in fact, is already a connotation), the traumatic photograph (fires, shipwrecks, catastrophes, violent deaths, all captured 'from life as lived') is the photograph about which there is nothing to say; the shock-photo is by structure insignificant: no value, no knowledge, at the limit no verbal categorization can have a hold on the process instituting the signification. One could imagine a kind of law: the more direct the trauma, the more difficult is connotation; or again, the 'mythological' effect of a photograph is inversely proportional to its traumatic effect.

Why? Doubtless because photographic connotation, like every well structured signification, is an institutional activity; in relation to society overall, its function is to integrate man, to reassure him. Every code is at once arbitrary and rational; recourse to a code is thus always an opportunity for man to prove himself, to test himself through a reason and a liberty. In this sense, the analysis of codes perhaps allows an easier and surer historical definition of a society than the analysis of its signifieds, for the latter can often appear as trans-historical, belonging more to an anthropological base than to a proper history. Hegel gave a better definition of the ancient Greeks by outlining the manner in which they made nature signify than by describing the totality of their 'feelings and beliefs' on the subject. Similarly, we can perhaps do better than to take stock directly of the ideological contents of our age; by trying to reconstitute in its specific structure the code of connotation of a mode of communication as important as the press photograph we may hope to find, in their very subtlety, the forms our society uses to ensure its peace of mind and to grasp thereby the magnitude, the detours and the underlying function of that activity. The prospect is the more appealing in that, as was said at the beginning, it develops with regard to the photograph in the form of a paradox – that which makes of an inert object a language and which transforms the unculture of a 'mechanical' art into the most social of institutions.

NOTES

1 It is a question, of course, of 'cultural' or culturalized structures, not of operational structures. Mathematics, for example, constitutes a denoted structure without any connotation at all; should mass society seize on it, however, setting out for instance an algebraic formula in an article on Einstein, this originally purely mathematical message now takes on a very heavy connotation, since it *signifies* science.
2 The description of a drawing is easier, involving, finally, the description of a structure that is already connoted, fashioned with a *coded* signification in view. It is for this reason perhaps that psychological texts use a great many drawings and very few photographs.

11 Umberto Eco

How culture conditions the colours we see

I

Colour is not an easy matter. James Gibson (1968) in *The Senses Considered as Perceptual Systems*, says that 'the meaning of the term colour is one of the worst muddles in the history of science'. If one uses the term 'colour' to mean the pigmentation of substances in the environment, one has not said anything about our chromatic perception. Johannes Itten (1961), in his *Kunst der Farbe*, distinguishes between pigments as chromatic reality and our perceptual response as chromatic effect. The chromatic effect, it seems, depends on many factors: the nature of surfaces, light, contrast between objects, previous knowledge, and so on.

I do not have any competence about pigments and I have very confused ideas about the laws governing chromatic effect; moreover I am neither a painter, nor an art critic. My personal relationship with the coloured world is a private affair as much as my sexual activity, and I am not supposed to entertain my readers with my personal reactivity towards the polychromous theatre of the world. Thus, as far as colours are concerned, I take the privilege of considering myself a blind man. I shall be writing about colours from a merely theoretical point of view, namely, from the point of view of a general semiotic approach.

Since I have assumed myself to be blind or at least a Daltonist, I shall mistrust my visual experience. I shall start from a verbal text, chapter 26, Book II, of Aulus Gellius' *Noctes Acticae*, a Latin encyclopaedia of the second century AD.

To deal with colours by making recourse to a text of this period is rather challenging. We are facing linguistic terms for colours, but we do not know what chromatic effects these words refer to. We know much about Roman sculpture and architecture, but very little about Roman painting. The colours we see today in Pompeii are not the colours the Pompeians saw; even if the pigments are the same, the chromatic responses are not. In the nineteenth century, Gladstone suggested that Greeks were unable to distinguish blue from yellow. Goetz and many others assumed that Latin speakers did not distinguish blue from green. I have found also somewhere that Egyptians used blue in their paintings but had no linguistic term to designate it, and that Assyrians, in order to name the colour blue, could do no better than transform the noun 'uknu', naming lapis lazuli, into an adjective.

All of this is highly speculative, but we need not test every case. Let me concentrate on the following passage from Aulus Gellius. The reader is advised to hold his temper, since the passage is highly confusing.

Gellius is reporting a conversation he had with Fronto, a poet and grammarian, and Favorinus, a philosopher. Favorinus remarked that eyes are able to isolate more colours than words can name. Red (*rufus*) and green (*viridis*), he said, have only two names but many species. He was, without knowing it, introducing the contemporary scientific distinction between identification (understood as categorization) and discrimination, of which I shall speak later.

Favorinus continues: *rufus* is a name, but what a difference between the red of blood, the red of purple, the red of saffron, and the red of gold! They are all differences of red but, in order to define them, Latin can only make recourse to adjectives derived from the names of objects, thus calling *flammeus* the red of fire, *sanguineus* the red of blood, *croceus* the red of saffron, *aureus* the red of gold. Greek has more names, Favorinus says, but Fronto replies that Latin, too, has many colour terms and that, in order to designate *russus* and *ruber* (red), one can also use *fulvus, flavus, rubidus, poeniceus, rutilus, luteus, spadix*.

Now if one looks at the whole history of Latin literature, one notices that *fulvus* is associated by Virgil and other authors with the lion's mane, with sand, wolves, gold, eagles, but also with jasper. *Flavae*, in Virgil, are the hair of the blond Dido, as well as olive leaves; and the Tiber river, because of the yellow-grey mud polluting its waters, was commonly called *flavus*. The other terms all refer to various gradations of red, from pale rose to dark red: notice, for instance, that *luteus*, which Fronto defines as 'diluted red', is referred by Pliny to the egg-yolk and by Catullus to poppies.

In order to add more precision, Fronto says that *fulvus* is a mixture of red and green, while *flavus* is a mixture of green, red and white. Fronto then quotes another example from Virgil (*Georgica*, III, 82) where a horse (commonly interpreted by philologists as a dapple-grey horse) is *glaucus*. Now *glaucus* in Latin tradition stands for greenish, light-green, blue-green and grey-blue; Virgil uses this adjective also for willow trees and for ulva or sea lettuce, as well as for waters. Fronto says that Virgil could also have used for his same purpose (his grey horse) *caerulus*. Now this term is usually associated with the sea, skies, the eyes of Minerva, watermelons and cucumbers (Propertius), while Juvenal employs it to describe some sort of rye bread.

And things get no better with *viridis* (from which comes the Italian *verde*, green), since in the whole of Latin tradition, one can find *viridis* associated with grass, skies, parrots, sea, trees.

I have suggested that Latin did not clearly distinguish blue from green, but Favorinus gives us the impression that Latin users did not even distinguish blue-green from red, since he quotes Ennius (*Annales*, XIV, 372–373) who describes the sea at the same time as *caeruleus* and *flavus* as marble. Favorinus agrees with this, since – he says – Fronto had previously described *flavus* as a mixture of green and white. But one should remember that, as a matter of fact, Fronto had said that *flavus* was green, white and red, and a few lines before that, had classified *flavus* among various gradations of red!

Let me exclude any explanation in terms of colour blindness. Too easy. Gellius and his friends were erudites; they were not describing their own perceptions, they were elaborating upon literary texts coming from different centuries. Can one say that they were considering cases of poetic invention – where, by a provocative use of language, fresh and uncommon impressions are vividly depicted? If that were the case, we would expect from them more excitation, more marvel, more appreciation for these stylistic *tours de force*. On the contrary, they propose all these cases as examples of the most correct and precise use of language.

Thus the puzzle we are faced with is neither a psychological nor an aesthetic one: it is a cultural one, and as such it is filtered through a linguistic system. We are dealing with verbal language in so far as it conveys notions about visual experiences, and we must, then, understand how verbal language makes the non-verbal experience recognizable, speakable and effable.

To solve Aulus Gellius' puzzle, we must pass through the semiotic structure of language. As a matter of fact, colour blindness itself represents a social puzzle, difficult both to solve and to detect, because of linguistic reasons. Let me quote this important passage from Arthur Linksz, which is later commented upon by Marshall Sahlins:

> To suppose color terms merely name differences suggested by the visible spectrum, their function being to articulate realities necessarily and already known as such is something like the idea that genealogical relations comprise a *de facto* grid of 'kinship types', inevitably taken in this significance by all societies, which differ merely in the way they classify (cope with) such universal facts of 'relationship.' The point, however, in color as in kinship, is that the terms stand in meaningful relations with other terms, and it is by the relations between terms within the global system that the character of objective reference is sedimented. Moreover, the concrete attributes thus singled out by the semantic differentiation of terms then function also as *signifiers* of social relations, not simply as the *signifieds* of the terms. In the event, it is not even necessary that those who participate in a given natural order have the same substantive experience of the object, so long as they are capable of making some kind of sensory distinction at the semiotically pertinent boundaries. Hence the cultural facility of color blinds, functioning on differences in brightness – in a world that everyone else sees as differentiated by hue. Red-and-green color-blind people talk of reds and greens and all shades of it [sic] using the same words most of us assign to objects of a certain color. They think and talk and act in terms of 'object color' and 'color constancy' as do the rest of us. They call leaves green, roses red. Variations in saturation and brilliance of their yellow gives [sic] them an amazing variety of impressions. While we learn to rely on differences of hue, their minds get trained in evaluating brilliance . . . . most of the red-and-green blind do not know of their defect and think we see things in the same shades they do. They have no reason for sensing any conflict. If there is an argument, they find *us* fussy, not *themselves* defective. They heard us call the leaves green and whatever shade

leaves have for them they call green. People of average intelligence never stop to analyze their sensations. They are much too busy looking for what these sensations mean.

(Linksz 1952)

Commenting on this passage in his beautiful essay on 'Colors and Cultures', Sahlins (1975) not only insists on the thesis that colour is a cultural matter, but remarks that every test of colour discrimination is rooted in a sort of referential fallacy. Psychologists frequently assume that classifications of colours and utterance of colour names are linked to the representation of an actual experience; they assume that colour terms in the first instance denote the immanent properties of a sensation. Therefore, many tests are contaminated by this confusion between *meaning* and *reference*. When one utters a colour term one is not directly pointing to a state of the world (process of reference), but, on the contrary, one is connecting or correlating that term with a cultural unit or concept. The utterance of the term is determined, obviously, by a given sensation, but the transformation of the sensory stimuli into a precept is in some way determined by the semiotic relationship between the linguistic expression and the meaning or *content* culturally correlated to it.

Our problem, to quote Sahlins again, is 'how then to reconcile these two undeniable yet opposed understandings: color distinctions are naturally based, albeit that natural distinctions are culturally constituted? The dilemma can only be solved by reading from the cultural meaning of color to the empirical tests of discrimination, rather than the other way around.'

II

I shall begin with verbal language for practical reasons, for it represents the most powerful and therefore the most familiar instrument people use for defining the surrounding world and for communicating to each other about it. It is not, however, impossible to imagine another sign system in which colours and other elements of the world were indicated not by words but, say, by fingers (the thumb means red, the forefinger blue, etc.). Since we have more sounds than fingers at our disposal, we are verbal animals. But things might have gone differently: in the course of evolution we could have elaborated, instead of a very flexible phonatory apparatus, a particular skill in emitting, by chemical means, thousands of odours. Even if this were the case, our analysis of semiotic systems would not basically change.

If you look into a traditional handbook on communication, you see that such a process is represented as shown in Figure 11.1.

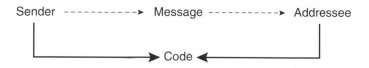

Figure 11.1

In order for a process of communication to be successful, a common code is the most elementary requirement. But the notion of code is still rather vague, abstract.

If dealing with the Morse code, the problem is rather simple: a code is a list of equivalences by virtue of which a given array of dots and dashes is made to correspond, element to element, to a given series of alphabetic letters. A natural language is a bit more complicated. We begin with a paradigm of phonemes which do not correspond to anything at all, then these phonemes are made to constitute a repertoire of meaningful units, lexemes. Lexemes are, in turn, made to correspond, roughly speaking, to certain cultural entities: let me call them, for the moment, meanings or concepts. Of course, the situation is not this simple – there are syntactical and co-textual rules, not to mention phenomena such as homonymy, polysemy and contextual meanings.

In order to make my discourse manageable for the present purpose, let me be outrageously simple and assume that in order to make communication possible, one needs a signification system. This principle holds for any sign system, from natural language to naval flag signals. A semiotic approach attempts to define the general conditions, for every system of signs, that allow processes of communication on the basis of a given system of signification. It is highly improbable to establish a communication process without an underlying signification system, whereas, theoretically speaking, it is not impossible to invent a signification system without using it in order to communicate – such a procedure, though, would seem a waste of time and energy.

A very schematic signification system can be represented as Figure 11.2.

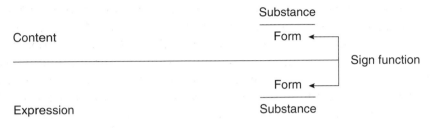

Figure 11.2

A system of general types of physical entities generates expressions: the general types are the form of the expression; their concrete and individual productions and manifestations are substances. Natural language, for instance, is based upon thirty and forty phonemes, organized by a phonological system establishing abstract types. We recognize these abstract types regardless of the various ways in which they are physically produced. Types, studied by phonology or phonemics, represent the *emic* aspect of language; concrete occurrences, studied by phonetics, represent the *etic* aspect. What is *emic* involves linguistic categories, whereas *etic* involves concrete sounds.

Phonemes are articulated to compose morphemes or – to be less technical – lexical entities or words. Type-phonemes and type-lexical expressions constitute a system of expression form, emically considered. The form of expression is used to convey contents, in the sense in which the sign is traditionally defined as *aliquid quid stat pro aliquo* or, as C.S. Peirce said, something which stands to somebody for something else in some respect or capacity. Units of the expression form are correlated to content units by a sign function.

What is content? Not the external world. Expressions do not *signify* things or states of the world. At most, they are *used* to communicate with somebody about states of the world. If I say that ravens are black and unicorns are white, I am undoubtedly uttering a statement about a state of the world. (In the first instance, I am speaking of the world of our experience, in the second I am speaking about a possible world of which unicorns are inhabitants – the fact that they are white is part of the state of affairs of that world.) However, a term like 'raven' or 'unicorn' does not necessarily refer to a 'thing': it refers instead to a cultural unit, to an aspect of our organization of the world.

The content of a signification system depends on our cultural organization of the world into categories. By 'world', I do not necessarily mean physical world: Euclid's world is not a physical one, but a *possible universe* organized into points, lines, planes, angles, and so forth. It is a self-sufficient universe in which there are neither ravens nor unicorns, but only cultural units such as the concept of similitude and none such as the concept of love or justice. I can communicate about the Euclidean universe, making true or false assertions (I can, for example, assert truly that the sum of the internal angles of a triangle is equal to 180° and falsely assert that two parallel lines can meet in a given point of that universe), but the units 'triangle' and 'line' are, in themselves, neither true nor false. They are simply the pertinent or relevant elements of the Euclidean universe. Thus a signification system allows its possible users to isolate and name what is relevant to them from a given point of view.

Let us consider a classic example given by many semantic hand-books: Eskimos apparently have four words to designate four types of snow, while Europeans have only one word and consider relevant only one specific state of H_2O in opposition to other states like ice and water. Of course a skier can recognize different qualities of snow, but he always sees, and speaks of, the same cultural unit, considered from different points of view according to certain practical needs. Eskimos, on the other hand, see, perceive and think of four different things in the same way in which I perceive, and speak of, two different things when, about to skate on a lake, I ascertain whether there is water or ice. This means that a given culture organizes the world according to given practices, or practical purposes, and consequently considers as pertinent different aspects of the world. Pertinence is a function of our practices.

According to a suggestion made by Luis Prieto (1975), if I have on a table before me a large crystal ashtray, a paper cup and a hammer, I can organize these pieces of furniture of my limited world into a twofold system of pertinences. If my practical purpose is to collect some liquid, I then isolate a positive class whose members are the paper cup and the ashtray, and a negative class whose only member is the hammer. If, on the contrary, my purpose is to throw a missile at an enemy, then the heavy ashtray and the hammer will belong to the same class, in opposition to the light and useless paper cup. Practices select pertinences. The practical purpose does not, however, depend on a free decision on my part: material constraints are in play, since I cannot decide that the hammer can act as a container and the paper cup as a missile. Thus practical purposes, decisions about pertinences and material constraints will interact in leading a culture to segment the continuum of its own experience into a given form of the content. To say that a signification system makes communication processes possible means that one can usually communicate only about those cultural units that a given signification system has made pertinent. It is, then, reasonable to suppose now that one can better perceive that which a signification system has isolated and outlined as pertinent.

Let us imagine an archaic community which has only two terms to designate every possible kind of human being: a term equivalent to 'man' and a term like 'barbarian' or 'alien'. The members of the community have two cultural units at their disposal: for them, the many-coloured universe of featherless two-legged mammals (among which we might distinguish black and Chinese, Dane and Dutch, European and American, East and West German) is a black and white universe split into 'us' and 'the others'. Let us for the moment disregard the fact that further properties can be associated to these cultural units, namely that 'men' are rational and friendly, while 'barbarians' are stupid, irrational and dangerous. The problem of the organization of content is, of course, more complicated than this, and from the perspective of contemporary compositional analysis, what I called cultural units are more finely subdivided into a network of minor semantic properties. Yet even when we limit the domain of semiotic problems to be discussed, our fictional community retains a note of verisimilitude. The ancient Greek subdivision of humankind into Hellenes and 'oi barbaroi' is more or less similar to my fictional model, as is the Nazi reorganization of humankind into Aryans and 'inferior races'.

Imagine a 'sci-fi' situation in which our planet is invaded by monsters from two different galaxies. The aliens of Galaxy no. 1 are round, greenish and have three legs and four eyes; the aliens of Galaxy no. 2 are elongated, brown and have six legs and one eye. Certainly we would be able to distinguish and describe both species, but as far as our defence is concerned, the aliens are all 'non-human'. When the men of the terrestrial outpost first encounter the alien *avant-garde*, they will probably perceive and signal those they meet as simply aliens or monsters. Before we forge new terms to define their differences, we would need scientific interaction, and at some point we would enrich and reformulate our content form. But without such a collective reshaping of our content system, our very ability to recognize aliens will be strongly influenced by our cultural categories.

In the same way, for the members of our fictional ancient society, it will be difficult to ascertain the difference between a Viking and a Phoenician, as well as the difference between their languages: at first they will all be 'barbaroi', speaking a non-language. Eventually, at a more advanced stage of inter-racial contact, someone will discover that Vikings are more aggressive and Phoenicians more eager to entertain commercial relationships, thus facilitating the reformulation of the content, the discovery of new pertinences, and the invention of new expressions to designate these pertinences. A sort of under-lying discriminative ability will lead to a more refined system of identification and categorization. But in the early stages of contact, categorization will overcome discrimination.

At this point, I must introduce a new concept, the opposition between restricted and elaborated code. In a further stage of inter-racial contacts, our fictional society could split into two castes. Priests and merchants will be able to distinguish Vikings from Phoenicians, probably for different purposes (merchants because they are inter-ested in dealing with the Phoenicians, and priests because they suppose that Vikings can be easily converted). These two castes will reorganize their content form, and coin new expressions to name these different cultural units. But the rest of the citizenry, in order to be employed as warriors, will still share a more restricted code; for them, 'men' *versus* 'barbarians' will remain the only pertinent opposition. Thus at the same moment in the same society there will be two different levels of social organization; therefore there will be two different ways of thinking, perceiving and speaking, based upon two different systems of signification or, better, upon two different stages of complexity of the same system. As the Italian play-wright Dario Fo once said: the worker knows a hundred words, his master a thousand – that is why he is the master. To know more words means to conceive of a more refined organization of the content. When our instinctive tendency to discriminate produces a more subtle categorization, we acquire a more powerful world view. In the course of this improvement, one changes one's codes.

Of course, such a passage from restricted to elaborated code happens not only infra-culturally but inter-culturally as well, and in space as well as time. Take the rodent universe. In Latin there is only one name to indicate two different kinds of animals that the English call, respectively, 'mouse' and 'rat' (Figure 11.3).

Latin	English
Mus	Mouse
	Rat

Figure 11.3

In Italian, we have two names, 'topo' and 'ratto', but many Italians today confuse the terms, using 'topo' for both animals. This linguistic simplification deters them from paying attention to the morphological differences between a 'little mouse' and a 'big one' – an attitude that can produce a number of sanitary and social consequences.

Thus it is possible to say that the Latin term *mus* (and perhaps *topo* today) referred to a sort of homogeneous pertinent portion of the content, while the English names 'mouse' and 'rat' refer to two different pertinent units (Figure 11.4).

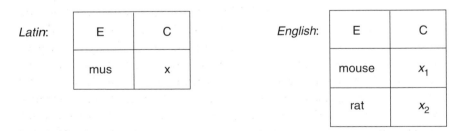

Latin:

E	C
mus	x

English:

E	C
mouse	x_1
rat	x_2

Figure 11.4

The organization of content has to do with the empty cases I have filled up with variables. The important semiotic problem here is how to describe the content of these empty cases, as we are obliged to analyse them through other expressions – in their turn having to be analysed by other expressions, and so on *ad infinitum*. I return to the problem of colour and to the page of Aulus Gellius I mentioned earlier; the problem of the categorization of colours involves such empty cases.

III

Perception occupies a puzzling position, somewhere midway between semiotic categorization and discrimination based upon mere sensory processes. Jean Petitot, who is working on the material roots of linguistic categorization based upon the mathematical theory of catastrophes, suggested to me that categorization and discrimination do not interact in the universe of sounds as they do in the universe of colours.[1]

We can, it seems, identify sounds with remarkable precision, but once we have perceived the emic difference between, say, *pa* and *ba*, we have difficulty in discriminating between the different etic ways in which *pa* and *ba* can be pronounced. Petitot suggests that this ability to categorize sounds is not culturally but innately grounded, and postulates a brain mechanism called 'perceptual catergorization' which would explain why verbal language is such a paramount semiotic system. Such innate ability in sound identification, and such a difficulty in sound discrimination, are crucial for human language.

It is important that we can identify the thirty or forty phonemes which constitute the phonological paradigm of a given language, but it would be embarrassing (linguistically speaking) to be exaggeratedly sensitive to minimal individual differences between the etic ways of uttering the same phoneme. That is why, were I speaking, you could understand your native language even though many of you would be able to guess that I was not nurtured at Oxford. Your ability to discriminate accents has nothing to do with your etic competence – at most it has to do with paralinguistics or tonemics, which are entirely different. The more you were to focus your attention on my sounds, thinking of them as phonemes of your native tongue, the more you would be recognizing them emically, independently of the accent; you would forget the accent and directly catch phonological categories. Of course there are individuals specially trained in discriminating tonemes (that is, the subtle nuances in the etic production of sounds), such as actors or social workers interested in people's national or regional origins. But theirs is an etic training which has nothing to do with the emic training connected with the acquisition of a language as an abstract type.

Our discrimination ability for colours seems to be greater: we can detect the fact that hues gradually change in the continuum of a rainbow, though we have no means to categorize the borderlines between different colours. Nevertheless, when a given subject is exposed to a continuum of sounds ranging from the syllable *ba* to the syllable *pa*, uttered in many etic ways, 'k' will be the 'catastrophic point', where so-called feature detectors in the human brain isolate the threshold between two emic categories (Figure 11.5).

k

ba... pa

Figure 11.5

Our innate capacity for perceptual categorization enables a subject to perceive a clear opposition between the two emic entities, *ba* and *pa*, and disregard etic discrimination. But if the same subject is intensively exposed to the stimulus *ba*, the catastrophe point will slip to the left when he is once again intensively exposed to the full range of sounds represented in Figure 11.5. This phenomenon is called 'selective adaptation': the subject will acquire a quite severe notion of the emic type *ba* (and, probably, a snobbish sensitivity to accents).

The opposite happens with colours. Let us consider two colours, *a* and *b*, which are mutually adjacent in the spectrum. If the stimulus *a* is repeated, the catastrophe point will slip to the right rather than to the left. This means that the more a subject becomes acquainted with a stimulus, the more eager he will be to assign similar stimuli to the category to which he has assigned the original stimulus. Categorial training produces categorization ability for both sounds and colours; but sound categories become more restricted, while colour categories become more tolerant, and sensitivity in discrimination decreases.

Of course a painter can be trained more in etic discrimination than in emic categorization, but in the experiments above, the reaction of the subject is determined by the fact that he is not freely concerned with sense data, but is influenced by the aims of the laboratory experiment. He is encouraged to isolate categorial entities and reacts with categories already defined by language, even though he speaks only to himself.

These experiences have nothing to do with what I previously said about sign functions: to perceive phonemes or colours has to do with the emic analysis of expressions, not with the correlation between expressions and contents. But I smell in these experiences the presence of a more complicated semiotic question.

IV

It has been said that colour discrimination, under laboratory conditions, is probably the same for all peoples no matter what language they speak, though psychologists also suggest that there is not only an ontogenetic but also a phylogenetic increase in discriminatory competence. The Optical Society of America classifies a range of between 7.5 and 10 million colours which can theoretically be discriminated.

A trained artist can discriminate and name a great many hues, which the pigment industry supplies and indicates with numbers, to indicate an immense variety of colours easily discriminated in the industry. But the Farnsworth-Munsell test, which includes 100 hues, demonstrates that the average discrimination rate is highly unsatisfactory. Not only do the majority of subjects have no linguistic means with which to categorize these 100 hues, but approximately 68 per cent of the population (excluding colour defectives) make a total error score of between 20 and 100 on the first test, which involves rearranging these hues on a continuous gradation scale. Cases of superior discrimination (only 16 per cent) scored from zero to 16. The largest collection of English colour names runs to over 3000 entries (Maerz and Paul 1953), but only eight of these commonly occur (Thorndike and Lorge 1962).

Thus average chromatic competence is better represented by the seven colours of the rainbow, with their corresponding wavelengths in millimicrons (Figure 11.6).

Average
chromatic competence

⌈ 800–650	Red
⌊ 640–590	Orange
⌈ 580–550	Yellow
⌈ 540–490	Green
⌈ 480–460	Blue
450–440	Indigo
⌊ 430–390	Violet

Figure 11.6

Square brackets indicate the thresholds where, according to modern experiments, there are clear jumps in discrimination. This segmentation does seem to correspond to our common experience, though it was not the experience of Latin speakers, if indeed it is true that they did not clearly distinguish between green and blue. It seems that Russian speakers segment the range of wavelengths we call 'blue' into different portions, *goluboj* and *sinij*. Hindus consider red and orange a unified pertinent unit. And against the 3000 hues that, according to David Katz, the Maori of New Zealand recognize and name by 3000 different terms (Katz and Katz 1960), there are, according to Conklin (1955), the Hanunóo of the Philippines, with a peculiar opposition between a public restricted code and more of less individual, elaborated ones:

> Color distinctions in Hanunóo are made at two levels of contrast. The first, higher, more general level consists of an all-inclusive coordinate, four-way classification which lies at the core of the color system. The four categories are mutually exclusive in contrastive contexts, but may overlap slightly in absolute (i.e., spectrally) or in other measurable terms. The second level, including several sublevels, consists of hundreds of specific color categories, many of which overlap and interdigitate.

Terminologically, there is 'unanimous agreement' (Lenneberg 1953 p. 469) on the designations for the four Level I categories, but considerable lack of unanimity – with a few explainable exceptions – in the use of terms of Level II.

(Conklin 1955 p. 341)

Let us disregard Level II, which seems a case of many elaborated codes differing from males to females and even from individual to individual. Let us consider the various formats of Level II as idiolectal and quasi-professional codes.

The three-dimensional color solid is divided by this Level I categorization into four unequal parts; the largest is *mabi:ru*, the smallest *malatuy* [see Figure 11.7]. While boundaries separating these categories cannot be set in absolute terms, the focal points (differing slightly in size, themselves) within the four sections, can be limited more or less to black, white, orange-red, and leaf-green respectively. In general terms, *mabi:ru* includes the range usually covered in English by black, violet, indigo, blue, dark green, gray, and deep shades of other colors and mixtures; *malagti*, white and very light tinges of other colors and mixtures; *marara*, maroon, red, orange, yellow, and mixtures in which these qualities are seen to predominate; *malatuy*, light green and mixtures of green, yellow, and light brown. All color terms can be reduced

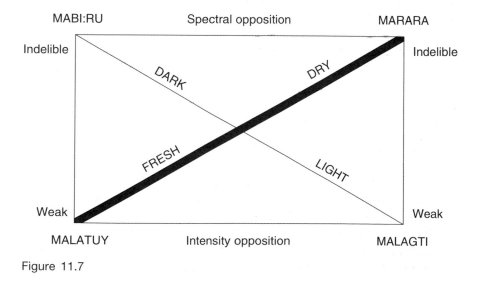

Figure 11.7

to one of these four, but none of the four is reducible. This does not mean that other color terms are synonyms, but that they designate color categories of greater specification within four recognized color realms.

(Conklin 1955 pp. 341–342)

Hanunóo segmentation follows our basic English paradigm only to a limited extent, since it involves black, white and grey in different ways. What is important for our present study is that the pertinentization of the spectrum depends on symbolic, i.e. cultural principles. Note that these cultural pertinentizations are produced because of practical purposes, according to the material needs of the Hanunóo community.

> The basis of this Level I classification appears to have certain correlates beyond what is usually considered the range of chromatic differentiation, and which are associated with linguistic phenomena in the external environment.
>
> First, there is the opposition between light and dark, obvious in the contrast of ranges of meaning of *lagti* and *biru*. Second, there is an opposition between dryness or desiccation and wetness or freshness (succulence) in visible components of the natural environment which are reflected in the terms *rara* and *latuy* respectively. This distinction is of particular significance in terms of plant life. Almost all living plant types possess some fresh, succulent and often 'greenish' parts. To eat any kind of raw, uncooked food, particularly fresh fruit or vegetables, is known as *sag-laty-un* (*latuy*). A shiny, wet, brown-colored section of newly cut bamboo is *malatuy* not *marara*. Dried-out or matured plant material such as certain kinds of yellowed bamboo or hardened kernels of mature or parched corn are *marara*. To become desiccated, to lose all moisture, is known as *mamara* < *para* 'desiccation'. A third opposition, dividing the two already suggested, is that of deep, unfading, indelible, and hence often more desired material as against pale, weak, faded, bleached, or 'colorless' substance, a distinction contrasting *mabi:ru* and *marara* with *malagti* and *malatuy*.

(Conklin 1955 p. 342)

We have then a system of cultural units – lightness, darkness, wetness, dryness – which are expressed by four fundamental colours;

these colours are, in turn, four cultural units expressed by four linguistic terms. This double organization of the content depends, as does any organization of this kind, on a system of disjunctions: it represents a structure. Just as a 'mouse', within a semantic space concerning rodents, is everything which is not a 'rat', and vice versa, so the pertinent content space of *malatuy* is determined by its northern borderline beyond which there is *marara*, and its southern borderline, below which there is *mabi:ru*.

Geopolitically speaking, Holland is a negative concept: it is the class of all points adjacent to, but not, Germany, Belgium or the North Sea. The same principle holds for all other geopolitical expressions such as Germany or Italy or the Soviet Union. In any system, whether geopolitical or chromatic or lexical, units are defined not in themselves but in terms of opposition and position in relation to other units. There can be no units without a system. The different ways in which cultures make the continuum of colours pertinent, thereby categorizing and identifying hues or chromatic units, correspond to different content systems. This semiotic phenomenon is not independent of perception and discrimination ability; it interacts with these phenomena and frequently overwhelms them.

Consider again our diagram of colours (Figure 11.8): it takes into account not only differences in the organization of content among different contemporary cultures, but also depicts different levels of complexity within a given culture as well as differences through the ages. It represents a reduced model of a tri-dimensional system of differences.

At this point we can probably tackle Aulus Gellius' puzzle. Rome, in the second century AD, was a very crowded crossroads of many cultures. The Empire controlled Europe from Spain to the Rhine, from England to North Africa and the Middle East. All these cultures, with their own chromatic sensitivities, were present in the Roman crucible, with their own chromatic sensitivities, were present in the Roman crucible. Diachronically speaking, Aulus Gellius was trying to put together the codes of at least two centuries of Latin literature and, synchronically speaking, the codes of different non-Latin cultures. Gellius must have been considering diverse and possibly contrasting cultural segmentations of the chromatic field. This would explain the contradictions in his analysis and the chromatic uneasiness felt by the modern reader. His colour-show is not a coherent one: we seem to be watching a flickering TV screen, with something wrong

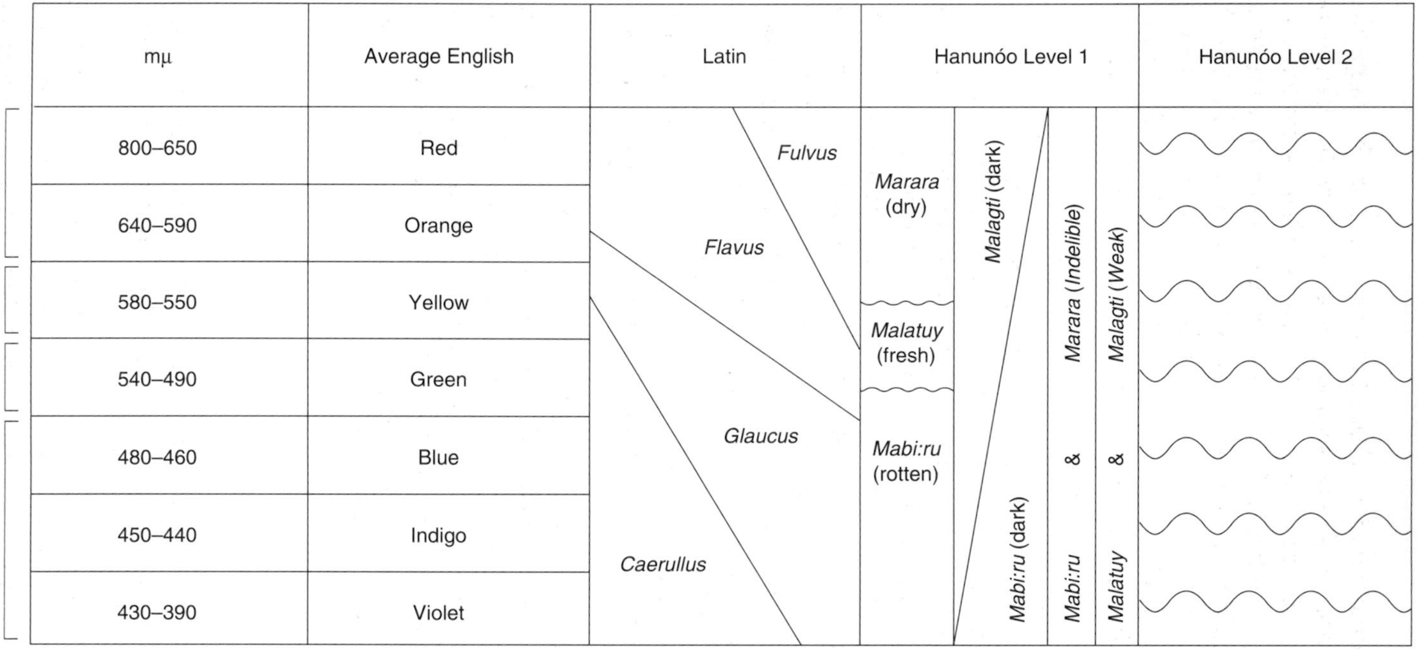

mμ	Average English	Latin	Hanunóo Level 1	Hanunóo Level 2
800–650	Red	Fulvus	Marara (dry)	
640–590	Orange	Flavus		
580–550	Yellow		Malatuy (fresh)	
540–490	Green	Glaucus		
480–460	Blue	Caerullus	Mabi:ru (rotten)	
450–440	Indigo			
430–390	Violet			

Hanunóo Level 1: Malagti (dark) — Mabi:ru (dark)

Mabi:ru & *Marara* (Indelible)

Malatuy & *Malagti* (Weak)

Figure 11.8

the electronic circuits, where tints mix up and the same face shifts, in the space of a few seconds, from yellow to orange or green. Determined by his cultural information, Gellius cannot trust to his personal perceptions, if any, and appears eager to see gold as red as fire, and saffron as yellow as the greenish shade of a blue horse.

We do not know and we shall never know how Gellius really perceived his *Umwelt*; unfortunately, our only evidence of what he saw and thought is what he said. I suspect that he was prisoner of his cultural mish-mash.

Yet it also seems to me (but obviously this hypothesis should be tested on more texts) that Latin poets were less sensitive to clear-cut spectral oppositions or gradations, and more sensitive to slight mixtures of spectrally distant hues. In other words, they were not interested in pigments but in perceptual effects due to the combined action of light, surfaces, the nature and purposes of object. Thus a sword can be *fulva* as jasper because the poet sees the red of the blood it may spill. That is why such descriptions remind us more of certain paintings of Franz Marc or of the early Kandinsky than of a scientific chromatic polyhedron. As a decadent man of culture, Gellius tends to interpret poetic creativity and invention as a socially accepted code and is not interested in the relationships which colours had with other content oppositions in different cultural systems. It would be interesting to transform a given Latin chromatic system, that of Virgil for example, into a structure more or less like the one I proposed for the Hanunóo system, where the names of hues must be associated to opposition between dark and light (also in psychological and moral sense), euphoric and dysphoric, excitation and calm, and so on. The names of colours, taken in themselves, have no precise chromatic content: they must be viewed within the general context of many interacting semiotic systems.

V

Are we, in any sense, freer than Gellius from the armour of our culture? We are animals who can discriminate colours, but we are, above all, cultural animals.

Human societies do not only speak of colours, but also with colours. We frequently use colours as semiotic devices: we communicate with flags, traffic lights, road signs, various kinds of emblems.

Now a socio-semiotic study of national flags remarks that national flags make use of only seven colours: red, blue, green, yellow, orange, black and white (Weitman 1973). For physical reasons, the proportion of these colours is as follows:

Colour combinations	Per cent
Red/white/blue	16.8
Red/white	9.5
Red/yellow/green	7.3
Red/white/green	6.6
Red/white/green/black	6.6
Blue/white	6.0
Red/yellow/blue	5.8
	58.6

Orange, hardly distinguishable from red, is rarely used. What counts in the perception of a flag is categorization, not discrimination. If we were to look up the flags of the Scandinavian countries, we would realize that the blue of the Swedish and Finnish flags (which is light) is different from the blue of the Icelandic and Norwegian ones (which is dark). Now look at Sweden's yellow cross on a light blue field – there is not a flag in the world with a yellow cross on a *dark blue* background, and for good reason. Everyone would recognize such a flag as the symbol for Sweden. (And, thinking of Norway's dark blue cross on a red field, a flag with a light blue cross on red would similarly be recognized as Norway's symbol.) In national flags, categorization overwhelms discrimination.

This simplification exists not only for reasons of easier perception: such 'easier perception' is supported by a previous cultural coding by virtue of which certain colours form a clear-cut system of oppositional units which are, in turn, clearly correlated with another system concerning values or abstract ideas.

In the study on national flags I have been referring to, it is interesting to check the symbolic values assigned by different countries to the same colour. Red, for example, symbolizes bravery, blood and courage in many countries (Afghanistan, Austria, Italy, Bulgaria, Burundi, Chile, Ecuador, etc.), but it also represents animals in Bolivia, faith in Ethiopia, soil in Dahomey. White, almost universally, stands for peace, hope and purity, but in Congo Kinshasha, hope is represented by blue which, for the majority of countries, stands for sky, sea and rivers. The colours of national flags are not colours: physical pigments; they are expressions correlated to cultural units, and as such are strongly categorized.

But the real problem is not – or not only – that our discrimination ability is limited to few colours. It is that the system of basic values to be expressed by colours is a limited one. The nature of these values (hope, peace, and so on) is irrelevant: what counts is the structural architecture of their basic oppositions, which must be clear.

One should remark that a greater variety of colours exists, or existed, in heraldry. But heraldry represents a case of an elaborated code for a cultivated minority able to discriminate more colours and associate more refined names to different hues, as well as memorize numerous aristocratic stocks.

The same strong categorization is at work in traffic lights and road signals. A traffic light can work and transmit its orders irrespective of the shade of green, red or yellow that, in terms of wavelengths, it emits. One would certainly stop at a traffic light with an orange light on, and continue moving even though the green light were a shade of blue. (Note that in the traffic light code, the signification of colours is reinforced by the position of the lights, which reduces the relevance of hues – and helps the colour-blind.) In any case, here too, in traffic regulation, people can only recognize a limited system of obligations. I do not think it is possible to found a system of communication on a subtle discrimination between colours too close to each other in the spectrum. This may seem strange since, as I have said, we potentially have a great capacity for discrimination, and with ten million colours it would be interesting to compose a language more rich and powerful than the verbal one, based as it is upon no more than forty phonemes. But the phonemes of verbal language are, in fact, a reasonable reduction of the great variety of possible sounds that our phonatory apparatus can produce. The seven colours of flags and signals are probably the most a human culture can recognize – by a general agreement as to categorizable expressive entities. This agreement has come about, probably, because verbal language has shaped our average sensitivity according to the macroscopic segmentation represented by the seven colours of the rainbow which is a Western conventional way of segmentation. The agreement has also come about because average verbal language, with its polysemy, works better for common people when many names stand synonymously for few basic concepts, rather than the opposite, when few names stand homonymously for thousands of concepts.

The fact that a painter (think of Paul Klee) can recognize and name more colours, the fact that verbal language itself is able not only to designate hundreds of nuances, but also describe unheard-of-tints by examples, periphrases and poetic ingenuity – all this represents a series of cases of elaborated codes. It is common to every society to have members able to escape the determination of the rules, to propose new rules, to behave beyond the rules.

In everyday life, our reactivity to colour demonstrates a sort of inner and profound solidarity between semiotic systems. Just as language is determined by the way in which society sets up systems of values, things and ideas, so our chromatic perception is determined by language. You may look up your flags again: suppose there is a football match between Italy and Holland. One will distinguish the Dutch flag from the Italian one, even though the red of either of them, or of both, were looking orange. If, on the contrary, the match were between Italy and Ireland, the Italian flag would be characterized by a dark red, since white, green and orange are the Irish colours.

If one wants to oppose, for shorthand purposes, a Mondrian to a Kandinsky, Mondrian would be recognizable even though its reds were more or less orange, but in the course of an aesthetic discourse on Mondrian, and in judging the correctness of an art book's reproduction, one should spend much careful analysis in discriminating the better and more faithful colour among Mondrian reproductions.

Thus the artistic activity, be it the poetry of Virgil or the research on pigments by Mondrian, works against social codes and collective categorization, in order to produce a more refined social consciousness of our cultural way of defining contents.

If people are eager to fight for a red, white and blue flag, then people must be ready to die even though its red, due to the action of atmospheric atmospheres, has become pinkish. Only artists are ready to spend their lives imagining (to quote James Joyce) 'an opening flower breaking in full crimson and unfolding and fading to palest rose, leaf by leaf and wave of light by wave of light, flooding all the heavens with its soft flushes, every flush deeper than the other'.

NOTE

1 Jean Petitot, work in progress (personal communication), with references to the work of A. Liberman, N. Studdart-Kennedy, K. Stevens (on perception of the speech code), Eimas, Massaro and Pisoni (on selective adaptation and features detectors), Eimas and Mehler (on innate bases of categorial perception).

12 Gunther Kress and Theo van Leeuwen

Reading images

THE 'OLD' AND THE 'NEW' VISUAL LITERACY IN BOOKS FOR THE VERY YOUNG

So far we have distinguished two kinds of visual literacy: one in which visual communication has been made subservient to language and in which images have come to be regarded as unstructured replicas of reality; another in which (spoken) language exists side by side with, and independent of, forms of visual representation which are openly structured, rather than viewed as more or less faithful duplicates of reality. We have looked at these kinds of visual literacy as historical and cultural alternatives. But they also exist side by side in our own culture, and we suggest that we are in the middle of a shift in valuation and uses from the one mode to the other, from the 'old' to the 'new' visual literacy, in many important social contexts. The examples we will now discuss suggest that the very first books children encounter may already introduce them to particular kinds of visual literacy.

Figure 12.1 shows a typical two-page spread from *Baby's First Book*, a book from the widely distributed Ladybird series which, on its inside cover, declares that 'the text and illustrations, though over-simple to grown-ups, will satisfy their [i.e. the toddler's] cravings for the repetition of what they already know, and will help them associate the words with the objects'.

Figure 12.2 shows a typical page from Dick Bruna's *On My Walk*. This book is one of a set of four, the others being *In My Home*, *In My Toy Cupboard* and *On the Farm*. It consists of eight pages, and, with the exception of the front and back covers, the pages contain no words whatsoever.

Figure 12.1   My bath (from *Baby's First Book*, Ladybird)

Compared to the picture of the bird in the tree [Figure 12.2], the picture of the bath is realistic, detailed and complex. If we were to analyse it into its components, if we were to try and identify all the different elements of this picture, we might encounter problems. Are the ripples in the water to be counted as components? Are the shadows, cast by the tub and towel? And if we were to try and identify the relations between these two components, what would we have to say, for example, about the relation between the duck and the soap? We ask these questions because they are the sort of questions with which one might start if one wanted to show that images are structured messages, amenable to constituent analysis. Isn't the structure here that of the cultural object 'bathroom', rather than one imposed by the conventions of a visual code? Isn't this picture unproblematically, transparently readable (recognizable), provided one knows what bathrooms look like?

This is the line Paris School semioticians such as Roland Barthes and Christian Metz took in the 1960s. Commenting on photography, Barthes said:

In order to move from the reality to its photograph it is in no way necessary to divide up this reality into units and to

Figure 12.2   Bird in a tree (Bruna, 1988)

constitute these units as signs, substantially different from the object they communicate. . . . Certainly, the image is not the reality but at least it is its perfect *analogon* and it is exactly this analogical perfection which, to commonsense, defines the photograph. Thus can be seen the special status of the photographic image: *it is a message without a code.*

(Barthes 1977 p. 17)

And he extends this argument to other pictorial modes, albeit with a qualification:

Are there other messages without a code? At first sight, yes: precisely the whole range of analogical reproductions of reality – drawings, paintings, cinema, theatre. However, each of those messages develops in an immediate and obvious way a supplementary message . . . which is what is commonly called the style of the reproduction.

(ibid.)

The picture of the bird in the tree, on the other hand, is much less naturalistic, much less detailed and much simpler than the

Figure 12.3 Computer-drawn dinner invitations

picture of the bath. It is stylized and conventional, and quite clearly a coded image. No depth, no shadows, no subtle nuances of colour: everything is plain and bold and simple. And the structure of the image, with its one central and four marginal images, does not imitate anything in the real world. It is a conventional visual arrangement, based on a visual code. As a result the components of the whole stand out as separate, distinct units, and the picture would seem quite amenable to constituent analysis. This is not just a matter of style: the structure of this picture could also be realized in more detailed styles. Bruna's book dates from 1953, well before the era of computer 'imaging', but the picture of the bird in the tree could have been composed with a computer, aligning ready-made simple icons in a compositional configuration – it is in fact quite similar to the computer-drawn dinner invitation in Figure 12.3 – and in computer imaging naturalistic details (texture, depth, etc.) can now be added or subtracted as independent variables.

Second, the picture of the bathroom is accompanied by words. Language comes first, authoritatively imposing meaning on the image, turning it into a typical instance of a bathroom by means of the generic label 'Bath'. As a result the picture could be replaced by other images of bathrooms without much loss of meaning (one verbal text, many images, many possible illustrations). Language bestows similarity and order on the diverse, heterogeneous world of images. Thus the book presents, on the one hand, an 'uncoded', naturalistic representation ('the world as it is' – empirical, factual, specific) and, on the other hand, a specific, authoritatively prescribed way of reading this 'uncoded' naturalistic picture. We will show later that, contrary to what Barthes and others argued in the 1960s, pictures of this kind are also structured, whether they are photographs, drawings, paintings or other kinds of pictures. For the moment, however, the important point is that they are not usually interpreted as such, that awareness of the structuredness of images of this kind is, in our society, suppressed and not part of 'commonsense'.

In Dick Bruna's *On My Walk*, by contrast, there are no words to authoritatively impose meaning on the image, and the image is no longer an illustration: the words, rather than the image, come second. Parents who read this book with their children could all tell a different story, even use different languages (one image, many verbal texts). The world of 'one image, many different verbal texts' ('commentaries') imposes a new mode of control over meaning, and turns the image, formerly a record of nature or a playground for children and artists, into a more powerful, but also more rigorously controlled and codified public language, while it gives language, formerly closely policed in many social institutions, a more private and less controlled, but also less powerful status. The 'readings' which parents produce when they read *On My Walk* with their children may all be different, yet these different readings will necessarily have common elements, deriving from their common basis – the elements included in the image, and the way these elements are compositionally brought together. Whatever story parents will tell about the page with the bird in the tree, it will necessarily have to be a story that creates a relation between, for instance, birds and aeroplanes (nature and technology) and birds and cats (prey and predator). It will also have to be a story in which the bird, safely in its tree, is the central character, literally and figuratively. In how many ways can cats and birds be related? Not that many, at

least not if one assumes that books like *On My Walk* serve to introduce children to the world around them, rather than to the possible
worlds of fantasies and utopias.

Cats can 'hunt', 'torture', 'kill' and 'eat' birds. Birds can 'escape'
cats or fail to do so. There are not that many stories to choose from.
On the other hand, parents and their children can choose the order
in which they want to deal with the various elements: the page is
'non-linear'. It does not impose a sequential structure. And they can
choose whether to tell the story of the bird and the cat as a political
story, a story of powerful predators coming from another continent
and native birds killed and threatened with extinction (as might be
done, for instance, in Australia), or as a story that legitimizes the
survival of the fittest. The story of the bird and the aeroplane, similarly, may be told from an environmentalist point of view, as a story
of evolutionary triumphs and human technological progress. Even
where such discourses are not explicitly invoked, they will still
communicate themselves to children through the parents' attitudes
towards the characters and the actions.

Not only the elements on the individual pages, but also the pages
themselves must be brought in relation to each other. The book as a
whole must be readable as a coherent sequence. This is prompted by
the title (*On My Walk*) as well as by the picture on the front cover,
which shows all the elements together. We have investigated this a
little further in connection with another book in the Bruna series,
On the Farm. This book contains the following central pictures: house,
farmer, cat, dog, apple tree, rooster, lamb, cow. Listing the ways in
which these pictures can plausibly be linked to each other, we found
that some (e.g. the apple tree and the house) can only be linked in
spatial, locative terms (e.g. the apple tree is next to the house).
Others (e.g. the animals and the house) can be related by verbs of
'dwelling' (e.g. the cow lies under the apple tree) or by the verbs
of 'motion' (e.g. the cat climbs up the apple tree). Two of the animals
(the cat and the dog) can relate to the other animals and to each
other by means of antagonistic or co-operative actions (e.g. the dog
barks at the cow; the dog leads the sheep). Only the farmer can relate
to all the other elements in an agentive way. He can buy them, own
them, build them, grow them, keep them, raise them, harvest them,
shear them, slaughter them, and so on. In other words, whatever
way the parents read these pictures, they will, in the end, have to
deal with the theme of spatial order, the theme of social interaction

(projected onto animals) and the theme of human mastery over the nature (as well as, via the marginal pictures, with the theme of pro-creation), and they will have to do all this in terms of the elements preselected by the book. An analysis of the way the elements can be opposed to each other shows that, whatever the classifications parents may construct, they will not be able to avoid engaging with the Western cultural distinctions between 'untamed nature', 'domesticated/cultivated nature' and 'human technology'. And they will also have to recognize the distinction between animate and inanimate, flora and fauna, and between pets, farm animals and wild animals.

It should be noted, however, that every page in the book (and in Bruna's other books) contain at least one relation that does not easily fit the received classifications, that forms somewhat of a challenge and a puzzle. What, for example, is the relation between a rabbit and a basket of flowers? A beetle and a fence? Such visual enigmas can challenge parents and children to exercise their imagi-nation, to include in their thinking elements that do not easily fit in with the traditional order of things, to tolerate some ambiguity, to allow the inclusion of the 'other' in their construction of the world.

The two books, then, are very different in their stance towards the image. The Bruna stance presents highly processed, highly essen-tialized, highly idealized representations, and provides parents and, later, children, with the opportunity to talk about the images in ways which are or seem appropriate to them, to apply specific values, specific discourses to highly abstracted images. The Ladybird stance presents ostensibly less processed, more naturalistic representations and provides parents (and, later on, children) with a specific prescribed way of reading the image. The one book presents itself as open and interactive, the other as closed and authoritarian. Yet, as we have seen, there is closure in the Bruna text too, even though less explicitly and visibly so. This closure lies in the limits which the selection and structure of the images impose on the apparently open readings, as well as in the discourses which are already 'in' the social-ized parents, and which, once orally transmitted to the children, will appear spontaneous and 'natural' to parents and children alike. Are they not, after all, merely engaged in an innocent reading of 'what is there' in the pictures? Thus the two books represent two different forms of social control over meaning, one which is openly and explicitly located in the text itself, and one which, more covertly and implicitly, lies in the way the book is less like a text than like a language, a system with which to *make* texts, and in the parental discourses that structure the way texts are made with this language.

These discourses, however, are not themselves part of Bruna's books, of the public text meant to transcend their diversity. Instead they are relegated to the realm of more private or subcultural 'lifestyles' where they do not powerfully threaten the order of the larger social world. There is never just 'heteroglossia' (many meanings), nor ever just 'homoglossia' (one authoritative meaning). Instead there is a role distribution among the different semiotics, a role distribution in which some semiotics are given a great deal of social power, but at the price of being subjected to greater institutional (and technological) control, while others are allowed relative freedom from control, but pay for this with diminished power. Today, we seem to move towards a decrease of control over language (e.g. the greater variety of accents allowed on the public media, the increasing problems in enforcing normative spelling), and towards an increase in codification and control over the visual (e.g. the use of image banks from which ready-made images can be drawn for the construction of visual texts, and, generally, the effect of computer imaging technology).

The two forms of control over meaning can be found elsewhere also. Compare, for example, the classic documentary film, in which an authoritative 'voice of God' narrator explains and interprets images of recorded reality, to the more modern 'direct cinema' documentary in which control over meaning lies in the selection of images and in the sometimes hardly noticeable ways in which these images are edited together. Or think of the way in which, in the field of 'cultural studies', an emphasis on analysing 'what the text says' is gradually being replaced by an emphasis on 'how different audiences read the same text', an emphasis, in other words, on the apparent freedom of interpretation which, by diverting attention away from the text itself, allows the limitations which the text imposes on this 'freedom of reading' to remain invisible, and therefore, perhaps, all the more efficacious and powerful. Or perhaps more insidiously, the transfer from 'what the text says' to 'what this theory constructs this text to be'.

It is interesting, in this connection, to consider the background of the Bruna books. They were first printed in 1953, in Amsterdam, and reprinted many times in their country of origin. The first British printing was in 1978. The time lag is perhaps no accident. Unlike the British, the Dutch have, for most of this century, recognized that their country does not have a 'common culture', but is divided into groups characterized by different and often opposing ideologies, *zuilen* (literally 'columns', 'pillars'), as the Dutch have called them. Dutch broadcasting, for example, had from its inception in the late 1920s a system in which different *levensbeschouwelijke* (i.e. 'orientated towards a particular view of life') groups ran broadcasting organizations which were allotted air time according to the size of their membership. Thus the same events would, on radio and later on television, be interpreted from a variety of different discursive ideological positions, while most other European countries had centralized, usually government-run, broadcasting organizations with one authoritative message. For a message to reach, in this context, the whole population, it had to be adaptable to a variety of cultural and ideological constructions, and, as we have seen, the Bruna books use the visual medium to achieve exactly that. Perhaps the belated success of the series in countries like Britain and Australia shows that there is now, in these countries too, beginning an awareness that they no longer have a 'common culture', and that, instead, they have become complex, diverse and discursively divided, and therefore in need of new forms of communication.

Part III

*The sign in
post-structuralism*

Signifiers and subjects

As we have seen, Lacan's essay, 'L'instance de la lettre' was written in 1957. Although the lecture on which the essay was based was given at a philosophy seminar it must be remembered that the proper context for it is psychoanalytic theory. Put another way, the essay is about subject formation.

The feature of 'L'instance de la lettre' which is, initially, the most striking is its digressive style and its breadth of allusion. The former has been the object of criticism in Anglo-American academia and it would be easy to dismiss Lacan's opacity as an attempt to cover uncertainty with jargon. Most writers on Lacan, however, urge the reader to bear with the slippery nature of his prose, arguing that, unlike the positivistic quasi-scientific discourse of the contemporary psychoanalytic establishment, it partakes of some of the strategies of the unconscious. In this way, the allusiveness of Lacan's prose is also appropriate because – unlike the International Psychoanalytic Association in the 1950s, according to Lacan – it follows Freud's exhortation to psychoanalysts that they should embrace information from the humanities rather than exclusively from the sciences (see Freud 1962 pp. 145–156).

In relation to the other theorists that we have discussed, there are two things which will be especially noticeable in this essay. The first is that Lacan insists on the fact that 'language' (not the linguistic sign alone) pre-exists the human being. As such, Lacan's argument about the insertion of the human subject into a pre-constituted differentiality (i.e. the play of differences that makes up language) is not dissimilar from some of Derrida's arguments at this point. Secondly, Lacan insists that the 'letter' is wholly material; that is to say that, in signs, a material entity (the signifier) always *enters* the concept (the signified). This is not entirely unrelated to Vološinov's assertion that speakers and listeners hear only what is true or untrue, pleasant or unpleasant; what is at work in signification is a concrete utterance that is material through and through.

Both of these points are discussed and extended by one of Lacan's most interesting expositors, Mikkel Borch-Jacobsen. In the extract (pp. 195–205) he begins by showing that the act of naming is an act of murder. This is because the fullness of being that accrues to any object or living thing can never be represented through language; language simply does not have the capacity to fully express, for example, the texture of a fruit or how a person is feeling at a given moment. Using the signifier 'cat', passes over the fact that one has simply encapsulated the whole of that animal's being in a three-letter, one-syllable word. In short, rendering something in language, effectively takes away that something's existence, an observation of the kind that Benveniste might have made. In the psychoanalytic situation such shortcomings of language's attempt to fully capture the world are often made manifest.

One definition of psychoanalysis is that it is a process which draws subjects' attention to their entanglement in language and, specifically, the commonly held belief in language's ability to refer to things or to have meaning. Borch-Jacobsen shows that, for Lacan, this entails two kinds of 'speech': that which is used with the faith that it is referential in orientation and is 'stuffed with meaning' (Borch-Jacobsen 1991 p. 139); and that which is 'stripped' of meaning, speech which refers to nothing beyond itself, but just *exists* as itself. These are called by Lacan (1977) 'empty speech' and 'full speech' respectively. Borch-Jacobsen maintains that the former's attempt to say something *other than* itself (to describe) and the latter's ability to say nothing but itself, is equivalent to Austin's (1980) concepts of 'constantive' and 'performative' statements (see this volume pp. 18–21 and 255–62). As we know Austin concluded that constantives were actually performatives in disguise. Borch-Jacobsen concurs: he argues, that all speech 'performs' *without* reference and (like Lacan and Derrida) he adheres to a strict version of Saussure's doctrine of differences between signs as the generator of significance.

The chief aim of Borch-Jacobsen in this extract is to show how Lacan thoroughly eradicates the pernicious belief in a signified which pre-exists language itself. He concludes not only that the signifier does not *represent* the signified but that the signified *does not even exist* ready for it to be represented by any signifier. In fact, the signified is engendered by the signifier. Because the signifier is nothing but itself – and, moreover, only itself in relation to other signifiers – signification therefore arises from an entity (the signifier) which can never mean anything on its own. Our 'reality' is thus constructed out of 'nothing' or, more accurately, a play of meaningless entities. To actualize this is to be a participant in 'full speech', accepting one's inability to ever fully refer to an object or person. Clearly this separation between a language which believes it can refer and a language which does not believe it has the powers of full reference is not dissimilar from the principles underpinning work by MacCabe, Heath and other *Screen* writers (see this volume pp. 15–18). However, Lacan and Borch-Jacobsen's banishment of the signified from the analysis of communication is most closely allied to Derrida's re-assessment of Saussure.

Further reading   Benvenuto and Kennedy 1986 pp. 103–125; Lemaire 1977 pp. 1–64; K. Silverman 1983 pp. 149–193; Weber 1991 pp. 39–58; Grosz 1990 pp. 92–101; Leader 1995; Payne 1993 pp. 74–85; Arrivé 1992 pp. 119–64; Greenfield 1984.

13 Jacques Lacan

The agency of the letter in the unconscious

THE MEANING OF THE LETTER

As my title suggests, beyond this 'speech', what the psychoanalytic experience discovers in the unconscious is the whole structure of language. Thus from the outset I have alerted informed minds to the extent to which the notion that the unconscious is merely the seat of the instincts will have to be rethought.

But how are we to take this 'letter' here? Quite simply, literally.[1]

By 'letter' I designate that material support that concrete discourse borrows from language.

This simple definition assumes that language is not to be confused with the various psychical and somatic functions that serve it in the speaking subject – primarily because language and its structure exist prior to the moment at which each subject at a certain point in his mental development makes his entry into it.

Let us note, then, that aphasias, although caused by purely anatomical lesions in the cerebral apparatus that supplies the mental centre for these functions, prove, on the whole, to distribute their deficits between the two sides of the signifying effect of what we call here 'the letter' in the creation of signification.[2] A point that will be clarified later.

Thus the subject, too, if he can appear to be the slave of language is all the more so of a discourse in the universal movement in which his place is already inscribed at birth, if only by virtue of his proper name.

Reference to the experience of the community, or to the substance of this discourse, settles nothing. For this experience assumes its essential dimension in the tradition that this discourse itself establishes. This tradition, long before the drama of history is inscribed in it, lays down the elementary structures of culture. And these very structures reveal an ordering of possible exchanges which, even if unconscious, is inconceivable outside the permutations authorized by language.

With the result that the ethnographic duality of nature and culture is giving way to a ternary conception of the human condition – nature, society, and culture – the last term of which could well be reduced to language, or that which essentially distinguishes human society from natural societies.

But I shall not make of this distinction either a point or a point of departure, leaving to its own obscurity the question of the original relations between the signifier and labour. I shall be content, for my little jab at the general function of *praxis* in the genesis of history, to point out that the very society that wished to restore, along with the privileges of the producer, the casual hierarchy of the relations between production and the ideological superstructure to their full political rights, has none the less failed to give birth to an esperanto in which the relations of language to socialist realities would have rendered any literary formalism radically impossible.[3]

For my part, I shall trust only those assumptions that have already proven their value by virtue of the fact that language through them has attained the status of an object of scientific investigation.

For it is by virtue of this fact that linguistics is seen to occupy the key position in this domain, [4] and the reclassification of the sciences and a regrouping of them around it signals, as is usually the case, a revolution in knowledge; only the necessities of communication made me inscribe it at the head of this volume under the title 'the sciences of man' – despite the confusion that is thereby covered over.[5]

To pinpoint the emergence of linguistic science we may say that, as in the case of all sciences in the modern sense, it is contained in the constitutive moment of an algorithm that is its foundation. This algorithm is the following:

$$\frac{S}{s}$$

which is read as: the signifier over the signified, 'over' corresponding to the bar separating the two stages.

This sign should be attributed to Ferdinand de Saussure although it is not found in exactly this form in any of the numerous schemas, which none the less express it, to be found in the printed version of his lectures of the years 1906–7, 1908–9, and 1910–11, which the piety of a group of his disciples caused to be published under the title, *Cours de linguistique générale*, a work of prime importance for the transmission of a teaching worthy of the name, that is, that one can come to terms with only in its own terms.

That is why it is legitimate for us to give him credit for the formulation S/s by which, in spite of the differences among schools, the beginning of modern linguistics can be recognized.

The thematics of this science is henceforth suspended, in effect, at the primordial position of the signifier and the signified as being distinct orders separated initially be a barrier resisting signification. And that is what was to make possible an exact study of the connections proper to the signifier, and of the extent of their function in the genesis of the signified.

For this primordial distinction goes well beyond the discussion concerning the arbitrariness of the sign, as it has been elaborated since the earliest reflections of the ancients, and even beyond the impasse which, through the same period, has been encountered in every discussion of the bi-univocal correspondence between the word and the thing, if only in the mere act of naming. All this, of course, is quite contrary to the appearances suggested by the importance often imputed to the role of the index finger pointing to an object in the learning process of the *infans* subject learning his mother tongue, or the use in foreign language teaching of so-called 'concrete' methods.

One cannot go further along this line of thought than to demonstrate that no signification can be sustained other than by reference to another signification:[6] in its extreme form this amounts to the proposition that there is no language (*langue*) in existence for which there is any question of its inability to cover the whole field of the signified, it being an effect of its existence as a language (*langue*) that it necessarily answers all needs. If we try to grasp in language the constitution of the object, we cannot fail to notice that this constitution is to be found only at the level of concept, a very different thing from a simple nominative, and that the *thing*, when reduced to the noun, breaks up into the double, divergent beam of the 'cause' (*causa*) in which it has taken shelter in the French word *chose*, and the nothing (*rien*) to which it has abandoned its Latin dress (*rem*).

These considerations, important as their existence is for the philosopher, turn us away from the locus in which language questions us as to its very nature. And we will fail to pursue the question further as long as we cling to the illusion that the signifier answers to the function of representing the signified, or better, that the signifier has to answer for its existence in the name of any signification whatever.

For even reduced to this latter formulation, the heresy is the same – the heresy that leads logical positivism in search of the 'meaning of meaning',[7] as its objective is called in the language of its devotees. As a result, we can observe that even a text highly charged with meaning can be reduced, through this sort of analysis, to insignificant bagatelles, all that survives being mathematical algorithms that are, of course, without any meaning.[8]

To return to our formula S/s: if we could infer nothing from it but the notion of the parallelism of its upper and lower terms, each one taken in its globality, it would remain the enigmatic sign of a total mystery. Which of course is not the case.

In order to grasp its function I shall begin by reproducing the classic, yet faulty illustration (see Figure 13.1) by which its usage is normally introduced, and one can see how it opens the way to the kind of error referred to above.

TREE

Figure 13.1

In my lecture, I replaced this illustration with another (Figure 13.2), which has no greater claim to correctness than that it has been transplanted into that incongruous dimension that the psychoanalyst has not yet altogether renounced because of his quite justified feeling that his conformism takes its value entirely from it. In Figure 13.2 we see that, without greatly extending the scope of the signifier concerned in the experiment, that is, by doubling a noun through the mere juxtaposition of two terms whose complementary meanings ought apparently to reinforce each other, a surprise is produced by an unexpected precipitation of an unexpected meaning: the image of twin doors symbolizing, through the solitary confinement offered Western Man for the satisfaction of his natural needs away from home, the imperative that he seems to share with the great majority of primitive communities by which his public life is subject to the laws of urinary segregation.

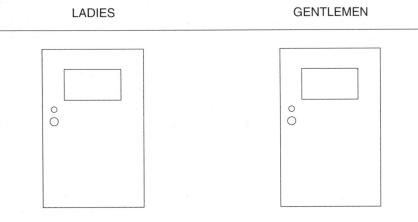

Figure 13.2

It is not only with the idea of silencing the nominalist debate with a low blow that I use this example, but rather to show how in fact the signifier enters the signified, namely, in a form which, not being immaterial, raises the question of its place in reality. For the blinking gaze of a short sighted person might be justified in wondering whether this was indeed the signifier as he peered closely at the little enamel signs that bore it, a signifier whose signified would in this call receive its final honours from the double and solemn procession from the upper nave.

But no contrived example can be as telling as the actual experi- ence of truth. So I am happy to have invented the above, since it awoke in the person whose word I most trust a memory of childhood, which having thus happily come to my attention is best placed here.

A train arrives at a station. A little boy and a little girl, brother and sister, are seated in a compartment face to face next to the window through which the buildings along the station platform can be seen passing as the train pulls to a stop. 'Look', says the brother, 'we're at Ladies!'; 'Idiot!' replies his sister, 'Can't you see we're at Gentlemen'.

Besides the fact that the rails in this story materialize the bar in the Saussurian algorithm (and in a form designed to suggest that its resistance may be other than dialectical), we should add that only someone who didn't have his eyes in front of the holes (it's the appropriate image here) could possibly confuse the place of the signifier and the signified in this story, or not see from what radiating centre the signifier sends forth its light into the shadow of incomplete significations.

For this signifier will now carry a purely animal Dissension, destined for the usual oblivion of natural mists, to the unbridled power of ideological warfare, relentless for families, a torment to the Gods. For these children, Ladies and Gentlemen will be henceforth two countries towards which each of their souls will strive on divergent wings, and between which a truce will be the more impossible since they are actually the same country and neither can compromise on its own superiority without detracting from the glory of the other.

But enough. It is beginning to sound like the history of France. Which it is more human, as it ought to be, to evoke here than that of England, destined to tumble from the Large to the Small End of Dean Swift's egg.

It remains to be conceived what steps, what corridor, the S of the signifier, visible here in the plurals[9] in which it focuses its welcome beyond the window, must take in order to rest its elbows on the ventilators through which, like warm and cold air, indignation and scorn come hissing out below.

One thing is certain: if the algorithm S/s with its bar is appropriate, access from one to the other cannot in any case have a signification. For in so far as it is itself only pure function of the signification, the algorithm can reveal only the structure of a signifier in this transfer.

Now the structure of the signifier is, as it is commonly said of language itself, that it should be articulated.

This means that no matter where one starts to designate their reciprocal encroachments and increasing inclusions, these units are subjected to the double condition of being reducible to ultimate differential elements and of combining them according to the laws of a closed order.

These elements, one of the decisive discoveries of linguistics, are *phonemes*; but we must not expect to find any *phonetic* constancy in the modulatory variability to which this term applies, but rather the synchronic system of differential couplings necessary for the discernment of sounds in a given language. Through this, one sees that an essential element of the spoken word itself was predestined to flow into the mobile characters which, in a jumble of lower-case Didots or Garamonds,[10] render validly present what we call the 'letter', namely, the essentially localized structure of the signifier.

With the second property of the signifier, that of combining according to the laws of a closed order, is affirmed the necessity of the topological substratum of which the term I ordinarily use, namely, the signifying chain, gives an approximate idea: rings of a necklace that is a ring in another necklace made of rings.

Such are the structural conditions that define grammar as the order of constitutive encroachments of the signifier up to the level of the unit immediately superior to the sentence, and lexicology as the order of constitutive inclusions of the signifier to the level of the verbal locution.

In examining the limits by which these two exercises in the understanding of linguistic usage are determined, it is easy to see that only the correlations between signifier and signifier provide the standard for all research into signification, as is indicated by the notion of 'usage' of a taxeme or semanteme which in fact refers to the context just above that of the units concerned.

But it is not because the undertakings of grammar and lexicology are exhausted within certain limits that we must think that beyond those limits signification reigns supreme. That would be an error.

For the signifier, by its very nature, always anticipates meaning by unfolding its dimension before it. As is seen at the level of the sentence when it is interrupted before the significant term: 'I shall never ...', 'All the same it is ...', 'And yet there may be ...'. Such sentences are not without meaning, a meaning all the more oppressive in that it is content to make us wait for it.[11]

But the phenomenon is no different which by the mere recoil of a 'but' brings to the light, comely as the Shulamite, honest as the dew, the negress adorned for the wedding and the poor woman for the auction-block.[12]

From which we can say that it is in the chain of the signifier that the meaning 'insists' but that none of its elements 'consists' in the signification of which it is at the moment capable.

We are forced, then to accept the notion of an incessant sliding of the signified under the signifier.

NOTES

1 '*À la lettre*' [Alan Sheridan: Tr.].
2 This aspect of aphasia, so useful in overthrowing the concept of 'psychological function', which only obscures every aspect of the question, becomes quite clear in the purely linguistic analysis of the two major forms of aphasia worked out by one of the leaders of modern linguistics, Roman Jakobson. See the most accessible of his works, the *Fundamentals of Language* (with Morris Halle), Mouton's Gravenhage, part II, chapters 1 to 4.
3 We may recall that the discussion of the need for a new language in communist society did in fact take place, and Stalin, much to the relief of those who adhered to his philosophy, put an end to it with the following formulation: language is not a superstructure.
4 By 'linguistics' I mean the study of existing languages (*langues*) in their structure and in the laws revealed therein; this excludes any theory of abstract codes sometimes included under the heading of communication theory, as well as the theory, originating in the physical sciences, called information theory, or any semiology more or less hypothetically generalized.
5 *Psychanalyse et sciences de l'homme.*
6 Cf. the *De Magistro* of St Augustine, especially the chapter 'De significatione locutionis' which I analysed in my seminar of 23 June 1954.
7 English in the original [Tr.].
8 So, Mr I.A. Richards, author of a work precisely in accord with such an objective, has in another work shown us its application. He took for his purposes a page from Mong-tse (Mencius, to the Jesuits) and called the piece, *Mencius on the Mind*. The guarantees of the purity of the experiment are nothing to the luxury of the approaches. And our expert on the traditional Canon that contains the text is found right on the spot in Peking where our demonstration-model mangle has been transported regardless of cost.

But we shall be no less transported, if less expensively, to see a bronze that gives out bell-tones at the slightest contact with thought, transformed into a rag to wipe the blackboard of the most dismaying British psychologism. And not without eventually being identified with the meninx of the author himself – all that remains of him or his object after having exhausted the meaning of the latter and the good sense of the former.
9 Not, unfortunately, the case in the English here – the plural of 'gentleman' being indicated other than by the addition of an 's' [Tr.].

10 Names of different type-faces [Tr.].
11 To which verbal hallucination, when it takes this form, opens a communicating door with the Freudian structure of psychosis – a door until now unnoticed (cf. 'On a Question Preliminary to any Possible Treatment of Psychosis', pp. 179–225).
12 The allusions are to the 'I am black, but comely . . .' of the *Song of Solomon*, and to the nineteenth-century cliché of the 'poor, but honest' woman [Tr.].

14 **Mikkel Borch-Jacobsen**

Linguisteries

We could begin this way: What do you call a cat? A cat, obviously.[1]
Yes; but what do you *call* 'a cat'? Is the named cat the same as the
unnamed cat, the cat *before* it was named? This is what ordinary
language believes (or makes us believe), as Maurice Blanchot (1981)
recalls in an article where, in his own way, he hails the publication
of Kojève's (1969) *Introduction to the Reading of Hegel*: 'Everyday
language calls a cat a cat, as if the living cat and its name were identical'.[2] But everyday language is wrong, as the (Hegelian) philosopher
and the writer know very well. The named cat is a dead cat, an
absent, negated cat: 'The word gives me what it signifies, but first
it suppresses it. . . . It is the absence of that being, its nothing
ness . . . Language begins only with a void. . . . In the beginning, I
don't speak in order to say something; rather, it is a nothing, that
asks to speak, nothing speaks, nothing finds its being in speech, and
the being of speech is nothing' (Blanchot 1981 pp. 36 and 38). The
upright, prosaic person who proposes to call a cat a cat – and not,
as a writer does, 'a dog'[3] – is therefore 'more mystifying than ever,
for the cat is not a cat (Blanchot 1981 p. 23). In fact, how can we
name the cat that has *disappeared* into speech? The real integrity of
language is the paradoxical and impossible integrity of the writer,
who creates *from nothing* (Blanchot 1981 p. 29) by constantly strug-
gling to name the death that he resuscitates as he goes along, and
which escapes from him as well, since his 'speech is the *life* of that
death' (Blanchot 1981 p. 41, my emphasis).[4] Thus, literary creation is
a perpetual idleness (or 'unworking') (*désoeuvrement*) that tries to
climb back beyond the work, toward Creation itself, and which can
accomplish this only through an aborted creation (or, what amounts
to the same thing, through an interminable apocalypse):

Hegel, ... in a text preceding the *Phenomenology*, wrote: 'The first act by which Adam made himself master of the animals was to give them a name; that is, he annihilated them in their existence (as "existants").' Hegel meant that, from that moment, the cat ceased to be simply a real cat and became an idea as well. Therefore, the meaning of speech demands, as preface to all speech, a sort of immense hecatomb, a preliminary deluge, plunging all of creation into a total sea. God created beings, but man had to annihilate them. In this way, they became meaningful for him, and he in turn created them out of that death into which they had disappeared.

(Blanchot 1981 p. 36)

IN THE BEGINNING WAS LANGUAGE

Let us recall that Lacan, in his 'Rome Discourse', was rectifying Goethe's formula: in the beginning was not the Action, but the Word (1977 pp. 61/271; see also this volume pp. 186–94) – by which he meant creative *speech*, the performative *speech act*. But two years later, in the second seminar, he modifies the accepted translation of St John's *logos*: in the beginning was not the word (*parole*), he maintained before his astonished listeners, but *language* (1988 pp. 309–314/355–361). This comment, apparently purely philological (and, as such, rather fanciful), actually introduces an important reversal, one whose importance will only increase. Creative speech is far from being what is opposed to representative language (revealing the nothing hidden by the latter); on the contrary, language 'gives' [speech] its radical condition' (1988 p. 313/360):

We can turn it [the inflection of *logos* in *verbum*] into something completely different from the reason of things, namely, this play of absence and presence which already provides the frame for *fiat*. For, in the end, *fiat* is made (*se fait*) on a backdrop of the unmade (*non-fait*) which is prior to it. In other words, I think that it isn't inconceivable that even the *fiat*, the most primary of creative speeches, is secondary. ... What's at issue [in language] is a succession of absences and presences, or rather of presence on a background of absence, of absence constituted by the fact

that a presence can exist. . . . It is the original contradiction of
0 and 1.

(Lacan 1988 pp. 312–313/359)

Therefore, language *in general*, and not just speech, is invested
with the power of bringing non-being (the zero) into being. More
precisely, speech does not create ex nihilo except against the backdrop of the simultaneity of presence and absence in language. This
is another way of saying that, for Lacan, language is heir to all the
characteristics previously attributed only to full/performative speech:
no matter what he says, no matter what his utterance, the subject
of the enunciation presents himself in it (only) as absence. This is
a sign (if we need one) that Lacan no longer believes in the possibility that one speech would be more 'true' than another, and that
this opposition within language is henceforth displaced onto the
'original' opposition between language as a whole and nothing (between 1 and 0).

At any rate, what is this 'language', heir to the defunct 'full
speech' (a 'language' where, inversely, full speech revives or survives
clandestinely)? Obviously, it cannot be the same 'language' that
Lacan had previously denounced as the 'wall of language' and the
'mistaken notion of "language as a sign".' How could the latter reveal
the nothing, since it stubbornly asserts that a cat is a cat and that
the word 'cat' *represents* the cat? It must be some other 'language'
(or another acceptation of the word 'language') – and Lacan's allusion to the binary alternation of cybernetic 'bits' immediately puts
us on the right track. Anyway, there is no reason to be so mysterious
about it, since it is something we all know (or think we know): this
'language', which the unconscious is structured like (or which is its
'condition'; 1970 p. 58), is actually the language of structural linguistics. Whatever distance Lacan may have tried to put, later on,
between himself and linguistics (to which he opposed his own
'linguistery'; 1975 p. 20), it is clear that the major model of reference
for his theory of language, from the mid-1950's on,[5] was indeed
linguistics in its Saussurian version: *langue* as a closed system of regulated oppositions, ordering a homogeneous multiplicity of signifying
unities independent of the reality that it designates.

As we know, this *langue*, the specific object of linguistic *science*,
is not spoken by anyone. It is a language that, in principle, should
be called dead,[6] separated as it is, by the Saussurian scalpel, from its

individual and discursive actualization, speech: 'Within the total phenomenon represented by language (*langage*), we first singled out two parts: *langue* and speech (*parole*). *Langue* is language, less speech' (Saussure 1974 p. 77).[7] How, then, did this *langue* come to inherit (under its Lacanian name, 'language') the essential traits of *speech*? That is what remains to be understood. In what respect (or at what price) can Saussure's *langue* manifest the subject of desire, since *langue* is constructed through the methodical exclusion of all subjectivity and every consideration of the individual utterance? We may very well suspect that this cannot happen without several 'linguisteries', and this is already indicated by the speed with which Lacan strides across the Saussurian distinction between *langue* and speech: Lacan's 'language' is never anything but *langue*, *plus* speech, a sort of strange 'speech-*langue*' ('*parlangue*')[8] in which speech becomes a dead *langue* and *langue* becomes nobody's speech.

But before we deal with this rash extension to discourse of the mechanisms that regulate *langue*, we must examine the other important modification that Lacan brings to Saussure's theory: the one that touches on the dissociation of signifier and signified, the two elements of the linguistic sign (which, according to Saussure, are inseparable). Indeed, this first modification, being a direct outgrowth of the critique of the 'language-sign' launched in the 'Rome Discourse', will allow for a better understanding of the conditions that 'language' must fulfil in order to take the place previously occupied by 'speech'. In short, just as 'full speech' was performative and non-constantive, so Saussure's *langue* does not gain entry into Lacan's doctrine before having been emptied of all representative functions and invested with a 'significance' (*significance*) that *creates* meaning.

Does this mean that Lacan was unfaithful to Saussure's teaching, or that he simply did not understand it (as some professional linguists – Mounin, for example – have protested)? First of all, Lacan's distortion of the Saussurian 'sign' really does nothing but determine the ambiguity of that concept, in agreement with the strictest post-Saussurian orthodoxy. For Saussure himself, the theory of the sign is anything but univocal. On the contrary, in the *Course in General Linguistics*, it is already more or less torn between two rival hypotheses. The first, which Saussure inherited from a long philosophical tradition, is the 'arbitrariness' (or 'unmotivatedness') of the sign. It consists in admitting, first, that the word 'cat' does not at all signify the real cat (even if it does designate or refer to it, which does not concern the Saussureian linguist): 'The linguistic sign unites, not a thing and a name, but a concept and a sound-image' (Saussure 1974 p. 66) – that is, once again, a 'signified' and a 'signifier'. In turn, this union (which, properly speaking, is the relation of signification) is by rights just as arbitrary as it is necessary (and, in fact, indissoluble) for every user of a given *langue*: the signifier 'has no natural connection *with the signified*' (Saussure 1974 p. 69, my emphasis); since what is pronounced '*b-ö-f* ['beef' in French] on one side of the border' is pronounced '*o-k-s* on the other' (Saussure 1974 p. 68). As for Saussure's second hypothesis, undoubtedly the more fruitful one, it pertains to the 'value' of the linguistic sign: the sign /bfːf/ (or /kæt/, or /hɔːrs/, since animals apparently must always carry the weight of these linguistic examples) is this sign in opposition to all the other signs that it is *not* (/biː/, /biːt/, /bIf/, and so on). In other words, the signification of a term is only the 'summary' of its value (Godel 1957 p. 237) – that is, of the paradigmatic and syntagmatic relationships between it and its surrounding terms (think of the dictionary, which enumerates words vertically according to their similarity and combines them horizontally with other words to specify their uses). Hence this conclusion: 'In language, there are only differences *without positive terms*' (Saussure 1974 p. 120).

It is easy to see that these two hypotheses are ultimately incompatible. Indeed, even when we admit that the theory of arbitrariness is not simply a new form of conventionalism,[9] the fact remains that to speak of an 'arbitrary' relation between the signifier and the signified is the same as to admit, if only negatively, that the first *represents* the second. By the same token, this inevitably means reviving the idea that there is a signified *independent* of the signifier that represents it, just when we are assenting that they form a unity as inseparable as the two sides of a sheet of paper (Saussure 1974 p. 113). It is precisely this mirage – of a signified independent of the signifier – that the hypothesis of value dispels. Indeed, it is through pure abstraction that Saussure can say that *the* signified 'beef' is here pronounced /biːf/, there /bœf/ or /ɔks/, as if this 'concept' had existed *before* Babel, independently of the dispersion of national/ maternal *langues*. In reality, for the speakers of a given *langue*, as Benveniste had already noted in 1939, there is no difference between the signifier /biːf/ and the signified 'beef': 'Between the signifier and the signified, the connection is not arbitrary; on the contrary, it is *necessary*. The concept (the "signified") *bœuf* [beef] is perforce identical in my [French] consciousness with the sound sequence (the "signifier") *böf*. . . . There is such a close symbiosis between them that the concept of *bœuf* is like the soul of the sound image *böf* (Benveniste 1939a; see also this volume pp. 63–9). In other words, there is strict adherence between the signifier and the signified, and if this is so, it is because, in accord with the theory of value, they vary in concert within a linguistic system with which they are in solidarity (hence the despair of translators, who know only too well that /bœuf/ will never have exactly the same *meaning* as /biːf/, even if they both refer to the same *thing*).

Signification, therefore, does not reside in the representation of a signified by a signifier, even an 'arbitrary' one. If we follow the hypothesis of value, the meaning of a sign is always (to use Peirce's vocabulary, quoted by Jakobson) in another sign that 'interprets' the first: 'The function of such an interpretant is performed by another sign or set of signs that occur together with a given sign, or might occur instead of it' (Jakobson 1953 p. 20).[10] Even more precisely, the signified is inseparable from the signifier, whose differential destiny it shares. As Lacan says, there is no signified 'day' before the signifying opposition that places day against the background of night's absence, and vice versa (1981 pp. 169–170), no signified 'man' without the signifying polarity that differentiates him from 'woman' (1981 pp. 223–224 and 282–283). And so it turns out that we can never lay our hands on *the* signified of a signifier except in another signifier,

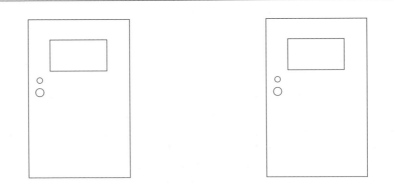

LADIES   GENTLEMEN

Figure 14.1

and so on. This is illustrated, in 'The Agency of the Letter', by the incongruous rewriting (Lacan 1977 p. 151/499) of the Saussurian schema of the sign (Figure 14.1).

The two doors, indistinguishable *in reality*, receive their imponderable 'meaning' – 'the imperative . . . of urinary segregation' (Lacan 1977 p. 151/500) – from the pure difference in places between the *two* signifiers 'Ladies' and 'Gentlemen'.

By the same token, if the signified of a signifier is itself a signifier, *what can the distinction between signifier and signified* (advanced by the Saussurian doctrine of arbitrariness) *correspond to*? As Benveniste noted in 1939, this distinction is actually only the relic, within a theory allergic to it, of a representationalist problematic of the sign. Therefore, Benveniste amends, arbitrariness concerns only the relation of the sign to the thing designated, and not the relation of the signifier to the signified, which itself is necessary and indissoluble. The signifier is not the 'arbitrary' representative of the signified, for the latter *is nothing* without the former, except through mirage or illusion. 'Meaning' is 'an internal component of linguistic form' (Benveniste 1939b n. 2) and therefore the signified is not to be sought anywhere but in the relations among signifiers.

We can see what Benveniste's rectification implies: it methodically reduces the theory of signification to a theory of value, and by the same token, as Jean-Claude Milner opportunely remarks, it justifies the notion 'that in order to designate any system structured like a language [let us correct this Lacanian slippage: like a *langue*], one adopts a single term – for example, "the signifier" ' (Milner 1979 n. 4). Now, as we know, this is the side taken by Lacan, who on this point merely draws the strict conclusions of the theory of value. Indeed, if the sign represents nothing – neither the referent nor even the signified – then there is nothing to sink one's teeth into but the signifier. Only the signifier survives the deluge (as Blanchot 1981 says) that swallows up every 'signifiable' (Lacan 1977 p. 288/692). As for the concept of the 'sign', it is totally abandoned; witness the double and significant destiny that it meets in Lacan. Either it is criticized as what the signifier is *not* – that is, 'what represents something for someone' (Lacan 1970 p. 65), a definition borrowed from Peirce but implicitly entailing that of the Saussurian sign – or it is simply *identified* with the concept of the signifier ('The signifier is a sign that refers to another sign': Lacan 1981 p. 188).

Therefore, the stakes are clear enough in this methodical reduction of sign to the signifier alone. For Lacan, it is a question of emptying the linguistic sign of every representative function, in order to invest it with the role previously imparted to speech: the role of producing (presenting) *nothing* from *nothing*. There is, Lacan repeats after Lévi-Strauss,[11] an 'autonomy' of the signifier relative to the signified (1981 p. 223; 1970 p. 55), in the sense that the signifier 'does not depend on the signification . . . but is its source' (1981 p. 282). This formula summarizes very well the double demonstration to which Lacan yields whenever he presents his doctrine of the signifier (see, for example, the first section of 'The Agency of the Letter', which is entirely constructed on the following pattern):

1 The signifier does not *depend* on the signified. Indeed, not only does 'the signifier [not] answer to the function of representing the signified', it cannot answer to 'any signification whatever' (Lacan 1977 p. 150/498; see also 1975 pp. 31–32). Taken in itself (that is, separated, as if that were possible, from other signifiers), the signifier 'signifies nothing' (1981 p. 210), and this is what Lacan tries to express by speaking of its 'materiality' (1988 pp. 82/104–105; 1966 p. 24), its 'localized' (1977 p. 153/501) and 'literal' structure: 'By "letter" I designate that material support that concrete discourse borrows from language' (1977 p. 147/495). Admittedly, these are ambiguous formulations, but they do signify, at any rate, that the signifier does not *incarnate* a prior ideality.[12] If, as Benveniste (1939a) proposes in his rectification of Saussure, 'the concept *boeuf* is like the soul of the sound-image *böf*', then, according to Lacan, we must add that the literal body of the signifier contains no soul (no meaning) before the spirit comes to it from its coupling with other bodies just as stupid as itself. The signifier is truly senseless (*in-sensé*), 'stupid' (*bête*; Lacan 1975 p. 24), and, just like a character on a typewriter keyboard, it makes sense only by effacing another signifier, taking its *place* on the written page, *next* to other signifiers (with all the other, no less stupid, 'typos' that this may imply – slips of the tongue and the pen, *Witz*, and so on).

2 The signifier is the *source* of the signified. The latter is never anything but an 'effect' of these couplings and encroachments of signifiers, a 'signified effect' (*effet de signifié*; Lacan 1975 pp. 22–23) in the sense in which we speak, for example, of a 'Larsen effect' or an 'optical illusion' (*efet d'optique*). This signified is truly nothing –

nothing that would *in effect* be caused or produced by the signifier. In accord with the theory of value, meaning is never anything but an illusion, produced 'between' signifiers, which themselves have no meaning – a sort of rainbow that eludes our grasp as soon as we try to approach it. 'Sense', Lacan maintains, 'emerges from nonsense' (1977 p.158/508), and here is the whole 'sense' (if we may call it that) of Lacan's rewriting of the Saussurian schema of the sign, in which Figure 14.2

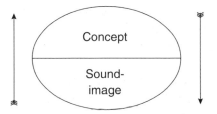

Figure 14.2

is transformed into the 'algorithm'

$$\frac{S}{s}$$

'which is read as: the signifier over the signified, "over" corresponding to the bar separating the two stages' (Lacan 1977 p. 149/497). S, the creative and capital signifier, hereafter precedes, in all its supremacy, its passive and secondary effect: the s of the signified.

NOTES

1 'Appeler un chat un chat' is approximately equivalent to the English expression 'to call a spade a spade' [Alan Bass: Tr.].
2 Blanchot (1981 p. 38); originally published as Blanchot (1947); reprinted in Blanchot (1949). *Le Droit à la mort* (the right to death) is an implicit quotation of Kojève in relation to Terror and the 'political right to death' (cf. Kojève, xx/558). More generally, the argument developed by Blanchot in this article/manifesto is entirely based on Kojève's commentary on Hegel. The first page number refers to the English translation (Kojève 1969), the second to the original French edition (Kojève 1947). Hereafter 'Kojève' is followed by two page numbers or by xx/page number where no English translation exists [Douglas Brick: Tr.].

3 'Thus is born the image that does not directly designate the thing, but rather what the thing is not, that speaks of a dog instead of a cat' (a metaphorical process that is not at all the sole property of writers; as Lacan used to say, the child likes to say that the dog says 'meow' and the cat 'bow-wow') (Blanchot 1981 p. 40).

4 Obviously, this is an allusion to Hegel's formula, 'the life that contains death and maintains itself therein', and the Kojèvian paraphrase, 'the death that lives a human life' (Kojève, xx/550).

5 Undoubtedly an effect of fashion: at the time, everyone was interested in Saussure, starting with Lacan's friends Lévi-Strauss and Merleau-Ponty. See especially Merleau-Ponty's 'Indirect Language and the Voices of Silence', 'On the Phenomenology of Language', and 'From Mauss to Lévi-Strauss' in *Signs*, as well as his course at the Sorbonne on 'La conscience et l'acquisition du langage', *Bulletin de psychologie* XVIII, 236 (1964), 3–6.

6 'Although dead languages are no longer spoken, we can easily assimilate their linguistic organisms' (Saussure 1974 p. 15).

7 Translation modified (quoted and discussed by Vincent Descombes, 1983 pp. 186 ff.). In this text, I have translated *parole* as 'speech', *langage* as 'language' and I have left *langue* in French. For Saussure's distinctions among the three terms, see Saussure (1974 pp. 7–17), where Wade Baskin has translated *parole* as 'speaking', *langage* as 'human speech', and *langue* as 'language' (Trans.).

8 A neologism that echoes those of Lacan: *parlêtre*, *lalangue*, etc. (Trans.).

9 'The arbitrariness of the sign amounts to positing that it cannot be thought of as other than it is, since there is no reason that it should be as it is. The arbitrariness neatly covers up a question that will not be asked – What is the sign when it is not the sign? What is language before it is language? – that is, the question usually expressed in terms of the origin. . . . Here again, confusion is frequent: the thesis of arbitrariness has the function of eliminating any question about the origin, and thus it has only a superficial resemblance to conventionalism' (Milner 1978 p. 59). It should be noted that Lacan was much more severe with Saussure on this point than was his commentator, Milner; see Lacan (1977 pp. 149–50; 1975 pp. 23 and 32; 1970 p. 63).

10 Jakobson's contribution is Chapter 2; the other authors are Claude Lévi-Strauss (Chapter 1) and C.F. Voegelin and Thomas A. Sebeok (Chapter 3).

11 Let us cite once more this passage from *Introduction to the Work of Marcel Mauss*, p. 37: 'Like language, the social *is* an autonomous reality (the same one, moreover); symbols are more real than what they symbolize, the signifier precedes and determines the signified'.

12 And for good reason: as Derrida (1987) has noted, this 'materiality' of the signifier/letter '*in fact corresponds to an idealization*. . . . "Cut a letter in small pieces, and it remains the letter is is" [a quote from the seminar on 'The Purloined Letter', in which Lacan states that this 'materiality' of the signified 'is *odd* (*singulière*) in many ways, the first of which is not to admit partition'; 1966 p. 14]; since this cannot be said of empirical materiality, it must imply an ideality (the intangibility of a self-identity displacing itself without alteration) . . . . If this ideality is not the content of meaning, it must be either a certain ideality of the signifier (what is identifiable in its form to the extent that it can be distinguished from its empirical events and re-editions), or the *point de capiton* ['*Capitonner* means to quilt; *point de capiton* is Lacan's term for the "quilted stitch" that links signifier to signified', Note by Alan Bass (trans.)] which staples the signifier to the signified. . . . One

can understand that Lacan finds this "materiality" "odd" [*singulière*]: he retains only its ideality' (Derrida 1987 p. 464). Derrida is right: what Lacan calls the 'materiality' of the signifier is nothing other than its 'incorporeal' ideality, according to Saussure ('The sign is by nature incorporeal', quoted in Godel 1957 p. 67). But Lacan is in no way ignorant of this, and that is exactly why he always underscores its *nullibiété* and its 'unquantifiable' character (Lacan 1966 pp. 23–24), or again, its 'subtlety' (Lacan 1977 p. 87). In reality, Lacan insists on the 'materiality' of the signifier only in order to reverse (with a gesture that one may, of course, find too rapid) the relation classically established between ideality and meaning: the ideality of the signifier/letter has no other 'meaning' but the strictly in-sensible *différance* of meaning (that is to say, the negativity of the subject). As for the relation Derrida establishes between the 'letter' and the *phonē* (the ideal indivisibility of the phoneme), it nevertheless seems to me to be the opposite of what he suggests in this article. Not only does Lacan make it clear later on (in 1972) that 'the signifier cannot in any way be limited to its phonetic prop' (Lacan 1975 p. 22), but in 'The Agency of the Letter in the Unconscious' (from 1957) he already *subordinates* the alleged phonemeticity of the signifier to the differential-spaced structure of the 'letter': 'These [ultimate differential] elements . . . are *phonemes* . . . the synchronic system of differential couplings necessary for the discernment of sounds in a given language. Through this, one see that an essential element of the spoken word itself was predestined to flow into the mobile characters which, in a jumble of lower-case Didots or Garamonds [names of different typefaces (Trans.)] render validly present what we call the 'letter', namely, the essentially localized structure of the signifier (Lacan 1977 p. 153). The seminar on identification returns at length to the literal character of the signifier (mark, trait), to deny that writing has in itself a function of ideographic representation *or of notation of the phoneme*. Hence, with respect to the proper name, 'what the advent of writing signifies is the following: the something that is already writing – if we consider the characteristic and the isolation of the signifying trait – once named becomes capable of supporting that famous sound on which M. Gardiner puts all stress concerning proper names . . . . The characteristic of the proper name is always more or less linked with this trait of its liaison, not with sound, but with writing' (Lacan 1961).

The play of différance

EDITOR'S INTRODUCTION

The interview with Derrida conducted by Julia Kristeva took place in 1968, was collected in the volume *Positions* in 1972 and subsequently translated into English (1981). It consists of a lucid, though breathless, exposition of Derrida's thoughts on the utility of semiology in our understanding of meaning. The second part of the title refers to the 'science' which Derrida (1976) had inaugurated in the previous year in his book, *Of Grammatology*, and it becomes clear that Derrida feels virtually the whole of Western metaphysics to have overlooked this method of investigating signification. Central to Derrida's argument is the idea that meaning is always to be understood as a constant play of difference, a continuous flux which makes up *différance*. As he explains, even those traditions of thinking that have attempted to advocate a 'differential' or 'diacritical' understanding of signification (e.g. Saussure), have actually held on to the concept of a 'transcendental signified'. By this he means that they have not seen meaning or signification as a *totally* differential *process*; instead, they have unwittingly reconstructed referential models in which the signifier operates, but it does so purely for the purposes of referring to a self-contained pre-existing 'concept' which exists independently of signification.

The quest for the 'transcendental signified' is ultimately a futile one. Rather like the quest in *The Wizard of Oz*, there is confidence that a final, pre-existent concept (the Wizard), lies at the end of the Yellow Brick Road (the play of meaning). Unfortunately, when Dorothy reaches her destination, and hence her answer, she finds that the Wonderful Wizard of Oz is, in fact, a little old man with a loudhailer. The 'meaning' of the quest for Dorothy can be experienced only whilst she is amidst the play of *différance*, on the Yellow Brick Road. This scenario may seem like a self-perpetuating one which has no end. However, Derrida is clear in this interview that the practice of semiology, the investigation of the sign systems that are at work in any signification, is not to be junked; instead, it must be used to explore new avenues and discover the existence of new chains of signification. If, in semiology, 'metaphysical presuppositions coexist with critical motifs', then for Derrida 'grammatology' is the working through of this split domain.

Such a division in the investigation of significance is witnessed in the second extract, by Brian Torode. In the extraordinary collection of essays by Torode and his fellow sociologist, David Silverman, from which this reading is taken, two forms of approaching communication are delineated. The first is called 'interpretation' and, as a rule, such an approach takes the *signifier* as 'indicator, or appearance of a signified essential reality' (Silverman and Torode 1980 p. 3). The example Silverman and Torode give of this approach is Saussure, particularly the way in which Saussure envisages communication taking place between the contents of two brains, a set-up which Derrida would describe as a manifestation of the metaphysics of 'presence'. Counterposed to this is the approach advocated by Silverman and Torode which they name 'interruption'. As the communicative interaction is conceived not as the meeting of two brains but, instead, the configuration of a language, the practice of 'interruption' seeks to enter the very fact of linguistic play. In this view, language is the object of enquiry but it is an object which is used in a multifaceted and socially situated way by speakers. 'Interruption' unsettles 'interpretation' with its straightforward relation between 'appearance' and 'reality'; it seeks to demonstrate that there is, in fact, a further level, a play of reference 'from one language to another language that suggests the reference of language to a reality other than language' (Silverman and Torode 1980 p. 9).

It becomes clear from Silverman and Torode's essays that two important influences on their theory are Vološinov and Derrida. In the essay that follows, a key component of Vološinov's thesis about language – the interplay of many 'voices' in communication – is utilized in the process of 'interrupting' the conventional 'appearance'/'reality' dyad.

Vološinov takes as his example, the case of 'reported speech' in fictional discourse, which sets up certain relations between voices such as the authorial prose and the speech of a given character. This is the same kind of area studied by Colin MacCabe (see this volume pp. 17–18) whose imperatives are not dissimilar from those of Vološinov. However, Vološinov's findings have a closer relationship with the work of Bakhtin, who began by positing the voices in Dostoevsky's novels as almost unique, eventually giving way to the possibility that it was in the very nature of *all* fictional discourse to be 'polyphonic' (see Bakhtin 1973). What Torode shows, is that the many voices in fiction do not simply harbour the potential for a democracy of speech but that, by undermining each other's 'reality', they expose the way 'appearance' and 'reality' are constituted as a practice in the discourse. Moreover, Torode implements a Derridean focus on the *play* of the text to reveal the management of the text's content (including voices) through the time of its narration (*economy*), and the deferral of gratification which contributes to the pleasure of the text (*sexuality*).

In the ensuing analysis of 'Little Red Riding Hood', Torode shows that it is the 'voice' of the Wolf that 'interrupts' the narrative. The Wolf constantly uncovers, or threatens to uncover, both the workings of textuality *and* the other voices' faith in 'appearance' and 'reality'. Torode's analysis is, in this way, an exemplary exercise in Derrida's 'grammatology', demonstrating that texts themselves can sometimes lay bare their own circulation of fictional 'transcendental signifieds'.

Further reading   Derrida 1982 pp. 1–28, pp. 307–330; Norris 1982 pp. 24–32; 1987 pp. 87–96; Moi 1985 pp. 105–107; Weedon *et al.* 1981; Dews 1987 pp. 1–108; Hasan 1987; Melrose 1993.

15 Jacques Derrida

Semiology and grammatology: interview with Julia Kristeva

Kristeva: Semiology today is constructed on the model of the sign and its correlates: *communication* and *structure*. What are the 'logo-centric' and ethnocentric limits of these models, and how are they incapable of serving as the basis for a notation attempting to escape metaphysics?

Derrida: All gestures here are necessarily equivocal. And sup-posing, which I do not believe, that someday it will be possible *simply* to escape metaphysics, the concept of the sign will have marked, in this sense, a simultaneous impediment and progress. For if the sign, by its root and its implications, is in all its aspects metaphysical, if it is in systematic solidarity with stoic and medieval theology, the work and the displacement to which it has been submitted – and of which it also, curiously, is the instrument – have had *delimiting* effects. For this work and displacement have permitted the critique of how the concept of the sign belongs to meta-physics, which represents a simultaneous *marking* and *loosening* of the limits of the system in which this concept was born and began to serve, and thereby also represents, to a certain extent, an uprooting of the sign from its own soil. This work must be con-ducted as far as possible, but at a certain point one inevitably encoun-ters 'the logocentric and ethnocentric limits' of such a model. At this point, perhaps, the concept is to be abandoned. But this point is very difficult to determine, and is never pure. All the heuristic and critical resources of the concept of the sign have to be exhausted, and exhausted equally in all domains and contexts. Now, it is inevitable that not only inequalities of development (which will always occur), but also the necessity of certain contexts, will render strategically indispensable the recourse to a model known elsewhere, and even at the most novel points of investigation, to function as an obstacle.

To take only one example, one could show that a semiology of the Saussurean type has had a double role. *On the one hand*, an absolutely decisive critical role:

1 It has marked, against the tradition, that the signified is insep-arable from the signifier, that the signified and signifier are the two sides of one and the same production. Saussure even purposely refused to have this opposition or this 'two-sided unity' conform to the relationship between soul and body, as had always been done. 'This two-sided unity has often been compared to the unity of the human person, composed of a body and a soul. The comparison is hardly satisfactory' (Saussure 1916 p. 145).

2 By emphasizing the *differential* and *formal* characteristics of semiological functioning, by showing that it 'is impossible for sound, the material element, itself to belong to language' and that 'in its essence it [the linguistic signifier] is not at all phonic' (p. 164); by desubstantializing both the signified content and the 'expressive substance' – which therefore is no longer in a privileged or exclu-sive way phonic – by making linguistics a division of general semiology (p. 33), Saussure powerfully contributed to turning against the metaphysical tradition the concept of the sign that he borrowed from it.

And yet Saussure could not not confirm this tradition in the extent to which he continued to use the concept of the sign. No more than any other, this concept cannot be employed in both an absolutely novel and an absolutely conventional way. One necessarily assumes, in a non-critical way, at least some of the implications inscribed in its system. There is at least one moment at which Saussure must renounce drawing all the conclusions from the critical work he has undertaken, and that is the not fortuitous moment when he resigns himself to using the word 'sign', lacking anything better. After having justified the introduction of the words 'signified' and 'signifier', Saussure writes: 'As for *sign*, if we retain it, it is because we find nothing else to replace it, everyday language suggesting no other' (pp. 99–100). And, in effect, it is difficult to see how one could evac-uate the *sign* when one has begun by proposing the opposition signified/signifier.

Now, 'everyday language' is not innocent or neutral. It is the language of Western metaphysics, and it carries with it not only a considerable number of presuppositions of all types, but also presuppositions inseparable from metaphysics, which, although little attended to, are knotted into a system. This is why *on the other hand*:

1 The maintenance of the rigorous distinction – an essential and juridical distinction – between the *signans* and the *signatum*, the equation of the *signatum* and the concept (p. 99),[1] inherently leaves open the possibility of thinking a *concept signified in and of itself*, a concept simply present for thought, independent of a relationship to language, that is of a relationship to a system of signifiers. By leaving open this possibility – and it is inherent even in the opposition signifier/signified, that is in the sign – Saussure contradicts the critical acquisitions of which we were just speaking. He accedes to the classical exigency of what I have proposed to call a 'transcendental signified', which in and of itself, in its essence, would refer to no signifier, would exceed the chain of signs, and would no longer itself function as a signifier. On the contrary, though, from the moment that one questions the possibility of such a transcendental signified, and that one recognizes that every signified is also in the position of a signifier (see Derrida 1967), the distinction between signified and signifier becomes problematical at its root. Of course this is an operation that must be undertaken with prudence for: (a) it must pass through the difficult deconstruction of the entire history of metaphysics which imposed, and never will cease to impose upon semiological science in its entirety this fundamental quest for a 'transcendental signified' and a concept independent of language; this quest not being imposed from without by something like 'philosophy', but rather by everything that links our language, our culture, our 'system of thought' to the history and system of metaphysics; (b) nor is it a question of confusing at every level, and in all simplicity, the signifier and the signified. That this opposition or difference cannot be radical or absolute does not prevent it from functioning, and even from being indispensable within certain limits – very wide limits. For example, no translation would be possible without it. In effect, the theme of a transcendental signified took shape within the horizon of an absolutely pure, transparent, and unequivocal translatability. In the limits to which it is possible, or at least *appears* possible, translation practices the difference between signified and signifier. But if this difference is never pure, no more so is translation and for the notion of translation we would have to substitute a

notion of *transformation*: a regulated transformation of one language by another, of one text by another. We will never have, and in fact have never had, to do with some 'transport' of pure signifieds from one language to another, or within one and the same language, that the signifying instrument would leave virgin and untouched.

2 Although he recognized the necessity of putting the phonic substance between brackets ('What is essential in language, we shall see, is foreign to the phonic character of the linguistic sign' [p. 21]. 'In its essence it [the linguistic signifier] is not at all phonic' [p. 164]), Saussure, for essential, and essentially metaphysical, reasons had to privilege speech, everything that links the sign to *phonē*. He also speaks of the 'natural link' between thought and voice, meaning and sound (p. 46). He even speaks of 'thought-sound' (p. 156). I have attempted elsewhere to show what is traditional in such a gesture, and to what necessities it submits. In any event, it winds up contradicting the most interesting critical motive of the *Course*, making of linguistics the regulatory model, the 'pattern' for a general semiology of which it was to be, by all rights and theoretically, only a part. The theme of the arbitrary, thus, is turned away from its most fruitful paths (formalization) toward a hierarchizing teleology: 'Thus it can be said that entirely arbitrary signs realize better than any others the ideal of the semiological process; this is why language, the most complex and most widespread of the systems of expression, is also the most characteristic one of them all; in this sense linguistics can become the *general pattern for all semiology*, even though language is only a particular system' (p. 101). One finds exactly the same gesture and the same concepts in Hegel. The contradiction between these two moments of the *Course* is also marked by Saussure's recognizing elsewhere that 'it is not spoken language that is natural to man, but the faculty of constituting a language, that is, a system of distinct signs . . .', that is, the possibility of the *code* and of *articulation*, independent of any substance, for example, phonic substance.

3 The concept of the sign (signifier/signified) carries within itself the necessity of privileging the phonic substance and of setting up linguistics as the 'pattern' for semiology. *Phonē*, in effect, is the signifying substance *given to consciousness* as that which is most intimately tied to the thought of the signified concept. From this point of view, the voice is consciousness itself. When I speak, not only am I conscious also of keeping as close as possible to my thought, or to the 'concept', a signifier that does not fall into the world, a signifier

that I hear as soon as I emit it, that seems to depend upon my pure and free spontaneity, requiring the use of no instrument, no accessory, no force taken from the world. Not only do the signifier and the signified seem to unite, but also, in this confusion, the signifier seems to erase itself or to become transparent, in order to allow the concept to present itself as what it is, referring to nothing other than its presence. The exteriority of the signifier seems reduced. Naturally this experience is a lure, but a lure whose necessity has organized an entire structure, or an entire epoch; and on the grounds of this epoch a semiology has been constituted whose concepts and fundamental presuppositions are quite precisely discernible from Plato to Husserl, passing through Aristotle, Rousseau, Hegel, etc.

4 To reduce the exteriority of the signifier is to exclude everything in semiotic practice that is not psychic. Now, only the privilege accorded to the phonetic and linguistic sign can authorize Saussure's proposition according to which the 'linguistic sign is therefore a two-sided *psychic* entity' (p. 99). Supposing that this proposition has a rigorous sense in and of itself, it is difficult to see how it could be extended to every sign, be it phonetic-linguistic or not. It is difficult to see therefore, except, precisely, by making of the phonetic sign the 'pattern' for all signs, how general semiology can be inscribed in a psychology. However, this is what Saussure does:

> One can thus conceive of a science that would study the life of signs at the heart of social life; it would form a part of social psychology, and consequently of general psychology; we will name it semiology (from the Greek *sēmeion*, 'sign'). It would teach what signs consist of, what laws regulate them. Since it does not yet exist, one cannot say what it will be; but it has a right to exist, its place is determined in advance. Linguistics is only a part of this general science, the laws that semiology will discover will be applicable to linguistics, and the latter will find itself attached to a well defined domain in the set of human facts. It is for the psychologist to determine the exact place of semiology' (p. 33).

Of course modern linguistics and semioticians have not remained with Saussure, or at least with this Saussurean 'psychologism'. The Copenhagen School and all of American linguistics have explicitly criticized it. But if I have insisted on Saussure, it is not only because even those who criticize him recognize him as the founder of general semiology and borrow most of their concepts from him; but above all because one cannot simply criticize the 'psychologistic' usage of the concept of the sign. Psychologism is not the poor usage of a good concept, but is inscribed and prescribed within the concept of the sign itself, in the equivocal manner of which I spoke at the beginning. This equivocality, which weighs upon the model of the sign, marks the 'semiological' project itself and the organic totality of its concepts, in particular that of *communication*, which in effect implies a *transmission charged with making pass, from one subject to another, the identity* of a *signified* object, of a *meaning* or of a *concept* rightfully separable from the process of passage and from the signifying operation. Communication presupposes subjects (whose identity and presence are constituted before the signifying operation) and objects (signified concepts, a thought meaning that the passage of communication will have neither to constitute, nor, by all rights, to transform). *A* communicates *B* to *C*. Through the sign the emitter communicates something to a receptor, etc.

The case of the concept of *structure*, that you also bring up, is certainly more ambiguous. Everything depends upon how one sets it to work. Like the concept of the sign – and therefore of semiology – it can simultaneously confirm and shake logocentric and ethnocentric assuredness. It is not a question of junking these concepts, nor do we have the means to do so. Doubtless it is more necessary, from within semiology, to transform concepts, to displace them, to turn them against their presuppositions, to reinscribe them in other chains, and little by little to modify the terrain of our work and thereby produce new configurations; I do not believe in decisive ruptures, in an unequivocal 'epistemological break', as it is called today. Breaks are always, and fatally, reinscribed in an old cloth that must continually, interminably be undone. This interminability is not an accident or contingency; it is essential, systematic, and theoretical. And this in no way minimizes the necessity and relative importance of certain breaks, of the appearance and definition of new structures . . .

Kristeva: What is the *gram* as a 'new structure of nonpresence'? What is *writing* as *différance*? What rupture do these concepts introduce in relation to the key concepts of semiology – the (phonetic) *sign* and *structure*? How does the notion of *text* replace, in grammatology, the linguistic and semiological notion of what is *enounced*?

Derrida: The reduction of writing – as the reduction of the exteriority of the signifier – was part and parcel of phonologism and logocentrism. We know how Saussure, according to the traditional operation that was also Plato's, Aristotle's, Rousseau's, Hegel's, Husserl's, etc., excludes writing from the field of linguistics – from language and speech – as a phenomenon of exterior representation, both useless and dangerous: 'The linguistic object is not defined by the combination of the written word and the spoken word, the latter alone constituting this object' (p. 45); 'writing is foreign to the internal system [of language]' (p. 44); 'writing veils our view of language: it does not clothe language, but travesties it' (p. 51). The tie of writing to language is 'superficial', 'factitious'. It is 'bizarre' that writing, which should only be an 'image', 'usurps the principal role' and that 'the natural relationship is inversed' (p. 47). Writing is a 'trap', its action is 'vicious' and 'tyrannical', its misdeeds are monstrosities, 'teratological cases', 'linguistics should put them under observation in a special compartment', (p. 54), etc. Naturally, this representativist conception of writing ('Language and writing are two distinct sign systems; the unique *raison d'être* of the second is to *represent* the first' [p. 45]) is linked to the practice of phonetic-alphabetic writing, to which Saussure realizes his study is 'limited' (p. 48). In effect, alphabetical writing seems to present speech, and at the same time to erase itself before speech. Actually, it could be shown, as I have attempted to do, that there is no purely phonetic writing, and that phonologism is less a consequence of the practice of the alphabet in a given culture than a certain ethical or axiological *experience* of this practice. Writing *should* erase itself before the plenitude of living speech, perfectly represented in the transparence of its notation, immediately present for the subject who speaks it, and for the subject who receives its meaning, content, value.

Now, if one ceases to limit oneself to the model of phonetic writing, which we privilege only by ethnocentrism, and if we draw all the consequences from the fact that there is no purely phonetic writing (by reason of the necessary spacing of signs, punctuation, intervals, the differences indispensable for the functioning of graphemes, etc.), then the entire phonologist or logocentrist logic becomes problematical. Its range of legitimacy becomes narrow and superficial. This delimitation, however, is indispensable if one wants to be able to account, with some coherence, for the principle of difference, such as Saussure himself recalls it. This principle compels us not only to privilege one substance – here the phonic, so called temporal, substance – while excluding another – for example, the graphic, so called spatial, substance – but even to consider every process of signification as a formal play of differences. That is, of traces.

Why traces? And by what right do we reintroduce grammatics at the moment when we seem to have neutralized every substance, be it phonic, graphic, or otherwise? Of course it is not a question of resorting to the same concept of writing and of simply inverting the dissymmetry that now has become problematical. It is a question, rather, of producing a new concept of writing. This concept can be called *gram* or *différance*. The play of differences supposes, in effect, syntheses and referrals which forbid at any moment, or in any sense, that a simple element be *present* in and of itself, referring only to itself. Whether in the order of spoken or written discourse, no element can function as a sign without referring to another element which itself is not simply present. This interweaving results in each 'element' – phoneme or grapheme – being constituted on the basis of the trace within it of the other elements of the chain or system. This interweaving, this textile, is the *text* produced only in the transformation of another text. Nothing, neither among the elements nor within the system, is anywhere ever simply present or absent. There are only, everywhere, differences and traces of traces. The gram, then, is the most general concept of semiology – which thus becomes grammatology – and it covers not only the field of writing in the restricted sense, but also the field of linguistics. The advantage of this concept – provided that it be surrounded by a certain interpretive context, for no more than any other conceptual element it does not signify, or suffice, by itself – is that in principle it neutralizes the phonologistic propensity of the 'sign', and *in fact counterbalances* it by liberating the entire scientific field of the 'graphic substance' (history and systems of writing beyond the bounds of the West) whose interest is not minimal, but which so far has been left in the shadows of neglect.

The gram as *différance*, then, is a structure and a movement no longer conceivable on the basis of the opposition presence/absence. *Différance* is the systematic play of differences, of the traces of differences, of the *spacing* by means of which elements are related to each other. This spacing is the simultaneously active and passive (the *a* of *différance* indicates this indecision as concerns activity and passivity, that which cannot be governed by or distributed between the terms of this opposition)[2] production of the intervals without which the 'full' terms would not signify, would not function. It is also the becoming-space of the spoken chain – which has been called temporal or linear; a becoming-space which makes possible both writing and every correspondence between speech and writing, every passage from one to the other.

The activity or productivity connoted by the *a* of *différance* refers to the generative movement in the play of differences. The latter are neither fallen from the sky nor inscribed once and for all in a closed system, a static structure that a synchronic and taxonomic operation could exhaust. Differences are the effects of transformations, and from this vantage the theme of *différance* is incompatible with the static, synchronic, taxonomic, ahistoric motifs in the concept of *structure*. But it goes without saying that this motif is not the only one that defines structure, and that the production of differences, *différance*, is not astructural: it produces systematic and regulated transformations which are able, at a certain point, to leave room for a structural science. The concept of *différance* even develops the most legitimate principled exigencies of 'structuralism'.

Language, and in general every semiotic code – which Saussure defines as 'classifications' – are therefore effects, but their cause is not a subject, a substance, or a being somewhere present and outside the movement of *différance*. Since there is no presence before and outside semiological *différance*, one can extend to the system of signs in general what Saussure says of language: 'Language is necessary for speech to be intelligible and to produce all its effects; but speech is necessary for language to be established; historically, the fact of speech always comes first.' There is a circle here, for if one rigorously distinguishes language and speech, code and message, schema and usage, etc., and if one wishes to do justice to the two postulates thus enunciated, one does not know where to begin, nor how something can begin in general, be it language or speech. Therefore, one has to admit, before any dissociation of language and speech, code and message, etc. (and everything that goes along with such a dissociation), a systematic production of differences, the *production* of a system of differences – a *différance* – within whose effects one eventually, by abstraction and according to determined motivations, will be able to demarcate a linguistics of language and a linguistics of speech, etc.

Nothing – no present and in-*different* being – thus precedes *différance* and spacing. There is no subject who is agent, author, and master of *différance*, who eventually and empirically would be over-taken by *différance*. Subjectivity – like objectivity – is an effect of *différance*, an effect inscribed in a system of *différance*. This is why the *a* of *différance* also recalls that spacing is temporization, the detour and postponement by means of which intuition, perception, consum-mation – in a word, the relationship to the present, the reference to a present reality, to a *being* – are always *deferred*. Deferred by virtue of the very principle of difference which holds that an element func-tions and signifies, takes on or conveys meaning, only by referring to another past or future element in an economy of traces. This economic aspect of *différance*, which brings into play a certain not conscious calculation in a field of forces, is inseparable from the more narrowly semiotic aspect of *différance*. It confirms that the subject, and first of all the conscious and speaking subject, depends upon the system of differences and the movement of *différance*, that the subject is not present, nor above all present to itself before *différance*, that the subject is constituted only in being divided from itself, in becoming space, in temporizing, in deferral; and it confirms that, as Saussure said, 'language [which consists only of differences] is not a function of the speaking subject.' At the point at which the concept of *différance*, and the chain attached to it, intervenes, all the conceptual oppositions of metaphysics (signifier/signified; sensible/intelligible; writing/speech; passivity/activity; etc.) – to the extent that they ulti-mately refer to the presence of something present (for example, in the form of the identity of the subject who is present for all his oper-ations, present beneath every accident or event, self-present objects and acts of its language, etc.) – become nonpertinent. They all amount, at one moment or another, to a subordination of the moment of *différance* in favor of the presence of a value or a *meaning* suppos-edly antecedent to *différance*, more original than it, exceeding and governing it in the last analysis. This is still the presence of what we called above the 'transcendental signified'.

Kristeva: It is said that the concept of 'meaning' in semiotics is markedly different from the phenomenological concept of 'meaning'. In what ways, however, are they complicit, and to what extent does the semiological project remain intrametaphysical?

Derrida: It is true that at first the phenomenological extension of the concept of 'meaning' appears much wider, much less determined.

All experience is the experience of meaning (*Sinn*). Everything that appears to consciousness, everything that is for consciousness in general, is *meaning*. Meaning is the phenomenality of the phenomenon. In the *Logical Researches* Husserl rejected Frege's distinction between *Sinn* and *Bedeutung*. Later this distinction seemed useful to him, not that he understood it as did Frege, but in order to mark the dividing line between meaning in its most general extention (*Sinn*) and meaning as an object of logical or linguistic enunciation, meaning as signification (*Bedeutung*). It is at this point that the complicity to which you allude may appear. Thus, for example:

1 Husserl, in order to isolate meaning (*Sinn* or *Bedeutung*) from enunciation or from the intention of signification (*Bedeutungs-intention*) that 'animates' enunciation, needs to distinguish rigorously between the signifying (sensible) aspect, whose originality he recognizes, but which he excludes from his logico-grammatical problematic, and the aspect of signified meaning (which is intelligible, ideal, 'spiritual'). Perhaps we had best cite a passage from *ideas* here:

> Let us start from the familiar distinction between the sensory, the so to speak bodily aspect of expression, and its nonsensory 'mental' aspect. There is no need for us to enter more closely into the discussion of the first aspect, nor upon the way of uniting the two aspects, though we clearly have title-headings here indicated for phenomenological problems that are not unimportant. We restrict our glance exclusively to 'meaning' [*Bedeutung*], and 'meaning something' [*Bedeuten*]. Originally these words relate only to the sphere of speech [*sprachliche Sphäre*], that of 'expression' [*des Ausdruckens*]. But it is almost inevitable, and at the same time an important step for knowledge, to extend the meaning of these words, and to modify them suitably so that they may be applied in a certain way to the whole noetico-noematic sphere, to all acts, therefore, whether these are interwoven [*verflochten*] with expression acts or not. With this in view we ourselves, when referring to any intentional experiences, have spoken all along of *Sinn* [sense], a word which is generally used as an equivalent for '*Bedeutung*' [meaning]. We propose in the interests of distinctness to favour the word *Bedeutung* (meaning at the conceptual level) when referring to the old concept, and more particularly in the complex speech-form

'logical' or *'expressing'* *meaning.* We use the word *Sinn* [sense or meaning *simpliciter*] in the future, as before, in its more embracing breadth of applications.

(Husserl 1931 p. 319)

Thus, whether or not it is 'signified' or 'expressed', whether or not it is 'interwoven' with a process of signification, 'meaning' is an intelligible or spiritual *ideality* which eventually can be united to the sensible aspects of a signifier that in itself it does not need. Its presence, meaning, or essence of meaning, is conceivable outside this interweaving as soon as the phenomenologist, like the semiotician, allegedly refers to a pure unity, a rigorously identifiable aspect of meaning or of the signified.

2 This layer of pure meaning, or a pure signified, refers, explicitly to Husserl and at least implicitly in semiotic practice, to a layer of prelinguistic or presemiotic (preexpressive, Husserl calls it) meaning whose presence would be conceivable outside and before the work of *différance*, outside and before the process or system of signification. The latter would only bring meaning to light, translate it, transport it, communicate it, incarnate it, express it, etc. Such a meaning – which in either case is phenomenological meaning, and, in the last analysis, that which originally is given to consciousness in perceptive intuition – would not be, from the outset, in the position of a signifier, would not be inscribed in the relational and differential tissue which would make of it, from the outset, a referral, a trace, a gram, a spacing. It could be shown that metaphysics has always consisted in attempting to uproot the presence of meaning, in whatever guise, from *différance*; and every time that a region or layer of pure meaning or a pure signified is allegedly rigorously delineated or isolated this gesture is repeated. And how could semiotics, as such, *simply* dispense with any recourse to the identity of the signified? The relationship between meaning and sign, or between the signified and the signifier, then becomes one of *exteriority*: or better, as in Husserl, the latter becomes the exteriorization (*Äusserung*) or the expression (*Ausdruck*) of the former. Language is determined as expression – the expulsion of the intimacy of an inside – and we return to all the difficulties and presuppositions we were just speaking of concerning Saussure. I have attempted to indicated elsewhere the consequences that link all of phenomenology to this privilege of *expression*, to the exclusion of 'indication' from the sphere

of pure language (of the 'logicity' of language), and to the privilege necessarily accorded to the voice, etc. This privilege was already at work in the *Logical Researches*, in the remarkable project of a 'purely logical grammar' that is more important and more rigorous than all the projects of a 'general reasoned grammar' of seventeenth- and eighteenth-century France, projects that certain modern linguists refer to, however.

Kristeva: If language is always 'expression', and if its closure is thereby demonstrated, to what extent, and by means of what kind of practice, could this expressivity be surpassed? To what extent would nonexpressivity signify? Would not grammatology be a nonexpressive 'semiology' based on logical-mathematical notation rather than on linguistic notation?

Derrida: I am tempted to respond in an apparently contradictory way. *On the one hand*, expressivism is never simply surpassable, because it is impossible to reduce the couple outside/inside as a simple structure of opposition. This couple is an effect of *différance*, as is the effect of language that impels language to represent itself as expressive re-presentation, a translation on the outside of what was constituted inside. The representation of language as 'expression' is not an accidental prejudice, but rather a kind of structural lure, what Kant would have called a transcendental illusion. The latter is modified according to the language, the era, the culture. Doubtless Western metaphysics constitutes a powerful systematization of this illusion, but I believe that it would be an imprudent overstatement to assert that Western metaphysics alone does so. *On the other hand*, and inversely, I would say that if expressivism is not *simply and once and for all* surpassable, expressivity is in fact always already surpassed, whether one wishes it or not, whether one knows it or not. In the extent to which what is called 'meaning' (to be 'expressed') is already, and thoroughly, constituted by a tissue of differences, in the extent to which there is already a *text*, a network of textual referral to *other* texts, a textual transformation in which each allegedly 'simple term' is marked by the trace of another term, the presumed interiority of meaning is already worked upon by its own exteriority. It is always already carried outside itself. It already differs (from itself) before any act of expression. And only on this condition can it constitute a syntagm or text. Only on this condition can it 'signify'. From this point of view, perhaps, we would not have to ask to what extent nonexpressivity could signify. Only nonexpressivity can signify, because in all rigor there is no signification unless there is synthesis, syntagm, *différance*, and text. And the notion of text, conceived with all its implications, is incompatible with the unequivocal notion of expression. Of course, when one says that only the text signifies, one already has transformed the values of signifying and sign. For if one understands the sign in its most severe classical closure, one would have to say the opposite: signification is expression; the text, which expresses nothing, is insignificant, etc. Grammatology, as the science of textuality, then would be a nonexpressive semiology only on the condition of transforming the concept of sign and of uprooting it from its congenital expressivism.

The last part of your question is even more difficult. It is clear that the reticence, that is, the resistance to logical-mathematical notation has always been the signature of logocentrism and phonologism in the event to which they have dominated metaphysics and the classical semiological and linguistic projects. The critique of nonphonetic mathematical writing (for example, Leibniz's 'characteristic') in Rousseau, Hegel, etc., recurs in a nonfortuitous manner in Saussure, for whom it coincides with a stated preference for natural languages (see Saussure 1916 p. 57). A grammatology that would break with this system of presuppositions, then, must in effect liberate the mathematization of language, and must also declare that 'the practice of science in fact has never ceased to protest the imperialism of the *Logos*, for example by calling upon, from all time, and more and more, nonphonetic writing' (see Derrida 1967 p. 12). Everything that has always linked *logos* to *phonē* has been limited by mathematics, whose progress is in absolute solidarity with the practice of a nonphonetic inscription. About these 'grammatological' principles and tasks there is no possible doubt, I believe. But the extension of mathematical notation, and in general the formalization of writing, must be very slow and very prudent, at least if one wishes it to take over *effectively* the domains from which it has been excluded so far. It seems to me that critical work on 'natural' languages by means of 'natural' languages, an entire internal transformation of classical notation, a systematic practice of exchanges between 'natural' languages and writing should prepare and accompany such a formalization. An infinite task, for it always will be impossible, and for essential reasons, to reduce absolutely the natural languages and nonmathematical notation. We must also be wary of the 'naive' side of formalism and mathematism, one of whose secondary functions in metaphysics, let us not forget, has been to complete and confirm the logocentric theology which they otherwise could context. Thus in Leibniz the project of a universal, mathematical, and nonphonetic characteristic is inseparable form a metaphysics of the simple, and hence from the existence of divine understanding,[3] the divine *logos*.

The effective progress of mathematical notation thus goes along with the deconstruction of metaphysics, with the profound renewal of mathematics itself, and the concept of science of which mathematics has always been the model.

Kristeva: The putting into question of the sign being a putting into question of scientificity, to what extent is or is not grammatology a 'science'? Do you consider certain semiotic works close to the grammatological project, and if, so which ones?

Derrida: Grammatology must deconstruct everything that ties the concept and norms of scientificity to ontotheology, logocentrism, phonologism. This is an immense and interminable work that must ceaselessly avoid letting the transgression of the classical project of science fall back into a prescientific empiricism. This supposes a kind of *double register* in grammatological practice: it must simultaneously go beyond metaphysical positivism and scientism, and accentuate whatever in the effective work of science contributes to freeing it of the metaphysical bonds that have borne on its definition and its movement since its beginnings. Grammatology must pursue and consolidate whatever, in scientific practice, has always already begun to exceed the logocentric closure. This is why there is no simple answer to the question of whether grammatology is a 'science'. In a word, I would say that it *inscribes* and *delimits* science; it must freely and rigorously make the norms of science function in its own writing; once again, it *marks* and at the same time *loosens* the limit which closes classical scientificity.

For the same reason, there is no *scientific* semiotic work that does not serve grammatology. And it will always be possible to turn against the metaphysical presuppositions of a semiotic discourse the grammatological motifs which science produces in semiotics. It is on the basis of the formalist and differential motif present in Saussure's *Cours* that the psychologism, phonologism and exclusion of writing that are no less present in it can be criticized. Similarly, in Hjelmslev's glossematics, if one drew all the consequences of the critique of Saussure's psychologism, the neutralization of expressive substances

– and therefore of phonologism – the 'structuralism', 'immanentism', the critique of metaphysics, the thematics of play, etc., then one would be able to exclude an entire metaphysical conceptuality that is naively utilized (the couple expression/content in the tradition of the couple signifier/signified; the opposition form/substance applied to each of the two preceding terms; the 'empirical principle', etc.: see Derrida 1967 pp. 83 ff.). One can say *a priori* that in every proposition or in every system of semiotic research – and you could cite the most current examples better than I – metaphysical presuppositions coexist with critical motifs. And this by the simple fact that up to a certain point they inhabit the same language. Doubtless, grammatology is less another science, a new discipline charged with a new content or new domain, than the vigilant practice of this textual division.

NOTES

1 That is, the intelligible. The difference between the signifier and the signified has always reproduced the difference between the sensible and the intelligible. And it does so no less in the twentieth century than in its stoic origins. 'Modern structuralist thought has clearly established this: language is a system of signs, and linguistics is an integral part of the science of signs, *semiotics* (or to use Saussure's terms, *semiology*). The medieval definition – *aliquid stat pro aliquo* – resuscitated by our epoch has shown itself to be still valid and fruitful. Thereby, the constitutive mark of every sign in general, of the linguistic sign in particular, resides in its double character: every linguistic unit is bipartite, and comports two aspects: one sensible and the other intelligible – on the one hand, the *signans* (Saussure's *signifier*), and on the other, the *signatum* (the *signified*)' (Jakobson 1963 p. 162).
2 In other words, *différance* combines and confuses 'differing' and 'deferring' in both their active and passive sense (Alan Bass, trans.).
3 'But for now it suffices to remark that the foundation of any characteristic is also that of the demonstration of God's existence; for simple thoughts are the elements of the characteristic, and simple forms are the source of things. Now, I maintain that all simple forms are compatible with each other. This is a proposition whose demonstration I could not well give without explaining at length the foundations of the characteristic. But if it is granted, it follows that the nature of God, which encloses all simple forms taken absolutely, is possible. Now, we proved above that God is, provided that he is possible. Therefore, he exists. Q.E.D.' (Letter to Princess Elizabeth, 1678).

16 Brian Torode

Textuality, sexuality, economy

VOLOŠINOV'S SOCIOLOGY OF SPEECHES

Vološinov's connections with the themes of our argument are indicated by noting his discussion of Saussure's approach.[1] He states that at the time of writing, 'the majority of Russian thinkers in linguistics are under the determinative influence of Saussure and his disciples' (1973 pp. 58–59). Vološinov formulates Saussure's main thesis as being, that 'language stands in opposition to utterance in the same way as does that which is social to that which is individual'. Therefore:

> Linguistics, as Saussure conceives it, cannot have the utterance as the object of study. What constitutes the linguistic element in the utterance are the normatively identical forms of language present in it. Everything else is 'accessory and random'.
>
> (Vološinov 1973 p. 60)

Saussure, in line with 'the sociological school of Durkheim', would 'decisively cast aside' the 'individual act of speaking, the utterance (*parole*)'. This discarded element, however, makes its reappearance in the history of language which 'is dominated by the "utterance" with its individuality and randomness'. Consequently, in a move of Saussure's which Vološinov finds characteristic of this 'abstract objectivism', history must be excluded 'as an irrational force distorting the logical purity of the language system' (ibid. p. 61).

Vološinov opposes himself as rigorously to the 'individualistic subjectivism' which would regard language as 'an ever-flowing stream of speech-acts in which nothing remains fixed and identical to itself' (ibid. p. 52). Objectivism and subjectivism both preserve the mystical notion of the uniqueness of the utterance, the first to denigrate it, the second to celebrate it. But for Vološinov, 'the individual utterance is by no means an individual fact not susceptible to sociological analysis by virtue of its individuality'. Against objectivism it must be insisted that 'individual utterances are what constitute the actual, concrete, reality of language, and . . . that they do have creative value in language'. But with objectivism it must be affirmed that 'the structure of the utterance . . . is a social structure'. Vološinov asserts (ibid. pp. 93–94) that 'the stylistic shaping of an utterance is shaping of a social kind, and the very verbal stream of utterances, which is what the reality of language actually amounts to, is a social stream'. We turn now to the distinctive account of the 'social structure' of the utterance which Vološinov elaborates.

The statement that 'any utterance, no matter how weighty and complete in and of itself, is only a moment in the continuous process of verbal communication' (ibid. p. 95) is unexceptional enough. But Vološinov draws from it a rigorous method for the interrogation of the utterance which is new. The utterance has no complete meaning in itself, for it is necessarily a response to previous utterances. The utterance is monologic only in appearance. In reality it is the product and continuation of dialogue. 'Any true understanding is dialogic in nature' (ibid. p. 102). But this dialogic nature is extremely elusive: the utterance itself invites consideration as a united whole. Vološinov proceeds, therefore, to focus attention on a kind of utterance which explicitly addresses the relation between utterances, namely reported speech.

Reported speech comprises 'the syntactic patterns . . . . the modifications of those patterns and the variants of those modifications, which we find in a language for the reporting of other people's utterances, and for incorporating those utterances, as the utterances of others, into a bound, monologic context' (ibid. p. 112). It is speech within speech, utterance within utterance, and at the same time also speech about speech, utterance about utterance (ibid. p. 115). It is therefore proposed 'to take the phenomenon of reported speech and postulate it as a problem from a sociological orientation', and on this basis 'to map out the sociological method in linguistics' (ibid. p. 113).

Vološinov's statement of this method is worth quoting at length: 'The productive study of dialogue presupposes . . . a more profound investigation of the forms used in reported speech, since these forms reflect basic and constant tendencies in the active reception of other speakers' speech':

> What we have in the forms of reported speech is precisely an objective document of this reception. Once we have learned to decipher it, this document provides us with information, not about accidental and mercurial subjective psychological processes in the 'soul' of the recipient, but about steadfast social tendencies in an active reception of other speakers' speech, tendencies that have crystallized into language forms.
>
> (ibid. p. 117)

In a passage which itself involves more than a trace of the Durkheimianism for which he criticized Saussure, he continues

> The mechanism of this process is located, not in the individual soul, but in society. It is the function of society to select and make grammatical (adapt to the grammatical structure of its language) just those factors in the active and evaluative reception of utterances that are socially vital and constant, and, hence, are grounded in the economic existence of the particular community of speakers.
>
> (ibid. p. 117)

In our view, the deciphering of the forms of reported speech as exemplifying steadfast social tendencies in the reception of other speakers' speech must be sharply distinguished from the documentary method interpretation of these tendencies in terms of functions of society and the grammatical structure of language. Vološinov only incompletely articulates the distinction between his approach and that of classical sociology. The distinction becomes clearer when we turn from these theoretical prognostications to consider an example of Vološinov's method of decipherment in practice.

The method is demonstrated in an examination of reported speech in the literary text. Here, Vološinov points out, it is used in particular to mark the relation between the authorial context on the one hand, and the reported speech of the characters on the other. Historically, this relation has taken three characteristic forms. In the first, a rigid separation is made between the speeches. Author's speech has its precise style, and that of the characters is in each case clearly distinct from it and from that of other characters. No attempt is made to reformulate one in terms of another. Although it superficially preserves the individuality of each speaker, Vološinov finds this to be an authoritarian and dogmatic organization of the dialogue, since all other characters appear only within the context defined by the author's speech, with which the text opens and to which it returns. It is characteristic, for example, of the Middle French writings of the seventeenth century.

A second possibility is one 'in which the dynamism of the interorientation between reporting and reported speech moves are exactly opposite in nature' (ibid. p. 120). Here,

> language devises means for infiltrating reported speech with authorial retort and commentary in deft and subtle ways. The reporting context strives to break down the self-contained compactness of the reported speech, to resolve it, to obliterate its boundaries.
>
> (ibid. p. 120)

This style, found by Vološinov to characterize 'the Renaissance (especially in the French language), the end of the eighteenth century and virtually the entire nineteenth century', breaks down authoritarian dogmatism, and exhibits instead 'a relativism supplying extremely favourable grounds for a positive and sensitive reception of all individualized verbal nuances of thought, belief, feeling (ibid. p. 121). This individualism, though playfully pitting one speech against another, none the less preserves the integrity of each though without the unambiguous hierarchy asserted by the first style.

More recently, particularly in the late-nineteenth century writers of Russia, Vološinov discovers a mode of writing which calls into question both the integrity of the speech of the 'characters' which it reports, and also 'it's' own authority to speak. In this style

> the verbal dominant may shift to the reported speech, which in that case becomes more forceful and more active than the authorial context framing it. This time the reported speech begins to resolve, as it were, the reporting context, instead of the other way around. The authorial context loses the greater objectivity it normally commands in comparison with reported speech.
>
> (ibid. p. 121)

In this case, the narrator's speech can become 'just as individualized, colourful, and non-authoritative as is the speech of the characters' (ibid. p. 121). Here, as he later puts it, 'we perceive the author's accents and intonations being interrupted by the . . . value judgements of another person' (ibid. p. 155).

It is this third mode of writing the relation between speeches which particularly interests both Vološinov and ourselves. He finds it expressed in a distinctive mode of direct speech, which he calls quasi-direct discourse, in which narrator's and character's speeches interfere to the extent that it is impossible to unambiguously determine which is at work in a particular word. In this case there is a double sense in which the authoritarian context of the text has been overthrown. The 'narrator' has become a character within the text, unable to stand back from it. But further, no such standing back is now possible. The unresolvably problematic character of the text defies the attempt to sum up in a single speech the interplay of speeches within it.

Vološinov draws attention to a striking implication of this problematicity. It is impossible to read such a text out loud with accuracy in the spoken voice. In the authoritarian text it is not difficult for the reader (say, the author himself) to adopt a distinctive style of speech, facial expression, gesticulation, for each of the roles he is to perform, including his own. Indeed if he reads his own part straightforwardly then the authority of his own speech will be enhanced by the more or less artificial ways in which he less successfully mimics others. In the relativistic text, the task of reading is more complex, but none the less clear-cut. It amounts to the performance of a number of characters, including that of the author, with equal vigour and plausibility. Here unlike the first case a degree of theatrical skill is required: a bad performance of any role will falsify it and so damage the text as a whole.

But to read the anti-authoritarian text is necessarily to falsify it. Insofar as the reader-author, by style of speech, facial expression, or gesture either identifies together two instances of discourse, or distinguishes two instances of discourse, then he resolves in speech what was written to be irresolvable. Vološinov concludes

> From all this, it necessarily follows that the absolute acting out of reported speech, where a work of fiction is read aloud, is admissible only in the rarest cases. Otherwise an inevitable conflict arises with the basic aesthetic design of the context.
>
> (ibid. p. 157)

Thus the writer who asserted earlier that 'the very verbal stream of utterances . . . is what the reality of language actually amounts to' has reached the surprising conclusion that what this reality actually amounts to is necessarily misrepresented by its verbal performance. The real relations which this performance conceals can be grasped only when language is examined as writing. This conclusion has implications going beyond the significance of the literary text. Speech generally misrepresents itself. The dialogic relations between speeches, exemplifying steadfast social tendencies, which Vološinov wants to make the object of his sociological method in linguistics are not directly visible as the relations between one utterance and another. Contradictory tendencies within the utterance and problematic relations between utterances make it necessary to define a new level of analysis. We refer to 'voices' as the speech unities which interplay, in the fashion which Vološinov admirably describes, in both the spoken and written word. Within a particular discourse the number of voices at work will not be arbitrary, nor will the modes of relationship between them.

We have elsewhere identified the 'appearance'/'reality' relation as a particularly crucial mode of relationship between voices, and it is one which precisely accounts for the examples which Vološinov has presented. In the classical text, characters in diverse voices articulate the varied appearances of the world to them, but only in the context of the single reality articulated by the narrators' voice. Authoritarian dogmatism arises in this situation, where every voice is re-interpreted by the voice of the author.

In the relativist text, the ability to re-interpret other voices is generalized from that of the author to all voices. A cacophony of competing claims is heard, but finally each acknowledges the independence of the other, in exchange for the assurance of its own. For each, its own voice is the single reality: the very multiplicity of the others confirm their merely apparent status.

In the anti-authoritarian text the claimed integrity of the voice is undermined. A play which can no longer be recognized as the cut and thrust of competing voices is at work. In the mutual interruption of one voice by another what is in question is no longer the insistent re-assertion by each of its own version of 'reality' underlying the 'appearance' presented by the other, but rather the practices whereby the relation between 'appearance' and 'reality' is constituted in either. This play is fundamentally textual rather than vocal in character. It is the play which Jacques Derrida has identified as the play of 'différance'.[2]

DERRIDA'S 'DIFFÉRANCE'

The problematic character of the spoken voice in its relation to the written text is a sustained theme of Derrida's writings: we can regard his discussion as building on the point which Vološinov's has reached.[3]

For us, textuality is the interplay of voices which constitute 'appearance' and 'reality' in discourse, spoken or written, an interplay however which is fundamentally disguised in speech, with the possibility of becoming apparent only in writing. Derrida calls this interplay *différance*.[4] The name is specifically chosen so that in speech it is audible: when the word is read aloud (in French), it sounds the same as 'difference'. Only in writing can *différance* appear.

Derrida draws attention to the fact that *différance* has two aspects. It is a temporal deferral of the moment when 'appearance' and 'reality', initially differentiated, will be brought into correspondence. It is equally a spatial-ontological deference of 'appearance' to the 'reality' which does not appear.

The text as traditionally understood involves a play of *différance* which is limited in scope, i.e. closed. The text opens with a gap between 'appearance' and 'reality', which is resolved in the course of the narrative, so that ultimately the difference is abolished. Typically, the text initially portrays diverse characters, each able to formulate a different 'appearance' of the world in which the tale is located. Through the unfolding of a plot, which may be simple or complex, the different appearances clash and contradict. Finally, the course of events produces a single 'reality', apparent equally to all. So understood, the text is a site of interaction in the course of which many distinct subjectivities come to recognize themselves in a single objectivity which is thus intersubjective.[5]

From the social-psychological point of view, the interpretation of the text focuses upon the 'subjects' and 'objects' constituted by the text. But Derrida shifts attention to the gap within the text which constitutes them. The text produces and consumes *différance*. The play of the text thus has two aspects. Derrida locates the first as *economic*. It arises from the temporal deferring aspect of *différance*, which constitutes the time of the text. He locates the second as *sexual*. It arises from the spatial-ontological deferring aspect of *différance*, which constitutes the pleasure of the text.

From the social psychological point of view, the text reiterates the recognition of subjectivity in intersubjective objectivity. It is necessarily closed because the functioning of the society as a whole depends upon this recognition. The text is thus necessary to society, and society to the text. A significant aspect of this necessity is that the play of *différance* should be closed: indeed it is the function of the social psychological text to close it.

But, Derrida points out, the text as the play of *différance* is not necessary to society. The non-necessity of *différance* has itself two aspects. From the temporal point of view, 'appearance' and 'reality' are ultimately identical. In this sense the time of the text is an economic surplus over what is necessary. From the spatial-ontological point of view, 'appearance' and 'reality' are ultimately different: 'reality' need never 'appear' at all. In this sense the pleasure of the text is a surplus over what is necessary.

The textual play of *différance* thus transcends the necessary closure of social-psychological recognition. The *différance* between 'appearance' and 'reality' is always already in play, and thus so are sexuality and economy, which transcend and threaten the functional needs of 'subjectivity' and 'intersubjectivity' respectively.

The text must then be re-read, against social psychological interpretation. In our terms, its play of *différance* must be interrupted. This interruption is a political intervention in the text, for the existence of *différance* is systematically denied by the upholders of the status quo, who reduce it to the 'psychological' and 'sociological' facets of a single smooth working consensual whole.

Two reductions are the butt of Derrida's particular criticism. The first, of speech to thought, is epitomized by the writing of Husserl. It is articulated in a short passage of thirty pages of his early *Logical Investigations* (1970 pp. 268–298). This attempts to displace language, for once and for all, from any claim to centrality as object of phenomenological investigation. Derrida finds in Husserl's appeal to soliloquy an 'autoaffection' which is fundamentally erotic in character. The pleasure of hearing one's own voice is non-necessary and thus capable of a pure intensity which is given expression by Husserl in his account of the ego.[6] Derrida's interrogation of Husserl is thus able to demonstrate, through the latter's writing (itself ostensibly anti-psychological), the sexual and differential character of what passes for self-same and psychological identity (Derrida 1973 *passim*).

The second, from writing to speech, is epitomized by the writing of Saussure, for whom this theme expresses directly – though as Derrida shows, in contradictory fashion – the thesis of the arbitrariness of the sign. For Saussure writing stands to speech as signifier to the signified. To give writing priority over speech is to value the signifier over the signified. This is precisely what Derrida, reading Saussure against himself, proposes to do. Following an identification which is explicit in Saussure himself, Derrida finds the establishment of the signifier–signified relation within language, in the absence of any natural identification, to be an operation which is fundamentally economic in character. The surplus of the signified over the signifier is non-natural and is the transformatory force of writing which Saussure himself reveals but tries to suppress in his drive to sociologize the establishment of what he calls value (Derrida 1976 *passim* but esp. pt I, ch. 2).

The sexual is thus the relation between voice and voice viewed from the standpoint of underlying difference where the economic is the relation between voice and voice viewed from the standpoint of underlying sameness. Derrida shows that these identifications, and the origin of the two reductions which cover them over, can each be derived from the writings of Jean-Jacques Rousseau, the eighteenth-century antecedent of both Saussure and Husserl. A scenario, presented by Rousseau as the 'origin of languages' illustrates these relations

> In the arid places where water could be had only from wells, people had to rejoin one another to sink the wells, or at least to agree upon their use. Such must have been the origin of societies and languages in warm countries.
>
> This is where the first ties were formed among families: there were the first rendezvous of the two sexes. Girls would come to seek water for the household, young men would come to water their herds. Their eyes, accustomed to the same sights since infancy, began to see with increased pleasure. The heart is moved by these novel objects; an unknown attraction renders it less savage; it feels pleasure at not being alone. Imperceptibly, water becomes more necessary. The livestock become thirsty more often. One would arrive in haste, and leave with regret. In that happy age when nothing marked the hours, nothing would oblige one to count them; the only measure of time would be the alteration

of amusement and boredom. Under old oaks, conquerors of the years, an ardent youth will gradually lose its ferocity. Little by little, they become less shy with each other. In trying to make oneself understood, one learns to explain oneself. There too original festivals developed. Feet skipped with joy, earnest gestures no longer sufficed, the voice accompanied them in impassioned accents: pleasure and desire mingled and were felt together. There at last was the true cradle of nations: from the pure crystal of the fountains, flowed the first fires of love.

> (Rousseau, quoted in Derrida 1976 p. 262)

Rousseau's text accounts for the origin of the voice in terms of an economically necessary encounter out of which a non-necessary pleasure is soon produced. Economy expresses the sameness between the practices of girls and boys: each must seek water and in so doing enter into relations with others different from themselves, unfamiliar to those 'accustomed to the same sights from infancy'. Pleasure arises out of the contemplation of this difference in its own right, an activity which is strictly non-necessary. The cultivation of this pleasure itself influences the temporality, that is the economy, of the encounter: the time made available for it is extended little by little.

But Rousseau's idyllic picture harmonizes the *différance* which it glimpses. The pursuit of pleasure precisely matches the economic surplus which allows for it: the result is a situation free of conflict and process. Derrida writes

What Rousseau describes here is neither the eve of society nor society already formed, but the movement of a birth, the continuous advent of presence. None of the oppositions of determined predicates can be applied clearly to what, between the state of nature and the state of society, is not a state but a passage which should have continued and lasted.

> (Derrida 1976 pp. 262–263)

The 'origin' is not a single moment in the distant past to which we can now only look back nostalgically. Rather, the textual, sexual, and economic work of originary *différance*, 'between the state of nature and the state of society', is always already in play. It is possible to re-open this play if we are able to interrupt the interpretations dedicated to closing it.

Derrida's practice of writing advances upon Vološinov's in a crucial respect. Although identifying and welcoming the over-throwing of the authoritarian voice, Vološinov himself practised it. For him the distinction between the classical 'objectivist' and 'subjectivist' texts and the contemporary texts which we could call 'materialist' was objective. But for Derrida, it is a textual distinction: it depends on the way in which we read these texts.

The classical text wants to be read as necessarily and safely closed, as successfully voicing subjective integrity. But we have to interrupt this closure to reveal the play of non-necessary and dangerous openness. In an attempt to demonstrate this practice, we turn now to read a classical text which, like Rousseau's, portrays a passage 'between the state of nature and the state of society'. Charles Perrault's *Little Red Riding Hood* (1975) is such a tale. We will present two readings of the story, in order to exemplify the two ways in which texts may be treated. The first is the social-psychological way which acknowledges itself as an interpretation of the text. The second, we shall argue, is a materialist interruption of the text.

Here it is not simply a matter of comparing two philosophical positions each of which upholds the text as an exemplification of itself. If this were so, then the text would be irrelevant. Rather, we claim that the interpretation can only read the text as an illustration of the idea which it brings to the text. Instead interruption is open to the play of the text itself.[7]

READING LITTLE RED RIDING HOOD

In his paper called 'Little Red Riding Hood's Metacommentary', Victor Larrucia states that his own concerns are at the 'peculiar inter-face between meaning and behaviour'. His approach (1975 p. 518), 'while acknowledging the prime significance of historical and social context, aims at the processes involved in communication itself in order to see the text as a message in circuit.' He explains that 'while the approach is basically centred on the text, it views the text only in terms of a communication process, and meaning here is seen as a constituent, not of the message, but rather of the process'. The approach 'requires two essential tools: one for decoding the text, the other for relating the decoded text to the communication process'. These essential tools he finds respectively in the structuralist analysis of myth by Claude Lévi-Strauss (1977) and in the pragmatic analysis of communication by Paul Watzlawick *et al.* (1968).

It will be argued here that Larrucia's approach is necessarily eclectic. His eclecticism arises from the attempt to reconcile two aspects of a supposedly total situation: a message and a communication process in which it circulates. It will be shown that this approach reduces the 'message' (here the text of the story) to a presupposed version of the 'process' (here the Europe of the late seventeenth century in which the story was produced). By contrast, it will be proposed that a text or message itself sufficiently constitutes the sense of the communicational context within which it circulates. Our interruption of the story will concern itself with the precise character of this context.

From Watzlawick *et al.*, Larrucia (1975) draws the assumption that, 'all messages have two aspects, a command and a report, the first being a message about the nature of the relationship between sender and receiver, the second the message of content' (p. 520). These two 'functions' can work 'conjunctively or disjunctively' (pp. 521–522). 'There is normally no problem . . . if there is a conjunctive operation.' But, problems arise when the ostensible *report* (p. 522): 'which might select one set of possibilities for role behaviour, is negated by the relationship established in the command aspect of the message.' This, he writes 'is the essential ingredient for a power struggle':

> Theoretically, this notion of power struggle derives from Gregory Bateson's idea of paradoxical injunction – double bind – wherein a message, through the very nature of a communicational process, creates an untenable behavioural situation: an example of this is 'Be spontaneous!', which denies the possibility for the receiver of acting spontaneously at the very instant it requires of the receiver spontaneous action.
>
> (Larrucia 1975 p. 522)

Larrucia proposes that 'this process holds at both "societal" and "individual" levels'. This enables him to reconcile the Watzlawick-Bateson theory of sender–recipient relations with Lévi-Strauss's account of the cultural significance of myth:

> As Lévi-Strauss says, 'Although experience contradicts theory, social life validates cosmology by its similarity of structure. Hence

cosmology is true'. Lévi-Strauss' use of the term 'contradiction' is equivalent to my use of the term 'paradox', that is, some logical inconsistency in the way members of a group relate to one another can neither be resolved without changing the fundamental structure of the group ... nor spoken of. We might say this paradox is the 'blindspot' for the group, the blindspot which generates social communication for the vision peculiar to the group.

Larrucia's reading of 'Red Riding Hood' proceeds by first examining the report aspect of the tale, employing Lévi-Strauss's notion of 'contradiction', and secondly examining its command aspect, employing the Watzlawick-Bateson notion of 'paradoxical injunction'.

The notion of a power struggle around the meaning of the text is intriguing. But Larrucia conceives it as occurring between the text itself (the report) and a meta-statement attached to the text (the command). Thus he is concerned with struggle between the text and something other than the text (another text). He sees the relation between these (texts) as either one of consistency (conjunction) or contradiction (disjunction). The reading attempted here, by contrast, will search for relations of struggle within and intrinsic to the text itself.

INTERPRETING MORALITY

Larrucia's Lévi-Straussian analysis re-writes the story in terms of units, each represented by a sentence, which when read from left to right and down the page tell the tale sequentially (diachronically), but which when read as contrasting pairs of vertical columns reveal the synchronic structure of contradictions which is the unconscious meaning of the tale.[8] The result is as follows:

Column 1	Column 2	Column 3	Column 4
1 Grandmother's illness causes mother to make Grandmother food	2 Little Red Riding Hood (LRRH) obeys mother and goes off to woods	3 LRRH meets (Wolf as) friend and talks	

Column 1	Column 2	Column 3	Column 4
4 Woodcutter's presence causes Wolf to speak to LRRH	5 LRRH obeys Wolf and takes long road to Grandmother's	6 Grandmother admits (Wolf as) LRRH	7 Wolf eats Grandmother
		8 LRRH meets (Wolf as) Grandmother	
	9 LRRH obeys Grandmother and gets into bed	10 LRRH questions (Wolf as) Grandmother	11 Wolf eats LRRH

(Larrucia 1975 p. 528)

Here,

> the first column involves mediated relationships, mediation being based on a sign (illness, . . . presence . . .): here the signs are recognized. In the second column are . . . relationships . . . where mediation is not based on a sign: here the sign is [*sic*] not recognized as signs. The third column contains . . . disguised relationship; . . . the sign disguises a real relationship. The last column involves direct relationships which are not disguised and which involve no sign.

(Larrucia 1975 p. 528)

Larrucia states that the first two columns represent respectively the over-rating and under-rating of mediated relationships. (Over-rating arises because no message was received from either Grandmother or Woodcutter; under-rating because 'no demands for exchange are made'.) The last two columns represent respectively the under-rating and over-rating of direct relations. (Under-rating arises because 'signs are not noticed as participating in a direct relationship', over-rating because there is no struggle.) The four columns can then 'be condensed into the following sets of opposition – Consent: Submit: Tricked: Coerced.'

This interpretation of the columns is in terms of a version of self, and of society which is exhibited by the tale. Larrucia states (ibid. p. 528): 'In the first two columns the subject has access to regulation and is not the object of control. In columns 3 and 4, a subject does not have access to regulation, and is in fact objectified by control.' These columns express 'unmediated' relationships. Note that in both instances for Larrucia the character in question is human: mother, Red Riding Hood, and grandmother are the actors to whom awareness or unawareness is attributed. In this sense, the Wolf is not a character in his reading of the story.

For Larrucia the Wolf in fact represents Nature in order that the tale can be read as a Lévi-Straussian Nature/Culture dialectic. This perspective assumes that nature provides the underlying reality of social life, while culture is its immanent appearance. Despite the complexities of the conception of the 'noble savage' entertained by Rousseau and Voltaire, its assumption remains that of Hobbes: natural individualistic conflict underlies superficial social cohesion. The commitment is to the social as the realm of freedom, as against the natural as the realm of unfreedom. On this basis Larrucia concludes that (p. 529) 'the contradiction which is the basis of the narrative structure might be put simply as Free: not-Free.' But of course Perrault's Wolf is not natural, neither is 'he' outside the cultural product which is the tale. The narrative structure of the text cannot be deduced from the Nature/Culture opposition conceived as a reality prior to it; rather it must be interrogated to show how the 'Nature'/'Culture' opposition arises within it.

For Larrucia the text arises at a specific point in the development of this opposition:

> Already in the Renaissance 'mastery of nature' was becoming a dominant theme – anything which can be seen as part of 'nature' is potentially exploitable, and . . . the report/command relationship depends on this opposition, Nature/Culture.
>
> (Larrucia 1975 p. 530)

The text expresses the social construction of the 'individual' self for the first time historically (and, we may add, biographically, in the life of each child to whom at a formative stage it is subsequently retold). It does so by way of a paradoxical injunction. The paradox can be expressed (p. 531), 'Be free, be entirely individual.' Concretely, the report (be free) contradicts the imperative employed by the command. Analytically, the 'be natural' of the report contradicts its cultural specificity as a command.

However, the paradox is not to be found within the text itself. Rather, it is to be found in the relation between the tale and the moral which Perrault appends to it (p. 532): 'The moral, which appears incidental to the tale, a supplement, in fact creates a disjunctive relationship between the ostensible content of the narrative and its meaning.' 'The moral', writes Larrucia, 'puts the narrative outside itself, and places itself in the domain of behaviour: it is didactic.' He concludes

> A relationship is created between behaviour and meaning, a relationship regarding both the significance of an act – social context – and the connection of the subject with the other – psychological context.
>
> (ibid. p. 532)

Thus a double-bind is constituted between the command, expressed by the motto, forbidding young lasses to listen to strangers, and the report, expressed by the story, of one who did. Unless Red Riding Hood's freedom to choose is acknowledged, the tale makes no sense. Unless this freedom is denied, the moral is unacceptable.

On this reading the story expresses the natural underlying reality, while the motto expresses the cultural conclusions to be drawn from it: the paradox is the particular form taken by the Nature/Culture opposition understood as the difference between these two. Lessons about Cultural (human) wolves are drawn from a tale about a Natural (animal) Wolf. But the Wolf is not an animal wolf, and the tale is not a natural tale. This reading imposes its own prior conception of the opposition to interpret it, instead of interrupting the opposition constituted by the text itself. We shall now attempt such an interruption.

RE-READING RED RIDING HOOD

Let us begin by reformulating Larrucia's categories (Figure 16.1)

Our row and column headings appear below and to the right of the table. Larrucia's headings appear above it and to the left. We propose that his 'mediation' is a gap between 'appearance' and 'reality' which is *real* in that the reader is aware of it, while 'sign' is his notion of a gap between 'appearance' and 'reality' which is *apparent* in the sense that the character in the story is also aware of it. This distinction is based on that made by the text of the story

	sign	no sign		
mediated relations	column 1	column 2	reality ≠ appearance	in *reality* i.e. to the reader
unmediated relations	column3	column 4	reality = appearance	
	reality ≠ appearance	reality = appearance		
	in *appearance*, i.e. to the character			

Figure 16.1

between the voice of the narrator, which formulates reality directly to the reader, and the voices of the characters, which formulate the appearance of that reality to them.[9]

Thus in Larrucia's column 1, the mother (incident 1) and the Wolf (incident 4) each introduce a gap between present appearance and future reality. The mother tells Red Riding Hood to go to the Grandmother. The Wolf tells Red Riding Hood that he too will go to the Grandmother.

In column 1 the narrator also introduces a gap between appearance and reality at each incident. At incident 1, he writes that the mother doted on the child, whereas the grandmother was 'even fonder, and made her a little red hood'. Thus beneath the appearance formulated in the mother's talk, an underlying current of conflict between mother and grandmother for the child is portrayed. At incident 4, as Larrucia notes, the Wolf's friendly words to the child are put in question for the reader by the narrator's direct statement of his desire to eat her up.

For both characters and reader, an appearance/reality gap opens the tale. For the characters this gap anticipates the time of the journey to the grandmother by both child and Wolf and encompasses the temporality of the tale. For the reader the gap is more foreboding. Little Red Riding Hood must wend her way warily through the woods. But the beginning and end may contain more dangers than the journey itself. In the text – and this is an event which Larrucia omits from his analysis – the time in the wood is the only freedom which she has.

In column 2, Larrucia collects incidents in which Little Red Riding Hood denies any gap between appearance and reality. She takes at face value words addressed to her, as she thinks, by each of the other three characters. In incidents 2 and 5, the reader has been warned of underlying realities which contradict these appearances, in the ways already noted. In incident 9, the reader has been told how the Wolf devoured the grandmother and then lay down in her bed.

Thus in column 2 a gap is introduced between the reader and the character. The character grasps only an appearance of the reality which is made available to the reader. The same character occupies this position on each occasion. Little Red Riding Hood thus exemplifies orientation to mere appearances.

In column 3, the Wolf on each occasion masquerades as other than he really is. He thus exhibits a gap between appearance and reality. Although the reader has been warned in general terms of the Wolf's desire, the narrator does not explain the motive underlying any of his particular actions. The reader is thus forced to accept these actions at face value as they occur.[10] In this sense, for the reader, reality equates with appearance for the incidents in this column.

The reader is thus put in the position of being more naive than the Wolf, whereas the reader was able to be less naive than Red Riding Hood. In column 3 the gap between the reader and the character is reversed. Now only appearance is made available to the reader. This Wolf thus exemplifies orientation to underlying reality.

In column 4, Larrucia collects incidents in which the Wolf reveals his underlying reality to himself, the Grandmother, Red Riding Hood, and the reader. Identity between reality and appearance is established for all, closing each of the gaps previously opened. Most fundamentally, the gap between appearance and reality for both reader and characters which began the tale has been resolved, first for one, then for the other, now for both.

But here, we have re-captured the sequence of the tale, which Larrucia – following Lévi-Strauss – wished to dissolve. Initially reality is opposed to appearance (to which reader and characters have different orientations). The text then moves through two formulations of appearance as opposed to reality (in the first, on behalf of a character, in the second, on behalf of the reader). Finally, reality is identified with appearance (one and the same for both characters and reader).

It is this movement of textuality, which we shall make the object of an alternative reading to Larrucia's. Larrucia's reading cannot grasp textuality as movement. In fact he cannot grasp textuality at all. The synchronic meaning which he attributes to the story can only be discovered outside the text itself.

INTERRUPTING TEXTUALITY

The tale is an interplay of discourses, being in order of appearance those of the narrator, of the mother, of Little Red Riding Hood, of the Wolf, and of the grandmother. However this distinction based on the identity of the speakers is not infallible. In his second and third appearances, the Wolf counterfeits the voices of Red Riding Hood and the grandmother respectively. The text marks this by his precise repetition of the words he has heard them use. The delight engendered by the final dialogue results precisely from the ambiguity of the Wolf's statements, between the innocuous speech of the grandmother and the explicit formulation of the evil intentions of the Wolf, into which it shades.

But if the identification of speeches with speakers is not reliable – and it is precisely the point of 'Little Red Riding Hood' that it is not – then serious problems are raised as to how to proceed in reading the text. In particular any attempt to input 'characters' to the speakers in the tale becomes suspect. Larrucia's interpretation depends precisely on such imputation: in his most rigorous statement, the tale concerns subjects who must choose between (social) regulation and (natural) control. This choice is neither 'social' nor 'natural'. (For Larrucia this fact can only be reiterated paradoxically.) Further, it is not a choice made by subjects.

The text can be (re-) read without the imposition of the category of the subject, but for this purpose new categories are necessary. Rather than imputing characters to the speakers (including Perrault and the narrator), and then reading the text as a relation between characters, these categories must formulate relations between speeches themselves. The categories for sameness and difference between characters, which Larrucia's social-psychological interpretation employs, are those of society and self.[11] ('Society' is the way in which two characters are the same, and 'self' the way in which they differ.) The categories for sameness and difference between speeches, which we propose are the basis for a materialist interruption of the text, are those of economy and sexuality. ('Economy' is the way in which two speeches are the same, and 'sexuality' the way in which they differ.)

'Self' and 'society' are concepts inherently bound up with social psychology's functionalist belief in harmonious closed systems divorced from historical transformation. Despite his awareness of contradiction and of history, Larrucia's 'paradoxical' formulation establishes the timeless closure of 'Red Riding Hood'. 'There can only be a perpetual oscillation between categories of freedom and non-freedom' (p. 534). 'Sexuality' disrupts functionalism by the fact that sexual pleasure is not necessary to the function of reproduction. 'Economy' disrupts functionalism by the fact that economic surplus is not necessary to the function of production. To interpret social psychological phenomena in terms of 'society' and 'self' is to presuppose their harmonious closure. To interrupt textual phenomena in search of 'surplus' and 'pleasure' is to discover their disharmonious openness. It is to reveal the political character of the modes of production (of surplus) and consumption (of pleasure) which they employ.

An interruption of 'Little Red Riding Hood' can reveal the politics of the text in these terms, and serve as a paradigm for the interrogation of other phenomena presently subsumed under the hegemony of social psychology.

Relations of sameness and difference between discourses are explicitly established by the text. The mother's speech, in terms of the 'cake', and the 'pot of butter', is subsequently repeated by Red Riding Hood to the Wolf, and by the Wolf counterfeiting Red Riding Hood to the grandmother. Finally the Wolf counterfeiting the grandmother again refers to the 'cake' and the 'pot of butter' in speaking to Red Riding Hood. In a textual sense, then, these two items play an economic role in establishing sameness between the discourses. The mother's speech to Red Riding Hood, Red Riding Hood's speech to the Wolf, and Red Riding Hood's speech to the Wolf counterfeiting the grandmother all refer to the 'Grandmother', and never refer to the Wolf. The speech of the Wolf to Red Riding Hood, and his speech to her counterfeiting the Grandmother, refer to himself ('I'), but not to the Grandmother. In a textual sense this difference establishes the sexual character of the tale.

Of the four characters in the tale, besides the narrator, only two are responsible for significant discourse. The Mother speaks only once at the outset, about the cake and the little pot of butter. These words had already been mentioned by the narrator, and are repeated five times by the characters. The Grandmother scarcely speaks. Thus the text presents three voices, those of narrator, Red Riding Hood, and Wolf. The narrator's voice formulates 'reality'. From the outset, he identifies the ambition of the Wolf to devour Red Riding Hood. Red Riding Hood's discourse formulates 'appearance'. To the very end, she maintains that she is speaking to her Grandmother. It is the Wolf's discourse which holds 'appearance' and 'reality' apart from one another, repeatedly deferring the moment when the two will correspond with one another to the very end of the narrative. The way in which it does so has both economic and sexual aspects.

ECONOMY

Red Riding Hood is on her way to visit her grandmother, bringing a cake and a little pot of butter. Given that her grandmother is ill, this is a necessary function within the domestic economy of the two households. The items are part of an ongoing exchange, for we are also told that it was the grandmother who made the child her little red hood. In his first conversation with her, the Wolf proposes to her an activity which is strictly surplus to her journey. He shall go this way, and she that. The little girl follows his suggestion and discovers her own freedom. She 'amused herself on the journey by gathering nuts, running after the butterflies, and making nosegays of the wild flowers which she found.' In his second conversation with her, counterfeiting the grandmother, he again proposes an activity which is strictly surplus to her necessary journey. She is to 'Put the cake and the little pot of butter on the bin, and come up on the bed with me.' Finally, from his own point of view, his gobbling up of Red Riding Hood is non-necessary. The text points out that this is not the case *vis-à-vis* the grandmother. 'He sprang upon the poor old lady, and ate her up in less than no time, for he had been more than three days without food.' By contrast to the 'less than no time' which the necessary devouring of the grandmother takes in the story, the non-necessary devouring of Red Riding Hood takes the whole time of the text.

SEXUALITY

Implicitly within the tale, but explicitly within Perrault's moral, the encounter between the Wolf and Red Riding Hood is a sexual one. Whereas in the English version she is invited to 'come up on the bed' by the Wolf, then she 'took off her cloak' and was astonished at her grandmother 'in her nightgown', in the French version she is told, 'Viens te coucher avec moi', meaning simply 'come to bed with me', then she 'se déshabille' and is astonished to see her grandmother 'en son déshabille'. The word may mean lightly clad, or simply, undressed. The sequence of astonished expression by the little girl, at the sight of arms, legs, ears, and eyes of the male wolf can express simply the astonishment of a girl for the first time in bed with a man. Marc Soriano (1968) points out that this level of meaning is enhanced in French oral versions of the tale, where Red Riding Hood's 'déshabillement' becomes a strip-tease. In relation to each item of her clothing, she asks where to place it. The Wolf replies, 'Jette-le au feu, mon enfant, tu n'en as plus besoin.' The conclusion of the text is its consumation, the consumption of Red Riding Hood. The sexual skill of the text is its ability to bring closer and closer, while still delaying ever so slightly, the climactic moment, thereby raising pleasure to a greater and greater intensity.

Economy and sexuality are constituted by the text itself. The text produces the surplus time in which the tale can unfold, by deferring the Wolf's initial urge to devour Red Riding Hood. It then consumes this surplus pleasurably, repeatedly deferring its conclusion. The telling of the tale is the deferring of Red Riding Hood's devouring. This deferral/deferance/*différance* is the work of the text.

TEXTUAL PRACTICE

Larrucia's reading of the tale is invited by the text itself which, with its appended moral, offers a series of interpretations of interpretations. To provide an alternative reading it is necessary to interrupt the levels of interpretation within the tale itself. Central among these is the moral's interpretation of the narrator's interpretation of the intentions of the Wolf. This can be questioned if it is acknowledged that the Wolf himself intervenes within the situation perhaps to a greater effect than the narrator.[12] We want to suggest that, whereas the narrator and writer of the moral interpret the situation in which they find themselves, the Wolf interrupts it.

For the narrator, 'old Father Wolf . . . would have very much liked to eat' Red Riding Hood. However this raises the question of whether the meaning of an action can be reduced to the intention of the actor. This question can be asked not only of sociological interpreters of actions or of literary texts, but of actors and characters within texts themselves. If must be insisted that the Wolf's actions do not reduce to his (animal) intentions. Whatever his intentions, the Wolf's actions consist in an intervention in the discourse of Little Red Riding Hood in order to transform it. The way in which he does so repays closer examination.

At the first encounter, we are not told the Wolf's opening words. Red Riding Hood's words are given, however. They are exactly repetitious of those addressed to her by her mother. In our earlier consideration of this encounter, following Larrucia, we formulated it as one in which Red Riding Hood obeyed the words of the Wolf, just as she had previously obeyed those of her mother. (These are incidents 2 and 5, making up column 2 of Larrucia's analysis of the story.) But re-consideration shows that this is misleading. The Wolf precisely questions blind obedience. He shows that there is more to the meaning of the mother's words than the appearance of those words. (He shows their indexicality.) Specifically, there is more than one way to obey the words (more than one path to the grandmother's house) and room to investigate the relative merits of each. As we have already noted, the little girl is thereby led to discover that she has surplus time on her hands, and she is able to employ this plea-surably in her own pursuits.

It is precisely the repeated words of the mother, whose meaning he has called into question in speaking to Red Riding Hood, that the Wolf himself repeats in speaking to the grandmother. He does so only to learn the stereotyped speech which the grandmother addresses, as she imagines, to Little Red Riding Hood.

Next the Wolf repeats these words to Red Riding Hood herself. But again his further remark calls this speech into question. He asks explicitly for the cake and the pot of butter to be set aside, and initiates another kind of speech with her. It is important not to be blinded by the knowledge that he is 'really' the Wolf to the fact that here he speaks as the grandmother and intervenes in her speech, in a way which transforms the discourse which she previously had with the child.

The Wolf opens the closure created by the social order speech of the mother and grandmother which had subsumed the little girl within it until then. Economically she had been no more than the bearer of items of exchange (the red hood one way, the cake and butter the other) between the two households: he shows her that she has surplus time of her own. Sexually she had been the object of desire of her mother and of her grandmother: he shows her that she can pursue her own pleasure.

These issues are no sooner opened than they are closed once more by the narrator's final words, which restore the unproblematic and 'wicked' animality of the Wolf. But the narrator's claim, which remains Larrucia's assumption, can be reversed. Instead of presupposing that the Wolf is really natural, and only feigns the veneer of culture, we may conclude that the narrator feigns his natural animal identity in order to exclude the Wolf from the cultural community. This is necessary in order to deny the Wolf's ability to transform the 'Nature'/'Culture' relation which the community is committed to preserve, a commitment upheld by social order theory from Perrault to the present day.

NOTES

1 'Valentin Vološinov' is regarded by some as the pseudonym of Mikhail Bakhtin. In any event Bakhtin (1971) is a useful short statement of the theoretical approach developed at greater length in Vološinov (1973).
2 Derrida's writing is itself anti-authoritarian in precisely this sense. Rather than interpreting a text of, say, Rousseau, in terms of his own presupposed version of reality, he interrupts it, allowing its own formulation of the 'appearance'/'reality' *différance* to come to the fore.
3 This theme is addressed most explicitly in Derrida (1976), but is already implied in Derrida (1973).
4 Cf. his 'Différance', in Derrida (1973).
5 Althusser's theory of ideology understands the text in precisely this way (see Silverman and Torode 1980 ch. 2).
6 The passion expressed by Husserl in his exclamations on behalf of the ego is illustrated by the passages discussed in Silverman and Torode (1980 ch. 5).
7 The aim of a 'genuine openness to the text itself' will be recognized as a linguistic version of Husserl's early programme of phenomenology, as

pursued further by Heidegger. However, in each of these writers the project of interruption is itself tainted with essentialism, which restores a form of interpretation. The project must therefore be continued, by way of an inter- ruption of the practice of interruption in each of these writers.

8 For a fuller account of the method, see Lévi-Strauss (1977 *passim*) and Larrucia (1975 pp. 523–528).

9 This is the method of the classical text, which 'Little Red Riding Hood' exem- plifies. To disrupt it, one has to conceive of a text in which the voice of the narrator is capable of misleading the reader. This is precisely what occurs in such a text as Robbe-Grillet's *Project for a Revolution in New York*, cf. Silverman and Torode (1980 ch. 12).

10 Of course it is possible to postulate a sophisticated reader who could antic- ipate the Wolf's moves. However if the reader in general were able to do this, then the plot would be pointless. To express this in terms which will be more rigorously defined below, there would be no pleasure in the text.

11 As already noted, the Wolf is excluded from subjectivity, self, and society. Although he does not explicate this argument, we might say that Larrucia's solution to the problematic identification of speakers (subjects) with speeches is that *qua* counterfeiter, the Wolf is not a speaker (subject), i.e. has no words of his own. Our view would be rather that by his ability to transform the speech of others, the Wolf better displays the potentialities of speaking than do the other characters.

12 This suggestion is not so fanciful as may appear, since given that the tale existed and exists in many oral versions prior to Perrault's writing it in a literary form, his re-writing of it and appending to it of a moral constitute a definite intervention within the tale which must be open to criticism.

Part IV

Sign users and speech acts

Saying and doing

EDITOR'S INTRODUCTION

The first chapter of Austin's *How to Do Things With Words* (this volume pp. 255–62) sets out the differences between 'performative' and 'constative' statements. Later in the book, Austin goes on to describe how performatives are characterized by an illocutionary force and constatives by a locutionary one. What it is important to remember when reading the following (as well as other early chapters in *How to Do Things with Words*) is that the separation is largely a rhetorical device. Austin is concerned in this early chapter to criticise a positivist version of language in which statements are either 'true' or 'false', and his own separation successfully carries this off. What Austin strives to show is that there are categories of 'statement' that, rather than 'communicating', *do* something. The argument that develops revolves around the fact that the separation that Austin identifies is no separation at all: in fact, all statements *do* (or perform) something, even those that appear to be constative in their orientation.

Embedded in Austin's simple propositions is the inference that the 'common sense' definition of 'communication', where the contents of one mind are *transmitted* to another, is highly problematic. This understanding of 'communication' is also criticized by Derrida for its advocacy and belief in what he calls 'presence' and, as we have noted (see pp. 19–20) both Austin and Derrida concur with regard to the question of language's impersonal fashion of functioning. We have also noted (see p. 184) that Lacan's concepts of 'empty' and 'full' speech seem to map onto Austin's 'constative' and 'performative'. In light of this, the final pages of the extract are especially important. When he writes about promises Austin mentions the intention of the speaker but, at the same time, he insists that these intentions do not make the promise 'true' or 'false'. Instead, the promise stands and all we can say about it is that it may be in 'bad faith'. Austin therefore attempts to show that the performative is not just the result of an operation by human beings but, in a sense, exists on its own terms.

Searle's article (originally published in 1965) extends some of Austin's principles. It looks at the rule-governed nature of illocution and posits three concepts which need to be taken into consideration. The first of these is the broad sweep of 'rules' working on an utterance which Searle divides into 'constitutive' and 'regulative' rules. The second concerns 'propositions', the predicates upon which a statement is based or, put another way, its 'content' irrespective of the illocution. The last concept is that of 'meaning' and it is here that we can see that Searle begins to explicitly depart from Austin. Using Grice's definition of the phenomenon, Searle argues that 'meaning' consists of an attempt by one speaker to have an effect on another speaker in an arena of communication bound by certain rules. He then goes on to analyse one kind of example – once again, it is 'the promise' – which evidences the combination that he has posited as constitutive of the illocutionary act.

It will be noticeable from the very outset that Searle refers to the acts that he discusses as 'expressions'. It is also clear that he cites Grice in order to highlight the *intention* of the addresser as well as the *effect* which might be made on the addressee. Searle is therefore forthright in his belief that what takes place between addresser and addressee is *communication*, the passage of an intended message from one mind to another mind which will be affected by this intention. He shares with Austin a belief in the centrality of rules in illocution but offers them only a partnership with 'intention' rather than an exclusive executive role. For Searle, the speaker and listener are not socially constituted *by* the illocutionary act but participate in the constitution *of* the act as an illocution. This understanding is necessary to the reading of Searle's later work (1969) where he begins to question the location of the language rules that Austin identifies.

Further reading   Grice 1968, 1975; Searle 1983a; Fish 1980 pp. 197–245; Thomas 1995 esp. pp. 28–54, 87–118; Mey 1993; Blakemore 1992; Petrey 1990; Iser 1978 pp. 54–62; Forrester 1990 pp. 149–153. The most advanced discussion of speech acts and communication theory is probably Sperber and Wilson 1995.

17 J. L. Austin

Performatives and constatives

What I shall have to say here is neither difficult nor contentious; the only merit I should like to claim for it is that of being true, at least in parts. The phenomenon to be discussed is very widespread and obvious, and it cannot fail to have been already noticed, at least here and there, by others. Yet I have not found attention paid to it specifically.

It was for too long the assumption of philosophers that the business of a 'statement' can only be to 'describe' some state of affairs, or to 'state some fact', which it must do either truly or falsely. Grammarians, indeed, have regularly pointed out that not all 'sentences' are (used in making) statements:[1] there are, traditionally, besides (grammarians') statements, also questions and exclamations, and sentences expressing commands or wishes or concessions. And doubtless philosophers have not intended to deny this, despite some loose use of 'sentence' for 'statement'. Doubtless, too, both grammarians and philosophers have been aware that it is by no means easy to distinguish even questions, commands, and so on from statements by means of the few and jejune grammatical marks available, such as word order, mood, and the like: though perhaps it has not been usual to dwell on the difficulties which this fact obviously raises. For how do we decide which is which? What are the limits and definitions of each?

But now in recent years, many things which would once have been accepted without question as 'statements' by both philosophers and grammarians have been scrutinized with new care. This scrutiny arose somewhat indirectly – at least in philosophy. First came the view, not always formulated without unfortunate dogmatism, that a statement (of fact) ought to be 'verifiable', and this led to the view that many 'statements' are only what may be called pseudo-statements. First and most obviously, many 'statements' were shown to be, as Kant perhaps first argued systematically, strictly nonsense, despite an unexceptionable grammatical form: and the continual discovery of fresh types of nonsense, unsystematic though their classification and mysterious though their explanation is too often allowed to remain, has done on the whole nothing but good. Yet we, that is, even philosophers, set some limits to the amount of nonsense that we are prepared to admit we talk: so that it was natural to go on to ask, as a second stage, whether many apparent pseudo-statements really set out to be 'statements' at all. It has come to be commonly held that many utterances which look like statements are either not intended at all, or only intended in part, to record or impart straightforward information about the facts: for example, 'ethical propositions' are perhaps intended, solely or partly, to evince emotion or to prescribe conduct or to influence it in special ways. Here too Kant was among the pioneers. We very often also use utterances in ways beyond the scope at least of traditional grammar. It has come to be seen that many specially perplexing words embedded in apparently descriptive statements do not serve to indicate some specially odd additional feature in the reality reported, but to indicate (not to report) the circumstances in which the statement is made or reservations to which it is subject or the way in which it is to be taken and the like. To overlook these possibilities in the way once common is called the 'descriptive' fallacy; but perhaps this is not a good name, as 'descriptive' itself is special. Not all true or false statements are descriptions, and for this reason I prefer to use the word 'Constative'. Along these lines it has by now been shown piecemeal, or at least made to look likely, that many traditional philosophical perplexities have arisen through a mistake – the mistake of taking as straightforward statements of fact utterances which are *either* (in interesting non-grammatical ways) nonsensical *or else* intended as something quite different.

Whatever we may think of any particular one of these views and suggestions, and however much we may deplore the initial confusion into which philosophical doctrine and method have been plunged, it cannot be doubted that they are producing a revolution in philosophy. If anyone wishes to call it the greatest and most salutary in its history, this is not, if you come to think of it, a large claim. It is not surprising that beginnings have been piecemeal, with *parti pris*, and for extraneous aims; this is common with revolutions.

PRELIMINARY ISOLATION OF THE PERFORMATIVE[2]

The type of utterance we are to consider here is not, of course, in general a type of nonsense; though misuse of it can, as we shall see, engender rather special varieties of 'nonsense'. Rather, it is one of our second class – the masqueraders. But it does not by any means necessarily masquerade as a statement of fact, descriptive or constative. Yet it does quite commonly do so, and that, oddly enough, when it assumes its most explicit form. Grammarians have not, I believe, seen through this 'disguise', and philosophers only at best incidentally.[3] It will be convenient, therefore, to study it first in this misleading form, in order to bring out its character-istics by contrasting them with those of the statement of fact which it apes.

We shall take, then, for our first examples some utterances which can fall into no hitherto recognized *grammatical* category save that of 'statement', which are not nonsense, and which contain none of those verbal danger-signals which philosophers have by now detected or think they have detected (curious words like 'good' or 'all', suspect auxiliaries like 'ought' or 'can', and dubious constructions like the hypothetical): all will have, as it happens, humdrum verbs in the first person singular present indicative active.[4] Utterances can be found, satisfying these conditions, yet such that

A. they do not 'describe' or 'report' or constate anything at all, are not 'true or false'; and
B. the uttering of the sentence is, or is a part of, the doing of an action, which again would not *normally* be described as, or as 'just', saying something.

This is far from being as paradoxical as it may sound or as I have meanly been trying to make it sound: indeed, the examples now to be given will be disappointing.

Examples:

(E. *a*) 'I do (sc. take this woman to be my lawful wedded wife)' – as uttered in the course of the marriage ceremony.[5]

(E. *b*) 'I name this ship the *Queen Elizabeth*' – as uttered when smashing the bottle against the stem.

(E. *c*) 'I give and bequeath my watch to my brother' – as occurring in a will.

(E. *d*) 'I bet you sixpence it will rain tomorrow.'

In these examples it seems clear that to utter the sentence (in, of course, the appropriate circumstances) is not to *describe* my doing of what I should be said in so uttering to be doing [6] or to state that I am doing it: it is to do it. None of the utterances cited is either true or false: I assert this as obvious and do not argue it. It needs argument no more than that 'damn' is not true or false: it may be that the utterance 'serves to inform you' – but that is quite different. To name the ship *is* to say (in the appropriate circumstances) the words 'I name, &c.' When I say, before the registrar or altar, &c., 'I do', I am not reporting on a marriage: I am indulging in it.

What are we to call a sentence or an utterance of this type?[7] I propose to call it a *performative sentence* or a performative utterance, or, for short, 'a performative'. The term 'performative' will be used in a variety of cognate ways and constructions, much as the term 'imperative' is.[8] The name is derived, of course, from 'perform', the usual verb with the noun 'action': it indicates that the issuing of the utterance is the performing of an action – it is not normally thought of as just saying something.

A number of other terms may suggest themselves, each of which would suitably cover this or that wider or narrower class of performatives: for example, many performatives are *contractual* ('I bet') or *declaratory* ('I declare war') utterances. But no term in current use that I know of is nearly wide enough to cover them all. One technical term that comes nearest to what we need is perhaps 'operative', as it is used strictly by lawyers in referring to that part, i.e. those clauses, of an instrument which serves to effect the transaction (conveyance or what not) which is its main object, whereas the rest of the document merely 'recites' the circumstances in which the transaction is to be effected.[9] But 'operative' has other meanings, and indeed is often used nowadays to mean little more than 'important'. I have preferred a new word, to which, though its etymology is not irrelevant, we shall perhaps not be so ready to attach some preconceived meaning.

CAN SAYING MAKE IT SO?

Are we then to say things like this:

'To marry is to say a few words', or

'Betting is simply saying something'?

Such a doctrine sounds odd or even flippant at first, but with sufficient safeguards it may become not odd at all.

A sound initial objection to them may be this; and it is not without some importance. In very many cases it is possible to perform an act of exactly the same kind *not* by uttering words, whether written or spoken, but in some other way. For example, I may in some places effect marriage by cohabiting, or I may bet with a totalisator machine by putting a coin in a slot. We should then, perhaps, convert the propositions above, and put it that 'to say a few certain words is to marry' or 'to marry is, in some cases, simply to say a few words' or 'simply to say a certain something is to bet'.

But probably the real reason why such remarks sound dangerous lies in another obvious fact, to which we shall have to revert in detail later, which is this. The uttering of the words is, indeed, usually a, or even *the*, leading incident in the performance of the act (of betting or what not), the performance of which is also the object of the utterance, but it is far from being usually, even if it is ever, the *sole* thing necessary if the act is to be deemed to have been performed. Speaking generally, it is always necessary that the *circumstances* in which the words are uttered should be in some way, or ways, *appropriate*, and it is very commonly necessary that either the speaker himself or other persons should *also* perform certain *other* actions, whether 'physical' or 'mental' actions or even acts of uttering further words. Thus, for naming the ship, it is essential that I should be the person appointed to name her, for (Christian) marrying, it is essential that I should not be already married with a wife living, sane and undivorced, and so on: for a bet to have been made, it is generally necessary for the offer of the bet to have been accepted by a taker (who must have done something, such as to say 'Done'), and it is hardly a gift if I *say* 'I give it you' but never hand it over.

So far, well and good. The action may be performed in ways other than by a performative utterance, and in any case the circumstances, including other actions, must be appropriate. But we may, in objecting, have something totally different, and this time quite mistaken, in mind, especially when we think of some of the more awe-inspiring performatives such as 'I promise to . . . '. Surely the words must be spoken 'seriously' and so as to be taken 'seriously'? This is, though vague, true enough in general – it is an important commonplace in discussing the purport of any utterance whatsoever. I must not be joking, for example, nor writing a poem. But we are apt to have a feeling that their being serious consists in their being uttered as (merely) the outward and visible sign, for convenience or other record or for information, of an inward and spiritual act: from which it is but a short step to go on to believe or to assume without realizing that for many purposes the outward utterance is a description, *true or false*, of the occurrence of the inward performance. The classic expression of this idea is to be found in the *Hippolytus* (1. 612), where Hippolytus says

ἡ γλῶσσ᾽ ὀμώμοχ᾽, ἡ δὲ φρὴν ἀνώμοτός,

i.e. 'my tongue swore to, but my heart (or mind or other backstage artiste) did not'.[10] Thus 'I promise to . . .' obliges me – puts on record my spiritual assumption of a spiritual shackle.

It is gratifying to observe in this very example how excess of profundity, or rather solemnity, at once paves the way for immorality. For one who says 'promising is not merely a matter of uttering words! It is an inward and spiritual act!' is apt to appear as a solid moralist standing out against a generation of superficial theorizers: we see him as he sees himself, surveying the invisible depths of ethical space, with all the distinction of a specialist in the *sui generis*. Yet he provides Hippolytus with a let-out, the bigamist with an excuse for his 'I do' and the welsher with a defence for his 'I bet'. Accuracy and morality alike are on the side of the plain saying that *our word is our bond*.

If we exclude such fictitious inward acts as this, can we suppose that any of the other things which certainly are normally required to accompany an utterance such as 'I promise that . . .' or 'I do (take this woman . . .)' are in fact described by it, and consequently do by their presence make it true or by their absence make it false? Well, taking the latter first, we shall next consider what we actually do say about the utterance concerned when one or another of its normal concomitants is *absent*. In no case do we say that the utterance was false but rather that the utterance – or rather the *act*,[11] e.g. the promise – was void, or given in bad faith, or not imple-mented, or the like. In the particular case of promising, as with many other performatives, it is appropriate that the person uttering the promise should have a certain intention, viz. here to keep his word: and perhaps of all concomitants this looks the most suitable to be that which 'I promise' does describe or record. Do we not actually, when such intention is absent, speak of a 'false' promise? Yet so to speak is *not* to say that the utterance 'I promise that . . .' is false, in the sense that though he states that he does, he doesn't, or that though he describes he misdescribes – misreports. For he *does* promise: the promise here is not even *void*, though it is given *in bad faith*. His utterance is perhaps misleading, probably deceitful and doubtless wrong, but it is not a lie or a misstatement. At most we might make out a case for saying that it implies or insinuates a falsehood or a misstatement (to the effect that he does intend to do something): but that is a very different matter. Moreover, we do not speak of a false bet or a false christening; and that we *do* speak of a false promise need commit us no more than the fact that we speak of a false move. 'False' is not necessarily used of statements only.

NOTES

1 It is, of course, not really correct that a sentence ever *is* a statement: rather, it is *used* in *making a statement*, and the statement itself is a 'logical construc-tion' out of the makings of statements.
2 Everything said in these sections is provisional, and subject to revision in the light of later sections.
3 Of all people, jurists should be best aware of the true state of affairs. Perhaps some now are. Yet they will succumb to their own timorous fiction, that a statement of 'the law' is a statement of fact.
4 Not without design: they are all 'explicit' performatives, and of that prepo-tent class later called 'exercitives'.
5 [Austin realized that the expression 'I do' is not used in the marriage cere-mony too late to correct his mistake. We have let it remain in the text as it is philosophically unimportant that it is a mistake. J. O. Urmson.]
6 Still less anything that I have already done or have yet to do.
7 'Sentences' form a class of 'utterances', which class is to be defined, so far as I am concerned, grammatically, though I doubt if the definition has yet been given satisfactorily. With performative utterances are contrasted, for example and essentially, 'constative' utterances; to issue a constative utter-ance (i.e. to utter it with a historical reference) is to make a statement. To issue a performative utterance is, for example, to make a bet.

8 Formerly I used 'performatory': but 'performative' is to be preferred as shorter, less ugly, more tractable, and more traditional in formation.

9 I owe this observation to Professor H. L. A. Hart.

10 But I do not mean to rule out all the offstage performers – the lights men, the stage manager, even the prompter; I am objecting only to certain officious understudies, who would duplicate the play.

11 We deliberately avoid distinguishing these, precisely because the distinction is not in point.

18 John Searle

What is a speech act?

INTRODUCTION

In a typical speech situation involving a speaker, a hearer, and an utterance by the speaker, there are many kinds of acts associated with the speaker's utterance. The speaker will characteristically have moved his jaw and tongue and made noises. In addition, he will characteristically have performed some acts within the class which includes informing or irritating or boring his hearers; he will further characteristically have performed acts within the class which includes referring to Kennedy or Khrushchev or the North Pole; and he will also have performed acts within the class which includes making statements, asking questions, issuing commands, giving reports, greeting, and warning. The members of this last class are what Austin (1980) called illocutionary acts and it is with this class that I shall be concerned in this paper, so the paper might have been called 'What is an Illocutionary Act?' I do not attempt to define the expression 'illocutionary act', although if my analysis of a particular illocutionary act succeeds it may provide the basis for a definition. Some of the English verbs and verb phrases associated with illocutionary acts are: state, assert, describe, warn, remark, comment, command, order, request, criticize, apologize, censure, approve, welcome, promise, express approval and express regret. Austin claimed that there were over a thousand such expressions in English.

By way of introduction, perhaps I can say why I think it is of interest and importance in the philosophy of language to study speech acts, or, as they are sometimes called, language acts or linguistic acts. I think it is essential to any specimen of linguistic communication that it involve a linguistic act. It is not, as has generally been supposed, the symbol or word or sentence, or even the token of the symbol or word or sentence, which is the unit of linguistic communication, but rather it is the *production* of the token in the performance of the speech act that constitutes the basic unit of linguistic communication. To put this point more precisely, the production of the sentence token under certain conditions is the illocutionary act, and the illocutionary act is the minimal unit of linguistic communication.

I do not know how to *prove* that linguistic communication essentially involves acts but I can think of arguments with which one might attempt to convince someone who was skeptical. One argument would be to call the skeptic's attention to the fact that when he takes a noise or a mark on paper to be an instance of linguistic communication, as a message, one of the things that is involved in his so taking that noise or mark is that he should regard it as having been produced by a being with certain intentions. He cannot just regard it as a natural phenomenon, like a stone, a waterfall, or a tree. In order to regard it as an instance of linguistic communication one must suppose that its production is what I am calling a speech act. It is a logical presupposition, for example, of current attempts to decipher the Mayan hieroglyphs that we at least hypothesize that the marks we see on the stones were produced by beings more or less like ourselves and produced with certain kinds of intentions. If we were certain the marks were a consequence of, say, water erosion, then the question of deciphering them or even calling them hieroglyphs could not arise. To construe them under the category of linguistic communication necessarily involves construing their production as speech acts.

To perform illocutionary acts is to engage in a rule-governed form of behavior. I shall argue that such things as asking questions or making statements are rule-governed in ways quite similar to those in which getting a base hit in baseball or moving a knight in chess are rule-governed forms of acts. I intend therefore to explicate the notion of an illocutionary act by stating a set of necessary and sufficient conditions for the performance of a particular kind of illocutionary act, and extracting from it a set of semantical rules for the use of the expression (or syntactic device) which marks the utterance as an illocutionary act of that kind. If I am successful in stating the conditions and the corresponding rules for even one kind of illocutionary act, that will provide us with a pattern for analyzing other kinds of acts and consequently for explicating the notion in general. But in order to set the stage for actually stating conditions and extracting rules for performing an illocutionary act I have to discuss three other preliminary notions: *rules, propositions* and *meaning*. I shall confine my discussion of these notions to those aspects which are essential to my main purposes in this paper, but, even so, what I wish to say concerning each of these notions, if it were to be at all complete, would require a paper for each; however, sometimes it may be worth sacrificing thoroughness for the sake of scope and I shall therefore be very brief.

RULES

In recent years there has been in the philosophy of language considerable discussion involving the notion of rules for the use of expressions. Some philosophers have even said that knowing the meaning of a word is simply a matter of knowing the rules for its use or employment. One disquieting feature of such discussions is that no philosopher, to my knowledge at least, has ever given anything like an adequate formulation of the rules for the use of even one expression. If meaning is a matter of rules of use, surely we ought to be able to state the rules for the use of expressions in a way which would explicate the meaning of those expressions. Certain other philosophers, dismayed perhaps by the failure of their colleagues to produce any rules, have denied the fashionable view that meaning is a matter of rules and have asserted that there are no semantical rules of the proposed kind at all. I am inclined to think that this skepticism is premature and stems from a failure to distinguish different sorts of rules, in a way which I shall now attempt to explain.

I distinguish between two sorts of rules: some regulate antecedently existing forms of behavior; for example, the rules of etiquette regulate interpersonal relationships, but these relationships exist independently of the rules of etiquette. Some rules on the other hand do not merely regulate but create or define new forms of behavior. The rules of football, for example, do not merely regulate the game of football but as it were create the possibility of or define that activity. The activity of playing football is constituted by acting in accordance with these rules; football has no existence apart from these rules. I call the latter kind of rules constitutive rules and the former kind regulative rules. Regulative rules regulate a pre-existing activity, an activity whose existence is logically independent of the existence of the rules. Constitutive rules constitute (and also regulate) an activity the existence of which is logically dependent on the rules.[1]

Regulative rules characteristically take the form of or can be paraphrased as imperatives, e.g. 'When cutting food hold the knife in the right hand', or 'Officers are to wear ties at dinner'. Some constitutive rules take quite a different form, e.g. a checkmate is made if the king is attacked in such a way that no move will leave it unattacked; a touchdown is scored when a player crosses the opponents' goal line in possession of the ball while a play is in progress. If our paradigms of rules are imperative regulative rules, such non-imperative constitutive rules are likely to strike us as extremely curious and hardly even as rules at all. Notice that they are almost tautological in character, for what the 'rule' seems to offer is a partial definition of 'checkmate' or 'touchdown'. But, of course, this quasi-tautological character is a necessary consequence of their being constitutive rules: the rules concerning touchdowns must define the notion of 'touchdown' in the same way that the rules concerning football define 'football'. That, for example, a touchdown can be scored in such and such ways and counts six points can appear sometimes as a rule, sometimes as an analytic truth; and that it can be construed as a tautology is a clue to the fact that the rule in question is a constitutive one. Regulative rules generally have the form 'Do X' or 'If Y do X'. Some members of the set of constitutive rules have this form but some also have the form 'X counts as Y'.[2]

The failure to perceive this is of some importance in philosophy. Thus, e.g., some philosophers ask 'How can a promise create an obligation?' A similar question would be 'How can a touchdown create six points?' And as they stand both questions can only be answered by stating a rule of the form 'X counts as Y'.

I am inclined to think that both the failure of some philosophers to state rules for the use of expressions and the skepticism of other philosophers concerning the existence of any such rules stem at least in part from a failure to recognize the distinctions between constitutive and regulative rules. The model or paradigm of a rule which most philosophers have is that of a regulative rule, and if one looks in semantics for purely regulative rules one is not likely to find anything interesting from the point of view of logical analysis.

There are no doubt social rules of the form 'One ought not to utter obscenities at formal gatherings', but that hardly seems a rule of the sort that is crucial in explicating the semantics of a language. The hypothesis that lies behind the present paper is that the semantics of a language can be regarded as a series of systems of constitutive rules and that illocutionary acts are acts performed in accordance with these sets of constitutive rules. One of the aims of this paper is to formulate a set of constitutive rules for a certain kind of speech act. And if what I have said concerning constitutive rules is correct, we should not be surprised if not all these rules take the form of imperative rules. Indeed we shall see that the rules fall into several different categories, none of which is quite like the rules of etiquette. The effort to state the rules for an illocutionary act can also be regarded as a kind of test of the hypothesis that there are constitutive rules underlying speech acts. If we are unable to give any satisfactory rule formulations, our failure could be construed as partially disconfirming evidence against the hypothesis.

PROPOSITIONS

Different illocutionary acts often have features in common with each other. Consider utterances of the following sentences:

1 Will John leave the room?
2 John will leave the room.
3 John, leave the room!
4 Would that John left the room.
5 If John will leave the room, I will leave also.

Utterances of each of these on a given occasion would characteristically be performances of different illocutionary acts. The first would, characteristically, be a question, the second an assertion about the future, that is, a prediction, the third a request or order, the fourth an expression of a wish and the fifth a hypothetical expression of intention. Yet in the performance of each the speaker would characteristically perform some subsidiary acts which are common to all five illocutionary acts. In the utterance of each the speaker *refers* to a particular person John and *predicates* the act of leaving the room of that person. In no case is that all he does, but in every case it is a part of what he does. I shall say, therefore, that in each of these cases, although the illocutionary acts are different, at least some of the non-illocutionary acts of reference and predication are the same. The reference to some person John and predication of the same thing of him in each of these illocutionary acts inclines me to say that there is a common *content* in each of them. Something expressible by the clause 'that John will leave the room' seems to be a common feature of all. We could, with not too much distortion, write each of these sentences in a way which would isolate this common feature: 'I assert that John will leave the room', 'I ask whether John will leave the room', etc.

For lack of a better word I propose to call this common content a proposition, and I shall describe this feature of these illocutionary acts by saying that in the utterance of each of (1)–(5) the speaker expresses the proposition that John will leave the room. Notice that I do not say that the sentence expresses the proposition; I do not know how sentences could perform acts of that kind. But I shall say that in the utterance of the sentence the speaker expresses a proposition. Notice also that I am distinguishing between a proposition and an assertion or statement of that proposition. The proposition that John will leave the room is expressed in the utterance of all of (1)–(5) but only in (2) is that proposition asserted. An assertion is an illocutionary act, but a proposition is not an act at all, although the act of expressing a proposition is a part of performing certain illocutionary acts.

I might summarize this by saying that I am distinguishing between the illocutionary act and the propositional content of an illocutionary act. Of course, not all illocutionary acts have a propositional content, for example, an utterance of 'Hurrah!' or 'Ouch!' does not. In one version or another this distinction is an old one and has been marked in different ways by authors as diverse as Frege, Sheffer, Lewis, Reichenbach and Hare, to mention only a few.

From a semantical point of view we can distinguish between the propositional indicator in the sentence and the indicator of illocutionary force. That is, for a large class of sentences used to perform illocutionary acts, we can say for the purpose of our analysis that the sentence has two (not necessarily separate) parts, the proposition indicating element and the function indicating device.[3] The function indicating device shows how the proposition is to be taken, or, to put it in another way, what illocutionary force the utterance is to have, that is, what illocutionary act the speaker is performing in the utterance of the sentence. Function indicating devices in English include word order, stress, intonation contour, punctuation, the mood of the verb, and finally a set of so-called performative verbs: I may indicate the kind of illocutionary act I am performing by beginning the sentence with 'I apologize', 'I warn', 'I state', etc. Often in actual speech situations the context will make it clear what the illocutionary force of the utterance is, without its being necessary to invoke the appropriate function indicating device.

If this semantical distinction is of any real importance, it seems likely that it should have some syntactical analogue, and certain recent developments in transformational grammar tend to support the view that it does. In the underlying phrase marker of a sentence there is a distinction between those elements which correspond to the function indicating device and those which correspond to the propositional content.

The distinction between the function indicating device and the proposition indicating device will prove very useful to us in giving an analysis of an illocutionary act. Since the same proposition can be common to all sorts of illocutionary acts, we can separate our analysis of the proposition from our analysis of kinds of illocutionary acts. I think there are rules for expressing propositions, rules for such things as reference and predication, but those rules can be discussed independently of the rules for function indicating. In this paper I shall not attempt to discuss propositional rules but shall concentrate on rules for using certain kinds of function indicating devices.

MEANING

Speech acts are characteristically performed in the utterance of sounds or the making of marks. What is the difference between *just* uttering sounds or making marks and performing a speech act? One difference is that the sounds or marks one makes in the performance of a speech act are characteristically said to *have meaning*, and a second related difference is that one is characteristically said to *mean something* by those sounds or marks. Characteristically when one speaks one means something by what one says, and what one says, the string of morphemes that one emits, is characteristically said to have a meaning. Here, incidentally, is another point at which our analogy between performing speech acts and playing games breaks down. The pieces in a game like chess are not characteristically said to have a meaning, and furthermore when one makes a move one is not characteristically said to mean anything by that move.

But what is it for one to mean something by what one says, and what is it for something to have a meaning? To answer the first of these questions I propose to borrow and revise some ideas of Paul Grice. In an article entitled 'Meaning', Grice (1957) gives the following analysis of one sense of the notion of 'meaning'. To say that *A* meant something by *x* is to say that '*A* intended the utterance of *x* to produce some effect in an audience by means of the recognition of this intention'. This seems to me a useful start on an analysis of meaning, first because it shows the close relationship between the notion of meaning and the notion of intention, and secondly because it captures something which is, I think, essential to speaking a language: in speaking a language I attempt to communicate things to my hearer by means of getting him to recognize my intention to communicate just those things. For example, characteristically, when I make an assertion, I attempt to communicate to and convince my hearer of the truth of a certain proposition; and the means I employ to do this are to utter certain sounds, which utterance I intend to produce in him the desired effect by means of his recognition of my intention to produce just that effect. I shall illustrate this with an example. I might on the one hand attempt to get you to believe that I am French by speaking French all the time, dressing in the French manner, showing wild enthusiasm for de Gaulle, and cultivating French acquaintances. But I might on the other hand attempt to get you to believe that I am French by simply telling you that I am French. Now, what is the difference between these two ways of my attempting to get you to believe that I am French? One crucial difference is that in the second case I attempt to get you to believe that I am French by getting you to recognize that it is my purported intention to get you to believe just that. That is one of the things involved in telling you that I am French. But of course if I try to get you to believe that I am French by putting on the act I described, then your recognition of my intention to produce in you the belief that I am French is not the means I am employing. Indeed in this case you would, I think, become rather suspicious if you recognized my intention.

However valuable this analysis of meaning is, it seems to me to be in certain respects defective. First of all, it fails to distinguish the different kinds of effects – perlocutionary versus illocutionary – that one may intend to produce in one's hearers, and it further fails to show the way in which these different kinds of effects are related to the notion of meaning. A second defect is that it fails to account for the extent to which meaning is a matter of rules or conventions. That is, this account of meaning does not show the connection between one's meaning something by what one says and what that which one says actually means in the language. In order to illustrate this point I now wish to present a counter-example to this analysis of meaning. The point of the counter-example will be to illustrate the connection between what a speaker means and what the words he utters mean.

Suppose that I am an American soldier in the Second World War and that I am captured by Italian troops. And suppose also that I wish to get these troops to believe that I am a German officer in order to get them to release me. What I would like to do is to tell them in German or Italian that I am a German officer. But let us suppose I don't know enough German or Italian to do that. So I, as it were, attempt to put on a show of telling them that I am a German officer by reciting those few bits of German that I know, trusting that they don't know enough German to see through my plan. Let us suppose I know only one line of German, which I remember from a poem I had to memorize in a high school German course. Therefore I, a captured American, address my Italian captors with the following sentence: 'Kennst du das Land, wo die Zitronen blühen?' Now, let us describe the situation in Gricean terms. I intend to produce a certain effect in them, namely, the effect of believing that I am a German officer; and I intend to produce this effect by means of their recognition of my intention. I intend that they should think that I am trying to tell them that I am a German officer. But does it follow from this account that when I say 'Kennst du das Land . . .' etc., what I mean is, 'I am a German officer', or even 'Ich bin ein deutscher Offizier', because what the words mean is, 'Knowest thou the land where the lemon trees bloom?' Of course, I want my captors to be deceived into thinking that what I mean is 'I am a German officer', but part of what is involved in the deception is getting them to think that that is what the words which I utter mean in German. At one point in the *Philosophical Investigations* Wittgenstein (1953) says 'Say "it's cold here" and mean "it's warm here".' The reason we are unable to do this is that what we can mean is a function of what we are saying. Meaning is more than a matter of intention, it is also a matter of convention.

Grice's account can be amended to deal with counter-examples of this kind. We have here a case where I am trying to produce a certain effect by means of the recognition of my intention to produce that effect, but the device I use to produce this effect is one which is conventionally, by the rules governing the use of that device, used as a means of producing quite different illocutionary effects. We must therefore reformulate the Gricean account of meaning in such a way as to make it clear that one's meaning something when one says something is more than just contingently related to what the sentence means in the language one is speaking. In our analysis of illocutionary acts, we must capture both the intentional and the conventional aspects and especially the relationship between them. In the performance of an illocutionary act the speaker intends to produce a certain effect by means of getting the hearer to recognize his intention to produce that effect, and furthermore, if he is using words literally, he intends this recognition to be achieved in virtue of the fact that the rules for using the expressions he utters associate the expressions with the production of that effect. It is this *combination* of elements which we shall need to express in our analysis of the illocutionary act.

HOW TO PROMISE

I shall now attempt to give an analysis of the illocutionary act of promising. In order to do this I shall ask what conditions are necessary and sufficient for the act or promising to have been performed in the utterance of a given sentence. I shall attempt to answer this question by stating these conditions as a set of propositions such that the conjunction of the members of the set entails the proposition that a speaker made a promise, and the proposition that the speaker made a promise entails this conjunction. Thus each condition will be a necessary condition for the performance of the act of promising, and taken collectively the set of conditions will be a sufficient condition for the act to have been performed.

If we get such a set of conditions we can extract from them a set of rules for the use of the function indicating device. The method here is analogous to discovering the rules of chess by asking oneself what are the necessary and sufficient conditions under which one can be said to have correctly moved a knight or castle or checkmated a player, etc. We are in the position of someone who has learned to play chess without ever having the rules formulated and who wants such a formulation. We learned how to play the game of illocutionary acts, but in general it was done without an explicit formulation of the rules, and the first step in getting such a formulation is to set out the conditions for the performance of a particular illocutionary act. Our inquiry will therefore serve a double philosophical purpose. By stating a set of conditions for the performance of a particular illocutionary act we shall have offered a partial explication of that notion and shall also have paved the way for the second step, the formulation of the rules.

I find the statement of the conditions very difficult to do, and I am not entirely satisfied with the list I am about to present. One reason for the difficulty is that the notion of a promise, like most notions in ordinary language, does not have absolutely strict rules. There are all sorts of odd, deviant, and borderline promises; and counter-examples, more or less bizarre, can be produced against my analysis. I am inclined to think we shall not be able to get a set of knock down necessary and sufficient conditions that will exactly mirror the ordinary use of the word 'promise'. I am confining my discussion, therefore, to the centre of the concept of promising and ignoring the fringe, borderline, and partially defective cases. I also confine my discussion to full-blown explicit promises and ignore promises made by elliptical turns of phrase, hints, metaphors, etc.

Another difficulty arises from my desire to state the conditions without certain forms of circularity. I want to give a list of conditions for the performance of a certain illocutionary act, which do not themselves mention the performance of any illocutionary acts. I need to satisfy this condition in order to offer an explication of the notion of an illocutionary act in general, otherwise I should simply be showing the relation between different illocutionary acts. However, although there will be no reference to illocutionary *acts*, certain illocutionary *concepts* will appear in the analysans as well as in the analysandum; and I think this form of circularity is unavoidable because of the nature of constitutive rules.

In the presentation of the conditions I shall first consider the case of a sincere promise and then show how to modify the conditions to allow for insincere promises. As our inquiry is semantical rather than syntactical, I shall simply assume the existence of grammatically well-formed sentences.

Given that a speaker S utters a sentence T in the presence of a hearer H, then, in the utterance of T, S sincerely (and non-defectively) promises that p to H if and only if:

1 Normal input and output conditions obtain

I use the terms 'input' and 'output' to cover the large and indefinite range of conditions under which any kind of serious linguistic communication is possible. 'Output' covers the conditions for intelligible speaking and 'input' covers the conditions for understanding. Together they include such things as that the speaker and hearer both know how to speak the language; both are conscious of what they are doing; the speaker is not acting under duress or threats; they have no physical impediments to communication, such as deafness, aphasia or laryngitis; they are not acting in a play or telling jokes, etc.

2 S expresses that p in the utterance of T

This condition isolates the propositional content from the rest of the speech act and enables us to concentrate on the peculiarities of promising in the rest of the analysis.

3 In expressing that p, S predicates a future act A of S

In the case of promising the function indicating device is an expression whose scope includes certain features of the proposition. In a promise an act must be predicated of the speaker and it cannot be a past act. I cannot promise to have done something, and I cannot promise that someone else will do something. (Although I can promise to see that he will do it.) The notion of an act, as I am construing it for present purposes, includes refraining from acts, performing series of acts, and may also include states and conditions: I may promise not to do something, I may promise to do something repeatedly, and I may promise to be or remain in a certain state or condition. I call conditions (2) and (3) the *propositional content conditions*.

4 H would prefer S's doing A to his not doing A, and S believes H would prefer his doing A to his not doing A

One crucial distinction between promises on the one hand and threats on the other is that a promise is a pledge to do something for you, not to you, but a threat is a pledge to do something to you, not for you. A promise is defective if the thing promised is something the promisee does not want done; and it is further defective if the promisor does not believe the promisee wants it done, since a non-defective promise must be intended as a promise and not as a threat or warning. I think both halves of this double condition are necessary in order to avoid fairly obvious counter-examples.

One can, however, think of apparent counter-examples to this condition as stated. Suppose I say to a lazy student 'If you don't hand in your paper on time I promise you I will give you a failing grade in the course'. Is this utterance a promise? I am inclined to think not; we would more naturally describe it as a warning or possibly even a threat. But why then is it possible to use the locution 'I promise' in such a case? I think we use it here because 'I promise' and 'I hereby promise' are among the strongest function indicating devices for *commitment* provided by the English language. For that reason we often use these expressions in the performance of speech acts which are not strictly speaking promises but in which we wish to emphasize our commitment. To illustrate this, consider another apparent counter-example to the analysis along different lines. Sometimes, more commonly I think in the United States than in England, one hears people say 'I promise' when making an emphatic assertion. Suppose, for example, I accuse you of having stolen the money. I say, 'You stole that money, didn't you?' You reply 'No, I didn't, I promise you I didn't'. Did you make a promise in this case? I find it very unnatural to describe your utterance as a promise. This utterance would be more aptly described as an emphatic denial, and we can explain the occurrence of the function indicating device 'I promise' as derivative from genuine promises and serving here as an expression adding emphasis to your denial.

In general the point stated in condition (4) is that if a purported promise is to be non-defective the thing promised must be something the hearer wants done, or considers to be in his interest, or would prefer being done to not being done, etc.; and the speaker must be aware of or believe or know, etc. that this is the case. I think a more elegant and exact formulation of this condition would require the introduction of technical terminology.

5 *It is not obvious to both S and H that S will do A in the normal course of events*

This condition is an instance of a general condition on many different kinds of illocutionary acts to the effect that the act must have a point. For example, if I make a request to someone to do something which it is obvious that he is already doing or is about to do, then my request is pointless and to that extent defective. In an actual speech situation, listeners, knowing the rules for performing illocutionary acts, will assume that this condition is satisfied. Suppose, for example, that in the course of a public speech I say to a member of my audience 'Look here, Smith, pay attention to what I am saying'. In order to make sense of this utterance the audience will have to assume that Smith has not been paying attention or at any rate that it is not obvious that he has been paying attention, that the question of his paying attention has arisen in some way; because a condition for making a request is that it is not obvious that the hearer is doing or about to do the thing requested.

Similarly with promises. It is out of order for me to promise to do something that it is obvious I am going to do anyhow. If I do seem to be making such a promise, the only way my audience can make sense of my utterance is to assume that I believe that it is not obvious that I am going to do the thing promised. A happily married man who promises his wife he will not desert her in the next week is likely to provide more anxiety than comfort.

Parenthetically I think this condition is an instance of the sort of phenomenon stated in Zipf's law. I think there is operating in our language, as in most forms of human behavior, a principle of least effort, in this case a principle of maximum illocutionary ends with minimum phonetic effort; and I think condition (5) is an instance of it.

I call conditions such as (4) and (5) *preparatory conditions*. They are *sine quibus non* of happy promising, but they do not yet state the essential feature.

6 *S intends to do A*

The most important distinction between sincere and insincere promises is that in the case of the sincere promise the speaker intends to do the act promised, in the case of the insincere promise he does not intend to do the act. Also in sincere promises the speaker believes it is possible for him to do the act (or to refrain from doing it), but I think the proposition that he intends to do it entails that he thinks it is possible to do (or refrain from doing) it, so I am not stating that as an extra condition. I call this condition the *sincerity condition*.

7   *S intends that the utterance of T will place him under an obligation to do A*

The essential feature of a promise is that it is the undertaking of an obligation to perform a certain act. I think that this condition distinguishes promises (and other members of the same family such as vows) from other kinds of speech acts. Notice that in the statement of the condition we only specify the speaker's intention; further conditions will make clear how that intention is realized. It is clear, however, that having this intention is a necessary condition of making a promise; for if a speaker can demonstrate that he did not have this intention in a given utterance, he can prove that the utterance was not a promise. We know, for example, that Mr Pickwick did not promise to marry the woman because we know he did not have the appropriate intention.

I call this the *essential condition*.

8   *S intends that the utterance of T will produce in H a belief that conditions (6) and (7) obtain by means of the recognition of the intention to produce that belief, and he intends this recognition to be achieved by means of the recognition of the sentence as one conventionally used to produce such beliefs*

This captures our amended Gricean analysis of what it is for the speaker to mean to make a promise. The speaker intends to produce a certain illocutionary effect by means of getting the hearer to recognize his intention to produce that effect, and he also intends this recognition to be achieved in virtue of the fact that the lexical and syntactical character of the item he utters conventionally associates it with producing that effect.

Strictly speaking this condition could be formulated as part of condition (1), but it is of enough philosophical interest to be worth stating separately. I find it troublesome for the following reason. If my original objection to Grice is really valid, then surely, one might say, all these iterated intentions are superfluous; all that is necessary is that the speaker should seriously utter a sentence. The production of all these effects is simply a consequence of the hearer's knowledge of what the sentence means, which in turn is a consequence of his knowledge of the language, which is assumed by the speaker at the outset. I think the correct reply to this objection is that condition (8) explicates what it is for the speaker to 'seriously' utter the sentence, i.e. to utter it and mean it, but I am not completely confident about either the force of the objection or of the reply.

9 *The semantical rules of the dialect spoken by S and H are such that T is correctly and sincerely uttered if and only if conditions (1)–(8) obtain*

This condition is intended to make clear that the sentence uttered is one which by the semantical rules of the language is used to make a promise. Taken together with condition (8), it eliminates counter-examples like the captured soldier example considered earlier. Exactly what the formulation of the rules is, we shall soon see.

So far we have considered only the case of a sincere promise. But insincere promises are promises nonetheless, and we now need to show how to modify the conditions to allow for them. In making an insincere promise the speaker does not have all the intentions and beliefs he has when making a sincere promise. However, he purports to have them. Indeed it is because he purports to have intentions and beliefs which he does not have that we describe his act as insincere. So to allow for insincere promises we need only to revise our conditions to state that the speaker takes responsibility for having the beliefs and intentions rather than stating that he actually has them. A clue that the speaker does take such responsibility is the fact that he could not say without absurdity, e.g. 'I promise to do *A* but I do not intend to do *A*'. To say 'I promise to do *A* is to take responsibility for intending to do *A*, and this condition holds whether the utterance was sincere or insincere. To allow for the possibility of an insincere promise then we have only to revise condition (6) so that it states not that the speaker intends to do *A*, but that he takes responsibility for intending to do *A*, and to avoid the charge of circularity I shall phrase this as follows:

6* *S intends that the utterance of T will make him responsible for intending to do A*

Thus amended (and with 'sincerely' dropped from our analysandum and from condition (9), our analysis is neutral on the question whether the promise was sincere or insincere.

RULES FOR THE USE OF THE FUNCTION INDICATING DEVICE

Our next task is to extract from our set of conditions a set of rules for the use of the function indicating device. Obviously not all of our conditions are equally relevant to this task. Condition (1) and conditions of the forms (8) and (9) apply generally to all kinds of normal illocutionary acts and are not peculiar to promising. Rules for the function indicating device for promising are to be found corresponding to conditions (2)–(7).

The semantical rules for the use of any function indicating device P for promising are:

Rule 1: P is to be uttered only in the context of a sentence (or larger stretch of discourse) the utterance of which predicates some future act A of the speaker S.

I call this the *propositional content rule*. It is derived from the propositional content conditions (2) and (3).

Rule 2: P is to be uttered only if the hearer H would prefer S's doing A to his not doing A, and S believes H would prefer S's doing A to his not doing A.

Rule 3: P is to be uttered only if it is not obvious to both S and H that S will do A in the normal course of events.

I call rules (2) and (3) *preparatory rules*. They are derived from the preparatory conditions (4) and (5).

Rule 4: P is to be uttered only if S intends to do A.

I call this the *sincerity rule*. It is derived from the sincerity condition (6).

Rule 5:   The utterance of P counts as the undertaking of an obligation to do A.

I call this the *essential rule*.

These rules are ordered: Rules 2–5 apply only if Rule 1 is satisfied, and Rule 5 applies only if Rules 2 and 3 are satisfied as well.

Notice that whereas rules 1–4 take the form of quasi-imperatives, i.e. they are of the form: utter P only if x, rule 5 is of the form:

the utterance of P counts as Y. Thus rule 5 is of the kind peculiar to systems of constitutive rules which I discussed above.

Notice also that the rather tiresome analogy with games is holding up remarkably well. If we ask ourselves under what conditions a player could be said to move a knight correctly, we would find preparatory conditions, such as that it must be his turn to move, as well as the essential condition stating the actual positions the knight can move to. I think that there is even a sincerity rule for competitive games, the rule that each side tries to win. I suggest that the team which 'throws' the game is behaving in a way closely analogous to the speaker who lies or makes false promises. Of course, there usually are no propositional content rules for games, because games do not, by and large, represent states of affairs.

If this analysis is of any general interest beyond the case of promising then it would seem that these distinctions should carry over into other types of speech act, and I think a little reflection will show that they do. Consider, e.g., giving an order. The preparatory conditions include that the speaker should be in a position of authority over the hearer, the sincerity condition is that the speaker wants the ordered act done, and the essential condition has to do with the fact that the utterance is an attempt to get the hearer to do it. For assertions, the preparatory conditions include the fact that the hearer must have some basis for supposing the asserted proposition is true, the sincerity condition is that he must believe it to be true, and the essential condition has to do with the fact that the utterance is an attempt to inform the hearer and convince him of its truth. Greetings are a much simpler kind of speech act, but even here some of the distinctions apply. In the utterance of 'Hello' there is no propositional content and no sincerity condition. The preparatory condition is that the speaker must have just encountered the hearer, and the essential rule is that the utterance indicates courteous recognition of the hearer.

A proposal for further research then is to carry out a similar analysis of other types of speech acts. Not only would this give us an analysis of concepts interesting in themselves, but the comparison of different analyses would deepen our understanding of the whole subject and incidentally provide a basis for a more serious taxonomy than any of the usual facile categories such as evaluative versus descriptive, or cognitive versus emotive.

NOTES

1 This distinction occurs in Rawls (1955) and Searle (1964).
2 The formulation 'X counts as Y' was originally suggested to me by Max Black.
3 In the sentence 'I promise that I will come' the function indicating device and the propositional element are separate. In the sentence 'I promise to come', which means the same as the first and is derived from it by certain transformations, the two elements are not separate.

Person, process and
practice

EDITOR'S INTRODUCTION

Benveniste's discussion of the category of person in linguistics has considerable consequences for the 'static', structuralist account of how
signification takes place in the engendering by the signifier of a stable
signified. Pronouns, as Benveniste shows, make up the most frequently
occurring items in language but, on each occasion on which they appear,
they enact a special relationship. Where the word 'tree' might refer to a
stable concept 'treeness', personal pronouns such as 'I' or 'you' can have
no general concept or signified. The only thing that 'I' signifies is the user
of the term 'I' who, at the moment of utterance, is referring to him/herself.
Similarly, with 'you', the speaker and hearer of the utterance containing this
term need to know to whom it refers in order for signification to occur.
Thus, pronouns give rise to the linguistic phenomenon of referring to the
direct situation in which the utterance happens, a phenomenon known as
deixis.

   Deixis also takes place whenever any one of numerous items appear
in an instance of *parole*: for example, *this* and *that*; *here* and *there*; *now*
and *then*; and all other 'deictic' categories which force an investigation of
the speech situation. Unsurprisingly, deixis is especially important when we
come to consider the role of subjects in language; as we have seen in
Lacan's account, language, because it pre-exists the child, offers the child
a means of referring to itself and effectively *determines* its thought (see
pp. 8–10 and 186–94). In order to speak about oneself, one must enter a
system which is divorced from oneself. Benveniste makes the same point
below when he observes the radical discrepancy in the dual functioning of
the category 'I': 'I' has a *referent* (the person who utters the word 'I') but

it also has a *referee* (the *linguistic category* of person which appears in that instance of *parole*). The first is a human being, the second is an item of language. Our experience of language is so primordial, however, that we tend to forget this.

The one exception to Benveniste's deictic rules is the third person, he or she. For Benveniste, the third person occurs in examples of *parole* which need not always refer to the instance of their uttering. Although a special case is made for the third person because of the potential generality of its meaning, one could argue, as Jakobson does below, that deictics *all* possess a general as well as a specific meaning (e.g. 'I' = the addresser). Jakobson's essay, which was published a year after Benveniste's, in 1957, refers to deictic categories as 'shifters', and places them firmly within a wider relationship of 'code' to 'message'. These relationships as they are described by Jakobson are pretty straightforward, but it is advisable to avoid the mistaken assumption that the malleable term 'code' can be equated in a direct way with *langue*. Here 'code' is conceived, not as the general system of language, but as a more local factor, entailing a specific kind of notation which, in turn, is tacitly agreed by addresser and addressee.

What Jakobson presents is a classification of verbal categories in terms of the 'code'–'message' relationship and its components: 'speech', 'narrated matter', the 'event' (that is to be narrated, as distinct from the narrated matter) and 'participants' of the event (including addresser, addressee and the participants as narrated in the speech). For those who are familiar with the work of the Russian Formalists or are aware of Jakobson's relation to this school, the separations of 'narrated matter', 'event' and 'participants', for example, will not be too surprising (see Shklovsky 1965; Merquior 1986 pp. 19-33). But the main purpose of Jakobson's essay is to draw up a typology of narrated events which do or do not refer to speech events. This distinction between utterances that refer to themselves as utterances and those which refer to narrated events while covering up the fact that they are utterances is one more version of the 'full' speech/'empty' speech opposition which provides the foundations for the extracts in the first section of Part V.

As a philosophy of language, the arguments of Benveniste and Jakobson are quite bleak. Human beings are offered one system which they must enter and must learn before they can even become subjects and refer to themselves. Furthermore, that act of reference will always be an impoverished one which never quite delivers the goods, largely because there is so much that it cannot signify. Counterposed to this is the theory of language outlined by Gunther Kress. Using Halliday's research into children's language (1975), Kress paints a different picture of how sign users take their place in the system. Kress' account is not so naive as to suggest that the whole edifice of language can be overthrown; nor does he suggest that it is sufficiently tyrannous to result in sporadic guerrilla warfare from its resistant users. What he does demonstrate is that, in the process of learning how to mean, children will gradually incorporate the rules of a language system that is bequeathed to them by their various teachers. However, that incorporation is a process of negotiation and accommodation: children often have their own ideas of how a language works and why it is appropriate to make the kind of assertions and logical connections that often amuse adults. In the examples that Kress examines, speakers are shown to be "agents of linguistic change", adapting to and adjusting a social institution; but what they hold in common with the versions of language described by Jakobson and Benveniste is the evidence *within* the communication of a social situation *outside*, giving shape to the particular instance of language use.

Further reading   Jakobson 1960; F. R. Palmer, 1990; Lyons 1981 pp. 171–242; 1977 pp. 636-718; Huddleston 1969; J. Palmer, 1987 pp. 75–95; Halliday 1975; Kress 1996; Kress and Knapp 1992; Green 1987; Vološinov 1987 pp. 93–115.

19 Émile Benveniste

The nature of pronouns

In the still open debate on the nature of pronouns, it is usual to consider these linguistic forms as constituting a class both formal and functional, in the manner of nominal or verbal forms, for example. Now all languages possess pronouns, and in all of them they are defined as referring to the same categories of expression (personal pronouns, demonstratives, etc.). The universality of these forms and these notions leads to the thought that the problem of pronouns is both a problem of language in general and a problem of individual languages; or better, that it is a problem of individual languages only because it is primarily a problem of language in general. It is as a phenomenon of language that we pose the problem here, in order to show that pronouns do not constitute a unitary class but are of different types depending on the mode of language of which they are the signs. Some belong to the syntax of a language, others are characteristics of what we shall call 'instances of discourse', that is, the discrete and always unique acts by which the language is actualized in speech by a speaker.

The situation of the personal pronouns should be considered first. It is not enough to distinguish them from the other pronouns by a denomination that separates them. It must be seen that the ordinary definition of the personal pronouns as containing the three terms, *I*, *you*, and *he*, simply destroys the notion of 'person'. 'Person' belongs only to *I/you* and is lacking in *he*. This basic difference will be evident from an analysis of *I*.

Between *I* and a noun referring to a lexical notion, there are not only the greatly varying formal differences that the morphological and syntactic structure of particular languages imposes; there are also others that result from the very process of linguistic utterance and which are of a more general and more basic nature. The utterance containing *I* belongs to that level or type of language which Charles Morris (1946) calls pragmatic, which includes, with the signs, those who make use of them. A linguistic text of great length – a scientific treatise, for example – can be imagined in which *I* and *you* would not appear a single time; conversely, it would be difficult to conceive of a short spoken text in which they were not employed. But the other signs of a language are distributed indifferently between these two types of texts. Besides this condition of use, which is itself distinctive, we shall call attention to a fundamental and moreover obvious property of *I* and *you* in the referential organization of linguistic signs. Each instance of use of a noun is referred to a fixed and 'objective' notion, capable of remaining potential or of being actualized in a particular object and always identical with the mental image it awakens. But the instances of the use of *I* do not constitute a class of reference since there is no 'object' definable as *I* to which these instances can refer in identical fashion. Each *I* has its own reference and corresponds each time to a unique being who is set up as such.

What then is the reality to which *I* or *you* refers? It is solely a 'reality of discourse', and this is a very strange thing. *I* cannot be defined except in terms of 'locution', not in terms of objects as a nominal sign is. *I* signifies 'the person who is uttering the present instance of the discourse containing *I*.' This instance is unique by definition and has validity only in its uniqueness. If I perceive two successive instances of discourse containing *I*, uttered in the same voice, nothing guarantees to me that one of them is not a reported discourse, a quotation in which *I* could be imputed to another. It is thus necessary to stress this point: *I* can only be identified by the instance of discourse that contains it and by that alone. It has no value except in the instance in which it is produced. But in the same way it is also as an instance of form that *I* must be taken; the form of *I* has no linguistic existence except in the act of speaking in which it is uttered. There is thus a combined double instance in this process: the instance of *I* as referent and the instance of discourse containing *I* as the referee. The definition can now be stated precisely as: *I* is 'the individual who utters the present instance of discourse containing the linguistic instance *I*'. Consequently, by introducing the situation of 'address', we obtain a symmetrical definition for *you* as the 'individual spoken to in the present instance of discourse containing the linguistic instance *you*'. These definitions refer to *I* and *you* as a category of language and are related to their position in language. We are not considering the specific forms of this category within given languages, and it matters little whether these forms must figure explicitly in the discourse or may remain implicit in it.

This constant and necessary reference to the instance of discourse constitutes the feature that unites to *I/you* a series of 'indicators' which, from their form and their systematic capacity, belong to different classes, some being pronouns, others adverbs, and still others, adverbial locutions.

The demonstratives, *this*, etc., are such indicators inasmuch as their organization correlates with that of the indicators of person, as in Lat. *hic/iste*. Here there is a new and distinctive feature in this series: it is the identification of the object by an indicator of ostension concomitant with the instance of discourse containing the indicator of person. By simultaneous ostension, *this* will be the object designated in the present instance of discourse and the reference implicit in the form (for example, *hic* as opposed to *iste*), which associates it with *I* and *you*. Outside this class, but on the same plane and associated in the same frame of reference, we find the adverbs *here* and *now*. Their relationship with *I* will be shown by defining them: *here* and *now* delimit the spatial and temporal instance coextensive and contemporary with the present instance of discourse containing *I*. This series is not limited to here and now; it is increased by a great number of simple or complex terms that proceed from the same relationship: *today, yesterday, tomorrow, in three days*, etc. It is pointless to define these terms and the demonstratives in general by deixis, as is generally done, unless one adds that the deixis is contemporary with the instance of discourse that carries the indicator of person; it is from this reference that the demonstrative takes its property of being unique and particular each time, which is the uniqueness of the instance of discourse to which it refers.

The essential thing, then, is the relation between the indicator (of person, time, place, object shown, etc.) and the *present* instance of discourse. For from the moment that one no longer refers, by the expression itself, to this relation of the indicator to the unique instance that manifests it, the language has recourse to a series of distinct terms that have a one-to-one correspondence with the first and which refer, not to the instance of discourse, but to 'real' objects, to 'historical' times and places. Hence correlations such as *I: he – here: there – now: then – today: the very day – yesterday: the day before –*

tomorrow: *the day after* – *next week*: *the following week* – *three days ago*: *three days before*, etc. The language itself reveals the profound difference between these two planes.

The reference to the 'speaker' implicit in this whole group of expressions has been treated too lightly and as being self-evident. We rob this reference of its inherent meaning if we do not see the feature by which it is distinguished from other linguistic signs. Yet it is a fact both original and fundamental that these 'pronominal' forms do not refer to 'reality' or to 'objective' positions in space or time but to the utterance, unique each time, that contains them, and thus they reflect their proper use. The importance of their function will be measured by the nature of the problem they serve to solve, which is none other than that of intersubjective communication. Language has solved this problem by creating an ensemble of 'empty' signs that are non referential with respect to 'reality'. These signs are always available and become 'full' as soon as a speaker introduces them into each instance of his discourse. Since they lack material reference, they cannot be misused; since they do not assert anything, they are not subject to the condition of truth and escape all denial. Their role is to provide the instrument of a conversion that one could call the conversion of language into discourse. It is by identifying himself as a unique person pronouncing *I* that each speaker sets himself up in turn as the 'subject'. The use thus has as a condition the situation of discourse and no other. If each speaker, in order to express the feeling he has of his irreducible subjectivity, made use of a distinct identifying signal (in the sense in which each radio transmitting station has its own call letters), there would be as many languages as individuals and communication would become absolutely impossible. Language wards off this danger by instituting a unique but mobile sign, *I*, which can be assumed by each speaker on the condition that he refers each time only to the instance of his own discourse. This sign is thus linked to the *exercise* of language and announces the speaker as speaker. It is this property that establishes the basis for individual discourse, in which each speaker takes over all the resources of language for his own behalf. Habit easily makes us unaware of this profound difference between language as a system of signs and language assumed into use by the individual. When the individual appropriates it, language is turned into instances of discourse, characterized by this system of internal references of which *I* is the key, and defining the individual by the particular linguistic construction he makes use of when he announces himself as the speaker. Thus the indicators *I* and *you* cannot exist as potentialities; they exist only insofar as they are actualized in the instance of discourse, in which, by each of their own instances, they mark the process of appropriation by the speaker.

The systematic nature of language causes the appropriation these indicators signal to appear in the instance of discourse in all the elements capable of 'agreeing' formally, especially in the verb, by means of processes that vary according to the type of idiom. We must emphasize this point: the 'verb form' is an inextricable part of the individual instance of discourse: it is always and necessarily actualized by the act of discourse and in dependence on that act. It cannot admit of any potential and 'objective' form. If the verb is usually represented by its infinitive as the lexical entry in a number of languages, this is purely by convention; the infinitive in language is something completely different from the infinitive in the lexicographic metalanguage. All the variations in the verbal paradigm – aspect, tense, gender, person, etc. – result from that actualization and from that dependence with respect to the instance of discourse, especially the 'tense' of the verb, which is always relative to the instance in which the verb form figures. A finite personal utterance is thus constituted on a double plane: it puts the denominative function of language into operation for references to the object, which language establishes as distinctive lexical signs, and arranges these references to the object with the aid of self-referential indicators corresponding to each of the formal classes that the idiom recognizes.

But is this always true? If language, as it is exercised, is by necessity produced in discrete instances, does not this necessity oblige it to consist only of 'personal' instances? We know empirically that this is not the case. There are utterances in discourse that escape the condition of person in spite of their individual nature; that is, they refer not to themselves but to an 'objective' situation. This is the domain that we call the 'third person'.

The 'third person' in fact represents the unmarked member of the correlation of person. That is why it is not a truism to affirm that the non-person is the only mode of utterance possible for the instances of discourse not meant to refer to themselves but to predicate the process of someone or something outside the instance itself, and this someone or something can always be provided with an objective reference.

Thus, in the formal class of pronouns, those said to be of the 'third person' are, by their function and by their nature, completely different from *I* and *you*. As has long been seen, forms like *he, him, that*, etc. only serve as abbreviated substitutes (Pierre is sick; *he* has a 'fever'); they replace or relay one or another of the material elements of the utterance. But this function is not attached only to pronouns; it can be served by elements of other classes – in French, on occasion by certain verbs ('cet enfant écrit maintenant mieux qu'il ne faisait l'année dernière' [similarly in English: that child writes better now than he *did* last year]). This is a function of syntactic 'representation' which extends to terms taken from different 'parts of speech' and which answers to a need for economy by replacing one segment of the utterance, or even an entire utterance, with a more manageable substitute. Hence the function of these substitutes has nothing in common with that of the indicators of person.

Certain languages show that the 'third person' is indeed literally a 'non-person'. [1] To take just one example among many, here is how the possessive pronominal prefixes are presented in two series (something like inalienable and alienable) in Yuma (California): first person, $?$-, $?an^v$-; second person, m-, man^y-; third person, zero, n^v. [2] The personal reference is a zero reference outside the *I/you* relationship. In other languages (Indo-European chiefly) the regularity of the formal structure and a symmetry of secondary origin produce the impression of three coordinated persons. This is especially the case with modern languages with an obligatory pronoun in which *he* seems to be a member of a paradigm with three terms, on a par with *I* and *you*, or in the inflection of the present in Indo-European with -*mi*, -*si*, -*ti*. In fact, the symmetry is only formal. What must be considered distinctive of the 'third person' is its property of (1) combining with any object reference, (2) never being reflective of the instance of discourse, (3) admitting of a sometimes rather large number of pronominal or demonstrative variants, and (4) not being compatible with the paradigm of referential terms like *here, now*, etc. Even a brief analysis of the forms that are imprecisely classed as pronominal leads thus to the recognition among them of classes of entirely different natures and, consequently, to the distinction between, on the one hand, language as a repertory of signs and a system for combining them and, on the other, language as an activity manifested in instances of discourse which are characterized as such by particular signs.

NOTES

1 See also this volume pp. 320–30.
2 According to Halpern (1946 p. 264).

20 Roman Jakobson

Shifters and verbal categories

1 SHIFTERS AND OTHER DUPLEX STRUCTURES

1.1 A message sent by its addresser must be adequately perceived by its receiver. Any message is encoded by its sender and is to be decoded by its addressee. The more closely the addressee approximates the code used by the addresser, the higher is the amount of information obtained. Both the message (M) and the underlying code (C) are vehicles of linguistic communication, but both of them function in a duplex manner; they may at once be utilized and referred to (= pointed at). Thus a message may refer to the code or to another message, and on the other hand, the general meaning of a code unit may imply a reference (*renvoi*) to the code or to the message. Accordingly four DUPLEX types must be distinguished; (1) two kinds of CIRCULARITY – message referring to message (M/M) and code referring to code (C/C); (2) two kinds of OVERLAPPING – message referring to code (M/C) and code referring to message (C/M).

1.2 (M/M) 'REPORTED SPEECH is speech within speech, a message within a message and at the same time it is also speech about speech, a message about a message', as Vološinov (1929) formulates it in his study of this crucial linguistic and stylistic problem. Such 'relayed' or 'displaced' speech, to use Bloomfield's (1933) terms, may prevail in our discourse, since we are far from confining our speech to events sensed in the present by the speaker himself. We quote others and our own former utterances, and we are even prone to present some of our current experiences in the form of self-quotation, for instance by confronting them with statements by someone else: 'Ye have heard that it hath been said*** But I say unto you***' There is a multiplex scale of linguistic processes for quoted and quasi-quoted speech, *oratio recta*, *obliqua*, and various forms of 'represented discourse' (*style indirect libre*). Certain languages, as for instance Bulgarian (s. Andrejčin 1938), Kwakiutl (s. Boas 1947), and Hopi (s. Whorf 1946), use particular morphological devices to denote events known to the speaker only from the testimony of others. Thus in Tunica all statements made from hearsay (and this covers the majority of sentences in the texts aside from those in direct discourse) are indicated by the presence of /-áni/, a quotative postfix used with a predicative word (Haas 1940).

1.3 (C/C) PROPER NAMES, treated in Gardiner's (1940) 'controversial essay' as a very knotty problem of linguistic theory, take a particular place in our linguistic code: the general meaning of a proper name cannot be defined without a reference to the code. In the code of English, 'Jerry' means a person named Jerry. The circularity is obvious: the name means anyone to whom this name is assigned. The appellative *pup* means a young dog, *mongrel* means a dog of mixed breed, *hound* is a dog used in hunting, while *Fido* means nothing more than a dog whose name is *Fido*. The general meaning of such words as *pup*, *mongrel*, or *hound*, could be indicated by abstractions like puppihood, mongrelness, or houndness, but the general meaning of *Fido* cannot be qualified in this way. To paraphrase Bertrand Russell (1940), there are many dogs called *Fido*, but they do not share any property of 'Fidoness'. Also the indefinite pronoun corresponding to names such as Jean, Jan, Joan, June, etc. – the 'what's-her name' or 'what-do-you-call-her' or 'how-d'ye-call-her' – includes a patent reference to the code.

1.4 (M/C) A message referring to the code is in logic termed an autonymous mode of speech. When we say, *The pup is a winsome animal* or *The pup is whimpering*, the word *pup* designates a young dog, whereas in such sentences as *Pup is a noun which means a young dog*, the word *pup* – one may state with Carnap (1937) – is used as its own designation. Any elucidating interpretation of words and sentences – whether intralingual (circumlocutions, synonyms) or interlingual (translation) – is a message referring to the code. Such a hypostasis – as Bloomfield (1933) pointed out – 'is closely related to quotation, the repetition of speech', and it plays a vital role in the acquisition and use of language.

1.5 (C/M) Any linguistic code contains a particular class of grammatical units which Jespersen (1922) labeled SHIFTERS: the general meaning of a shifter cannot be defined without a reference to the message.

Their semiotic nature was discussed by Burks (1949) in his study on Peirce's classification of signs into symbols, indices, and icons. According to Peirce (1931), a symbol (e.g. the English word *red*) is associated with the represented object by a conventional rule, while an index (e.g. the act of pointing) is in existential relation with the object it represents. Shifters combine both functions and belong therefore to the class of INDEXICAL SYMBOLS. As a striking example Burks (1949) cites the personal pronoun. *I* means the person uttering *I*. Thus on one hand, the sign *I* cannot represent its object without being associated with the latter 'by a conventional rule', and in different codes the same meaning is assigned to different sequences such as *I, ego, ich, ja* etc.: consequently *I* is a symbol. On the other hand, the sign *I* cannot represent its object without 'being in existential relation' with this object: the word *I* designating the utterer is existentially related to his utterance, and hence functions as an index (cf. Benveniste 1956; see also this volume pp. 283–91).

The peculiarity of the personal pronoun and other shifters was often believed to consist in the lack of a single, constant, general meaning. Husserl (1913): 'Das Wort "ich" nennt von Fall zu Fall eine andere Person, und es tut dies mittels immer neuer Bedeutung'. For this alleged multiplicity of contextual meanings, shifters in contradistinction to symbols were treated as mere indices (Bühler 1934). Every shifter, however, possesses its own general meaning. Thus *I* means the addresser (and *you*, the addressee) of the message to which it belongs. For Bertrand Russell (1940), shifters, or in his terms 'egocentric particulars', are defined by the fact that they never apply to more than one thing at a time. This, however, is common to all the syncategorematic terms. E.g. the conjunction *but* each time expresses an adversative relation between two stated concepts and not the generic idea of contrariety. In fact, shifters are distinguished from all other constituents of the linguistic code solely by their compulsory reference to the given message.

The indexical symbols, and in particular the personal pronouns, which the Humboldtian tradition conceives as the most elementary and primitive stratum of language, are, on the contrary, a complex category where code and message overlap. Therefore pronouns belong to the late acquisitions in child language and to the early losses in aphasia. If we observe that even linguistic scientists had difficulties in defining the general meaning of the term *I* (or *you*), which signifies the same intermittent function of different subjects, it is quite obvious that the child who has learned to identify himself with his proper name will not easily become accustomed to such alienable terms as the personal pronouns: be may be afraid of speaking of himself in the first person while being called *you* by his interlocutors. Sometimes he attempts to redistribute these appellations. For instance, he tries to monopolize the first person pronoun: 'Don't dare call yourself I. Only I am I, and you are only you.' Or he uses indiscriminately either *I* or *you* both for the addresser and the addressee so that this pronoun means any participant of the given dialogue. Or finally *I* is so rigorously substituted by the child for his proper name that he readily names any person of his surroundings but stubbornly refuses to utter his own name: the name has for its little bearer only a vocative meaning, opposed to the nominative function of *I*. This attitude may persevere as an infantile survival. Thus Guy de Maupassant confessed that his name sounded quite strange to him when pronounced by himself. The refusal to utter one's own name may become a social custom. Zelenin (1930) notes that in the Samoyede society the name was taboo for its carrier.

1.6 *Jim told me 'flicks' means 'movies'.* This brief utterance includes all four types of duplex structures: reported speech (M/M), the autonymous form of speech (M/C), a proper name (C/C), and shifters (C/M), namely the first person pronoun and the preterit, signaling an event prior to the delivery of the message. In language and in the use of language, duplicity plays a cardinal role. In particular, the classification of grammatical, and especially verbal, categories requires a consistent discrimination of shifters.

2 ATTEMPT TO CLASSIFY VERBAL CATEGORIES

2.1 In order to classify the verbal categories two basic distinctions are to be observed:

1 speech itself (^{s}), and its topic, the narrated matter (^{n});

2 The event itself (E), and any of its participants (P), whether 'performer' or 'undergoer'.

Consequently four items are to be distinguished: a narrated event (E^n), a speech event (E^s), a participant of the narrated event (P^n), and a participant of the speech event (P^s), whether addresser or addressee.

2.1.1 Any verb is concerned with a narrated event. Verbal categories may be subdivided into those which do and those which do not involve the participants of the event. Categories involving the participants may characterize either the participants themselves (P^n) or their relation to the narrated event (P^nE^n). Categories abstracting from the participants characterize either the narrated event itself (E^n)or its relation to another narrated event (E^nE^n). For categories characterizing only one narrated item – either the event (E^n) itself or its participants (P^n)themselves – the term DESIGNATORS will be used, while those categories which characterize a narrated item (E^n or P^n) with respect to another narrated item (E^nE^n or P^nE^n) will be termed CONNECTORS.

Designators indicate either the quality or the quantity of the narrated item and may be termed QUALIFIERS and QUANTIFIERS respectively.

Both designators and connectors may characterize the narrated event (*procès de l'énoncé*) and/or its participants either without or with reference to the speech event (*procès de l'énonciation*) (. ./E^s) or its participants (. ./P^s). Categories implying such a reference are to be termed SHIFTERS; those without such a reference are NON-SHIFTERS.

With regard to these basic dichotomies any generic verbal category can be defined.

2.2 (P^n) Among categories involving the participants of the narrated event, GENDER and NUMBER characterize the participants themselves without reference to the speech event – gender qualifies, and number quantifies the participants. E.g. in Algonquian, verbal forms indicate whether the performer on the one hand, and the undergoer on the other, are animate or inanimate (Bloomfield 1946); and the singleness, duality, or multiplicity of performers as well as undergoers is expressed in Koryak conjugation (Bogoraz 1922).

2.2.1 (P^n/P^s) PERSON characterizes the participants of the narrated event with reference to the participants of the speech event. Thus first person signals the identity of a participant of the narrated event with the performer of the speech event, and the second person, the identity with the actual or potential undergoer of the speech event.

2.3 (E^n) STATUS and ASPECT characterize the narrated event itself without involving its participants and without reference to the speech event. Status (in Whorf's 1946 terminology) defines the logical quality of the event. E.g. in Gilyak, the affirmative, presumptive, negative, interrogative, and negative-interrogative statuses are expressed by special verbal forms (Krejnovič 1934). In English the assertive status uses the 'do' – combinations which in certain conditions are optional for an affirmative assertion but compulsory for a negative or questioned assertion. Aspects quantify the narrated event.

2.3.1 (E^nE^s) TENSE characterizes the narrated event with reference to the speech event. Thus the preterit informs us that the narrated event is anterior to the speech event.

2.4 (P^nE^n) VOICE characterizes the relation between the narrated event and its participants without reference to the speech event or to the speaker.

2.4.1 (P^nE^n/P^s) MOOD characterizes the relation between the narrated event and its participants with reference to the participants of the speech event: in Vinogradov's formulation, this category 'reflects the speaker's view of the character of the connection between the action and the actor or the goal'.

2.5 (E^nE^n) There is no standardized name for this category; such labels as 'relative tense' cover only one of its varieties. Bloomfield's (1946) term 'order' or rather its Greek model 'taxis' seems to be the most appropriate. TAXIS characterizes the narrated event in relation to another narrated event and without reference to the speech event, thus Gilyak distinguishes three kinds of independent taxis – one requires, one admits, and one excludes a dependent taxis, and the dependent taxes express various relationships with the independent verb – simultaneity, anteriority, interruption, concessive connection, etc. A similar Hopi pattern is described by Whorf (1946).

2.5.1 (E^nE^{ns}/E^s) EVIDENTIAL is a tentative label for the verbal category which takes into account three events – a narrated event, a speech event, and a narrated speech event (E^{ns}), namely the alleged source of information about the narrated event. The speaker reports an event on the basis of someone else's report (quotative, i.e. hearsay evidence), of a dream (revelative evidence), of a guess (presumptive evidence) or of his own previous experience (memory evidence). Bulgarian conjugation distinguishes two semantically opposite sets of forms: 'direct narration' ($E^{ns} = E^s$) *vs* 'indirect narration' ($E^{ns} \neq E^s$). To our question, what happened to the steamer Evdokija, a Bulgarian first answered: *zaminala* 'it is claimed to have sailed', and then added: *zamina* 'I bear witness; it sailed.' (Cf. H. G. Lunt 1952 on the systematic distinction made in the Macedonian verbal pattern between 'vouched for' and 'distanced' events.)

2.6 The interrelation of all these generic categories may be illustrated by the over-all scheme shown in Figure 20.1.

	P involved		P not involved	
	Designator	*Connector*	*Designator*	*Connector*
Qualifier:	Gender		Status	
Quantifier:	Number		Aspect	
		Voice		Taxis
Shifter:	Person		Tense	
Shifter:		Mood		Evidential

Figure 20.1

With special regard to the opposition shifters *vs* non-shifters, we condense this model into a simpler table (Figure 20.2).

	P involved		P not involved	
	Designator	*Connector*	*Designator*	*Connector*
Non-shifter:	P^n	P^nE^n	E^n	E^nE^n
Shifter:	P^nP^s	$P^nE^nP^s$	P^nE^s	$E^nE^{ns}E^s$

Figure 20.2

21 Gunther Kress

Social processes and linguistic change: time and history in language

THE DISCURSIVE CONSTRUCTION OF LINGUISTIC HISTORY: SAUSSURE AND HIS READERS

Much of my argument so far has been constructed around the apparent paradox of the social determination of linguistic processes on the one hand and the significance of individual linguistic action on the other. The paradox remains as long as we think of the social (and with it the linguistic system) outside time, 'out of time'. It then has the appearance of a static, fixed system. Such 'snapshot views' underlie the most influential theory in this area in this century, that of Ferdinand de Saussure. He had spent his early years as a scholar working within the last significant period of the study of the histories of (mainly) European languages. His own early work represented an important consolidation of the monumental achievements of nearly a century of intensive research in Europe. Historical linguistics of the nineteenth century was concerned to show the relationship between European languages by tracing each to an assumed common ancestry, and to demonstrate the regularities governing language changes. In that process it demonstrated the 'family' connections between languages as distant as modern Hindi, long-extinct Middle-Eastern languages such as Hittite, and European languages such as Russian, Italian, German, and English, through their links with languages such as ancient Sanskrit and Greek for instance. What this work revealed and inevitably focused on was language as a system constantly in a process of change.

Against this picture of a diachronous system, seen in and through time, subject to constant change, Saussure posited the notion of the synchronous language system with time held still momentarily, a system of regularity and internal consistency, fixed and not subject to change. That was the picture put forward by Saussure in a series of lectures given at the University of Geneva. These were later edited from their lecture notes by two of Saussure's students, Charles Bally and Albert Sechehaye, and published by them after Saussure's death as the enormously influential *Course in General Linguistics*. It needs to be said at once that this book contains the contradictions that I have outlined, the unresolved opposition of diachrony and synchrony, and with it the unresolved opposition of language as a socially and historically determined phenomenon and language as an autonomous system. In my view it is quite unclear how Saussure might have resolved these tensions had he written the book himself – the book is after all a compilation from lecture notes by two students who were making *their* sense, their reading of these lectures. In the book there is a constant tension between these contradictory tendencies, sufficient to suggest that these matters were not settled for Saussure.

What *is* clear however is how the book has been read consistently since then. One reading, that of the synchronous autonomous system, outside time and outside of its social historical context, has been predominant. In that reading the individual language user meets the system as a monolithic, immutable given, which she or he may use but cannot alter. By and large this is the view of the individual's relation which has continued to hold sway, explicitly or implicitly.

My reason for giving this little history is a two-fold one. Firstly, I think that it provides a rather neat example of my discussion in the preceding chapters of the effects of discourses and ideologies on writing *and* on reading. Saussure's text is constructed precisely out of and in the difference between contradictory discourses: the romantic nineteenth-century discourses of freedom, change and of the social (in this case language) as a species of the natural, and the discourses (embodied in this case in the writings, for instance, of Durkheim) of the rule-governed system, of the social as subject to its own laws, and of the individual as subject to the social. The fact that one reading proved predominant is explained in my account by the predominance of the latter set of discourses at the time when Saussure's lectures appeared as a written, objectified text. What seems to have been very much a live dialogue for Saussure himself became for his readers a settled unidimensional text. Secondly, I believe that it is both important and helpful to see the historical, ideological and discursive constructedness of views which have taken on the mantle of the obvious. Awareness of this kind allows us to find a different, our own, reading position, and with that some useful space for independent analysis and thinking.

In this case it is the role of the individual *vis-à-vis* social and linguistic processes that I wish to focus on, and to locate in a different discourse.

SPEAKERS AS AGENTS OF LINGUISTIC CHANGE

There are no doubt very many ways in which linguistic change can be thought about. In this chapter, I will focus on just two: a change to the ideological, discursive and generic position of individual speakers, in other words a change to the 'linguistic make-up' of individuals; and a change to the linguistic system through changes in discourses, genres and ideologies brought about by 'speaking agents'.

Every text involves development, progression and change. It is one of the demands of texts that there is change. This can appear in quite trivial ways; for instance, as I read back over my manuscript I eliminate repetitions. Where I find that I have written the same word twice within reasonably close proximity I change one to a near synonym. So for instance I have quite recently changed a repeated use of *significant* to *important*. The conventional explanation for that is that repetitions 'jar'; though I myself do not find that repetition jarring. I suspect that the real reason is that repetition signals absence of development and progression, and thus contravenes a fundamental convention of texts.

Progression is a formal characteristic of most genres. Take this little narrative written, or typed rather, by a seven-year-old boy.

Seven-year-old boy's narrative
Once upon a time there lived two poeple axnd their son
they were verxyxexexx poor.
In their ganden they groo cavig and bens
One day they looked in their muny bocxks and there wxxxas
5   onlex
One xpene in it.
What shal we do?

xWe will have to sell the table.
Tomorrow we will sell in the market.
10   The ~~nexset~~ next day the boy went to the market
He sold the table but there was not anuf muny.
He was just ~~as~~ xx about to go home wxhen he notist that
the xxxstall ~~nexsk~~ next-door was selling some thing
difrnt.
15   He went to the stall and xxx said what are ~~xyxx xxxx~~ you
selling.
We are selling pots pans and friing-pans
How much is that pot it is 4 penes Iwill bxy it.
xxx It was a hot sony day so he put his coat in it.
20   When he got home he looked in the pot and there was two coat's
Daddy look mummy look then they tuck one coat out.
And anuth coat aperd then they put their shous in and
there was twis-as many as befro.
THey solld shoescoat's and hats.
25   they lived happly ever rft..

The progression is obvious, and generically determined: from description of initial state, to complication/crisis, to resolution and final inversion of the initial situation: *One day they looked in their muny bocks and there was onle one pene in it*, to: *They solld shoescoat's and hats. they lived happly every rft* . . . The conventionality might obscure the real significance of this text, namely that there is thoroughgoing progression throughout the text, which proceeds with an algebraic precision. The constant and insistent experience of such texts suggests to the child that in texts 'something always happens', that things at the end are not what they were at the beginning. This experience sets up a pattern of expectation for all texts. Texts that do not meet this expectation are considered inconclusive, repetitive, texts which 'don't get anywhere'. These are negative judgments in Anglo-Australian culture; though there is no reason why other cultures might not attach different valuations to such texts.

The two important points are: firstly, the habitually-established expectation of 'progression', that progression of time also implies progression of some other kind. That is a deeply-coded notion in western thought, and narrative is just one, though a most important instance of it. Secondly, the writer is the agent of the progression. So although the genre demands progression, the writer implements the genre, and thereby causes there to be progression in the text. The individual therefore is the one who causes progression in the text. When this becomes generalised to all texts the importance of the point is obvious: individuals are causally involved in progression change, and consequently where that progression or change affects the formal constitution of discourse or genre, it is still the individual who is agentive in this process.

Education is quintessentially about the progression and change of individuals in relation to dominant systems of classification. That progression is most visible in interactively-constructed texts. Here is an example from a childcare centre. The three participants are the teacher, Sarah (who is four years and six months old) and Aaron (who is four years and five months old). After an initial discussion about bedwetting between Aaron, Sarah and the teacher, the talk focuses on the pictures on a poster the teacher has been pinning up.

Talk

	Teacher:	Look at this (pointing to picture of mother and young rhino)
	Sarah:	His mother's a lot of toothes.
	Teacher:	How many teeth? How many have they got?
5	Sarah:	One two three, four
	Teacher:	What are they up the top?
	Sarah:	One two three four five
	Teacher:	Five at the top and four at the bottom
	Aaron:	No they're pimples
10	Teacher:	Do you think they're pimples?
	Aaron:	Yeah
	Teacher:	But they're where his teeth should be . . . do you think they're just a different colour?
	Aaron:	Well . . . that . . . those are pimples cos those are
15		pink
	Teacher:	Um . . . could be too . . . and what do you call those things there?
	Sarah:	Whiskers
	Teacher:	You do too and what's that Sarah?
20	Sarah:	A ear
	Teacher:	It's a funny looking ear isn't it?
	Aaron:	Yes . . . a little ear

Sarah: Thats got two . . . one, two . . . two ears
Teacher: Do you think they'd be friendly? . . . these
25   rhinoceroses?
Aaron & Sarah: No
Teacher: Why not?
Aaron: Cos they'll eat people
Teacher: How do you know? What makes them look unfriendly?
30 Aaron: Their teeth . . . they can eat people
Teacher: They *are* big. What about this animal?
Sarah: That hasn't got any teeth
Teacher: Hasn't he?
Sarah: No
35 Teacher: Do you think he'd be friendly?
Sarah & Aaron: Yes
Teacher: Look what he *has* got
Sarah: He's got little claws
Teacher: Claws
40 Sarah: See . . . but that . . . but he's still our friendly . . .
Teacher: He's still friendly even if he's got claws?
Sarah: Look . . . they're not flendry
Aaron: Yes they are
Teacher: Do you think lions are friendly Aaron?
45 Aaron: Yeah . . . because . . . if they . . . if people hurt
          them they hurt them back
Teacher: And it's quite safe you think if you don't hurt them?
Aaron: Yes
Teacher: I don't know

This extract shows a series of textual episodes constructed around the introduction of a (classificatory) term and a brief exchange about its integration into one classificatory system or another. For instance, in lines 3–16 Sarah introduces *toothes*. The teacher implicitly accepts this classification (of a part of the picture) by the question of how many teeth there are. Aaron challenges the classification, line 9, *No they're pimples*. The interaction now focuses on two differing classificatory principles, the teacher's authoritative (note the *should*) *they're where his teeth should be* and Aaron's *cos those are pink*. The teacher does not accept Aaron's classification, leaving the matter unresolved: *Um . . . could be too . . .* To take another example, lines 31–49. Here the question is whether lions are to be classified as friendly or not, and on what grounds. The teacher's principle seems to be that 'claws' indicates the category 'unfriendly'; Sarah seems to equate absence of teeth with friendliness; and Aaron's principle seems to involve the question whether the animal initiates the unfriendliness or merely acts in retaliation. The teacher again leaves the question of which classification system 'lion' is to be assigned to up in the air; though as she indicates her agreement quite clearly in other cases (lines 19–21) the children are no doubt aware of the absence of the teacher's agreement.

Clearly there is progression in these examples: it is not overtly carried to one conclusion, though there will be other occasions when the status of these terms will be raised again. At issue here are the systems of linguistic and cultural valuations. The teacher acts as an agent of cultural reproduction, though the children too are active in this process. In this text the two children attempt to sustain their classification; the teacher does not overtly insist on asserting her classification. For the three participants some changes will have occurred during the construction of this text: the teacher may have taken some notice of the force of Aaron's argument and hence amended her classification of 'lion' somewhat; Aaron and Sarah will equally have taken note of the teacher's classification, and made adjustments to their cultural/linguistic classificatory system. Over a long time-period, in their experience of growing into culture and society (and with them, into language) they will find it difficult to sustain their classifications – they will become 'acculturated' and 'socialised'. The process as such is not a conscious one, though in the interaction the differences are made obvious and become the focus of the interaction.

Children, like all those with lesser power, are at a disadvantage: their classifications, even though they may be supported by better reasons, do not generally carry the day. For them it is a matter of falling in with the classificatory systems of those who are more powerful. That however is, as I have attempted to show, not merely a passive 'acquisition' of language, but an active (re)construction of that system in dialogue, in interaction, and in sustained resistance – which is however always a merely temporary resistance over a particular term. The process of language learning which is most congenial to my views is that of Michael Halliday (1975) in his *Learning How to Mean*. He too regards the language learner as an active participant, engaged in constructing a system of meaning-making for herself or himself, in response to interactive, social processes and demands. Although there are significant theoretical differences between Halliday's account and mine, I believe that the two are ultimately compatible in broad terms. The relevant and most significant aspects for both approaches lie, I believe, in the role given to the individual learner in the process of social and language learning. In my view the learner is active and agentive, rather than a merely passive recipient. He or she constructs the linguistic system for herself or himself in constant tension between the classifications which seem appropriate to the child at any one time and those of the larger groups into which the child is growing. Although the final outcome is that children are fully socialised into the rules, values,and meanings of their social group, the path that they have taken in travelling there leaves them situated in quite a different way than they are in a theory which regards them as merely acquiring an existent system or passively acquiescing in having a system imposed on them. In my account the language learner is always active at any stage in the process. Consequently significance attaches to everything that she or he does. Whereas within other theoretical positions it is possible to account for the child's behaviour in terms of its 'shortfall' or 'deviance' from the adult's model, and to brand that behaviour as 'error', in my account there is a need to attend carefully to the actions of the learner, for they express three crucial things at least: the child's system of classification with its cognitive, conceptual, cultural and social implications, the child's understanding of the adult systems, and the tension between these two.

Moreover, if we wish to regard the adult speaker/writer, hearer/listener as a potentially agentive participant in processes of ideological and discursive/linguistic change – as I do – we need an account which plausibly brings him or her to that position. If we assume that language learners are essentially passive we cannot account for their activeness as mature speakers.

In my examples so far I have tried to illustrate progression and change within a single text. The most spectacular example of progression is that of individual language learners. To conclude this section I wish to illustrate progression and change in relation to genre. The three brief examples of written texts are, broadly, in the genre of scientific description. They were written by the same child at the ages of seven, twelve and fifteen respectively.

Three written texts

The Ant

The ant have a nest
under the ground.
The nest has many tunnels.
There are different kinds of ane in the nest.
There is a queen ant and male ants and worker and ants.

Beaked whales

(1) The Beaked Whales live out in mid-ocean, where the tasty squid are found. (2) Squid, it seems, provide most of their meals. (3) Men do not know much about their family because even the scientists who study whales have seen very few Beaked Whales. (4) Generally members of this family have long, narrow snouts, or 'beaks'. (5) They have very few teeth, just one or two on each side of the lower jaw, and these sometimes poke out like small tusks.
(6) The largest of this family is the Baird's Beaked Whale. (7) It grows to 42 ft. in length. (8) Most beaked Whales range between 15 and 30 ft. (9) The Bottlenose gets to be about 30 ft. long, and its cousin known as Cuvier's Beaked Whale grows to about 26 ft.
(10) Cuvier's Whale is rarely seen, though it is believed that it lives in all oceans. (11) It is unusual in colour so if you should see one, you should be able to recognise it. (12) Most whales have dark grey backs and pale undersides. (13) Cuvier's Beaked Whales instead has a light back and underside and two small tusk-teeth poke up outside the mouth of the males.
(14) Bottlenose is even more odd. (15) You may possibly see one travelling in a small school of ten or twelve whales.

Here I do not wish to give a description of the three texts in terms of the development of genre or of generic features of the texts themselves. Rather I am interested how the writer is defined or placed cognitively, conceptually and socially by his relative control of the genre. The writer's use of modality differs markedly between 'The Ant' and 'Beaked Whales'. The former has the single modality of factuality or certainty expressed by the so-called universal present tense, *The Ant have* a nest. The latter has a range of modalities from certainty: sentence 1 *The Beaked Whales live* out in; to a hypothetical modality: *it seems* [to me and other scientific writers] sentence 2; to a blurring, generalising modality: sentence 4 *Generally members of this family*, sentence 8 *Most beaked whales*; to possibility: *you should be able to recognise it*, sentence 11; to conjecture: sentence 10 *it is believed*. The difference reflects both the writer's stance *vis-à-vis* the material he is discussing, and in this, his stance *vis-à-vis* the communities in which the genres function. That is, the unidimensional modality of the first text indicates that the writer has only the single position *vis-à-vis* the material, that of description, definition, and factuality. He has neither the possibility of distancing himself from the material nor therefore the possibility of a nuanced valuation. The possibility of a differentiated stance towards the material and therefore of differentiated stances towards social groups does not arise. The multidimensional modality of the second text on the other hand indicates that the writer has a number of finely nuanced positions which he can take up *vis-à-vis* the material. The possibility of finely discriminating valuations is therefore present.

The first text is not 'addressed'; that is, no audience seems to be envisaged, or structured into the text. The reading position is identical with the writing position. The second text is addressed: *so if you should see one, You may possibly see*. The writing position is largely that of the anonymous scientist/writer: sentence 2 *Squid, it seems*; sentence 10 *Cuvier's whale is rarely seen, though it is believed*; though at this stage this writing position is not entirely consistently maintained. In sentence 3 the writer mentions *the scientists who study whales*, that is, he is not a member of that group. In the second text the writer has distance from the material, and also from his audience. There is thus a double-coded self/other distinction, which gives the writer a quite specific positioning.

In the third text the uncertainty of identification with the community defined by the genre has gone. The example here is part of a larger text of about 3500 words, with illustrative technical drawings. In each case only the opening lines of each of the four chapters are reproduced here.

Telecommunication

The electric telegraph

Before the invention of the Electric Telegraph the fastest means of conveying a message had been shouting, the speed of sound, and signalling with flags and the like. Both of these methods only good over
5   very short distances and relied on good weather conditions. The Electric Telegraph seemed instantaneous in comparison to previous methods.

Telegraphy involves completing one or more electrical circuits being completed and broken to transmit a code . . .

The telephone

10 Even though the electric telegraph was extremely fast at transmitting messages, all the messages had to be coded and sent along line one at a time with each word taking several seconds. So when the tele-phone came into operation it increased the speed of communication as well as making it more personal
15 Charles Grafton Page (1812–1865) discovered, in 1837, that rapid changes in the magnetism of iron caused it to give out a musical note. Also that the pitch of the note depended on the frequence with which these changes occurred. In 1860 Phillip Reis (1834–1874) was the first to transmit a musical melody electrically over a distance.
20 He stretched an animal membrane over a small cone to which he attached a platinum wire with sealing sax. The wire was part of an electrical circuit and when the membrane vibrated the wire completed and broke the circuit at the same frequence as the sound. At the other end of the circuit was a knitting needle with a coil of wires rapped
25 around it, and through the fact that Page had discovered the knitting needle reproduced the sound. Three years later he claimed that words can also be made out . . .

The radio or wireless

The telegraph and telephone had revolutionised communication but they
30 both had one big drawback in that they couldn't be used to communi-cate with moving vehicles such as trains or boats.
The story of radio perhaps begins with Joseph Henry (1779–1878) who, in 1842, showed that electrical discharges were oscillations.

The television

35 The first developments of the television came at about the same time as the radio, but it took much longer to develop than the radio . . .

The writer is fully in control of the genre. It is a multimodal text: line 7 *Telegraphy involves completing*, and line 32 *The story of radio perhaps begins*; line 10 *Even though the electric telegraph was extremely*; line 5–6 *The electric telegraph seemed instantaneous*; line 26 *Three years later he claimed*. These clearly indicate the writer's stance towards his material and towards his audience; and he now writes as a member of the scientific community. Within this he establishes his own writing position, for instance most obviously in line 32 *The story of radio perhaps begins* where *perhaps* indicates his own careful judgment; or lines 5–6 *The Electric Telegraph seemed instantaneous in comparison*.

The modalities of 'The Ant' text suggest a world of certainty, certain because no questions as yet arise for the writer, in which the writer is at one with what he is writing. The modalities of the third text suggest a complex world, made up of some certainties, some generally-accepted hypotheses, historically given 'facts', and carefully made personal valuations. In each of the two texts the individual has a specific positioning: as an unself-conscious individual in the first, and as a highly self-conscious member of a complex of social groupings in the second.

THE LINGUISTIC SYSTEM AND TIME

There are, as I mentioned at the outset of this chapter, very many aspects of this topic which I will not be able to discuss. For instance, in many texts one or both participants actively resist change – as in the case where a politician resists the pressing of an interviewer to shift his or her position over some problematic matter, or to concede a point in a contentious area. Advertisers may not wish to imply any change in their product, so that a McEagleburger is always a McEagleburger and texts are constructed to assert this. Conservative politics – at whatever level – are about texts of this kind. However, such texts still bear the obligatory signs of 'progression', however superficial.

One aspect which I will address very briefly is the effect of individual action on the discursive and generic system overall. Imagine that because of her or his social positioning a speaker is placed in such a way that she or he uses a certain set of discourses, sexist discourses included. Because of that social positioning he or she also tends to assume specific roles in interactions and in texts, let us assume, the roles which are always the less powerful. There is therefore an habitual, though socially-determined, conjunction of a certain subject position and certain textual and reading positions. That conjunction determines the use of certain forms of language. Over time that habitual use becomes codified, and then becomes a code.

To make this concrete: sexist discourse suggests subject positions for women. That is, it suggests to women to be and to act in certain ways, to relate to others in a particular manner, and so on. This will strongly shape the kinds of language a woman will use or that will be used about women. Assume further that the woman, by the effects of class and gender is habitually placed in certain ways in genres, for instance, generally not to be a committee member, let alone the chairperson; not usually to be interviewer but interviewee in say, an interview in the doctor's surgery; not to be the professional; but to be engaged in household labour, to be patronised by all, to be always a part of the world of the private and not to have a public role. Her modes of speaking clearly will be shaped by this experience. If the situation persists, the mode of speaking will become habitual and 'natural' for her. If the situation is one where many speakers are involved, the same general kinds of texts will be being produced on many occasions. A recognisably distinct manner of speaking, a new code, will have emerged. New speakers will grow into a situation where the code already exists as the usual, the 'natural' or even the 'proper' way for women to talk. In this way a code is established by individuals acting as social agents in time, whose actions are nevertheless always socially conditioned.

In much the same way modes of talking can become altered. The theoretical analyses of feminist writers, and the social practices of feminists over a long period are bringing about a recognisable change in the discourses around gender, and in social practices.

LANGUAGE, TIME AND EDUCATION

Social systems are complex, and language is no exception. Furthermore, these systems are constantly in process, in tension, constantly open to challenge and change. In the attempt to understand the complexities of any system there is always not only the temptation but also the need to generalise and to abstract, and thereby to think of the system itself abstractly or as an abstraction, out of time and out of context. The process is entirely understandable; the result is invariably a falsification. Throughout this little book I have suggested that language has to be seen as one social system in interaction with other social systems, in constant process, and in time. The major theoretical paradoxes then disappear: we can see that at any one point language has autonomy and yet that in time and in use it is constantly intermeshed with all other social systems, which exert their effect on language. We can understand how in the speaker's own personal time language exerts its rules and classifications and yet how at any one moment the individual is agentive in the construction of texts in relation to language change.

In thinking about language there are different kinds of time, which apply in differing ways. We know that languages change, and that the language of Shakespeare is noticeably different from the language of Australians in the 1980s. We vaguely perceive that older generations use language differently to the way we do: sometimes that realisation emerges as an irritation about the other's speech, as excessively 'slangy' or as unnecessarily deliberate and quaintly constructed. We know that differing groups use differing 'jargons'; counter-cultural groups of every generation create distinctive forms of language only to find their forms reincorporated into the mainstream by fashion conscious mainstream speakers. We know that in some of the interactions that we have participated in things did not go the way we wanted, that we could have put things better, or said things more clearly. In other words, in some exchange constructed around discursive difference, the course of the interaction did not favour our position. All these are examples of language in time and in (social) process. These different times move at quite different rates, with different momentum and energy. At times certain tendencies merge, and permanent changes occur.

What is important is to think of language always as a complex system, in movement, sometimes contradictory and sometimes in a single direction. In all of these processes the individual is crucial and instrumental. Education is that social institution which is about the change and progression of its client members in the direction of mainstream culture, and into its classifications. The institution of education absolutely depends on a theory of language in which notions of change and progression are at the centre.

Part V

The inscription of the audience in the message

Cinematic inscription

EDITOR'S INTRODUCTION

Although he was a linguist, the influence of Benveniste on film theory in the 1970s cannot be overestimated. The extract on 'Relationships of person in the verb' which dates from 1946, seems, at first sight, to consist of a series of micro-linguistic studies. However, Benveniste's identification of verbal persons is a work of general linguistics with considerable ramifications. As we have seen (pp. 283–91), Benveniste makes a special case for the third person, 'he/she', which he pronounces a 'non-person'. Unlike 'I' or 'you', 'he/she' does not have a specific person to whom it refers; person as such, then, is really inherent only in 'I' and 'you'. 'I' and 'you' possess a uniqueness because they refer to someone different on each occasion; 'he/she' is commonly understood as a person, but does not possess this quality of uniqueness. Benveniste also notes that the category of 'you' (the second person) can be used elsewhere than in a sentence which is directly addressing a present person; for example, the statement 'You usually have to queue when you sign on' uses 'you' as a generality. In this sense, the general ('one') is imputed with the quality of the personal. Similarly, with 'we', it is not possible for a speaker to actually conceive of several 'I's; in truth, 'we' entails that there is a conception of 'I' accompanied by several 'non-I's.

What Benveniste once more shows in this essay is that the constructions which make up a language are often forgotten or overlooked by its users. Clearly, everything that refers to 'he/she' is not part of 'I' and 'you', the purely personal; however, there are times when the personal is made to inhabit the impersonal. This notion, although not directly attributed to Benveniste, is at play in the extract by Nick Browne (pp. 331–51). Browne examines traditional notions of cinematic editing and shot organization in relation to the Western, *Stagecoach* (1939), and focuses on a section of the film in which what the audience sees is implicated in what the characters see. Traditionally, such an approach would focus on the way cinematic narration might guide the audience by presenting a certain organization of shots. What Browne argues is that the narrator's role is contained *in and by* the characters in the narrative. The audience (spectator, reader) does not take up a narrative 'centre' in relation to the film, nor does the audience simply reside in one character's point of view for the duration of a shot; instead, according to Browne, the spectator has the potential to be in several places at once and take on a 'plural subjectivity'.

The reason for this plural subjectivity is that the film tries to present itself as a free-standing entity, as if it were delivered from a thoroughly neutral perspective. At the same time, the sequence in question attempts to present a particular character's perspective which the audience might share. Should the spectator adopt the perspective of the character at a given moment then, effectively, the spectator is infusing the fictive non-person (the character) with attributes of (the spectator's) person. It is not too difficult, therefore, to see the links between Browne's argument about the 'spectator-in-the-text' and Benveniste's comments on linguistic person. But we must be clear that the main advance arising from this convergence is concerned not so much with the thorny problem of 'identification' but how film as an 'independent fiction' can 'nevertheless be in-habited' by the spectator. Note also that Browne maintains an understanding of spectators not simply as an 'effect' of the film, but as agents in the auditorium who have brought along their own 'ideological baggage' to the movie. Of course, what Browne does not discuss (nor is it his purpose to do so) are the psychological structures involved in spectators' inhabiting of the text and the manifold roles of the audience's ideological baggage.

Although Browne's article originally appeared in the French journal *Communications* (and was reprinted in the American magazine, *Film Quarterly*), his concerns are allied to those of contributors to the British film journal, *Screen*, in the 1970s. One of the *Screen* writers, Stephen Heath, was especially concerned with the psychological structures of audience engagement that we have mentioned and the extract by him reprinted here addresses these (the second section of Part VI of this volume, on the other hand, is a good place to begin an exploration of the way spectators/readers bring pre-existing attitudes, values and experiences to the reading process). In a densely argued passage, Heath demonstrates some of the theoretical consequences of 'classical' ('mainstream', 'narrative') cinema's 'containment' of the processes of production. Integral to his conception of spectatorship is the action of 'suture', a term derived from the Lacanian psychoanalyst, Jacques-Alain Miller. As we have already observed (see pp. 16–17), Heath sees in the human subject a separation between the subject's discourse and the individual human being; by various means – one of which is viewing a film – subjects try to 'perform' their subjectivity by imagining that language and themselves are one, thus papering over the separation. That process of humans joining themselves to language (or 'the chain of discourse') is akin to the stitching together (or *suturing*) of two sides of a wound in human flesh. Suturing in the cinema therefore takes place in two areas: firstly, It allows human beings to 'perform' (paper over) their own separation from the mode of representing themselves; secondly, suture entails that the unmanageable enormity of all the events in the world which are available for representation are subject to *containment* within the cinematic frame and within narrative.

The radical separation from discourse which the human constantly seeks to overcome takes place, for Heath, on this terrain. Suture is the action which is instrumental in creating a 'field' or space within the movement of cinematic images; this is nowhere more evident than in the common shot/reverse shot sequences where a character will look at an object or other character whereupon the succeeding shot will show what was looked at. What takes place in psychoanalytical terms is that the absence of what is looked at (or the separation from what is represented) is immediately filled, as if on demand, by the revelation in the next shot. Moreover, the meandering of narrative as a whole – its inexorable impetus to denouement coupled with necessary digressions – contributes to the same creation of a field of absence and presence. It is within this field or space, of course, that the kind of 'inscriptions' of the audience that Browne identifies, are said to take place.

Further reading   Benveniste 1971 pp. 205–214; K. Silverman 1983 pp. 43–53; MacCabe 1979; Willemen 1978; Easthope 1983 pp. 41–47; Lapsley and Westlake 1988 pp. 49–52; Mulvey 1989; Marcus 1991; J. A. Miller 1977/8; S. Heath 1981 pp. 76–112; Frow 1984; Branigan 1992 pp. 86–160; Mayne 1993 pp. 13–30.

22 Émile Benveniste

Relationships of person in the verb

Along with the pronoun, the verb is the only class of words embodying the category of person. But the pronoun has so many other characteristics belonging exclusively to it and conveying relationships so different that it would require an independent study. It is verbal person alone that we shall consider, although we shall make occasional use of pronouns.

In all languages that possess a verb, the forms of the conjugation are classed according to their reference to person, the enumeration of the persons properly constituting the conjugation; and three persons are distinguished in the singular, in the plural, and sometimes in the dual. It is well known that this classification is inherited from Greek grammar in which the inflected verbal forms make up the πρόσωπα, the personae, the 'figurations' under which the 'verbal' notion is realized. The series of πρόσωπα or personae in a way furnishes a parallel to that of the πτώσεις or *casus* of the nomina inflection. In the grammatical nomenclature of India, the notion is also expressed by the three *perusa* or 'persons', called respectively *prathamapurusa* 'first person' (= our 3rd pers.), *madhyamapurusa*, 'intermediate person' (= our 2nd pers.), and *uttamapurusa* 'last person' (= our 1st pers.); this is the same sequence as the Greek but in reverse order; the difference is fixed by tradition, the Greek grammarians citing verbs in the first person, those of India in the third.

This classification, as it was worked out by the Greeks for the description of their language, is today still considered not only to be verified by all the languages endowed with a verb but also to be natural and set down in the order of things. In the three relationships it institutes, it sums up the ensemble of the positions that determine a verbal form provided with a mark of person, and it is valid for the verb of any language whatsoever. There are always, then, three persons and there are only three. However, the summary and non-linguistic nature of a category thus established must be proclaimed. By aligning on a single level and in an unchanging order 'persons' defined by their succession and related to those *beings* which are 'I', 'you', and 'he', we only transpose into a pseudo-linguistic theory differences which are *lexical* in nature. These denominations do not indicate to us the necessity of the category or the content that it implies or the relationships which link the different persons. Inquiry must be made as to how each person is opposed to all the others and as to what principle their opposition is based on, since we can only apprehend them by what differentiates them.

Meanwhile a preliminary question arises: can a verb exist without distinction of persons? This amounts to asking whether the category of person is really necessary and inherent in the verb or whether it simply constitutes a possible modality in it, frequently realized but not indispensable, as are, after all, many of the verbal categories. Actually, although examples are very rare, it is possible to pick out languages in which the expression of person can be absent from the verb. Thus, in the Korean verb, according to Ramstedt, 'the grammatical persons . . . have no grammatical distinction in a language where all forms of the verb are indifferent to person and number' (Ramstedt n.d. p. 61). It is certain that the principal verbal distinctions in Korean are of a 'social' order; the forms are extremely diversified according to the rank of the subject and the interlocutor and vary according to whether one is speaking to a superior, an equal, or an inferior. The speaker effaces himself and makes abundant use of impersonal expressions; in order not to stress indiscreetly the relationship of the positions, he is often content with forms that are undifferentiated as to person, which may be understood correctly only through a refined sense of the proprieties. It is not necessary, however, to take this custom as an absolute rule as Ramstedt does; first, because Korean possesses a complete series of personal pronouns which can be put into play, and that is essential; and secondly, because, even in the sentences he cites, the ambiguity is not such as one might imagine it to be.[1] This *pogətta* 'I shall see; you will see; he will see; one can see; one is to see' (ibid., p. 71), generally means 'I shall see'; while 'you will see' [sing.] is expressed by *porida*. The sentence, *I bəanyn yo so hagəni-wa tasi-nən hazi ani hagetta* (not *hagesso*) 'this time I forgive you, but I shall not forgive you again' (ibid., p. 97), signifies instead, with the replacement of *hagetta* by *handa* '(I observe that) he forgives you this time but he will not forgive you again,' because the nominal and abstract stem *hagi* is hardly suitable to the first person. One must indeed understand *I san-son yl mǝkkǝni-wa irhǝm yn mollasso* to mean 'although I eat this fish, I don't know its name' (ibid., p. 96), but by substituting *molatti* for *mollasso*, the sentence would be in the 2nd sing.: 'although *you* eat this fish, *you* don't know its name.' The same with the sentence, *ilbon e sardaga pyoŋn yl edesso* 'I lived in Japan and I got this sickness' (ibid., p. 98) will signify '*you* got this sickness . . .' when *edesso* is replaced by *odokǝsso*. All these restrictions in usage and the necessity for the employment of pronouns contribute to the introduction of variations of person in a verb which is in principle undifferentiated. Among the Paleo-Siberian languages, according to Jakobson (1942 p. 617), the verbal forms in Gilyak do not in general distinguish person or number, but 'neuter' modes oppose the first to the non-first person in the singular; other languages in the same group also distinguish only two persons; sometimes, as in Yukaghir, the first and second merge, sometimes, as in Ket, the first and the third. But all these languages possess personal pronouns. In sum, it does not seem that there is any language that we know of that is endowed with a verb in which the distinctions of person are not indicated in one way or another in the verbal forms. One can thus conclude that the category of person really does belong among the fundamental and necessary notions of the verb. That is an observation which suffices for us, but it goes without saying that the originality of each verbal system in this respect should be studied in its own right.

A linguistic theory of verbal person can be constituted only on the basis of the oppositions that differentiate the persons; and it will be summed up in its entirety in the structure of these oppositions. In order to uncover this structure, we could start with the definitions used by the Arab grammarians. For them, the first person is *al-mutakallimu* 'the one who speaks'; the second, *al-muḫāṭabu* 'the one who is addressed'; but the third is *al-yāʾibu* 'the one who is absent.' A precise notion of the relationships among persons is implied by these denominations; precise especially in that it reveals the disparity between the first and second persons and the third. Contrary to what our terminology would make us believe, they are not homogeneous. This is what must be made clear first.

In the first two persons, there are both a person involved and a discourse concerning that person. 'I' designates the one who speaks and at the same time implies an utterance about 'I'; in saying 'I', I cannot *not* be speaking of myself. In the second person, 'you' is necessarily designated by 'I' and cannot be thought of outside a situation set up by starting with 'I'; and at the same time, 'I' states something as the predicate of 'you'. But in the third person a predicate is really stated, only it is outside 'I-you'; this form is thus an exception to the relationship by which 'I' and 'you' are specified. Consequently, the legitimacy of this form as a 'person' is to be questioned.

We are here at the center of the problem. The form that is called the third person really does contain an indication of a statement about someone or something but not related to a specific 'person'. The variable and properly 'personal' element of these denominations is here lacking. It is indeed the 'absent' of the Arab grammarians. It only presents the invariable inherent in every form of a conjugation. The consequence must be formulated clearly: the 'third person' is not a 'person'; it is really the verbal form whose function is to express the *non-person*. This definition accounts for the absence of any pronoun of the third person – a fundamental fact that it suffices to notice – and the very peculiar situation of the third person of the verb in most languages, of which we shall give a few examples.

In Semitic, the 3rd sing. of the perfect does not have an ending. In Turkish, the 3rd sing. generally has a zero marker, in contrast to the 1st sing. *-m* and the 2nd sing. *-n*; hence in the durative present of 'to love': 1. *sev-iyor-um*, 2. *sev-iyor-sun*, 3. *sev-iyor*; or in the determined preterite: 1. *sev-di-m*, 2. *sev-di-n*, 3. *sev-di*. In Finno-Ugric, the 3rd sing. has the form of the simple stem: Ostiak 1. *eutlem*, 2. *eutlen*, 3. *eutl*; the subjective conjugation of 'to write' in Hungarian: 1. *ír-ok*, 2. *ír-sz*, 3. *ír*. In Georgian, in the subjective conjugation (the only one in which consideration of the person as subject occurs exclusively), the two first persons, in addition to their endings, are characterized by prefixes: 1. *v-*, 2. *h-*; but the 3rd sing. has only the ending. In Caucasian of the northwest (Abxaz and Cherkess in particular), the personal signs for the two first persons have a constant and regular form, but for the third person there are many signs and quite a number of difficulties. Dravidian uses a nominal form of the noun of agency for the 3rd sing., in contrast to the two first persons.

In Eskimo, W. Thalbitzer clearly indicates the nonpersonal nature of the 3rd sing.: 'Of a neutral character, lacking any mark of personality, is the ending of the third person singular -*oq* . . . which quite agrees with the common absolute ending of the noun. . . . These endings for the third person indicative must be regarded as impersonal forms: *kapiwoq* "there is a stab, one is stabbed"' (*H.A.I.L.* 1: 1032, 1057).[2] In all of those Amerindian languages in which the verb functions by endings or by personal prefixes, this mark is generally lacking in the 3rd person. In Burushaski, the 3rd sing. of all verbs is subject to the signs of the nominal classes, while the two first persons are not (Lorimer n.d. 1: 240, sec. 269). Many other similar phenomena could easily be found in other families of languages. Those which have just been cited suffice to make it obvious that the first two persons are not on the same plane as the third, that the third person is always treated differently and not like a real verbal 'person', and that the uniform classification into three parallel persons does not fit the verb of these languages.

In Indo-European, the anomalous 3rd sing. of Lithuanian gives evidence along the same lines. In the archaic inflection of the perfect, if one analyzes the endings into their elements, 1. -*a*, 2. -*tha*, 3. -*e*, one obtains: 1 $\vartheta_2 e$, 2. -$t\vartheta_2 e$, opposed to 3. -*e*, which functions as a zero ending. If the Sanskrit periphrastic future is envisaged on the synchronic plane without any reference to the nominal sentence, one will observe the same lack of agreement between the 3rd sing. and the two other persons: 1. *kartā́smi*, 2. *kartā́si*, 3. *kartā́*. It is not fortuitous either that in the inflection of 'to be' in modern Greek to the two first persons, εἶμαι and εἶσαι, is opposed a third person, εἶναι, common to the singular and plural and of a distinct structure. Conversely, the difference can be manifested by a specially marked form of the 3rd sing.; thus, English (*he*) *loves* in contrast to (*I, you, we, they*) *love*. All these concordant phenomena must be considered in order to perceive the strangeness of the 'normal' inflection in Indo-European, for example, that of the athematic present *es-mi, es-si, es ti* with three symmetrical persons which, far from representing a fixed and necessary type, is an anomaly at the very center of the languages. The third person has been made to conform to the first two for reasons of symmetry and because every Indo-European verbal form tends to make the sign of the subject stand out since it is the only one it can show. We have here a regularity of an extreme and exceptional nature.

It follows that, very generally, person is inherent only in the positions 'I' and 'you'. The third person, by virtue of its very structure, is the nonpersonal form of verbal inflection.

Indeed, it is always used when the person is not designated and especially in the expression called impersonal. Here again we come up against the question of the impersonals, an old problem and a sterile debate as long as we persist in confusing 'person' and 'subject'. In ὕει, *tonat* 'it rains', the process is indeed stated as nonpersonal, a pure *phenomenon* whose occurrence is not connected with an agent; and locutions like Ζεὺς ὕει are doubtless recent and, as it were, reverse rationalizations. The authenticity of ὕει arises from the fact that it positively expresses the process as taking place outside the 'I-you', which are the only indicators of persons.

In effect, one characteristic of the persons 'I' and 'you' is their specific 'oneness': the 'I' who states, the 'you' to whom 'I' addresses himself are unique each time. But 'he' can be an infinite number of subjects – or none. That is why Rimbaud's 'je est un autre [I is another]' represents the typical expression of what is properly mental 'alienation', in which the 'I' is dispossessed of its constitutive identity.

A second characteristic is that 'I' and 'you' are reversible: the one whom 'I' defines by 'you' thinks of himself as 'I' and can be inverted into 'I', and 'I' becomes a 'you'. There is no like relationship possible between one of these two persons and 'he' because 'he' in itself does not specifically designate anything or anyone.

Finally, one should be fully aware of the peculiar fact that the 'third person' is the only one by which a *thing* is predicated verbally.

The 'third person' must not, therefore, be imagined as a person suited to depersonalization. There is no aspheresis of the person; it is exactly the non-person, which possesses as its sign the absence of that which specifically qualifies the 'I' and the 'you'. Because it does not imply any person, it can take any subject whatsoever or no subject, and this subject, expressed or not, is never posited as a 'person'. This subject only adds *in apposition* a precision judged necessary for the understanding of the content, not for the determination of the form. Hence *volat avis* does not mean 'the bird flies', but 'it flies (scil.) the bird.' The form *volat* would be enough in itself and, although it is nonpersonal, includes the grammatical notion of subject. Nahua and Chinook behave in the same way, always incorporating the subject pronoun (and also, if need be, the object pronoun) in the verbal form, the subject and object substantives being treated as appositions: Chinook *tgigénxaute ikanáte tEmewálEma* 'the spirits watch over the soul,' lit. 'they it watch over (*tgi*, 'they it'), the soul (*ikanáte*), the spirits (*t-mewálEma)*' (cf. Boas, *H.A.I.L.* 1: 647). Everything outside the person strictly considered, that is, outside 'I-you', receives as predicate a verbal form of the 'third person' and cannot receive any other.

This quite special position of the third person explains some of its special uses in the area of *parole*. It can be assigned to two expressions with opposite values. *He* (or *she*) can serve as a form of address with someone who is present when one wishes to remove him from the personal sphere of 'you'. On the one hand, it can show a kind of respect: it is the polite form (employed in Italian and German or in the forms of 'His Majesty') which raises the interlocutor above the status of person and the relationship of man to man. On the other hand, it is used to show scorn, to slight someone who does not even deserve that one address oneself 'personally' to him. From its function as a nonpersonal form, the 'third person' takes this ability to become a form of respect, which makes another being more than a person, as well as a form of insult, which can annihilate him as a person.

It can now be seen what the opposition between the first two persons of the verb and third consists of. They contrast as members of a correlation, the *correlation of personality*: 'I-you' possesses the sign of person; 'he' lacks it. The 'third person' has, with respect to the form itself, the constant characteristic and function of representing a nonpersonal invariant, and nothing but that.

But if 'I' and 'you' are both characterized by the sign of person, one really feels that in their turn they are opposed to one another within the category they constitute by a feature whose linguistic nature should be defined.

The definition of the second person as the person to whom the first addresses himself undoubtedly fits the most common use. But common does not mean single and invariable. The second person can be used outside address and can be made to enter into a variety of the 'impersonal'. For instance, *vous* in French functions as an anaphoric of *on* (e.g., 'on ne peut se promener sans que quelqu'un *vous* aborde' [one cannot go out for a walk without someone accosting you]). In many languages, 'you' can serve, as it does in English, to denote an indefinite agent (like Fr. *on*): Lat. memoria minuitur nisi

eam *exerceas*; crederes 'you [= one] would believe (on croirait)';
Gr. εἴποις ἄν 'you [= one] would say (on dirait)'; mod. Gr. λές 'you
say [= one says] (on dit),' πᾶς 'you go [= one goes] (on va)'; in
Russian, informulaic or proverbial locations: *govoriš s nim – on ne
slušaet* 'you speak [= one speaks] to him, he does not listen (on lui
parle, it n'écoute pas),' *podumaeš, čto on bolen* 'you [= one] would
think he was ill (on croirait qu'il est malade)' (Mazon, *Grammaire
russe*, sec. 157). It is necessary and sufficient, that one envisage a
person other than 'I' for the sign of 'you' to be assigned to that person.
Thus every *person* that one imagines is of the 'you' form, especially,
but not necessarily, the person being addressed 'you' can thus be
defined as 'the non-*I* person'.

There are grounds, then, for observing an opposition between
the '*I*-person' and the 'non-*I* person'. On what basis is it established?
A special correlation which we call, for want of a better term, the
correlation of subjectivity belongs to the *I-you* pair in its own right.
What differentiates 'I' from 'you' is first of all the fact of being, in
the case of 'I', *internal* to the statement and external to 'you'; but
external in a manner that does not suppress the human reality of
dialogue. The second person with the uses cited in Russian, etc., is
a form which assumes or calls up a fictive 'person' and thereby institutes an actual relationship between 'I' and this quasi-person;
moreover, 'I' is always *transcendent* with respect to 'you'. When I get
out of 'myself' in order to establish a living relationship with a
being, of necessity I encounter or I posit a 'you', who is the only
imaginable 'person' outside of me. These qualities of internality and
transcendence properly belong to 'I' and are reversed in 'you', who
is the only imaginable 'person' outside of me. These qualities of internality and transcendence properly belong to 'I' and are reversed in
'you'. One could thus define 'you' as the *non-subjective person*, in
contrast to the *subjective person* that 'I' represents; and these two
'persons' are together opposed to the 'non-person' form (= he).

It would seem that all the relations established among the three
forms of the singular should remain the same when they are transposed to the plural (the dual forms pose a problem only as being
dual, not as persons). Yet we know very well that the passage from
the singular to the plural in the personal pronouns does not involve
a simple pluralization. Furthermore, in a number of languages a
twofold distinction (inclusive and exclusive) of particular complexity
has been created in the verbal form of the first person plural.

As in the singular, the central problem here is that of the first person. The simple fact that different words are very generally used for 'I' and 'we' (and also for 'thou' and 'you') suffices to except the pronouns from the ordinary processes of pluralization. There are indeed some exceptions, but they are very rare and partial: for example, in Eskimo, the stem is the same in the singular *uwaŋa* 'I' and the plural *uwaŋut* 'we', and it enters into a formation of the nominal plural. But *illi* ('thou') and *iliⁱᵂsse* 'you' contrast in quite another way. In any case, identicality of pronominal forms in the singular and plural remains the exception. In the great majority of languages, the pronominal plural does not coincide with the nominal plural, at least as it is ordinarily represented. It is clear, in effect, that the oneness and the subjectivity inherent in 'I' contradict the possibility of a pluralization. If there cannot be several 'I's conceived of by an actual 'I' who is speaking, it is because 'we' is not a multiplication of identical objects but a *junction* between 'I' and the 'non-I', no matter what the content of this 'non-I' may be. This junction forms a new totality which is of a very special type whose components are not equivalent: in 'we' it is always 'I' which predominates since there cannot be 'we' except by starting with 'I', and thus 'I' dominates the 'non-I' element by means of its transcendent quality. The presence of 'I' is constitutive of 'we'.

It is common knowledge that in very different languages, the 'non-I', which is implicit and necessary in 'we', is capable of receiving two precise and distinct contents. 'We' is expressed in one way for 'I + you' and in another for 'I + they'. These are the inclusive and exclusive forms, which differentiate the pronominal and verbal plural of the first person in a large number of Amerindian and Australian languages, as well as in Papu, Malay-Polynesian, Dravidian, Tibetan, Manchurian and Tunguz, Nama, etc.

This use of 'inclusive' and 'exclusive' cannot be considered satisfactory; it rests in fact on the inclusion or exclusion of 'you', but with respect to 'they' the designations could be exactly the reverse. It is nevertheless difficult to find more appropriate terms. It seems more important to us to analyze this 'inclusive-exclusive' category from the point of view of the relationships of person.

Here the essential fact to recognize is that the distinction of the inclusive and exclusive forms is modeled in reality on the relationship we have established between the first and second singular and between the first and third singular, respectively. These two pluralizations of the first person singular serve in each case to join the opposed terms of the two correlations which have been isolated. The exclusive plural ('I + they') consists of a junction of two forms which oppose one another as personal and nonpersonal by virtue of the 'correlation of person'. For example, in Siuslaw (Oregon), the exclusive form in the dual (-a^uxûn, -axûà) and in the plural (-nxan) consists of that of the 3rd dual (-a^ux) and plural (-nx) augmented by the final of the 1st sing. (-n) (cf. L. J. Frachtenberg, *H.A.I.L.* 2: 468). In contrast, the inclusive form ('I + you') effects the junction of persons between whom exists the 'correlation of subjectivity'. It is interesting to observe that in Algonquian (Fox), the independent inclusive pronoun 'we' *ke-gunāna* has as its sign the *ke-* of the 2nd pers. *ke-gwa* 'thou', and *ke-guwāwa* 'you', while the exclusive 'we' *ne-gunāna* has *ne-*, that of the 1st pers. *ne-gwa* 'I' (*H.A.I.L.* 1: 817); it is a 'person' that predominates in each of the two forms, 'I' in the exclusive (entailing junction with the non-person) and 'you' in the inclusive (entailing junction of the nonsubjective person with 'I' implicit). This is only one of the very diverse realizations of this plurality. Others are possible. But we can see here the differentiation operating on the very principle of person: in the inclusive 'we' opposed to 'he, they', it is 'thou' which stands out, while in the exclusive 'we' opposed to 'thou, you', it is 'I' which is stressed. The two correlations that organize the system of persons in the singular are thus seen in the double expression of 'we'.

But the undifferentiated 'we' of other languages, Indo-European for example, must be viewed in a different perspective. What does the pluralization of the person of the verb consist of here? This 'we' is something other than a junction of definable elements, and the predominance of 'I' is very strong in it, to the point that, under certain conditions, this plural can take the place of the singular. The reason for this is that 'we' is not a quantified or multiplied 'I'; it is an 'I' expanded beyond the strict limits of the person, enlarged and at the same time amorphous. As a result there are two opposed but not contradictory uses outside the ordinary plural. On the one hand, the 'I' is amplified by 'we' into a person that is more massive, more solemn, and less defined; it is the royal 'we'. On the other hand, the use of 'we' blurs the too sharp assertion of 'I' into a broader and more diffuse expression: it is the 'we' of the author or orator. This can also be considered an explanation for the frequent contaminations or entanglements of the singular and plural, or of the plural and impersonal, in popular or peasant language: *nous, on va* (pop. Tuscan, *noi si canta*), or the *je sommes* of northern French, with its counterpart *nous suis* in Franco-Provençal, expressions in which the need to give 'we' an indefinite meaning is mixed with the voluntarily vague assertion of a prudently generalized 'I'.

In a general way, the verbal person in the plural expresses a diffused and amplified person. 'We' annexes an indistinct mass of other persons to 'I'. In the passage from 'thou' to 'you', be it the collective 'you' or the polite 'you', we recognize a generalization of 'thou', either metaphoric or real, with regard to which, especially in languages of Western culture, 'thou' often takes the value of a strictly personal and hence familiar address. As for the non-person (the third person), verbal pluralization, when it is not the grammatically regular predicate of a plural subject, accomplishes the same function as in the 'personal' forms: it expresses the indecisive generality of 'one' (of the type *dicunt* 'they say'). It is this non-person which, extended and unlimited by its expression, expresses an indefinite set of non-personal beings. In the verb, as in the personal pronoun, the plural is a factor of limitlessness, not multiplication.

The expressions of verbal person are thus basically organized by two fixed correlations:

1 The *correlation of personality* opposing the *I-you* persons to the non-person *he*;
2 The *correlation of subjectivity* operating within the preceding and opposing *I* to *you*.

The ordinary distinction of the singular and plural should be, if not replaced, at least interpreted in the order of persons by a distinction between *strict person* (= 'singular') and *amplified person* (= 'plural'). Only the 'third person', being a non-person, admits of a true plural.

NOTE

1 I have made certain of this by questioning Mr Li-Long-Tseu, a cultured Korean and himself a linguist to whom I am indebted for the following corrections. In transcribing Korean, I have reproduced his pronunciation.
2 *H.A.I.L.* is the *Handbook of American Indian Languages*, Bureau of American Ethnology, 1911–38.

23 Nick Browne

The spectator-in-the-text: *the rhetoric of* Stagecoach

The sequence from John Ford's *Stagecoach* shown in the accompanying stills raises the problem of accounting for the organization or images in an instance of the 'classical' fiction film and of proposing the critical terms appropriate for that account. The formal features of these images – the framing of shots and their sequencing, the repetition of set-ups, the position of characters, the direction of their glances – can be taken together as a complex structure and understood as a characteristic answer to the rhetorical problem of telling a story, of showing an action to a spectator. Because the significant relations have to do with seeing – both in the ways the characters 'see' each other and the way those relations are shown to the spectator – and because their complexity and coherence can be considered as a matter of 'point of view', I call the object of this study the 'specular text'.

Explanations of the imagery of the classical narrative film are offered by technical manuals and various theories of editing. Here though, I wish to examine the connection between the act of narration and the imagery, specifically in the matter of the framing and the angle of view determined by set-ups, by characterizing the narrating agency or authority which can be taken to rationalize the presentation of shots. An explanation of this kind necessarily involves clarifying in some detail the notion of the 'position of the spectator'. Thus we must characterize the spectator's implied position with respect to the action, the way it is structured, and the specific features of the process of 'reading' (though not in the sense of 'interpretation'). Doing so entails a description (within the terms of the narrative) of the relation of literal and fictional space that comprehends what seems, ambiguously, like the double origin of filmic images.

An inquiry into the forms of authority for the imagery and the corresponding strategies which implicate the viewer in the action has few precedents, yet it raises general but basic questions about filmic narration that begin to clarify existing accounts of the relation of narrative to image. The sequence from *Stagecoach* is interesting as a structure precisely because, in spite of its simplicity (it has no narrative or formal eccentricity) it challenges the traditional premises of critical efforts to account for the operation and effects of 'classical' film style.

The traditional rationale for the presentation of imagery is often stated by the camera's relation to the spectator. For instance, a basically dramatic account has it that the shots should show essentially what a spectator would see if the action were played on a stage, and if at each moment he had the best view of the action (thus changing angles only supply 'accents'). Editing would follow the spectator's natural course of attention as it is implied by the action of the *mise-en-scène*. In such a mode the question of agency – that is, who is 'staging' and making these events appear in this way – is referred not to the author or narrator but to the action itself, fully embodied in the characters. Everything that happens must be exhibited clearly for the eye of the spectator. On this theory, all the structures of the presentation are directed to a place external to the scene of the action – to the final authority, the ideal spectator. Oudart's recent account (*Film Quarterly*, Fall 1974) proposed that imagery is paradigmatically referred to the authority of the glance of the 'absent one', the off-screen character within the story who in the counter shot is depicted within the frame; the spectator 'identifies' with the visual field of the 'owner' of the glance. The 'system of the suture' is an explanation that establishes the origin of the imagery by reference to the agency of character but, surprisingly, it does not consider (indeed it seems to deny) the final agency, the authority of the narrator. The traces of the action of the narrator may seem to be effaced by this system, but such an effect can only be the result of a certain more general rhetoric. Thus I am proposing an account in which the structure of the imagery, whatever its apparent forms of presentation, refers jointly to the action of an implied narrator (who defines his position with respect to the tale by his judgements) and to the imaginative action occasioned by his placing and being placed by the spectator. Neither the traditional nor the more recent theories seem fully adequate to this problematic.

1

4a

DALLAS: Thank you.

2

4b

RINGO: Set down here, ma'am.

3a

4c

3b

5

6a

8a

6b

8b

7a

9

HATFIELD: May I find you another place Mrs. Mallory? It's cooler by the window.

7b

10

11a

LUCY: Thank you.

12b

11b

11c

12a

Thus the problem that arises from *Stagecoach* is to explain the functioning of the narrator and the nature and effects of spectator placement: specifically describing and accounting for in detail a filmic rhetoric in which the agency of the narrator in his relation to the spectator is enacted jointly by the characters and the particular sequence of shots that show them. To describe this rhetoric in a rigorous and illuminating way means clarifying in filmic terms the notions of 'narrative authority', 'point of view', and 'reading', and showing that these concepts are of use precisely because they arise naturally from the effort to account for the concrete structures of the text.

The moment in the story that the sequence depicts is the taking of a meal at the Dry Fork station on the stage's way to Lordsburg. Earlier in the film, the prostitute Dallas (the woman in the dark hat) has been run out of town by the Ladies' Law and Order League and has been put aboard the stagecoach. There she joined, among others, a cavalry officer's wife named Lucy (in the white hat) and Hatfield, her chivalrous but distant escort. Just before the present scene, the Ringo Kid (John Wayne) who has broken out of jail to avenge his brother's murder, has been ordered aboard by the sheriff when discovered by the side of the road. The sequence begins immediately after a vote among the members of the group to decide whether to go on to Lordsburg and ends shortly before the end of the scene when the group exits the station. For purposes of convenience I have called shots 4, 8, and 10, which are from the same set-up, series A, and shots 3, 7, 9 and 11, series B.

One of the rationales that might be proposed to account for the set-ups, the spatial fields they show, the sequence of shots, is their relation to the 'psychology' of the characters. How, if at all, are the set-ups linked to the visual attention, as with the glance, or say the interests of a character in the story? In the shot/reverse shot pattern which is sometimes, wrongly I think, taken as an exclusive paradigm of the 'classical' style, the presence of the shot on the screen is 'explained' or read as the depiction of the glance of the off-screen character, who, a moment later, is shown in the reverse shot. But because only a few shots of this sequence (or of most films) follow this pattern we shall be pressed to a different formulation. The general question is how the two set-ups of the two major series of shots – series A from the head of the table and series B from the left side – are to be explained.

Series A is related to the visual attention of the woman at the head of the table, Lucy. The connection between the shots and her view, especially in the modulation of the force and meaning of that view, must however be established. These shots from A are readable as the depiction of Lucy's glance only retrospectively, after series B has shown her at the head of the table and after the animation conveyed in the dolly forward has implied its significance. The point remains, however, that the shots of series A are finally clearly authorized by a certain disposition of attention of one of the characters.

In contrast to series A, the series B shots from the left of the table are like the opening and closing shots (1, 12) in not being associated with or justified spatially as the depiction of anyone's glance. Can the placement of these shots be justified either as the 'best angle' for the spectator or as the depiction of some other more complex conception of 'psychology' of character than an act of attention in a glance? Persons to whom these shots might be attributed as views would be Dallas, or the outlaw Ringo, for they satisfy one condition: they are out of the A-series frame. As series A shows, in this style the association of a shot with a glance is effected by a coincidence of geographical places, eye and camera. But here, quite plainly, neither Dallas nor Ringo are in a position to view from this angle. And in each shot, Lucy is in the frame.

To attribute the shots of series B – to justify their placement spatially, to some conception of character psychology requires some other justification than the mere representation of somebody's glance. What kind of psychological account could explain the alternation of these precise framings? What kind of mental disposition, ensemble of attitude, judgement, and intention, is this framing significant of? Whose disposition? On what basis would such an attribution be effected? If establishing the interpretation of the framing depended on or was referred to a character's 'state of mind', which in fact changes significantly over the course of the sequence for each of the major characters (Dallas, Ringo, and Lucy) how would it be possible to accommodate those changing feelings to the fixity of set-up? The fact of the fixity of set-up denies that the explanation for camera placement can as a principle be referred to a psychology of character(s) based on the kind of emotional changes – surprise, repudiation, naivete, humiliation – that eventuate in the sequence.

As another hypothesis we could say that the particular compositional features of series B are a presentation not of the 'mind' of any single character but of a state of affairs within the group, a relationship among the parties. What is the state of affairs within this society that the framing depicts? There are two significant features of the composition from set-up B: the relation of Lucy in the immediate foreground to the group behind her, a group whose responsiveness to events repeats the direction of her own attention, and her relation, spatially, to Dallas and Ringo who, excluded by the left edge of the frame, are outside. The permanent and underlying fact about the *mise-en-scène* which justifies the fixity of camera placement is its status as a social drama of alliance and antagonism between two social roles – Lucy, an insider, a married woman and defender of custom; and Dallas, outsider and prostitute who violates the code of the table. The camera set-ups and the spatial fields they reveal, the compositional exclusion of the outlaw couple and their isolation in a separate space, with the implied assertion of Lucy's custodial relation to the body of legitimate society, respond to and depict in formal terms the social 'positions' of the characters. In the kind of dramatic presentation they effect, the features of the framing are not justified as the depiction of personal psychology considered as changes of feeling; instead, by their emphasis on social positions, or types, they declare a psychology of intractable situations.

The framing of series B from the left of the table does not represent literally or figuratively any single person's view; rather, it might be said, it depicts, by what it excludes and includes, the interplay of social positions within a group. This asymmetry of social position of Lucy over Dallas extends as well to formal and compositional features of the sequence. Though set-up B represents both positions, Dallas's negatively, it makes Lucy's position privileged in the formal mechanism of narrative exposition. The fundamental narrative feature of the sequence is a modification and inflection of the logic of shot/counter shot. Here it is an alternation of series A and B around, not two characters, but either Lucy's eye or body. That is, in series A Lucy is present as an eye, as the formal beholder of the scene. Alternately, in B, Lucy is shown bodily dominating the foreground, and as the eye to which the views of series A are referred. Formally the narration proceeds by alternatingly shifting Lucy's presence from the level of the depicted action, as body (B), to the level of representation, as the invisible eye (A), making Lucy's presence the central point of spatial orientation and legibility. In shots 5 and 6, the close-up of the exchange of looks between the two women, the formal asymmetry is the difference of their frontality, and the shot of Lucy is from a place that Dallas could not literally occupy. Lucy's frontality (5) marks a dispossession, a displacement, that corresponds to Dallas's social 'absence' in the entire sequence – to her exclusion from the frame in B, to her isolation as the object of Lucy's scornful glance in A. By contrast to Lucy's presence everywhere, as body and eye, Dallas's eye is never taken as the source of authority for a shot. Her eye is averted. She is always, in both A and B, the object of another's gaze – a condition that corresponds to the inferiority of her social position, and to her formal invisibility – she can not authorize a view.

The shots of set-up B, which might be called 'objective', or perhaps 'nobody's' shots, in fact refer to or are a representation of Lucy's social dominance and formal privilege. B shows a field of vision that closely matches Lucy's *conception* of her own place in that social world: its framing corresponds to her alliance with the group and to her intention to exclude the outsiders, to deny their claim to recognition. It is in other words not exactly a description of Lucy's subjectivity but an objectification of her social self-conception. Though Lucy is visible in the frame, series B might be said, metaphorically, to embody her point of view.

This explanation seems cogent as far as it goes. But there are some further issues that arise from the passage, in the way it is experienced, that suggest that the foregoing analysis of the justification of these formal features is incomplete as an account of the grounds for the effects the passage produces and theoretically limited in terms of explaining the strategies of framing and other premises of the narration.

Simply put, the experience of the passage is a feeling of empathy for Dallas's exclusion and humiliation, and a repudiation of Lucy's prejudice as unjust, two feelings brought together by a sense of inevitability of the conflict. There is in other words a curious opposition between the empathetic response of a spectator toward Dallas with the underlying premises of the mechanism of the narrative which are so closely related, formally, to Lucy's presence, point of view, and interests. It is this sense of incongruity between feeling and formal structure that occasions the following effort to consider the sequence in terms of the ways it produces its effects, that is rhetorically.

One question about a formal matter, which draws attention to the limitations of a structural account based on a conception of the social order, is why the outsiders are seen from a position that is associated with Lucy's place at the table, her gaze. This fact, and the action of the audience within the film, casts doubt on two theories of agency. Our attention as spectators, in the shots of series B, does not follow the visual attention of any depicted characters. These shots might perhaps be read as statements of the 'interests' of characters, the nature of their social positions, but that is already a kind of commentary or interpretation that needs explanation. The actions of the men at the bar, the audience within the film, disprove the traditional rationale for editing stated by reference to an ideal spectator: as 'placed' spectators we anticipate, not follow, the movements of their attention (2,3); the object of their attention is sometimes out of the frame (3B) we see and what they see is shown only from a view significantly different from any simply 'accented' or 'best view', indeed from a place they could not occupy; and sometimes (7b, 8) they have turned away, uninterested, but the screen doesn't go black. In general, an adequate account of the formal choices of the passage must be quite different from an account of the event as if it were staged for the natural attention of a spectator, depicted or real. To ask why the spectator sees in the way he does refers to a set of premises distinguishable from an account based on the attention of either a character or an ideal spectator. It refers to the concrete logic of the placement of the implied spectator and to the theory of presentation that accounts for the shaping of his response. Such an account makes the 'position' of the spectator, the way in which he is implicated in the scene, the manner and location of his presence, his point of view, problematical.

It is this notion of the 'position of the spectator' that I wish to clarify in so far as that notion illuminates the rhetorical strategies, particularly choice of set-up (implying scale and framing) that depicts the action. In contemporary French film theory, particularly in the work of Comolli and Baudry, the notion of the 'place' of the spectator is derived from the central position of the eye in perspective and photographic representation. By literally substituting the epistemological subject, the spectator, for the eye, in an argument about filmic representation, the filmic spectator is said to be 'theological', and 'centred' with respect to filmic images. Thus the theory of the filmic spectator is treated as if subject to the Derridian critique of center, presence etc. French theory is wrong to enforce this analogy based on the position of the eye in photographic perspective, because what is optical and literal in that case corresponds only to the literal place of the spectator in the projection hall, and not at all to his figurative place in the film, nor to his place as subject to the rhetoric of the film, or reader or producer of the sense of the discourse. Outside of a French ideological project which fails to discriminate literal and figurative space, the notion of 'place' of the spectator and of 'center', is an altogether problematic notion whose significance and function in critical discussion has yet to be explicated.

The sequence from *Stagecoach* provides the terms in which the notion of the position of the spectator might be clarified, provided we distinguish, without yet expecting full clarification, the different senses of 'position'. A spectator is (a) seated physically in the space of the projection hall and (b) placed by the camera in a certain fictional position with respect to the depicted action; moreover (c), insofar as we see from what we might take to be the eye of a character, we are invited to occupy the place allied to the place he holds, in for example, the social system, and finally (d), in another figurative sense of place, it is the only way that our response can be accounted for, we can identify with a character's position in a certain situation.

In terms of the passage at hand, the question is then: how can I describe my 'position' as spectator in identifying with the humiliated position of one of the depicted characters, Dallas, when my views of her belong to those of another, fictional character, Lucy, who is in the act of rejecting her? What is the spectator's 'position' in identifying with Dallas in the role of the passive character? Dallas in averting her eyes from Lucy's in shot 6 accepts a view of herself in this encounter as 'prostitute' and is shamed. However, in identifying with Dallas in the role of outcast, presumably the basis for the evocation of our sympathy and pity, our response as spectator is not one of shame, or anything even analogous. We do not suffer or repeat the humiliation. I understand Dallas's feeling but I am not so identified with her that I re-enact it. One of the reasons for this restraint is that though I identify with Dallas's abject position of being seen as an unworthy object by someone whose judgment she accepts, I identify with her as the object of another's action. Indeed, in a remarkable strategy, I am asked to see Dallas through Lucy's eyes. That as spectator I am sharing Lucy's view and just as importantly, her manner of viewing, is insisted on most emphatically by the dolly forward (4) and by disclosures effected by shot/counter shot, thus placing us in a lively and implicated way in a position fully associated with Lucy's place at the head of the table.

Insofar as I identify with Dallas, it is not by repeating her shame, but by imagining myself in her position (situation). The early scenes of the film have carefully prepared us to believe that this exclusion is an unjust act. When the climactic moment arrives, our identification with Dallas as an object of view is simultaneously established as the ground for repudiating the one whose view we share and are implicated in. Though I share Lucy's literal geographical position of viewing at this moment in the film, I am not committed to her figurative point of view. I can in other words repudiate Lucy's view of or judgment on Dallas, without negating it as a view, in a way that Dallas herself, captive of the other's image, cannot. Because our feelings as spectators are not 'analogous' to the interests and feelings of the characters, we are not bound to accept their view either of themselves or of others. Our 'position' as spectator then is very different from the previous senses of 'position': it is defined neither in terms of orientation within the constructed geography of the fiction, nor of social position of the viewing character. On the contrary, our point of view on the sequence is tied more closely to our attitude of approval or disapproval and it is very different from any literal viewing angle or character's point of view.

Identification asks us as spectators to be two places at once, where the camera is and 'with' the depicted person – thus its double structure of viewer/viewed. As a powerful emotional process it thus throws into question any account of the position of the spectator as centered at a single point or at the center of any simply optical system. Identification, this passage shows, necessarily has a double structure in the way it implicates the spectator in both the position of the one seeing and the one seen. This sequence however does establish a certain kind of 'center' in the person of Lucy. Each of the shots is referred alternatingly to the scene before her eye, or the scene of her body, but it is a 'center' that functions as a principle of spatial legibility, and is associated with a literal point within the constructed space of the fiction. This center stands, though, as I have suggested, in a very complicated relation to our 'position' as spectator. That is, the experience of the passage shows that our identification, in the Freudian sense of an emotional investment, is not with the center, either Lucy or the camera. Rather, if, cautiously, we can describe our figurative relation to a film in geographical terms, of 'in', 'there', 'here', 'distance', (and this sequence, as part of its strategy as a fiction, explicitly asks us to by presenting action to us from the literal view of a character) then as spectators, we might be said to formally occupy someone else's place, to be 'in' the film, all the while being 'outside' it in our seats. We can identify with a character and share her 'point of view' even if the logic of the framing and selection of shots of the sequence deny that she has a view or a place within the society that the *mise-en-scène* depicts. There are significant differences between structures of shots, views, and identification: indeed, this sequence has shown, as a principle, that we do not 'identify' with the camera but with the characters, and hence do not feel dispossessed by a change in shots. For a spectator, as distinct perhaps from a character, point of view is not definitively or summarily stated by any single shot or even set of shots from a given spatial location.

The way in which we as spectators are implicated in the action is as much a matter of our position with respect to the unfolding of those events in time as in their representation from a point in space. The effect of the mode of sequencing, the regular opposition of insiders and outsiders, is modulated in ways that shape the attitudes of the spectator/reader toward the action. This durational aspect emphasizes the process of inhabiting a text with its rhythms of involvement and disengagement in the action, and suggests that the spectator's position, his being in time, might appropriately be designated the 'reader-in-the-text'. His doubly structured position of identification with the features and force of the act of viewing and with the object in the field of vision, are the visual terms of the dialectic of spectator placement. The rhetorical effort of shots 2–6 is directed in establishing the connection between shots and a 'view' to endowing the position at the head of the table with a particular sense of a personalized glance. Shot 2, like 4, cannot at the moment it appears on the screen be associated with Lucy's glance. The shot/counter shot sequencing discloses Lucy's location, and the turn of the head (3b) establishes a spatial relation between A and B; the animation, or gesture, implied by the dolly forward, combined with the emotional intensity implied by the choice of scale (5, 6) are read in terms of a personalized agency and clarified by what is shown in the visible field, Lucy's stern face (5). It is a rhetoric that unites the unfolding shots and gives meaning to this depicted glance – affront.

It creates with the discrete shots (2, 3, 4) the impression of a coherent act of viewing, a mental unity whose meaning must make itself felt by the viewer at the moment of confrontation (5, 6) to effect the sense of repudiation of Lucy's view and the abjectness of Dallas. It takes time – a sequence of shots, in other words – to convey and specify the meaning of an act of viewing.

Reading, as this instance shows, is in part a process of retrospection, situating what could not be 'placed' at the moment of its origin and bringing it forward to an interpretation of the meaning of the present moment. As such it has a complex relation to the action and to the spatial location of viewing. But the process of reading also depends on forgetting. After the climactic moment (5, 6) signaling Dallas's averting her eyes, a different temporal strategy is in effect. Lucy has looked away in 7b and in subsequent shots from the head of the table, our attention is directed not so much to the act of showing, and what it means – unawareness (2), recognition (4), rejection (6) – but rather in 8 and 10 is directed at the action within the frame. The spectator's forgetting of what the dramatic impact depended on just a few moments before (here the personalized force that accompanied the act of showing the shot as a glance) is an effect of placement that depends on an experience of duration which occludes a previous significance and replaces it with another, a process we might call fading.

The modulation of the effects of fading are what, to take another example, is at issue in the interpretation of the shots of both series A and B. I have argued above that the set-up and field of B correspond to Lucy's understanding of her place in the social system – to her point of view in the metaphorical sense. This interpretation corresponds to the general impression of the first six shots, taken together, as representing Lucy's manner of seeing. Shot 7 initiates a new line of dramatic action that poses the question of what Lucy will do now, and also begins a process not exactly of re-reading, but a search for a new reading of the meaning of the set-ups. At this moment (7b), Lucy has turned her attention away from Dallas and is now turned toward Hatfield; and Ringo, previously occupied with his table etiquette (2, 4) is looking (8b, 10) intently out of frame right. The initial sense of the set-up B is partially replaced by, but coexists with another: that the depicted action in the frame is now being viewed by someone looking from outside the frame, namely Ringo, who is waiting expectantly for something to happen. The view from the left of the table is readable, not exactly as Lucy's self-conception as before, and not as a depiction of Ringo's glance, but as a representation of his interest in the scene, his point of view (again, in the metaphorical sense). Similarly, shots 8 and 10, showing Dallas and Ringo, no longer seem to characterize Lucy as the one doing the seeing, as in 4 and 6; they have become impersonal. The rigidity and opposition of set-ups A and B correspond to the rigidity of social position, but our reading of the changing secondary significances of the framing is an effect of fading that is responsive to acts of attention and seeing depicted within the frame.

Our anticipation, our waiting to see what will happen, is provoked and represented on the level of the action by the turning around of the audience-in-the-film (Billy and Doc Boone in (3b, 9)). Our own feeling, because of our visual place to the left of the table, is closer to Ringo's than to theirs. Certainly the distention and delay of the climactic moment by a virtual repetition (9, 11a) of those shots of a hesitating Lucy (unnecessary for simple exposition) produce a sense of our temporal identification with Ringo (8b, 10), necessary for the success of the moment as drama – its uncertainty and resolution. The drama depends for the lesson it demonstrates not on Lucy's self-regard before a general public as previously, but on being watched by the parties to be affected. It is Ringo's increasingly involved presence as an authority for a view, even though he mistakenly thinks he is being ostracized, that makes the absent place left by Lucy's departure so evidently intended as a lesson in manners, so accusingly empty. By these strategies and effects of duration – retrospection, fading delay, and anticipation – the reading of emphasis on the act of showing or what is shown, the significance of angle and framing, can be modulated. Together these means define features of a rhetoric which, though different from the placement effected by visual structures also locate and implicate the reader/spectator in the text.

The spectator's place, the locus around which the spatial/temporal structures of presentation are organized, is a construction of the text which is ultimately the product of the narrator's disposition toward the tale. Such structures, which in shaping and presenting the action prompt a manner and indeed a path of reading, convey and are closely allied to the guiding moral commentary of the film. In this sequence the author has effaced himself, as in other instances of indirect discourse, for the sake of the characters and the action. Certainly he is nowhere visible in the same manner as the characters. Rather he is visible only through the materialization of the scene and in certain masked traces of his action. The indirect presence to his audience that the narrator enacts, the particular form of self-effacement, could be described as the masked displacement of his narrative authority as the producer of imagery from himself to the agency of his characters. That is, the film makes it appear as though it were the depicted characters to whom the authority for the presentation of shots can be referred – most evidently in the case of a depiction of a glance, but also, in more complex fashion, in the reading of shots as depictions of a 'state of mind'. The explanation of the presence of the imagery is referred by the film not to the originating authority who stands invisible, behind the action, but to his masks within the depicted space.

In accord with the narrator's efforts to direct attention away from his own activity, to mask and displace it, the narrator of *Stagecoach* has a visible persona, Lucy, perform a significant formal function in the narration: to constitute and to make legible and continuous the depicted space, by referring shots on the screen alternately to the authority of her eye or the place of her body. The literal place of the spectator in the projection hall, where in a sense all the shots are directed, is a 'center' that has a figurative correspondence on the level of the discourse in the 'place' that Lucy occupies in the depicted space. But because Lucy performs her integrative function not exactly by her being at a place, the head of the table, but by enacting a kind of central consciousness that corresponds to a social and formal role, a role which for narrative purposes can be exploited by shifting the views representing the manner of her presence, the notion of 'center' might be thought of not as a geographical place, but as a structure or function. As such, this locus makes it possible for the reader himself to occupy that role and himself to make the depicted space coherent and readable. For the spectator, the 'center' is not just a point either in the projection hall or in the depicted geography, but is the result of the impression produced by the functioning of the narrative and of his being able to fictionally occupy the absent place.

Locating this function, 'inscribing' the spectator's place on the level of the depicted action, has the effect of making the story seem to tell itself by reference not to an outside author but to a continuously visible, internal narrative authority. This governing strategy, of seeming to internalize the source of the exposition in characters, and thus of directing the spectator's attention to the depicted action, is supported by other features of the style: shot/counter shot, matching of glances, continuity.

Consequently, the place of the spectator in his relation to the narrator is established by, though not limited to, identifications with characters and the views they have of each other. More specifically his 'place' is defined through the variable force of identification with the one viewing and the one viewed – as illustrated in the encounter between Lucy and Dallas. Though the spectator may be placed in the 'center' by the formal function Lucy performs, he is not committed to her view of things. On the contrary, in the context of the film, that view is instantly regarded as insupportable. Our response to Dallas supports the sense that the spectator's figurative position is not stated by a description of where the camera is in the geography of the scene. On the contrary, though the spectator's position is closely tied to the fortunes and views of characters, our analysis suggests that identification, in the original sense of an emotional bond, need not be with the character whose view he shares, even less with the disembodied camera. Evidently, a spectator is several places at once – with the fictional viewer, with the viewed, and at the same time in a position to evaluate and respond to the claims of each. This fact suggests that like the dreamer, the filmic spectator is a plural subject: in his reading he is and is not himself.

In a film, imagining ourselves in a character's place by identification, in respect to the actual situation, is a different process, indeed a different order of fiction than taking a shot as originating from a certain point within the fictional geography. The relation though between the literal space of the projection hall and the depicted space of the film image is continuously problematic for a definition of the 'thatness' of the screen and for an account of the place of the spectator. If a discourse carries a certain impression of reality it is an effect not exactly of the image, but rather of the way the image is placed by the narrative or argument. My relation to an image on the screen is literal because it can be taken as being directed to a physical point, my seat (changing that seat doesn't alter my viewing angle on the action), as though I were the fixed origin of the view. On the other hand, the image can also be taken as originating from a point in a different kind of space, recognizably different in terms of habitability from that of the projection hall: it is from a fictional and changeable place implied by an origin contained in the image. The filmic image thus implies the ambiguity of a double origin – from both my literal place as spectator and from the place where the camera is within the imaginative space.

One structural result of the ambiguous relation of literal and depicted space and of the seemingly contradictory efforts of the text to both place and displace the spectator is the prohibition against the 'meeting', though no such act is literally possible, of actor's and spectator's glances, a prohibition that is an integral feature of the sequence as a 'specular text'. In its effect on the spectator, the prohibition defines the different spaces he simultaneously inhabits before the screen. By denying his presence in one sense, the prohibition establishes a boundary at the screen that underscores the fact that the spectator can have no actual physical exchange with the depicted world, that he can do nothing relevant to change the course of the action. It places him irretrievably outside the action.

At the same time, the prohibition is the initial premise of a narrative system for the representation of fictional space and the means of introducing the spectator imaginatively into it. The prohibition effects this construction and engagement by creating an obliquity between our angle of viewing and that of the characters which works to make differences of angle and scale readable as representations of different points of view. As such it plays a central part in our process of identification or non-identification with the camera and depicted characters. It provides the author with an ensemble of narrative forms – an imaginary currency consisting of temporary exchange, substitution, and identification – that enables us, fictionally, to take the place of another, to inhabit the text as a reader.

Establishing agency either by the authority of character or of spectator corresponds in its alternative rhetorical forms to the articulation of the ambiguity of the double origin of the image. In a particular text it is the narration that establishes and arbitrates the spectator's placement between these two spaces. *Stagecoach* makes definite efforts to imply that not only is the spectator not there, not present in his seat, but that the film-object originates from an authority within the fictional space. The narration seems to insist that the film is a free-standing entity which a spectator, irrelevant finally to its construction, could only look on from the outside. On the other hand, in the ways that I have described, the film is directed in all its structures of presentation toward the narrator's construction of a commentary on the story and toward placing the spectator at a certain 'angle' to it. The film has tried not just to direct the attention, but to place the eye of the spectator inside the fictional space, to make his presence integral and constitutive of the structure of views. The explanation the film seems to give of the action of narrative authority is a denial of the existence of a narrator different from character and an affirmation of the dominating role of fictional space. It is a spatial mode not determined by the ontology of the image as such but is in the last instance an effect of the narration.

Masking and displacement of narrative authority are thus integral to establishing the sense of the spectator 'in' the text, and the prohibition to establishing the film as an independent fiction, different from dream in being the product of another, that can nevertheless be inhabited. Fascination by identification with character is a way the integrity of fictional space is validated and because the spectator occupies a fictional role, is a way too that the film can efface the spectator's consciousness of his position. As a production of the spectator's reading, the sense of reality that the film enacts, the 'impression of the real', protects the account the text seems to give of the absent narrator.

The cumulative effect of the narrator's strategy of placement of the spectator from moment to moment is his introduction into what might be called the moral order of the text. That is, the presentational structures which shape the action both convey a point of view and define the course of the reading, and are fundamental to the exposition of moral ideas – specifically a discussion about the relation of insiders to outsiders. The effect of the distinction between pure and impure is the point of the sequence, though as a theme it is just part of the total exposition. The sequence thus assists in the construction of attitudes toward law and custom and to those who live outside their strictures. It introduces the question of the exercise of social and customary (as distinguished from legal) authority. To the extent we identify with Ringo and Dallas – and the film continuously invites us to by providing multiple grounds: the couple's bravery, competence, and sincerity – the conventional order and the morality it enforces is put in doubt. Without offering a full interpretation of the theme of *Stagecoach* which would I think be connected with the unorthodox nature of their love and the issue of Ringo's revenge and final exemption from the law by the sheriff,

I can still characterize the spectator's position at this particular moment in the film.

It amounts to this: that though we see the action from Lucy's eyes and are invited by a set of structures and strategies to experience the force and character of that view, we are put in the position finally of having to reject it as a view that is right or that we could be committed to. The sequence engages us on this point through effecting an identification with a situation in which the outsider is wronged and thus that challenges Lucy's position as the agent of an intolerant authority. We are asked, by the manner in which we must read, by the posture we must adopt, to repudiate Lucy's view, to see behind the moral convention that supports intolerance, to break out of a role that may be confining us. As such, the importance of the sequence in the entire film is the way it allies us emotionally with the interests and fortunes of the outsiders as against social custom, an identification and theme that, modulated in subsequent events, continues to the end of the film. The passage, lifted out of its context, but drawing on dispositions established in previous sequences, is an illustration of the process of constructing a spectator's attitudes in the film as a whole through the control of point of view. Whether or not the Western genre can in general be characterized by a certain mode of identification, as for example in the disposition or wish to see the right done, and whether *Stagecoach* has a particularly significant place in the history of the genre by virtue of its treatment of outsiders, is an open question. In any case the reader's position is constituted by a set of views, identifications, and judgments that establish his place in the moral order of the text.

Like the absent narrator who discloses himself and makes his judgments from a position inseparable from the sequence of depicted events that constitute the narrative, the spectator, in following the story, in being subject of and to the spatial and temporal placement and effects of exposition, is in the process of realizing an identity we have called his position. Following the trajectory of identifications that establishes the structure of values of a text, 'reading' as a temporal process could be said to continuously reconstruct the place of the narrator and his implied commentary on the scene. In this light, reading, as distinct from interpretation, might be characterized as a guided and prompted performance that (to the extent a text allows it, and I believe *Stagecoach* does) recreates the point of view enacted in a scene. As a correlative of narration, reading could be said to be the process of reenactment by fictionally occupying the place of the narrator.

Certain formal features of the imagery – framing, sequencing, the prohibition, the 'invisibility' of the narrator – I have suggested, can be explained as the ensemble of ways authority implicitly positions the spectator/reader. As a method, this analysis of *Stagecoach* points to a largely unexplored body of critical problems associated with describing and accounting for narrative and rhetorical signifying structures. The 'specular text', and the allied critical concepts of 'authority', 'reading', 'point of view', and 'position of the spectator', however provisional, might be taken then as a methodological initiative for a semiotic study of filmic texts.

24 Stephen Heath

Narrative space

Classical cinema does not efface the signs of production, it contains them. . . . It is that process that is the action of the film for the spectator – what counts is as much the representation as the represented, is as much the production as the product. Nor is there anything surprising in this: film is not a static and isolated object but a series of relations with the spectator it imagines, plays and sets as subject in its movement. The process of film is then perfectly available to certain terms of excess – those of that movement in its subject openings, its energetic controls. 'Style' is one area of such controlled excess, as again, more powerfully, are genres in their specific version of process. The musical is an obvious and extreme example with its systematic 'freedom' of space – crane choreography – and its shifting balances of narrative and spectacle; but an example that should not be allowed to mask the fundamental importance of the experience of process in other genres and in the basic order of classical cinema on which the various genres are grounded. Which is to say, finally, that radical disturbance is not to be linked to the mere autonomization of a formal element such as camera movement; on the contrary, it can only be effectively grasped as a work that operates at the expense of the classical suppositions of 'form' and 'content' in cinema, posing not autonomies but contradictions in the process of film and its narrative-subject binding.

The construction of space as a term of that binding in classical cinema is its implication for the spectator in the taking place of film as narrative; implication-process of a constant refinding – space regulated, orientated, continued, reconstituted. The use of look and point-of-view structures – exemplarily, the field/reverse field figure (not necessarily dependent, of course, on point-of-view shots)[1] – is fundamental to this process that has been described in terms of *suture*, a stitching or tying as in the surgical joining of the lips of a wound.[2] In its movement, its framings, its cuts, its intermittences, the film ceaselessly poses an absence, a lack, which is ceaselessly recaptured for – one needs to be able to say 'for in' – the film, that process binding the spectator as subject in the realization of the film's space.

In psychoanalysis, 'suture' refers to the relation of the individual as subject to the chain of its discourse where it figures missing in the guise of a stand-in; the subject is an effect of the signifier in which it is represented, stood in for, taken place (the signifier is the narration of the subject: cf. J. A. Miller 1966, translated as Miller 1977/8).

Ideological representation turns on – supports itself from – this 'initial' production of the subject in the symbolic order (hence the crucial role of psychoanalysis, as potential science of the construction of the subject, with historical materialism), directs it as a set of images and fixed positions, metonymy stopped into fictions of coherence. What must be emphasized, however, is that stopping – the functioning of suture in image, frame, narrative, etc. – is exactly a *process* it counters a productivity, an excess, that it states and restates in the very moment of containing in the interests of coherence – thus the film frame, for example, exceeded from within by the outside it delimits and poses and has ceaselessly to recapture (with post-Quattrocento painting itself, images are multiplied and the conditions are laid for a certain mechanical reproduction that the photograph will fulfil, the multiplication now massive, with image machines a normal appendage of the subject). The process never ends, is always *going on*; the construction-reconstruction has always to be renewed; machines, cinema included, are there for that – and their ideological operation is not only in the images but in the suture.

The film poses an image, not immediate or neutral,[3] but posed, framed and centred. Perspective-system images bind the spectator in place, the suturing central position that is the sense of the image, that sets its scene (in place, the spectator *completes* the image as its subject). Film too, but it also moves in all sorts of ways and directions, flows with energies, is potentially a veritable festival of affects. Placed, that movement is all the value of film in its development and exploitation: reproduction of life and the engagement of the spectator in the process of that reproduction as articulation of coherence. What moves in film, finally, is the spectator, immobile in front of the screen. Film is the regulation of that movement, the individual as subject held in a shifting and placing of desire, energy, contradiction, in a perpetual retotalization of the imaginary (the set scene of image and subject). This is the investment of film in narrativization; and crucially for a coherent space, the unity of place for vision.

Once again, however, the investment is in the process. Space comes in place through procedures such as look and point-of-view structures, and the spectator with it as subject in its realization. A reverse shot folds over the shot it joins and is joined in turn by the reverse it positions; a shot of a person looking is succeeded by a shot of the object looked at which is succeeded in turn by a shot of the person looking to confirm the object as seen; and so on, in a number of multiple imbrications. *Fields* are made, *moving* fields, and the process includes not just the completions but the definitions of absence for completion. The suturing operation is in the process, the give and take of absence and presence, the play of negativity and negation, flow and bind. Narrativization, with its continuity, closes, and is that movement of closure that shifts the spectator as subject in its terms: the spectator is the *point* of the film's spatial relations – the turn, say, of shot to reverse shot – their subject-passage (point-of-view organization, moreover, doubles over that passage in its third/first person layerings). Narrativization is scene and movement, movement and scene, the reconstruction of the subject in the pleasure of that balance (with genres as specific instances of equilibrium) – *for* homogeneity, containment. What is foreclosed in the process is not its production – often signified as such, from genre instances down to this or that 'impossible' shot – but the terms of the unity of that production (narration on narrated, enunciation on enounced), the other scene of its vision of the subject, the outside – heterogeneity, contradiction, history – of its coherent address.

NOTES

1 Salt (1976) distinguishes three varieties of field/reverse field and assigns an order and approximate dates for their respective appearances:

> It is necessary to distinguish between different varieties of angle: reverse angle cuts; the cut from a watcher to his point of view was the first to appear; the cut from one long shot of a scene to another more or less oppositely angled long shot, which must have happened somewhat later – the first example that can be quoted is *Røverens Brud* (Viggo Larsen,

1907); and the cut between just-off-the-eye-line angle – reverse angle shots of two people interacting – the earliest example that can be quoted occurs in *The Loafer* (Essanay, 1911).

(Salt 1976 p. 98)

2   For details of the introduction and various accounts of suture see S. Heath (1981 pp. 87–101).

3   'Another characteristic of the film image is its neutrality' (*Encyclopedia Britannica* (Macropedia) vol. 12 (Chicago 1974) p. 478).

Bodies, subjects and
social context

EDITOR'S INTRODUCTION

Since the early 1970s there has been a huge amount of academic work undertaken on the cinema in general but also, more specifically, on spectatorship. It is here that a great deal of the most complex theories of audience 'inscription' have been developed. However, it is by no means an unknown process within other disciplines and the cine-psychoanalytic approach to inscription is not the only one. In the essay 'Language as social semiotic' (this volume pp. 359–83), the sociolinguist M. A. K. Halliday argues that language is always encoded with the 'social context'. Rather than a scenario where a reader can 'become inscribed' in the text, Halliday's work seeks to demonstrate that learning a language and learning a culture are inseparable and simultaneous: from early childhood language users are therefore always carving out a place for themselves, both in language and in culture. A social role is always already inscribed in their language use.

The essay begins with a list of the necessary components for a socio-semiotic investigation of language: text, situation, register, code, linguistic system and social structure. Most of these also have their own subdivisions, so, without doubt, what Halliday presents is a very complex understanding of language as a 'social semiotic'. These details, however, are crucial to an understanding of the inscription of language users into language use; the child goes through the process of learning not just the meaning of individual linguistic signs but also how they can be made to function in relation to situation, register, social structure and so on. This is, on the one hand, how children ascend to adult language but, at the same time, it is how children take their place in the social structure. In his analysis of the language development of a child from nine months to three and a half years old, Halliday notes how the child's mother says 'Leave that stick outside; stop teasing the cat; and go and wash your hands. It's time for tea'. That the child responds to these words is a measure of how much he has learned of language's functioning and how he is implicated in his mother's words. But mark closely how the understanding of these words is bound up with a range of social imperatives to do with space (outside), time (for tea), cleanliness (wash your hands), behaviour (stop teasing the cat) and so on.

These social imperatives which inscribe users into language are examined at greater length by Allan Luke (pp. 384–95). Luke's article examines the rationale for literacy training and the possibility that it might also constitute a form of moral discipline. He offers a number of examples from classroom practice, particularly the 'story time' that is so much a feature of early education in the West. This, Luke shows, is not just the site of a pleasurable literacy instruction but also the working through of a disciplinary regime. Integral to the operation of this regime is a policing of the body: the children as listeners are coerced into taking up positions and maintaining postures demanded by the teacher. In this way, the listeners are bodily inscribed into the storytelling event. This is borne out in the way that the children's bodies visibly respond to certain of the stresses in the teacher's verbalization of the narrative. In addition to the bodily inscription, though, Luke emphasizes that the regime is often gendered in a specific fashion: the boys in the class are usually the object of restrictions on space and are generally those who move their body to the key parts of the story. Moreover, this inscription is collective: children are encouraged to join in with the verbalization of parts of the narrative (provided they observe 'proper' behaviour), and they experience portions of language explicitly as a group in such instances. What Luke shows, in short, is that our entry into language is often a physical, as well as a mental one.

The third extract (pp. 396–402) clearly invokes the notion of inscription but does not elaborate it as a rigorously observed mechanism. Judith Williamson looks at the paradox that occurs with the juxtaposition of 'art' and advertising and shows that audiences are offered a special kind of opportunity to 'enter' into texts. She asserts that advertising sells 'choices' rather than just commodities and this is mirrored in the examples which she puts under analysis. These usually consist of an advertisement whose text not only requires straightforward decoding of 'what it is' but also entails an inordinate amount of ideological work to be carried out by the decoder. Whereas the common understanding of advertising involves an apprehension of its instrumental intent to sell products, 'art', Williamson argues, is perceived as something 'higher', above the world of mammon. As such, items designated as 'art' invite a kind of interaction from audiences which is, supposedly, removed from that of popular culture. This kind of interaction is also determined by class, education aspirations and so on. When 'art' appears in advertisements, then, it sets up a tension between the reading of the advert in terms of its instrumental intent and the putatively non-profit orientated nature of 'art'. Moreover, the act of recognizing or demonstrating one's recognition of the 'art' work does two things: it allows the reader to 'enter' the text of the advertisement; and it satisfies the reader who can decode the text, appealing in turn to a range of social factors such as snobbery, taste and class position.

Further reading   Hall 1981; Muecke 1982; Fairclough 1992 pp. 137–168; Hodge and Kress 1988 pp. 240–260; Lemke 1995 pp. 19–36; Pêcheux 1982 pp. 55–129; Pateman 1983; Williamson 1978 pp. 40–70.

25 M. A. K. Halliday

Language as social semiotic

1 INTRODUCTORY

Sociolinguistics sometimes appears to be a search for answers which have no questions. Let us therefore enumerate at this point some of the questions that do seem to need answering.

1 How do people decode the highly condensed utterances of every-day speech, and how do they use the social system for doing so?
2 How do people reveal the ideational and interpersonal environment within which what they are saying is to be interpreted? In other words, how do they construct the social contexts in which meaning takes place?
3 How do people relate the social context to the linguistic system? In other words, how do they deploy their meaning potential in actual semantic exchanges?
4 How and why do people of different social class or other subcul-tural groups develop different dialectal varieties and different orientations towards meaning?
5 How far are children of different social groups exposed to different verbal patterns of primary socialization, and how does this deter-mine their reactions to secondary socialization especially in school?
6 How and why do children learn the functional–semantic system of the adult language?
7 How do children, through the ordinary everyday linguistic inter-action of family and peer group, come to learn the basic patterns of the culture: the social structure, the systems of knowledge and of values, and the diverse elements of the social semiotic?

2 ELEMENTS OF A SOCIOSEMIOTIC THEORY OF LANGUAGE

There are certain general concepts which seem to be essential ingredients in a sociosemiotic theory of language. These are the text, the situation, the text variety or register, the code (in Bernstein's (1971) sense), the linguistic system (including the semantic system), and the social structure.

2.1 Text

Let us begin with the concept of *text*, the instances of linguistic interaction in which people actually engage: whatever is said, or written, in an operational context, as distinct from a citational context like that of words listed in a dictionary.

For some purposes it may suffice to conceive of a text as a kind of 'supersentence', a linguistic unit that is in principle greater in size than a sentence but of the same kind. It has long been clear, however, that discourse has its own structure that is not constituted out of sentences in combination; and in a sociolinguistic perspective it is more useful to think of text as *encoded* in sentences, not as composed of them. (Hence what Cicourel (1969) refers to as omissions by the speaker are not so much omissions as encodings, which the hearer can decode because he shares the principles of realization that provide the key to the code.) In other words, a text is a semantic unit; it is the basic unit of the semantic process.

At the same time, text represents choice. A text is 'what is meant', selected from the total set of options that constitute what can be meant. In other words, text can be defined as actualized meaning potential.

The meaning potential, which is the paradigmatic range of semantic choice that is present in the system, and to which the members of a culture have access in their language, can be characterized in two ways, corresponding to Malinowski's distinction between the 'context of situation' and the 'context of culture' (1923, 1935). Interpreted in the context of culture, it is the entire semantic system of the language. This is a fiction, something we cannot hope to describe. Interpreted in the context of situation, it is the particular semantic system, or set of subsystems, which is associated with a particular type of situation or social context. This too is a fiction; but it is something that may be more easily describable (cf. 2.5 below). In sociolinguistic terms the meaning potential can be represented as the range of options that is characteristic of a specific situation type.

2.2 Situation

The situation is the environment in which the text comes to life. This is a well-established concept in linguistics, going back at least to Wegener (1885). It played a key part in Malinowski's ethnography of language, under the name of 'context of situation'; Malinowski's notions were further developed and made explicit by Firth (1957 p. 182), who maintained that the context of situation was not to be interpreted in concrete terms as a sort of audiovisual record of the surrounding 'props' but was, rather, an abstract representation of the environment in terms of certain general categories having relevance to the text. The context of situation may be totally remote from what is going on round about during the act of speaking or of writing.

It will be necessary to represent the situation in still more abstract terms if it is to have a place in a general sociolinguistic theory; and to conceive of it not as situation but as situation *type*, in the sense of what Bernstein (1971) refers to as a 'social context'. This is, essentially, a semiotic structure. It is a constellation of meanings deriving from the semiotic system that constitutes the culture.

If it is true that a hearer, given the right information, can make sensible guesses about what the speaker is going to mean – and this seems a necessary assumption, seeing that communication does take place – then this 'right information' is what we mean by the social context. It consists of those general properties of the situation which collectively function as the determinants of text, in that they specify the semantic configurations that the speaker will typically fashion in contexts of the given type.

However, such information relates not only 'downward' to the text but also 'upward', to the linguistic system and to the social system. The 'situation' is a theoretical sociolinguistic construct; it is for this reason that we interpret a particular situation type, or social context, as a semiotic structure. The semiotic structure of a situation type can be represented as a complex of three dimensions: the ongoing social activity, the role relationships involved, and the symbolic or rhetorical channel. We refer to these respectively as 'field', 'tenor' and 'mode' (following Halliday *et al.* 1964, as modified by Spencer and Gregory 1964; and cf. Gregory 1967). The field is the social action in which the text is embedded; it includes the subject-matter, as one special manifestation. The tenor is the set of role relationships among the relevant participants; it includes levels of formality as one particular instance. The mode is the channel or wavelength selected, which is essentially the function that is assigned to language in the total structure of the situation; it includes the medium (spoken or written) which is explained as a functional variable. (Cf. Halliday 1978 pp. 33 and 62–64.)

Field, tenor and mode are not kinds of language use, nor are they simply components of the speech setting. They are a conceptual framework for representing the social context as the semiotic environment in which people exchange meanings. Given an adequate specification of the semiotic properties of the context in terms of field, tenor and mode we should be able to make sensible predictions about the semantic properties of texts associated with it. To do this, however, requires an intermediary level – some concept of text variety, or register.

2.3   Register

The term 'register' was first used in this sense, that of text variety, by Reid (1956); the concept was taken up and developed by Jean Ure (Ure and Ellis 1974), and interpreted within Hill's (1958) 'institutional linguistic' framework by Halliday *et al.* (1964). The register is the semantic variety of which a text may be regarded as an instance.

Like other related concepts, such as 'speech variant' and '(sociolinguistic) code' (Ferguson 1971 chs 1 and 2; Gumperz 1971 pt I), register was originally conceived of in lexicogrammatical terms. Halliday *et al.* (1964) drew a primary distinction between two types of language variety: dialect, which they defined as variety according to the user, and register, which they defined as variety according to the use. The dialect is what a person speaks, determined by who he is; the register is what a person is speaking, determined by what he is doing at the time. This general distinction can be accepted, but, instead of characterizing a register largely by its lexicogrammatical properties, we shall suggest, as with text, a more abstract definition in semantic terms (see Halliday 1978 p. 35: Table 1).

A register can be defined as the configuration of semantic resources that the member of a culture typically associates with a situation type. It is the meaning potential that is accessible in a given social context. Both the situation and the register associated with it can be described to varying degrees of specificity; but the existence of registers is a fact of everyday experience – speakers have no difficulty in recognizing the semantic options and combinations of options that are 'at risk' under particular environmental conditions. Since these options are realized in the form of grammar and vocabulary, the register is recognizable as a particular selection of words and structures. But it is defined in terms of meanings; it is not an aggregate of conventional forms of expression superposed on some underlying content by 'social factors' of one kind or another. It is the selection of meanings that constitutes the variety to which a text belongs.

2.4 Code

'Code' is used here in Bernstein's (1971) sense; it is the principle of semiotic organization governing the choice of meanings by a speaker and their interpretation by a hearer. The code controls the semantic styles of the culture.

Codes are not varieties of language, as dialects and registers are. The codes are, so to speak, 'above' the linguistic system; they are types of social semiotic, or symbolic orders of meaning generated by the social system (cf. Hasan 1973). The code is actualized in language through the register, since it determines the semantic orientation of speakers in particular social contexts; Bernstein's (1971) own use of 'variant' (as in 'elaborated variant') refers to those characteristics of a register which derive from the form of the code. When the semantic systems of the language are activated by the situational determinants of text – the field, tenor and mode – this process is regulated by the codes.

Hence, the codes transmit, or control the transmission of, the underlying patterns of a culture or subculture, acting through the socializing agencies of family, peer group and school. As a child comes to attend to and interpret meanings, in the context of situation and in the context of culture, at the same time he takes over the code. The culture is transmitted to him with the code acting as a filter, defining and making accessible the semiotic principles of his own subculture, so that as he learns the culture he also learns the grid, or subcultural angle on the social system. The child's linguistic experience reveals the culture to him through the code, and so transmits the code as part of the culture.

2.5 The linguistic system

Within the linguistic system, it is the *semantic system* that is of primary concern in a sociolinguistic context. Let us assume a model of language with a semantic, a lexicogrammatical and a phonological stratum; this is the basic pattern underlying (often superficially more complex) interpretations of language in the work of Trubetzkoy, Hjelmslev, Firth, Jakobson, Martinet, Pottier, Pike, Lamb, Lakoff and McCawley (among many others). We can then adopt the general conception of the organization of each stratum, and of the realization between strata, that is embodied in Lamb's stratification theory (Lamb 1971, 1974).

The semantic system is Lamb's 'semological stratum'; it is conceived of here, however, in functional rather than in cognitive terms. The conceptual framework was referred to in Halliday (1978 ch. 3), with the terms 'ideational', 'interpersonal', and 'textual'. These are to be interpreted not as functions in the sense of 'uses of language', but as functional components of the semantic system – 'metafunctions' as we have called them. (Since in respect both of the stratal and of the functional organization of the linguistic system we are adopting a ternary interpretation rather than a binary one, we should perhaps explicitly disavow any particular adherence to the magic number three. In fact the functional interpretation could just as readily be stated in terms of four components, since the ideational comprises two distinct sub-parts, the experiential and the logical; see Halliday 1973; 1976; 1978 ch. 7.)

What are these functional components of the semantic system? They are the modes of meaning that are present in every use of language in every social context. A text is a product of all three; it is a polyphonic composition in which different semantic melodies are interwoven, to be realized as integrated lexicogrammatical structures. Each functional component contributes a band of structure to the whole.

The ideational function represents the speaker's meaning potential as an observer. It is the content function of language, language as 'about something'. This is the component through which the language encodes the cultural experience, and the speaker encodes his own individual experience as a member of the culture. It expresses the phenomena of the environment: the things – creatures, objects, actions, events, qualities, states and relations – of the world and of our own consciousness, including the phenomenon of language itself; and also the 'metaphenomena', the things that are already encoded as facts and as reports. All these are part of the ideational meaning of language.

The interpersonal component represents the speaker's meaning potential as an intruder. It is the participatory function of language, language as doing something. This is the component through which the speaker intrudes himself into the context of situation, both expressing his own attitudes and judgements and seeking to influence the attitudes and behaviour of others. It expresses the role relationships associated with the situation, including those that are defined by language itself, relationships of questioner–respondent, informer–doubter and the like. These constitute the interpersonal meaning of language.

The textual component represents the speaker's text-forming potential; it is that which makes language relevant. This is the component which provides the texture; that which makes the difference between language that is suspended *in vacuo* and language that is operational in a context of situation. It expresses the relation of the language to its environment, including both the verbal environment – what has been said or written before – and the nonverbal, situational environment. Hence the textual component has an enabling function with respect to the other two; it is only in combination with textual meanings that ideational and interpersonal meanings are actualized.

These components are reflected in the lexicogrammatical system in the form of discrete networks of options. In the clause, for example, the ideational function is represented by transitivity, the interpersonal by mood and modality, and the textual by a set of systems that have been referred to collectively as 'theme'. Each of these three sets of options is characterized by strong internal but weak external constraints: for example, any choice made in transitivity has a significant effect on other choices within the transitivity systems, but has very little effect on choices within the mood or theme systems. Hence the functional organization of meaning in language is built in to the core of the linguistic system, as the most general organizing principle of the lexicogrammatical stratum.

2.6 Social structure

Of the numerous ways in which the social structure is implicated in a sociolinguistic theory, there are three which stand out. In the first place, it defines and gives significance to the various types of social context in which meanings are exchanged. The different social groups and communication networks that determine what we have called the 'tenor' – the status and role relationships in the situation – are obviously products of the social structure; but so also in a more general sense are the types of social activity that constitute the 'field'. Even the 'mode', the rhetorical channel with its associated strategies, though more immediately reflected in linguistic patterns, has its origin in the social structure; it is the social structure that generates the semiotic tensions and the rhetorical styles and genres that express them (Barthes 1970).

Secondly, through its embodiment in the types of role relationships within the family, the social structure determines the various familial patterns of communication; it regulates the meanings and meaning styles that are associated with given social contexts, including those contexts that are critical in the processes of cultural transmission. In this way, the social structure determines, through the intermediary of language, the forms taken by the socialization of the child (see Bernstein 1971, 1975).

Thirdly, and most problematically, the social structure enters in through the effects of social hierarchy, in the form of caste or class. This is obviously the background to social dialects, which are both a direct manifestation of social hierarchy and also a symbolic expression of it, maintaining and reinforcing it in a variety of ways: for example, the association of dialect with register – the fact that certain registers conventionally call for certain dialectal modes – expresses the relation between social classes and the division of labour. In a more pervasive fashion, the social structure is present in the forms of semiotic interaction, and becomes apparent through incongruities and disturbances in the semantic system. Linguistics seems now to have largely abandoned its fear of impurity and come to grips with what is called 'fuzziness' in language; but this has been a logical rather than a sociological concept, a departure from an ideal regularity rather than an organic property of sociosemiotic systems. The 'fuzziness' of language is in part an expression of the dynamics and the tensions of the social system. It is not only the text (what people mean) but also the semantic system (what they can mean) that embodies the ambiguity, antagonism, imperfection, inequality and change that characterize the social system and social structure. This is not often systematically explored in linguistics, though it is familiar enough to students of communication and of general semantics, and to the public at large. It could probably be fruitfully approached through an extension of Bernstein's theory of codes (cf. Douglas 1972). The social structure is not just an ornamental background to linguistic interaction, as it has tended to become in sociolinguistic discussions. It is an essential element in the evolution of semantic systems and semantic processes.

3   A SOCIOLINGUISTIC VIEW OF SEMANTICS

In this section we shall consider three aspects of a sociological semantics: the semantics of situation types, the relation of the situation to the semantic system, and the sociosemantics of language development. The discussion will be illustrated from a sociolinguistic study of early language development.

3.1   The semantics of situation types

A sociological semantics implies not so much a general description of the semantic system of a language but rather a set of context-specific semantic descriptions, each one characterizing the meaning potential that is typically associated with a given situation type. In other words, a semantic description is the description of a register.

This approach has been used to great effect by Turner in a number of studies carried out under Bernstein's (1971) direction in London

(Turner 1973). Turner's contexts in themselves are highly specific; he constructs semantic networks representing, for example, the options taken up by mothers in response to particular questions about their child control strategies. At the same time they are highly general in their application, both because of the size of the sample investigated and, more especially, because of the sociological interpretation that is put upon the data, in terms of Bernstein's theories of cultural transmission and social change (see Halliday 1978 pp. 82–83: Figure 7).

The sociolinguistic notion of a situation type, or social context, is variable in generality, and may be conceived of as covering a greater or smaller number of possible instances. So the sets of semantic options that constitute the meaning potential associated with a situation type may also be more or less general. What characterizes this potential is its truly 'sociolinguistic' nature. A semantics of this kind forms the interface between the social system and the linguistic system; its elements realize social meanings and are realized in linguistic forms. Each option in the semantic network, in other words, is interpreted in the semiotics of the situation and is also represented in the lexicogrammar of the text. (Note that this is not equivalent to saying that the entire semiotic structure of the situation is represented in the semantic options, and hence also in the text, which is certainly not true.)

Figure 25.1 shows an outline semantic network for a particular situation type, one that falls within the general context of child play; more specifically, it is that of a small child manipulating vehicular toys in interaction with an adult. The network specifies some of the principal options, together with their possible realizations. The options derive from the general functional components of the semantic system (2.5 above) and are readily interpretable in terms of the grammar of English; we have not attempted to represent the meaning potential of the adult in the situation, but only that of the child. The networks relate, in turn, to a general description of English, modified to take account of the child's stage of development.

3.2 Structure of the situation, and its relation to the semantic system

The semiotic structure of a situation type can be represented in terms of the three general concepts of field, tenor and mode (cf 2.2 above).

The 'child play' situation type that was specified by the semantic networks in figure 9 might be characterized, by reference to these concepts, in something like the following manner:

Field   Child at play: manipulating moveable objects (wheeled vehicles) with related fixtures, assisted by adult; concurrently associating (i) similar past events, (ii) similar absent objects; also evaluating objects in terms of each other and of processes.

Tenor   Small child and parent interacting: child determining course of action, (i) announcing own intentions, (ii) controlling actions of parent; concurrently sharing and seeking corroboration of own experience with parent.

Mode   Spoken, alternately monologue and dialogue, task-oriented; pragmatic, (i) referring to processes and objects of situation, (ii) relating to and furthering child's own actions, (iii) demanding other objects; interposed with narrative and exploratory elements.

Below is a specimen of a text having these semiotic properties. It is taken from a study of the language development of one subject, Nigel, from nine months to three and a half years; the passage selected is from age 1;11. [Note: ` = falling tone; ´ = rising tone; ˇ = fall-rise tone; tonic nucleus falls on syllables having tone marks; tone group boundaries within an utterance shown by. . . . For analysis of intonation, see Halliday 1967.]

Nigel [*small wooden train in hand, approaching track laid along a plank sloping from chair to floor*]:   Here the ràilway line . . . but it not for the trăin to go on that.
Father: Isn't it?
Nigel: Yès tís. . . . I wonder the train will carry the lòrry [*puts train on lorry (sic)*].
Father: I wonder.
Nigel: Oh yes it wíll. . . . I don't wànt to send the train on this flóor . . . you want to send the train on the ràilway line [*runs it up plank onto chair*] . . . but it doesn't go very well on the chăir. . . . [*makes train go round in circles*] The train all round and ròund . . . it going all round and ròund . . . [*tries to reach other train*] have that tráin . . . have the blue tráin ('give it to me') [*Father does so*] . . . send the blue train down the ráilway line . . . [*plank falls off chair*] lèt me put the railway line on the cháir ('you put the railway

line on the chair!') [*Father does so*] ... [*looking at blue train*] Daddy put sèllotape on it ('previously') ... there a very fierce lìon in the train ... Daddy go and see if the lion still thére. ... Have your éngine ('give me my engine').

Father: Which engine? The little black engine?

Nigel: Yés ... Daddy go and find it fór you ... Daddy go and find the black éngine for you.

Nigel's linguistic system at this stage is in a state of transition, as he approximates more and more closely to the adult language, and it is unstable at various points. He is well on the way to the adult system of mood, but has not quite got there – he has not quite grasped the principle that language can be used as a *substitute* for shared experience, to impart information not previously known to the hearer;

Table 25.1 Determination of semantic features by elements of semiotic structures of situation (text in 3.2)

	Situational	Semantic	
Field	manipulation of objects	process type and participant structure	Ideational
	assistance of adult	benefactive	
	movable objects and fixtures	type of relevant object	
	movability of objects & their relation to fixtures	type of location and movement	
	recall of similar events	past time	
	evaluation	modulation	
Tenor	Interaction with parent	person	Interpersonal
	determination of course of action	mood and polarity	
	enunciation of intention	demand, 'I want to'	
	control of action	demand, 'I want you to'	
	sharing of experience	statement/question, monologue	
	seeking corroboration of experience	statement/question, dialogue	
Mode	dialogue	ellipsis (question–answer)	Textual
	reference to situation	exophoric reference	
	textual cohesion: objects	anaphoric reference	
	textual cohesion: processes	conjunction	
	furthering child's actions	theme (in conjunction with transitivity and mood; typically, parent or child in demands, child in two-participant statements, object in one-participant statements)	
	orientation to task		
	spoken mode	lexical collocation and repetition information structure	

systems:

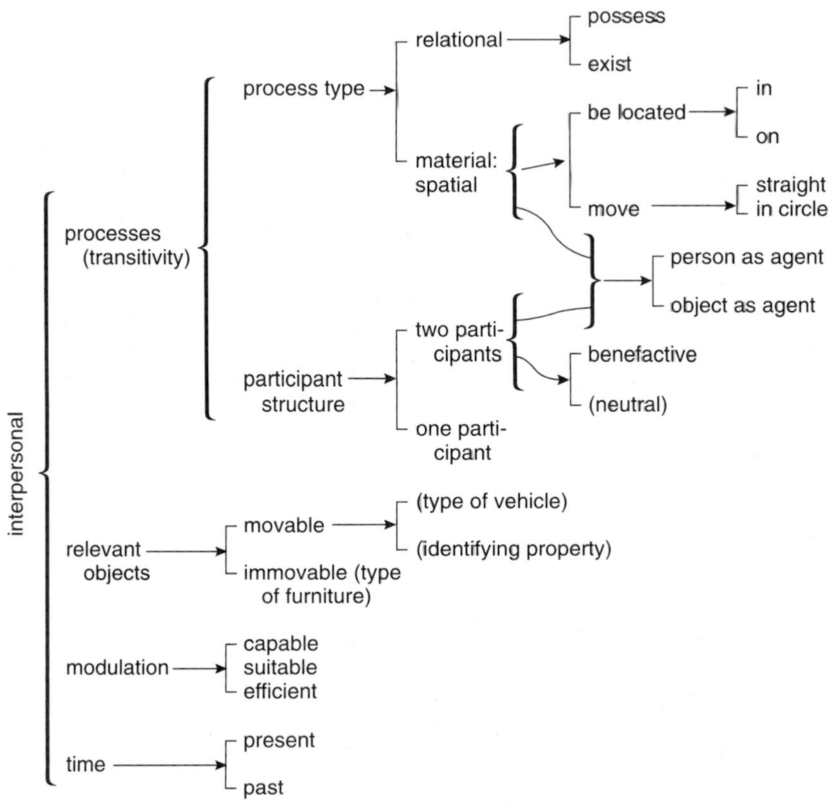

realizations in text:

be located / 2 participants	put
be located / 1 participant	be (in, on)
be located : in	in
be located : on	on
move / 2 participants : person	send
move / 2 participants : object	carry
move / 1 participant	go
move : straight	down
move : in circle	round and round
possess / 2 participants	(give)
possess / 1 participant	have
exist / 2 participants	find
exist / 1 participant	be (there's)
benefactive ('for me')	for you
movable : type of vehicle	train, engine, lorry
movable : identifying property	blue, black
immovable	chair, floor
	railway line
capable	will
suitable	(be) for
efficient	(go) well
past	(past tense)
present	(present tense)

processes (transitivity)

process type

relational — possess / exist

be located — in / on

material: spatial — move — straight / in circle

person as agent / object as agent

participant structure — two participants — benefactive / (neutral)

one participant

relevant objects — movable (type of vehicle) / (identifying property)

immovable (type of furniture)

modulation — capable / suitable / efficient

time — present / past

interpersonal

Figure 25.1a Semantic systems and their realizations, as represented in Nigel's speech (see section 3.2 for text)

systems:

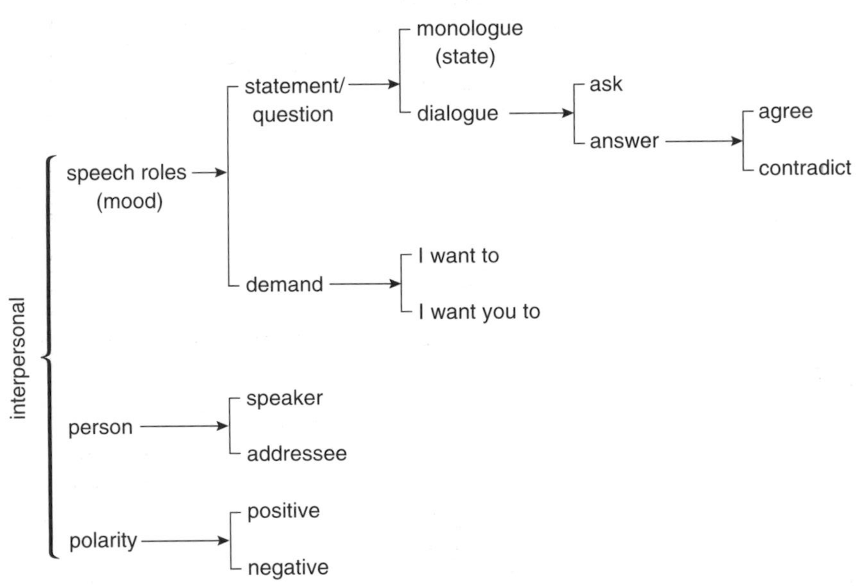

realizations in text:

statement/question	(falling tone)
demand	(rising tone)
monologue / positive	(indicative)
monologue / negative	(indicative+) *not*
ask	*I wonder* (+ indicative)
answer (cf. textual component)	*yes* [/*no*] (+ indicative)
I want to / positive	(*I*/*you*) want; (subjectless non-finite, e.g. *have that*)
I want to / negative	(*I*/*you*) *don't want*
I want you to	*let me* [*sic*]; (proper name); (*I*/*you*) want (proper name) to
speaker	*I*; *you* [*sic*]
addressee	*you*; (proper name, e.g. *Daddy*)

Figure 25.1b Interpersonal systems and their realizations

systems:

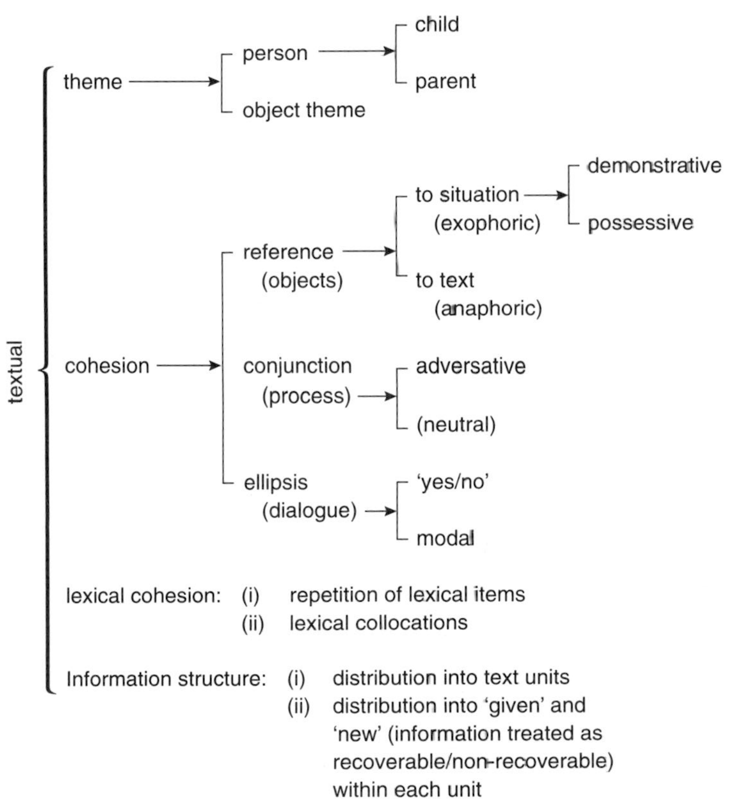

realizations in text:

textual

theme
— person
— child
— parent
— object theme

cohesion
— reference (objects)
  — to situation (exophoric)
    — demonstrative
    — possessive
  — to text (anaphoric)
— conjunction (process)
  — adversative
  — (neutral)
— ellipsis (dialogue)
  — 'yes/no'
  — modal

lexical cohesion:
(i) repetition of lexical items
(ii) lexical collocations

Information structure:
(i) distribution into text units
(ii) distribution into 'given' and 'new' (information treated as recoverable/non-recoverable) within each unit

person theme : child — I/you (initial); (subjectless non-finite)

person theme : parent — (proper name intial)

object theme — (object name initial)

exophoric : demonstrative — this, that, the, here

exophoric : possessive — your ('my')
anaphoric — it, that, the
adversative — but; (fall-rise tone)

ellipsis : 'yes/no' — yes [no]
ellipsis : modal — (modal element, e.g. it is . . . it will)

lexical : repetition of items — (e.g. train . . . train)
lexical : collocations — (e.g. chair. . . floor; train . . . railway line

information structure: text units — (organization in tone groups)
information structure: given–new — (location of tonic nucleus)

Figure 25.1c   Textual systems and their realizations

and therefore he has not yet learnt the general meaning of the yes/no question. He has a system of person, but alternates between *I/me* and *you* as the expression of the first person 'I'. He has a transitivity system, but confuses the roles of agent (actor) and medium (goal) in a non-middle (two-participant) process. It is worth pointing out perhaps that adult linguistic systems are themselves unstable at many points – a good example being transitivity in English, which is in a state of considerable flux; what the child is approximating to, therefore, is not something fixed and harmonious but something shifting, fluid and full of indeterminacies.

What does emerge from a consideration of Nigel's discourse is how, through the internal organization of the linguistic system, situational features determine text. If we describe the semiotic structure of the situation in terms of features of field, tenor and mode, and consider how these various features relate to the systems making up the semantic networks shown in Figure 25.1, we arrive at something like the picture presented in Table 25.1 (p. 370).

There is thus a systematic correspondence between the semiotic structure of the situation type and the functional organization of the semantic system. Each of the main areas of meaning potential tends to be determined or activated by one particular aspect of the situation:

Semantic components		*Situational elements*
ideational	systems activated by features of	field
interpersonal	"	tenor
textual	"	mode

In other words, the type of symbolic activity (field) tends to determine the range of meaning as content, language in the observer function (ideational); the role relationships (tenor) tend to determine the range of meaning as participation, language in the intruder function (interpersonal); and the rhetorical channel (mode) tends to determine the range of meaning as texture, language in its relevance to the environment (textual). There are of course many indeterminate areas – though there is often some system even in the indeterminacy: for example, the child's evaluation of objects lies on the borderline of 'field' and 'tenor', and the system of 'modulation' likewise lies on the borderline of the ideational and interpersonal components of language (Halliday 1969). But there is an overall pattern. This is not just a coincidence: presumably the semantic system evolved as symbolic interaction among people in social contexts, so we should expect the semiotic structure of these contexts to be embodied in its internal organization. By taking account of this we get an insight into the form of relationship among the three concepts of situation, text and semantic system. The semiotic features of the situation activate corresponding portions of the semantic system, in this way determining the register, the configuration of potential meanings that is typically associated with this situation type, and becomes actualized in the text that is engendered by it.

3.3 Sociosemantics of language development

A child learning his mother tongue is learning how to mean; he is building up a meaning potential in respect of a limited number of social functions. These functions constitute the semiotic environment of a very small child, and may be thought of as universals of human culture.

The meanings the child can express at this stage derive very directly from the social functions. For example, one of the functions served by the child's 'proto-language' is the regulatory function, that of controlling the behaviour of other people; and in this function he is likely to develop meanings such as 'do that some more' (continue or repeat what you've just been doing), and 'don't do that'. How does he get from these to the complex and functionally remote meanings of the adult semantic system?

These language-engendering functions, or 'proto-contexts', are simultaneously the origin both of the social context and of the semantic system. The child develops his ability to mean by a gradual process of generalization and abstraction, which in the case of Nigel appeared to go somewhat along the following lines. Out of the six functions of his proto-language (instrumental, regulatory, interactional, personal, heuristic and imaginative), he derived a simple but highly general distinction between language as a means of doing and language as a means of knowing – with the latter, at this stage, interpretable functionally as 'learning'. As he moved into the phase of transition into the adult system, at around 18 months, he assigned every utterance to one or other of these generalized functional categories, encoding the distinction by means of intonation: all 'learning' utterances were on a falling tone, and all 'doing' utterances on a rising tone. As forms of interaction, the latter required a response (increasingly, as time went on, a *verbal* response) while the former did not.

From the moment when this semantic principle was adopted, however, it ceased to satisfy, since Nigel already needed a semiotic system which would enable him to do both these things at once – to use language in both the learning mode and the doing mode within a single utterance. Without this ability he could not engage in true dialogue; the system could not develop a dynamic for the adoption and assignment of semiotic roles in verbal interaction. At this point, two steps were required, or really one complex step, for effectively completing the transition to the adult system. One was a further abstraction of the basic functional opposition, such that it came to be incorporated into his semantic system, as the two components of 'ideational' and 'interpersonal'; in the most general terms, the former developed from the 'learning' function, the latter from the 'doing' function. The other step was the introduction of a lexicogrammar, or syntax, making it possible for these two modes of meaning to be expressed simultaneously in the form of integrated lexicogrammatical structures.

The term 'sociosemantics of language development' refers to this process, whereby the original social functions of the infant's proto-language are reinterpreted, first as 'macro-functions', and then as 'meta-functions', functional components in the organization of the semantic system. These components, as remarked earlier (2.5), are clearly seen in the adult language; the options show a high degree of mutual constraint within one component but a very low degree of constraint between components. At the same time, looked at from another point of view, what the child has done is finally to dissociate the concept of 'function' from that of 'use'; the functions evolve into components of the semantic system, and the uses into what we are calling social contexts or situation types. For a detailed treatment of this topic see Halliday (1975).

4   TOWARDS A GENERAL SOCIOLINGUISTIC THEORY

In this final section we shall try to suggest how the main components of the sociolinguistic universe relate to one another, the assumption being that this network of relations is the cornerstone of a general sociolinguistic theory.

4.1   Meaning and text

The *text* is the linguistic form of social interaction. It is a continuous progression of meanings, combining both simultaneously and in succession. The meanings are the selections made by the speaker from the options that constitute the *meaning potential*; text is the actualization of this meaning potential, the process of semantic choice (see Halliday 1978 ch. 7).

The selections in meaning derive from different functional origins, and are mapped onto one another in the course of their realization as lexicogrammatical structure. In our folk linguistic terminology, the 'meaning' is represented as 'wording' – which in turn is expressed as 'sound' ('pronouncing') or as 'spelling'. The folk linguistic, incidentally, shows our awareness of the tri-stratal nature of language.

4.2   Text and situation

A text is embedded in a context of *situation*. The context of situation of any text is an instance of a generalized social context or situation type. The situation type is not an inventory of ongoing sights and sounds but a semiotic structure; it is the ecological matrix that is constitutive of the text.

Certain types of situation have in their semiotic structure some element which makes them central to the processes of cultural transmission; these are Bernstein's (1971) 'critical socializing contexts'. Examples are those having a regulative component (where a parent is regulating the child's behaviour), or an instructional component (where the child is being explicitly taught).

4.3 Situation as semiotic structure

The semiotic structure of the situation is formed out of the three sociosemiotic variables of field, tenor and mode. These represent in systematic form the type of activity in which the text has significant function (field), the status and role relationships involved (tenor) and the symbolic mode and rhetorical channels that are adopted (mode). The field, tenor and mode act collectively as determinants of the text through their specification of the register (4.5 below); at the same time they are systematically associated with the linguistic system through the functional components of the semantics (4.4).

4.4 Situation and semantic system

The semiotic components of the situation (field, tenor and mode) are systematically related to the functional components of the semantics (ideational, interpersonal and textual): *field* to the *ideational* compo-nent, representing the 'content' function of language, the speaker as observer; *tenor* to the *interpersonal* component, representing the 'participation' function of language, the speaker as intruder; and *mode* to the *textual* component, representing the 'relevance' function of language, without which the other two do not become actualized. There is a tendency, in other words, for the field of social action to be encoded linguistically in the form of ideational meanings, the role relationships in the form of interpersonal meanings, and the symbolic mode in the form of textual meanings.

4.5 Situation, semantic system and register

The semiotic structure of a given situation type, its particular pattern of field, tenor and mode, can be thought of as resonating in the semantic system and so activating particular networks of semantic options, typically options from within the corresponding semantic components (4.4). This process specifies a range of meaning poten-tial, or *register*: the semantic configuration that is typically associated with the situation type in question.

4.6   Register and code

The specification of the register by the social context is in turn controlled and modified by the *code*: the semiotic style, or 'sociolinguistic coding orientation' in Bernstein's term, that represents the particular subcultural angle on the social system. This angle of vision is a function of the social structure. It reflects, in our society, the pattern of social hierarchy, and the resulting tensions between an egalitarian ideology and a hierarchical reality. The code is transmitted initially through the agency of family types and family role systems, and subsequently reinforced in the various peer groups of children, adolescents and adults.

4.7   Lanugage and the social system

The foregoing synthesis presupposes an interpretation of the social system as a *social semiotic*: a system of meanings that constitutes the 'reality' of the culture. This is the higher-level system to which language is related: the semantic system of language is a realization of the social semiotic. There are many other forms of its symbolic realization besides language; but language is unique in having its own semantic stratum.

This takes us back to the 'meaning potential' of 4.1. The meaning potential of language, which is realized in the lexicogrammatical system, itself realizes meanings of a higher order; not only the semiotic of the particular social context, its organization as field, tenor and mode, but also that of the total set of social contexts that constitutes the social system. In this respect language is unique among the modes of expression of social meanings: it operates on both levels, having meaning both in general and in particular at the same time. This property arises out of the functional organization of the semantic system, whereby the meaning potential associated with a particular social context is derived from corresponding sets of generalized options in the semantic system.

4.8   Language and the child

A child begins by creating a proto-language of his own, a meaning potential in respect of each of the social functions that constitute his developmental semiotic. In the course of maturation and socialization he comes to take over the adult language. The text-in-situation by which he is surrounded is filtered through his own functional–semantic grid, so that he processes just as much of it as can be interpreted in terms of his own meaning potential at the time.

As a strategy for entering the adult system he generalizes from his initial set of functions an opposition between language as doing and language as learning. This is the developmental origin of the interpersonal and indeational components in the semantic system of the adult language. The concept of function is now abstracted from that of use, and has become the basic principle of the linguistic organization of meaning.

4.9   The child and the culture

As a child learns language, he also learns *through* language. He interprets text not only as being specifically relevant to the context of situation but also as being generally relevant to the context of culture. It is the linguistic system that enables him to do this; since the sets of semantic options which are characteristic of the situation (the register) derive from generalized functional components of the semantic system, they also at the same time realize the higher order meanings that constitute the culture, and so the child's focus moves easily between microsemiotic and macrosemiotic environment.

So when Nigel's mother said to him 'Leave that stick outside; stop teasing the cat; and go and wash your hands. It's time for tea', he could not only understand the instructions but could also derive from them information about the social system: about the boundaries dividing social space, and 'what goes where'; about the continuity between the human and the animal world; about the regularity of cultural events; and more besides. He does not, of course, learn all this from single instances, but from the countless sociosemiotic events of this kind that makes up the life of social man. And as a corollary to this, he comes to rely heavily on social system for the decoding of the meanings that are embodied in such day-to-day encounters.

In one sense a child's learning of this mother tongue is a process of progressively freeing himself from the constraints of the immediate context – or, better, of progressively redefining the context and the place of language within it – so that he is able to learn through language, and interpret an exchange of meanings in relation to the culture as a whole. Language is not the only form of the realization of social meanings, but it is the only form of it that has this complex property: to mean, linguistically, is at once both to reflect and to act – and to do both these things both in particular and in general at the same time. So it is first and foremost through language that the culture is transmitted to the child, in the course of everyday interaction in the key socializing agencies of family, peer group and school. This process, like other semiotic processes, is controlled and regulated by the code; and so, in the course of it, the child himself also takes over the coding orientation, the subcultural semiotic bias that is a feature of all social structures except those of a (possibly non-existent) homogeneous type, and certainly of all complex societies of a pluralistic and hierarchical kind.

4.10 Summary

Halliday (1978 ch. 3: Figure 4) was an attempt to summarize the discussion in diagrammatic form; the arrow is to be read as 'determines'. What follows is a rendering of it in prose.

Social interaction typically takes a linguistic form, which we call *text*. A text is the product of infinitely many simultaneous and successive choices in meaning, and is realized as lexicogrammatical structure, or 'wording'. The environment of the text is the context of situation, which is an instance of a social context, or *situation type*. The situation type is a semiotic construct which is structured in terms of *field*, *tenor* and *mode*: the text-generating activity, the role relationships of the participants, and the rhetorical modes they are adopting. These situational variables are related respectively to the *ideational*, *interpersonal*, and *textual* components of the *semantic system*: meaning as content (the observer function of language), meaning as participation (the intruder function) and meaning as texture (the relevance function). They are related in the sense that each of the situational features typically calls forth a network of options from the corresponding semantic component; in this way the semiotic properties of a particular situation type, its structure in terms of field, tenor and mode, determine the semantic configuration or *register* – the meaning potential that is characteristic of the situation type in question, and is realized as what is known as a 'speech variant'. This process is regulated by the *code*, the semiotic grid or principles of the organization of social meaning that represent the particular subcultural angle on the social system. The subcultural variation is in its turn a product of the *social structure*, typically the social hierarchy acting through the distribution of family types having different familial role systems. A child, coming into the picture, interprets text-in-situation in term of his generalized functional categories of *learning* (*mathetic*) and *doing* (*pragmatic*); from here by a further process of abstraction he constructs the functionally organized semantic system of the adult language. He has now gained access to the social semiotic; this is the context in which he himself will learn to mean, and in which all his subsequent meaning will take place.

I have been attempting here to interrelate the various components of the sociolinguistic universe, with special reference to the place of language within it. It is for this reason that I have adopted the mode of interpretation of the social system as a semiotic, and stressed the systematic aspects of it: the concept of system itself, and the concept of function within a system. It is all the more important, in this context, to avoid any suggestion of an idealized social functionalism, and to insist that the social system is not something static, regular and harmonious, nor are its elements held poised in some perfect pattern of functional relationships.

A 'sociosemiotic' perspective implies an interpretation of the shifts, the irregularities, the disharmonies and the tensions that characterize human interaction and social processes. It attempts to explain the semiotic of the social structure, in its aspects both of persistence and of change, including the semantics of social class, of the power system, of hierarchy and of social conflict. It attempts also to explain the linguistic processes whereby the members construct the social semiotic, whereby social reality is shaped, constrained and modified – processes which, far from tending towards an ideal construction, admit and even institutionalize myopia, prejudice and misunderstanding (Berger and Luckmann 1966 ch. 3).

The components of the sociolinguistic universe themselves provide the sources and conditions of disorder and of change. These may be seen in the text, in the situation, and in the semantic system, as well as in the dynamics of cultural transmission and social learning. All the lines of determination are *ipso facto* also lines of tension, not only through indeterminacy in the transmission but also through feedback. The meaning of the text, for example, is fed back into the situation, and becomes part of it, changing it in the process; it is also fed back, through the register, into the semantic system, which it likewise affects and modifies. The code, the form in which we conceptualize the injection of the social structure into the semantic process, is itself a two-way relation, embodying feedback from the semantic configurations of social interaction into the role relationships of the family and other social groups. The social learning processes of a child, whether those of learning the language or of learning the culture, are among the most permeable surfaces of the whole system, as one soon becomes aware in listening to the language of young children's peer groups – a type of semiotic context which has hardly begun to be seriously studied. In the light of the role of language in social processes, a sociolinguistic perspective does not readily accommodate strong boundaries. The 'sociolinguistic order' is neither an ideal order nor a reality that has no order at all; it is a human artefact having some of the properties of both.

26 Allan Luke

The body literate: discourse and inscription in early literacy training

CLASSROOM INSCRIPTIONS

In contemporary psychologically-based pedagogy, teachers inscribe and read the student 'body as the surface of the mind' (Baker and Luke 1991). Early literacy training as the site of body mapping and writing, as comprising material practices for the constitution of the literate, is exemplified in various cross-cultural and historical settings. As S. B. Heath (1981), Wagner *et al.* (1986 pp. 254–255) and other ethnographic researchers have demonstrated, the technologies, icons and products of literacy constitute a 'material culture'. Here I make the case that ceremonial inscription of the body is a key, and frequently over-looked and undertheorised, element of literacy training.

For many children in Western cultures, the dispositional training of the habitus first comes into play in the routines of family literacy events, however natural such sites and practices may appear (Heath 1982; P. Miller *et al.* 1986). One reader recalls his first encounters with text:

> Ann-Marie made me sit down in front of her, on my little chair; she leant over, lowered her eyelids and went to sleep. From this mask-like face issued a plaster voice. . . . After a moment, I realised, it was the book that was talking. Sentences emerged that frightened me; they were like real centipedes; they swarmed with syllables and letters, spat out their dipthongs and made their double consonants hum; fluting, nasal, broken up with sighs and pausings . . . words left their mark on objects, transforming

actions into rituals and events into ceremonies. Someone began to ask questions: . . . it was as if a child were being quizzed: what would he have done in the woodcutter's place? Which of the two sisters did he prefer? Why? Did he agree with Babette's punishment. But this child was not entirely me and I was afraid to reply. I did reply, though; my feeble voice grew faint and I felt I was turning into something else. . . . When she stopped reading, I quickly took back the books and carried them off under my arm without a word of thanks. . . . In the long run, I came to enjoy this release which tore me out of myself

(Sartre 1967 p.44)

The scientific and literary pedigree of this environment notwithstanding, this reconstruction might fit well into Heath's (1982) 'Maintown' community, where the heuristic exchanges of childhood story reading prepare the child for what counts as school literacy. Here, the child is practicing an academic language game. An integral part of such games is differing trainings in bodily position and paralinguistics. For example, in Heath's (1982) study, for white, working-class families, sitting properly and not squirming was part of the ritual of bedtime reading; for black working-class children, verbal storying entailed learning and inventing bodily patterns of mime, dance and movement to frame the tale. What is occurring in early literacy (and oral storying) events is the construction of the habitus, the articulation and instantiation of a system of bodily discipline.

What is curious in the above instance is Sartre's reconstruction of early reading as a *disembodied* construction of the Other: as a calling upon of the 'child who wasn't entirely me,' with the effect of tearing 'one out of oneself'. The ritual effect here is the bodily and linguistic (and, for Sartre, ontological) constitution of the literate by turning the child/student 'into someone else'. This would appear an instance of literacy training as a technology of the self, one geared for what Foucault called the inscription of the 'dissociated Self' par excellence.

Such inscriptions of the habitus also occur in contemporary classroom literacy events. As part of our survey of Australian classrooms in two urban sites, 18 boundaried literacy-related 'lessons' were audiotaped in two sites, one urban and one rural; transcription was aided by the use of field notes. All lessons observed and taped can be described as discrete classroom events, which according to the self-report data on the large-scale survey tend to occur as regular, routinised practices in progressive early childhood literacy training: for example, 'morning news', 'modeled writing' sessions, 'writing conferences', 'story-time', and 'shared book experience' (cf. S. Michaels 1981). Here I focus on two examples of the latter, which use an enlarged print book for a group collaborative reading as developed by Holdaway (1976). This practice reportedly is common in the two jurisdictions studied, and I construe many of the patterns which emerge in these transcripts as attempts at 'model' practice under the scrutiny of the researcher.

Transcript 1: Billy Goats

[Fifteen 5- and 6-year-old children are arrayed around the teacher on the floor in a rugged area; they are working with an enlarged print book about 'Billy Goats'. The teacher sits before them on a chair, turning pages of the book which is mounted on an easel.]

1   S1: I've gotta pair of socks like that.
2   T: David, will you just sit up straight. Michael, just sit up straight and face the front. When we first look at this, I was looking at this book and there's something different about the goats. But around here [points to picture] . . . what were all the goats wearing? [turns page]
3   S2: Go . . . gooo
4   S3: Ah beard, . . . a little beard, and they all gotta little beard.
5   T: [loudly] A beard. What do they all got on the first page? What do they all got around their necks?
6   S1: Ah bells, a one has . . .
7   S3: //Bells
8   T: [loudly] Bells. Well actually I was wrong. I thought that no one has bells, but I got it straight anyway. So . . . has the little billy goat got a bell? Michael, if you can't sit down you can practice sitting up straight at recess. OK? Sit down. But . . . ssshhh . . . What's the big billy goat got?

This site is bounded both temporally (i.e. shared book 'time') and spatially (i.e this 'time' occurs within the confines of the rug reading area; children who move out of this instructional locus are physically and verbally rearranged both before and during the events).

The onset of the event is taken with the rearrangement of student bodies into the 'correct' reading habitus, and with the discursive construction of a collectivity such that this rearrangement can be targeted and retargeted as the lesson proceeds. In turn 2, the teacher's pronominalisation of 'we' shifts fluidly to 'I' within a single clause. Here, the subjectivities of teacher and student reader(s) are collapsed, effecting an equivalence, a fluid conflation of teacher–student reader. It is this conjoint subjectivity which is interrogated (turns 2, 5, 8), and from this interactively constructed subjectivity that student responses are sourced. Against this, we find 'difference' marked in turn 8. Those who have not internalised the teachers' gaze, those who are not willing participants in the technology, are singled out, not as 'I' or 'we' but 'you'. Where the technology of the self fails, the technology of power steps in. Where the gaze apparently has not been internalised by the children, it is externally asserted by the teacher.

This construction is achieved in part through a set of injunctions: in turn 2, a composite set of bodily inscriptions is undertaken. 'Sit up straight', 'face the front', are preludes to gestural and linguistic imperatives on 'how *we* look' and 'where *we* look'. Posture, movement and visual gaze thus are monitored and directed. So what is occurring here can be described beyond its archetypal IRE (Injunction Response Event) exchange structure. In effect who is to take the R turn (which subjectivity? which reader? which body?) is constructed by and within the classroom discourse.

This classroom literacy event constitutes what will count as reading for its participants (Baker and Freebody 1989). Within the IRE pattern, the language game entails guessing the single word response prompted by teacher gesture and talk (Mehan 1979). I have here stressed the bodily constraints of such literacy events. This event, like many following the 'shared book' pattern leads on to a choral reading led by the teacher.

Transcript 2: Billy Goat Narrative

'Now I'm coming to gobble you up,' roared the Troll. 'Well come along I've got two spears and I'll poke your eyeballs out at your ears. I've got besides two great flat stones and I'll crush you to bits, body and bones.'

That is what the Big Billy Goat said, and that is what the Big Billy Goat did, and after that he went up the hillside.

The billy goats got so fat they could hardly walk home again. And if the fat hasn't fallen off them, why they're still fat.

As Bourdieu (1977) notes, part of the training of the bodily habitus entails training of the mouth. In this particular event, 'We read' (McHoul 1991), and this reading entails the aforementioned collectivisation not only of the body, but of eyes, mouth and body; 'we' see, we move and we mouthe. The 'reading' is boisterous, and led by the (louder) teacher's voice and gestures which set cadence, stress, intonation and pitch. Notably, even those boys who had trouble sitting (and dissociating) participate here. They strain their bodies upward and open their mouths widely. The teachers volume and pitch stresses the alliterative passage, 'bits, bodies, and bones', shouted by all, and punctuated by many of the boys with bodies stretching upwards towards the teacher and text. The girls, by contrast, tend to sit more shrunkenly, their hands at their sides and in their laps.

Multiple levels of inscription are occurring here, not the least of which is bodily. Certainly the ideational content of the text constitutes one form of 'writing' of the subject, a selective introduction to particular ways of speaking, acting, and being. On its lexicogrammatical surface, the culture represented is indeed masculinist and violent, constructing ideological 'subject positions' (Kress 1985) and 'classification schemes' (Fairclough 1989). But perhaps what is significant is not the 'content' of the technology per se, but rather how it shapes and constructs its subjects. In the following event, group and individual reading are interleaved in a way which foregrounds those very workings of this technology of the self.

Transcript 3: Mr. Singh's Garden

[Ten children, aged 5–6 sit on the rug area around the teacher. Again, she is poised next to an enlarged print book mounted on an easel. She sits on a chair above the children and has a pointer in her hand.]

1   T: On your bottoms please, so that we can all see [gestures to the text, begins tracking lines in text with her hand]

2   Students and Teacher: In Mr. Singh's garden, there was a red rose. 'Ah,' said the caterpiller, 'I see a red rose.'

3   S1:   Nah, Kylie [shouts]

4   T: Shhss, Kylie, we don't need help. Be quiet. Evelyn, you read the next page [turns page].

5   S2:   'Ah,' said the bird, 'I see the caterpiller.'

6   T: Brendan, you read the next page [turns page].

7   S3:   'Ah,' said a cat, 'I see a bird.'

8   T: All together now, I'll pick some nice children out for individual reading [turns page].

9   Students and Teacher: 'Ah,' said the dog, 'I see a cat.' 'I see a dog,' said Mr. Singh, 'and it's in my garden.'

10   T: Good girl Emma, for reading 'Mr. Singh.' I read 'Mrs. Singh' by mistake.

11   S4:   Mister.

Prohibitions on the body are central here. One not only must sound like a reader to an authoritative ear, but one is enjoined to adopt the correct bodily habitus for participation in reading: 'on your bottoms please, so that we can all see' (Turn 1).

Collective reading (Turns 2 & 9) is alternated with individual reading (Turns 5 & 7). In this manner, the very exchange structure of the lesson fuses together for its participants, individual and group subjectivities, transposing the 'I' into a collective 'we'. Those 'nice children' who are picked out for solo performance are those who are seen to have internalised the discipline of collective readership. These children are mapped differently than those who are disciplined on behalf of the collectivity (Turn 4: 'we don't need help').

In Turn 10, Emma is singled out from the collective reading and praised for showing signs of having assumed the gaze. She apparently has internalised the procedure sufficiently to correct the teacher's misreading. Here the relationship is reversed, and the teacher confesses to having misread. What is interesting is that Emma has taken on the authorised 'voice' of the teacher, the technology of the self is in place. Her performance stands in direct contrast to the male speaker in Turn 3, who, like the boys in Transcript 1, shows no (bodily or linguistic) sign of internal discipline: he yells out. But here he succeeds in calling attention to the undiscipline of the girl next to him, who becomes the object of a technology of power, the reprimand, albeit on behalf of the collective 'we' (Turn 4).

The patterns of inscription described here are gendered. In the above lessons, as throughout the lesson corpus, the technologies of power are predominantly asserted on boy participants (Walkerdine 1981). In the events examined above, the girls tended to be more willing participants, and, like Emma in the latter transcript, their compliant bodily schemas signalled that their willing participation and the technology of the self are at work.

If the foregoing analyses of classroom events were done using the templates of psychology – whether Skinnerian, Chomskian, Vygotskian, or Piagetian – if they were operating from normative definitions of literacy and the optimal means for its instruction, the events and sites described would take on a very different appearance. Depending on which psychology was called into play, they would appear appropriate or inappropriate, efficient or inefficient at achieving 'learning' and 'reading'. Yet the suspension of a priori acceptance of the legitimacy of 'true' educational discourses, whether those revealed in the surveys of these and other teachers, or in educational texts, enables what Foucault (1977) termed a 'genealogical' reading of what is accomplished in the regimes of practice.

A very different diagram emerges, one which foregrounds the training and building of a literate habitus. Particular postures, silences, gestures, and visible signs of 'being in' the lesson and the collective body are on display. Proximics, the organisation and delimitation of space and time in the classroom are encompassing aspects of the gaze: from 'sitting on one's bottom' to 'sitting up straight', awaiting one's turn to speak. These are monitored for by the teacher who, with her or his discourse templates and meta-phors for 'reading' and the 'child', scans and maps bodies on (psychological/humanist) grids of specification, accordingly issuing prohibitions 'to "watch one's tongue", to "mind one's p's and q's", to pursue correctness through constant self-corrections' (Bourdieu 1977 p. 656). His or her age, size, position, and official status as leader of the event – his or her displays of superior knowledge and power with both 'reading' and 'teaching' – grants his or her eyes, ears and mouth moral authority. They come to stand as embodied sources of power (Kroker and Cook 1986 pp. 79–87), at times mirroring, at times filtering, at times marking and punctuating. But beyond this authoritative reading by the teacher of the physical and semiotic, a material 'seeing' and 'hearing' is marked on the canvas of student body. Throughout, students take on directional gaze towards the text, the pronunciation, cadences and intonation patterns of the teacher's voice (e.g. 'bits, bodies and bones'), and the hearing of the text, alternating group and individual performance. Subjectivity is reestablished in terms of a collective identity, and possession of this identity is marked on and by the body – moving and still, seeing and hearing, speaking and silent.

(RE)MEMBERING THE BODY

I have here offered a poststructuralist discourse analysis of early literacy training. It does not target for criticism a particular approach to literacy instruction or its participants. Rather it tables a different map for reading classroom literacy events, one which views the truth claims of pedagogy and research themselves as discourse constructions with tangible, political consequences. It also sets out to retheorise what occurs in the material culture of classroom events as bodily transcription and to show how that culture constitutes the morally regulated, literate subject. In this way, the theory-driven analysis undertaken here moves towards Foucault's project of 'genealogical' analysis of the body inscribed by history and 'traced' by language. I conclude with comments on the implications of this model for theorising and studying literacy events, and for reframing the sociocultural consequences of literacy instruction.

The model of literacy training presented here can be used to reread data from social histories of literacy and cross cultural ethnographies of communication. Reconsider, for instance, the rote acquisition of Quranic literacy among the Vai:

> children . . . bend over their individual boards with passages from the Quran written on them. For 2 hours or more the singsong of their changing can be heard, accompanied occasionally by the admonishment from the teacher, or the snap of a small whip landing on the backside of an errant student.
>
> (Scribner and Cole 1981 p. 30)

Here the body and voice are subject to the instructional technology, a technology tied directly to the discipline, in Foucault's sense, of the Quran. These non-secular ceremonies, moreover, have their parallels in Western settings: for instance, in the choral repetition, rote memorisation and veneration of the Book taught to fundamentalist children in southern-US Sunday schools (Zinsser 1986). We find parallel examples in 19th century British and Canadian pedagogy, where standardised bodily stances were to be assumed for oral recitation, slate-writing, pensmanship, and other literate practices (de Castell and Luke 1986). There too, pedagogy entailed the construction and discipline of a bodily and linguistic habitus. Furthermore, this bodily aspect of literacy training has clear precedents in some oral cultures' initiations into archetypal texts. Describing the recitation of the Bagre among the LoDagaa, Goody (1988 p. 171) notes the focal role of the shea nut, 'needed (verbally at least) to make the "oil" (in fact, whitewash) that is used to mark the bodies of the new members'.

Setting the tenor for the last decade of research in the ethnography of literacy, S.B. Heath (1981 p. 27) maintained that reading and writing, 'like other systems of communication' are 'organised ... in culture-specific ways and according to certain norms of interpretation' and that the events of literacy training assemble, enact and rehearse 'methods of learning these norms and having them reinforced.' But despite the proliferation of ethnographic and interactional analysis of literacy events in schools, the body has not been viewed as a constitutive or focal object of study. While we see the body in descriptions of tribal culture like Goody's and occasionally in descriptions of community life like Heath's, it disappears when we turn to the modernist school, the very site of the crossgenerational representation and reproduction of the Cartesian mind/body dualism. As several theorists of popular culture have noted, the discourses, 'styles' and practices of schooling exclude and rationalise bodily pleasure and desire (e.g Hebdige 1979). By stressing the heard (voice), the seen (text), and the unseen (mind), by readily explaining ethnographic and linguistic evidence via psychological metanarrative, much interactionist classroom research has participated, however tacitly, in that exclusion. The reconceptualisation of literacy training proposed here is an attempt to reinstate the body as a political object of literacy and linguistic research.

The inscription of children in literacy training has taken on differing configurations in various cultural and historical settings.

The 'Great Debate' over literacy education in English-speaking countries continues apace, and most recently has featured reforms which stress more child-centred, holistic approaches. The 'shared book' instructional events described here have come to be associated with reform movements in New Zealand and Australia. Advocates argue for the replacement of individuated 'skill and drill' activities with what teachers in this study described as 'natural learning' approaches, some of which reframe classroom events as 'social contexts'. But as part of an interactionist tradition, they typically stop short of an analysis of classroom events which reconnects with a broader political theorisation of the consequence of the distribution of discourse and literacy. The analyses I offer here may lead us to query whether such 'child-centred' instructional events are indeed (more or less) 'natural' or whether they signal a shift in emphasised discursive technology, a reshaping of moral regulation and with it, patterns of social reproduction.

Such progressive approaches and their apparent opposite numbers, traditional skills and classicist approaches, may act as equivalent and oscillating 'armatures of [governmental] power' (Hunter 1989; McHoul 1991). But they also signal differences in pedagogical technologies, supplanting what I have called here technologies of power with more subtle technologies of the self. Certainly, in the events discussed here 'reading' is remade into collective activity, harkening back to the forms of choral and oral reading predominant before the early 20th century prescription of silent reading (Luke 1988). In this regard, they suggest a discipline similar to that noted by Davis (1987 p. 221) in her description of literacy learning in 16th century France: 'the protestant method for guaranteeing orthodoxy was in the last instance censorship and punishment; but in the first instance it was *the combination of reading with listening to a trained teacher.*' In the protestant literacy training described by Davis and the progressive training analysed here, the premium placed on membership in a collective engaged in 'learning by doing', on noncoercive participation – however 'kinder and gentler' – still marks out a form of political and moral construction of the literate habitus, what Foucault (1979) calls a 'means of correct training.'

Of course, in local sites such approaches never occur in the 'pure' forms prescribed in the 'truths' of educational discourse. Disciplinary power is neither unitary nor total, but rather diffuse and site specific. The 'progressive' teaching examined here exemplifies how a single boundaried lesson may be the site for multiple pedagogical technologies aimed at single bodies, alternating strategies designed to collapse them into a unitary, collective entity of the literate subjectivity, whether the 'natural learner' or the 'decoder'. Implements of technologies of signs (e.g. the enlarged print book, the blackboard, the pointer), move in concert with those of technologies of power (e.g. the reprimand, the injunction), and those of technologies of the self (the internalised gaze). In this light, perhaps what differentiates contending models in the great debate over literacy teaching (e.g. 'skills', 'cultural literacy', 'great books,' 'whole language') is more fundamental than overt difference in ideology and content. Drawing from a full historical arsenal, each centres on differing technologies for shaping and regulating bodies.

To return to the literacy/reproduction nexus posited Bourdieu and Passeron (1977): such technologies no doubt have concrete sociocultural parts to play in the representation and reproduction of classed and gendered textual labour. The ritualised oral reading procedures here could be seen to mirror particular home practices (e.g. the bedtime story) and various secular and nonsecular practices in the community and polity (e.g. church responsive reading; singing of a national anthem). Curiously, though, however well the body may remember, the language games mapped here do not appear to have direct correlates to reading-at-work or reading-at-home. I would argue that the forms of 'cultural capital' garnered here (e.g. oral reading, intonation patterns, correct posture) are not taken out directly for credit on the 'linguistic market'. Rather, their capitalisation would seem to be in acquiring the bodily habitus for student reading and thereby ensuing discipline and promotion within the institution. If this is the case, the mode of inscription described here is a closed text, one sourced in, characteristic of, and servicing the disciplinary regime of the school.

The imprint is in part a matter of, as Graff (1981) so eloquently puts it, training in being trained. Of course, the effect may indeed be the inscription of particular values, beliefs, and attitudes. Particularly focal in children's texts and interaction are the interlocking possible worlds of class, gender and ethnicity presented: the Billy Goat narrative is but one exemplar of textual ideology at work. But I have tried here to draw attention to the normalisation of the body as pedagogic strategy and practice. The key is in what Foucault

(1988 pp. 16–17) calls 'the prohibition and strong incitation to speak' as a means of turning the gaze on oneself, of 'telling the abbot everything he had in mind', and thereby monitoring oneself in the confessional. And what more effective way of extending the body politic to its members.

27 Judith Williamson

... But I know what I like: the function of 'art' in advertising

Advertising is part of a system which not only sells us *things* – it sells us 'choices': or, to be more precise, sells us the idea that we are 'free' to 'choose' *between* things. To nourish this 'freedom' advertising must, like other key ideological forms, cover its own tracks and assert that these choices are the result of personal taste. As a contemporary advert puts it: *'One instinctively knows when something is right'*. In our society 'high' and 'low' cultural forms share the same speech: for this pompous phrase could equally have leapt straight from the mouth of that most instinctive bourgeois character: The Artist.

Unlike advertising, Art has a reputation for being above things vulgar and mercenary, a form eternal rather than social, whose appreciation springs from the discerning heart, not the cultural background. This ethereal notion can be brought down with a bump by the merest glimpse, on the one hand at the Art market, distinguished from other fields of commercial gain only by the intriguing fact that it successfully deals in the 'priceless', and on the other hand, at that equally effective cultural economy whereby anything that too many people like is rapidly devalued as 'Art'. Classical music which makes it onto '100 Favourites' LPs becomes scorned by 'serious' music lovers; reproductions even of 'valued' paintings, like Van Gogh's 'Sunflowers', disappear from the walls of the cognoscenti when they become widely enough loved to be sold in Woolworth's.

It is on this 'cultural economy' that advertising feeds its endless appetite for social values. Ads are in the business not of creating, but of re-cycling social categories, relying on systems of value already in existence as sources for the 'auras', at once intangible and precise, which must be associated with the goods for sale. Any system which is already structured in terms of up-market and down-market is especially useful, the more so if it has a high investment in denying its own workings. Advertising pitches its products at specific social classes (carefully graded from A to E) yet, as with Art, choice and taste must appear as personal attributes of the individual. So 'Art' is a particularly appropriate system for ads: while appearing to be 'above' social distinctions, it provides a distinct set of social codes which we all understand.

For what is interesting is the degree of agreement at both ends of the social scale as to what 'Art' is. Art is felt to be 'difficult', its meaning not accessible by mere everyday use of the perceptive faculties. It is something which the great majority of people feel is somehow above them, out of reach and beyond their grasp. This perfectly mirrors the opinion of those select few who can be assured of their good taste simply by its exclusiveness.

It is in the light of these implications that the Benson and Hedges campaign appears in its full brilliance. Usually seen as an application of a surrealist style of advertising, it is in fact much more: an application of social assumptions about class, taste and Art. All ads are surreal in a sense: they connect disparate objects in strange formal systems, or place familiar objects in locations with which they have no obvious connection. We are so familiar with perfume bottles haunting desert islands and motor cars growing in fields of buttercups that their surreal qualities go unremarked. (Dali's 'Apparition of a Face and Fruit Dish on a Beach' could be the description of an everyday advertisement.) What the B&H ads do, obliquely, is *refer* to surrealism as an 'Art' structure, and more particularly, they draw on the crux of surrealism – the assumption of an underlying sense. In the original Surrealist paintings, this sense was a psychoanalytic one, the logic of a dream. The fact that it wasn't immediately apparent guaranteed the depth of its existence.

B&H ads like the Mousetrap, the Birdcage, the Christmas Tree (Figure 27.1) (and more recently, the Winston ads) make a formal play on doing exactly what all ads do: re-place a product in a context with which is had no 'natural' connection, so that it takes on meaning from its surroundings. The difference is that the B&H ads don't seek to naturalize this re-location, they play on its strangeness. The product doesn't come to mean 'parrot' or 'electric plug'. It is the context of 'Art' in which the product is being inserted.

Figure 27.1

And in this context, it is the very difficulty in understanding the images, and the absence of obvious connections, which indicates the genuinely 'cultured' status of the ads, and therefore, of the product. The ads are visual puzzles, they imply meanings one doesn't have access to. This suggests 'High Art' and thereby, exclusivity. A product for the discerning, the tasteful, the few. The legal restrictions on linking tobacco with social success are brilliantly by-passed. A B&H ad doesn't *depict* a social class (as, for example, Martini ads do) but implicitly, and flatteringly, *addresses* one, through its reference to Art and the assumed response. (Similarly, Players No. 6 (Figure 27.2) have managed to imply exactly the social class of consumer they used to depict, in their imitation series which is much less 'difficult': while referring to the Benson and Hedges campaign, their 'down-market' version is reassuring, for people who didn't feel they 'got' the smarter images.)

In terms of class and taste, the Three Ducks ad (Figure 27.3) is the most revealing. Flying ducks are tacitly a joke about 'bad' taste among those who assume theirs is 'good'. Just as the formal peculiarity of the picture is unsettling, with its distorted angles, stark

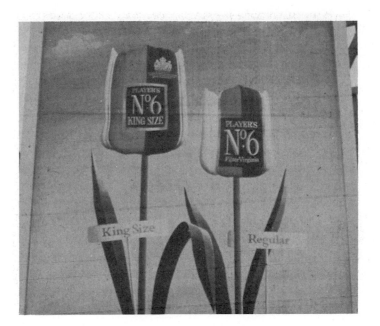

Figure 27.2

primary colours and lack of realism, so the cosy lower-classness of the whole lifestyle implied by the ducks, is both scorned and threatened by the social snobbery (wrapped in a visual snobbery) of the image. This ad confirms the connection between Artistic and social values which underpins the whole series.

Quite the opposite effect is produced by the 'Mona Lisa' ad (Figure 27.4). This is a familiar reference, a picture that even the 'uneducated' have heard of. But more than that: here again, the connotations derived from its use of the 'Art' image exactly fit the overall social tone of the ad. The Mona Lisa's smile is a well-known mystique, famous, like Art, for its incomprehensibility. But here we have a perfectly ordinary, homey explanation! She is thinking of a real dairy cream cake. The inscrutable is suddenly brought into terms of everyday life, and, although this is clearly a joke, it is one with very deep-lying implications, about Art, inferiority, and the *relief* at being able to joke about something one feels is alien. And this relief is exactly like the pleasure of letting oneself go, and having a nice (but naughty) éclair. In relation to High Culture and Art, this ad is as reassuring as a cream cake. Even the caption recognizes both

Figure 27.3

the transgression of tampering with 'Art' (naughty) and, simultane-ously, the comforting sense such transgression brings (nice). This ad draws on exactly the same assumptions about 'Art' as the B&H ones, but invites the response of a different social group (and in particular, women).

The 'Picasseau' ad (Figure 27.5), like the 'Mona Lisa' ad, jokes about a well-known style with a familiarity that at once disarms and impresses: it successfully combines both ends of the spectrum. Even people who have never heard of cubism have heard of Picasso and

Figure 27.4

Figure 27.5

know he often painted in strange square shapes, making the familiar (a woman, a guitar) alien. Here it's done so simply that anyone can 'get' it: the alien is re-familiarized. Yet it's done so stylishly that it also reads like an in-joke for the arty. Anyone can grasp the visual joke – even the bubbles are square. Cleverly, this ad provides multiple values: snobbery, or reassurance. It depends how much you know about Art . . .

Part VI

Readers and reading

Interpretation, ideation and the reading process

EDITOR'S INTRODUCTION

The debate – or quarrel – that took place in 1981 between literary theorists, Wolfgang Iser and Stanley Fish, illustrates some of the consequences of firmly locating meaning in the text, in the reader or somewhere in between. Fish (1981) launched the debate with a scathing review article of Iser's 1978 book, *The Act of Reading*, which appeared at a time when Iser was becoming a prominent name in American literary criticism. As Fish explains, Iser's popularity probably stemmed from the fact that he presented the human alternative to the Derridean deconstruction which many thought to have taken hold in the American academy. In his balanced view of meaning as lying somewhere between the pole of the 'artistic' (text created by the author) and the 'esthetic' (text realized by the reader) it does seem that Iser sits on the fence (Iser 1974 p. 274). Fish challenges him on this and, in so doing, fires one of the opening shots in a battle over 'pluralism' and 'value' that rages in American academia even as I write. The crux of the issue is whether there are as many possible readings of a text as there are readers, or whether there may be a small number of 'correct' or 'legitimate' readings of a text (or even just one 'correct' reading). In the fierce debate which currently grips America, proponents of each of these views condemn holders of the other view as tyrants (see Fish 1994; Hughes 1994 and the essays collected in Dunant 1994).

Fish argues that Iser tries to straddle both perspectives in his theory of literary communication, giving equal partnership to readers and traditional authors in the production of meaning. This is also part and parcel of a humanist project which is focused on the specific functions of 'gaps' or 'indeterminacies' that exist in literary texts. Not only do readers fill these gaps/indeterminacies in the text–reader interaction but also it is almost as if, in so doing, readers fill a 'gap' in themselves. The view of human agents improving themselves in the act of reading literature echoes traditional teachings such as those of F. R. Leavis (see During 1993) except for two things: the notion of 'gaps' affords much more autonomy to readers in the production of meaning (as opposed to the customarily held belief in the author's genius or creativity); and Iser implies that modern literature has been characterized by the proliferation of gaps, thus enhancing the gap-filling activity of the reader. We can see in these formulations how Iser bridges diverse schools. Leavis would have almost certainly embraced the humanist side of Iser's treatise which stressed the reader's improvement, while rejecting Iser's thesis on modern literature and the in-put of the reader; Barthes and the *Screen* writers would, conversely, recognize elements of their own projects regarding the *writerly*/'revolutionary' text (modern litera-ture) while rejecting the humanist angle.

The other area that is crucial to the Fish–Iser debate concerns such concepts as 'imagination', 'perception', 'ideation' and so on. Iser insists that, in spite of the reader's activity certain features of a text are 'given', words are empirically 'there'. The mnemonic sentence he offers to illustrate this arises from the example of the way in which different lines may be drawn between stars in a constellation: 'The "stars" in a literary text are fixed; the lines that join them are variable' (Iser 1974 p. 282). Similarly, Fish's position can be memorised in his statement that 'the stars in a literary text are not fixed; they are just as variable as the lines that join them'. For Fish, the reader supplies everything; this is because there can be nothing that precedes interpretation. As soon as human beings apprehend an item in the world they have already embarked on a process of interpreting it. There can be no 'given' as such. In this way, the human being's interpre-tation of objects in the world is co-extensive with the act of interpretation of objects in a literary text. Both are instances of the same kind of inter-pretative activity.

Although the Fish–Iser debate does not conclude with a comfortable synthesis of both views (not to mention the fact that it is conducted in such an unbecoming fashion, particularly on Iser's side), it is still of great value. It summarizes some of the key issues that are at stake in the loca-tion of meaning. It also provides students of communication theory with a clear opportunity to determine where they stand in relation to them.

Further reading Iser 1974, 1978, 1989; Fish 1980; Freund 1987, especially pp. 134–151; Holub 1984, especially pp. 101–106; Allen 1987; Eagleton 1983 pp. 54–90.

28 Stanley Fish

Why no one's afraid of Wolfgang Iser

THE MEANING OF THE LETTER

At a time when we are warned daily against the sirens of literary theory, Wolfgang Iser is notable because he does not appear on anyone's list. He is not included among those (Derrida, de Man, Bloom, Miller, Fish) who are thought of as subverting standards, values and the rule of common sense; nor do we find him cited as one of those (Abrams, Hirsch, Booth, Graff, Crews, Shattuck) who are fighting the good fight against the forces of deconstructive nihilism. His absence from the field of pitched battle does not mean that he goes unread: on the contrary his two major works, *The Implied Reader* and *The Act of Reading* outsell all other books on the prestigious list of the Johns Hopkins Press with the exception of *Grammatology* (a book that is, I suspect, more purchased than read). Iser is, in short, a phenomenon: he is influential without being controversial, and at a moment when everyone is choosing up sides, he seems to be on no side at all or (it amounts to the same thing) on every side at once.

How does he do it? (I might have asked, 'how does he get away with it?', but that would have been to tip my hand.) The answer lies, I think, in the terms in which he conceives of his project which is no less than to free the literary text from the demand that it yield or contain a referential meaning, an embodied truth. Such a demand, Iser complains, reduces literary texts 'to the level of documents' (Iser 1978 p. 13) and thus robs them 'of that very dimension that sets them apart from the document, merely the opportunity they offer us to experience for ourselves the spirit of the age, social conditions, the author's neuroses, etc.' (p. 13). The emphasis here is on the word 'experience' for what is left out of the traditional or classical account is the actualizing role played by the reader in the production – as opposed to the mere perception or uncovering – of literary meaning. 'How can the meaning possibly be experienced if – as is always assumed by the classical norm of interpretation – it is already there, namely waiting for a referential exposition?' (p. 18). Meaning in a literary text does not simply lie there, it must be brought out in an act of concretization (p. 21). It follows then that the critic's 'object should . . . be not to explain a work, but to reveal the conditions that bring about its various possible effects', effects that require the participation of a reader in whose experience 'the text comes to life' (p. 19).

As Iser sees it, the advantage of his theory is that it avoids identifying the aesthetic object either with the text, in its formal and objective self-sufficiency, or with the idiosyncratic experience of individual readers. The literary work 'cannot be identical with the text or with the concretization, but must be situated somewhere between the two. It must inevitably be virtual in character, as it cannot be reduced to the reality of the text or to the subjectivity of the reader' (p. 21). In the question informing much of contemporary literary theory – what is the source of interpretive authority, the text or the reader – Iser answers 'both'. He does not, however, conceive of the relationship between them as a partnership in which each brings a portion of the meaning which is then added to the portion brought by the other: for in his theory meaning is something neither of them *has* (it is not an embodied object), rather it is something that is produced or built up or assembled by a *process* of interaction in which the two parties play quite different, but interdependent roles. The role of the text is to 'designate *instructions* for the *production* of the signified' (p. 65) which in the case of literature is the aesthetic object: the role of the reader is to follow these directions and so to produce it. 'It' in this last sentence does not stand for a thing but for an event, a happening: the emphasis of the model is finally temporal rather than spatial (although, as we shall see, it contains spatial elements and, the literary work is not to be identified with any one point in the 'dyadic interaction' but with the entire process. 'The text can never be grasped as a whole – only as a series of changing viewpoints, each one restricted in itself and so necessitating further perspectives. This is the process by which the reader realizes an overall situation' (p. 68).

The relationship then is one of script to performer, but in literary texts, Iser explains, the script is not explicit in an exhaustive way, and therefore the reader's activities are not wholly constrained by its directions. Indeed, the literary text is distinguished from the non-literary, and especially from the texts of science (p. 87) by the presence (actually an absence) in it of 'gaps' or 'indeterminacies' or 'blanks' which are then filled or filled in by a reader according to his 'individual disposition' (p. 123). That is, the 'structure of the text allows for different ways' of fulfilling its 'potential' (p. 37). The different perspectives embedded in the text are set alongside one another in ways that demand that they be organized, and it is the reader who must 'build up' the connections, 'the syntheses which eventually individualize the aesthetic object' (p. 118). So that 'while the meaning of the literary work remains related to what the printed text says. . . . it requires the creative imagination of the reader to put it all together' (p. 142).

It is statements like these (which are found everywhere in the book) that account in part for the attractiveness of Iser's theory: it seems able to accommodate emphases that have often been perceived as contradictory in the writings of other theorists. It is at once spatial – in that it conceives of the text as an object with a particular shape (the shape of the 'designated instructions') – and temporal – in that the production of literary meaning is a process that the text only sets in motion. It is for the same reason a theory that can claim a measure of objectivity – its operations begin with something that is 'given' – and yet at the same time it requires the subjective contribution of the reader who must do his individual part: it is therefore a theory that sets limits to interpretation – as Iser repeatedly says the subjective element is not 'arbitrary' (pp. 23–24) because it is 'guided' or 'prestructured' (p. 21) or 'moulded' (p. 122) by the structures the text contains (p. 21) – and yet within these limits it allows, and indeed demands, the exercise of interpretive freedom.

It is in sum a capacious and liberal theory that in its generosity seems particularly well suited to the pluralism of most American literary criticism. Pluralism is by and large an attempt to steer a middle way between the poles of objectivity and subjectivity. That is, pluralists wish neither to embrace a theory in which literary texts have one and only one correct reading (because that would be as they see it to violate the essence of literature), nor to embrace a theory in which text can receive as many correct or legitimate readings as there are readers (because then words like 'correct' and 'legitimate' would lose their force). It is their contention, therefore, that while a literary text is distinguished by its openness to a number of readings, it is not open to any and all readings: there may be a plurality of significances that can legitimately be specified for a literary work, but that plurality is not an infinity. It follows then that what pluralist practice requires is a theory that can accommodate the diversity of interpretation and yet at the same time identify the constraints that prevent interpretation from being arbitrary.

Iser's is obviously such a theory, and moreover it has the additional advantage of answering to the demand of recent criticism that the reader be given his due. Pluralism is not necessarily a reader-oriented doctrine. In its new critical manifestation, it is rather a testimony to the richness of the literary text which is said to contain the multiple meanings that a competent reader will discern. Since these meanings are particularly complex and many leveled, it is not surprising, the argument goes, that no one critical approach or perspective can do justice to them. The (limited) tolerance of diverse views that characterizes this brand of pluralism is a concession not to the reader's creative imagination, but to the difficulty of his task (a task that is by definition incapable of completion). In Iser's theory, however, the reader is given a more prominent role because what the text contains is not a meaning, however complex, but a set of directions for assembling a meaning, directions he will carry out in his own way. 'Thus, the meaning of a literary text is not a definable entity but, if anything, a dynamic happening' (p. 22).

At times, however, Iser reserves the word 'meaning' for the 'intersubjective structure' that provokes the reader's activities, while referring to the product of those activities – the building up of the aesthetic object – as 'significance'. 'The intersubjective structure of meaning assembly can have many forms of significance according to the social and cultural code or the individual norms which underlie the formation of this significance' (p. 151). This is another point at which Iser touches base with a familiar critical formula, but redefines it in such a way as to remove some of the difficulties it has seemed to offer. The distinction (derived from Frege) between meaning and significance is associated in Anglo-American criticism with E. D. Hirsch for whom it is a distinction between intended or authorial meaning and the meanings that might be educed by readers who are 'pursuing their own interests unchecked by intentions'

(Booth 1978 p. 19). It is thus not an innocent distinction, but one heavily weighted in the direction of authorial or historical meaning to which, Hirsch believes, we have an *ethical* obligation. (Would we want others to ignore or distort *our* intentions?) In Iser's formulation, however, we are relieved of the necessity to choose between an intended meaning and the meanings that issue from our subjectivities because the intended meaning is not a referential statement or an encoded attitude or a representation of a state of affairs, but a script for performance, and therefore it lives only in its manifestations and in every one of its manifestations. Every time a reader builds his own structure of significance, he is simultaneously being faithful to authorial meaning, and indeed, he can be faithful only in that way. Rather than being opposed to authorial meaning, interpreter's meaning is necessary to its actualization. In the same way, Iser avoids the hard choice, also implicit in Hirsch's distinction, between historical and ahistorical interpretation. The readers contemporary to an author are in no more a privileged position than the readers of later generations: for both sets of readers are provoked to an act of construction rather than an act of retrieval; and since the blueprint for construction is significantly incomplete – it displays gaps and blanks and indeterminacies – no instance of construction is more accurate, in the sense of being truer to an historically embodied meaning, than any other. Even the first reader of a work is called upon to complete the connections left unspecified in the text according to his 'individual disposition'. This does not mean, as Iser is quick to point out, that the history of successive constructions or assemblings or actualizations is of no interest; it is just that it is an empirical rather than a theoretical question – it is a study of the individual realizations of a literary work rather than what makes those realizations possible in the first place – and it is therefore a question that belongs properly to the 'aesthetics of reception' (Iser 1978 p. x), a branch of inquiry identified with the work of H. R. Jauss and others. Iser thus manages the considerable feat of operating at a level that escapes historical contingency while at the same time acknowledging the legitimacy of historically conditioned readings both as a phenomenon and as an object of study.

In addition, his theory boasts an historical component of its own. It is his contention that in the nineteenth and twentieth centuries literary texts became more and more indeterminate, and as a result 'the reader's viewpoint became less clearly oriented, which meant correspondingly greater demands on his own structuring activity' (p. 205). Moreover, as the reader's activity becomes more strenuous he receives to a greater degree the chief benefit of literary experience, which is, according to Iser, the opportunity to 'take a fresh look at the forces which guide and orient him, and which he may hitherto have accepted without question' (p. 74). These 'forces' are the 'thought systems' or 'prevailing norms' that have provided the reader with 'a framework for the social action' (p. 71) and a basis for the conduct of human relations (p. 73). In the literary text these systems and norms are arranged in such a way as to provoke the reader to an examination of their limitations and distortions. Thus while 'the literary work arises out of the reader's own social or philosophical background, it will serve to detach prevailing norms from their functional context, thus enabling the reader to observe how such social regulators function, and what effect they have on the people subject to them' (p. 74). In the case of works written long ago the reader will be doubly enabled: 'he will be able not only to reconstruct . . . the historical situation that provided the framework for the text but also to experience for himself the specific deficiencies brought about by [its] historical norms' (p. 74).

Again, Iser is impressive in his ability to affirm both sides of a traditional opposition, in this case the opposition between literature and life. On the one hand, literature is not mimetic or representational ('it is no mere copy of life'), for rather than reproducing or mirroring or urging the thought system of an age (as one might do in a journalistic essay, or political speech), it 'almost invariably tends to take as its dominant "meaning" those possibilities that have been neutralized or negated by that system' (p. 72); but on the other hand, literature is valuable because of the perspective it affords on life; it is the means by which we achieve a distance on our 'habitual dispositions', a distance that enables us to recognize and supply their deficiencies. This is even truer when the work is built up out of the systems of an earlier age; for in the act of grasping a reality that is not our own (p. 74) we are moved to rethink and revise the conceptual framework that underlies 'the ordinary process of day-to-day living' (p. 74). In short, not only does literature 'call into question' (p. 61) conventional notions of validity and coherence; in doing so it promotes change and growth in the individual:

The significance of the work ... does not lie in the meaning
sealed within the text, but in the fact that the meaning brings
out what had previously been sealed within us. When the subject
is separated from himself, the resultant spontaneity is guided and
shaped by the text in such a way that it is transformed
into a new and real consciousness. Thus each text constitutes
its own reader. ... This structure pinpoints the reciprocity
between the constituting of meaning and the heightening of
self awareness which develops in the reading process
(Iser 1978 pp. 157–159).

In other words, as the reader puts the work together, he is himself
put together; as the text 'begins to exist as a gestalt in the reader's
consciousness' (p. 121), the gestalt that *is* the reader's consciousness
is in the process of being altered by the structure it is building; in
response to an indeterminate set of directions, the reader is moved
to assemble the virtual object in his own way, but as that object takes
shape it begins to have a reciprocal effect on the way that the reader
considers his own: the reader may be following his individual disposition in the act of construction, but that disposition is itself changed
in an interaction with what it has constructed: 'Hence, the constitution of meaning not only implies the creation of a totality emerging
from interacting textual perspectives ... but also, through formulating this totality, it enables us to formulate ourselves, and thus
discover an inner world of which we had hitherto not been conscious'
(p. 158).

As the claims for literature expand to include the fostering of
self-consciousness, so do the claims for Iser's theory which is now
not only an aesthetic, an ontology, and a history, but a psychology
and an epistemology as well. Indeed the range of problems that
Iser apparently solves is remarkable; but even more remarkable is
the fact that he achieves his solutions without sacrificing any of the
interests that might be urged by one or another of the traditional
theoretical positions. His theory is mounted on behalf of the reader,
but it honours the intentions of the authors; the aesthetic object is
constructed in time, but the blueprint for its construction is spatially
embodied; each realization of the blueprint is historical and unique;
but it itself is given once and for all: literature is freed from the
tyranny of referential meaning, but nevertheless contains a meaning
in the directions that trigger the reader's activities: those activities

are determined by a reader's 'stock of experience' (p. 38) but in the course of their unfolding, that stock is transformed. The theory, in short, has something for everyone, and denies legitimacy to no one.

And yet, in the end it falls apart, and it falls apart because the distinction on which it finally depends – the distinction between the determinate and the indeterminate – will not hold. The distinction is crucial because it provides both the stability and flexibility of Iser's formulations. Without it he would not be able to say that the reader's activities are constrained by something they do not produce; he would not be able at once to honor and to bypass history by stabilizing the set of directions the text contains; he would not be able to define the aesthetic object in opposition to the world of fact, but tie its production securely to that world: he would have no basis (independent of interpretation) for the thesis that since the end of the eighteenth century literature has been characterized by more and more gaps: he would not be able to free the text from the constraints of referential meaning and yet say that the meanings produced by innumerable readers are part of its potential.

It is important to realize how 'firm' the determinacy/indeterminacy distinction is for Iser. When he is at his most phenomenological (pp 114; 118; 151–154; 202–203) it sometimes seems that the very features of the text emerge into being in a reciprocal relationship with the reader's activities; but in his more characteristic moments Iser insists on the brute-fact status of the text, at least insofar as it provides directions for the assembling of the 'virtual object'. Thus he declares in one place, 'the stars in a literary text are fixed: the lines that join them are variable'; and in another, 'the structure of the text sets off a sequence of mental images which lead to the text translating itself into the reader's consciousness'; and in still another 'the text itself . . . offers "schematized aspects" through which the actual subject matter of the work can be produced'. Each of these statements (and there are countless others) is a version of the basic distinction, reaffirmed unequivocally by Iser in the *Diacritics* interview (June 1980), 'between a significance which is to be supplied, and a significance which *has* been supplied' (p. 72) or, in other words, between what is already given and what must be brought into being by interpretive activity.

Iser is able to maintain this position because he regards the text as a *part of the world* (even though the process it sets in motion is not), and because he regards the world, or external reality, as itself determinate, something that is given rather than supplied. It is the objective status of the world that accounts for the difference between literary and non-literary mental activity. In ordinary experience 'the given empirical object' acts as a constraint on any characterization of it; whereas in literary experiences objects are produced by the mental images we form, images that endow the 'nongiven ... with presence' (Iser 1978 p. 137). Sentences, uttered in everyday life are assessed in terms of their fidelity to empirical facts, but 'for the literary text there can be no such "facts"; instead we have a sequence of schemata which have the function of stimulating the reader himself into establishing the "facts"' (p. 141). The point is that these 'schemata' are themselves facts of a determinate kind and they are therefore ontologically (rather than merely temporally) prior to the (literary) facts whose production they guide.

Iser's most developed example of this process concerns the presentation of Allworthy in Fielding's *Tom Jones*.

> Allworthy is introduced to us as a perfect man, but he is at once brought face to face with a hypocrite, Captain Blifil, and is completely taken in by the latter's feigned piety. Clearly, then, the signifiers are not meant solely to designate perfection. On the contrary, they denote instructions to the reader to build up the signified which presents not a quality of perfection, but in fact a vital defect, Allworthy's lack of judgement.
>
> (Iser 1978 p. 65)

This is an instance, in Iser's vocabulary, of the 'changing perspectives' (p. 114) that are juxtaposed in such a way as to stimulate the reader's search for consistency (p. 120). Thus, two 'character perspectives', that of Allworthy as *homo perfectus* and Blifil as apparent Saint, 'confront one another' (p. 121), and the reader is led to reject the simple designation of perfection and to formulate for himself a revised conception of Allworthy's character. It is a perfect illustration of what distinguishes a literary from a non-literary text. In a non-literary text, the connections are all supplied (by the structure of empirical reality), and as a result the reader is left with nothing to do; but in the literary text 'textual segments' are presented without explicit indications of the relationship between them, and as a result 'gaps' open up which it is the responsibility of the reader to close and fill.

It is all very neat until one begins to examine the textual segments that constitute the category of the 'given'. Consider the characterization of Allworthy as a perfect or allworthy man. In order for Iser's account to be persuasive, perfection in humankind must be understood (at least at first) to be incompatible with being taken in by a hypocrite: for only then will the 'Allworthy perspective' and the 'Blifil perspective' be perceived as discontinuous. But one can easily imagine a reader for whom perfection is inseparable from the vulnerability displayed by Allworthy and for such a reader there would be no disparity between the original description of Allworthy and his subsequent behaviour. That is, the text would display 'good continuation' (a characteristic, according to Iser, of non-literary texts) and would not, at least at this point, present a gap or blank for the reader to fill up. I am not urging this reading against Iser's but merely pointing out that it is a possible one and that its possibility irreparably blurs the supposedly hard lines of his theory: for if the 'textual signs' do not announce their shape but appear in a variety of shapes according to the differing expectations and assumptions of different readers and if gaps are not built into the text, but appear (or do not appear) as a consequence of particular interpretive strategies, then there is no distinction between what the text gives and what the reader supplies; he supplies *everything*; the stars in a literary text are not fixed; they are just as variable as the lines that join them.

Let me make clear what I am *not* saying. I am *not* saying that it is impossible to give an account of *Tom Jones* which depends on a distinction between what is in the text and what the reader is moved, by gaps in the text, to supply; it is just that the distinction itself is an assumption which, when it informs an act of literary description will *produce* the phenomena it purports to describe. That is to say, every component in such an account – the determinacies or textual segments, the indeterminacies or gaps and the adventures of the reader's 'wandering viewpoint' – will be the products of an interpretive strategy that demands them, and therefore no one of those components can constitute the independent given which serves to ground the interpretive process.

The point can be made again with another of Iser's examples, a chapter in *Vanity Fair* entitled 'Arcadian Simplicity'. The 'textual segment' is, according to Iser, a 'signal from the author', a 'pointer' that 'ensures that the reader will never lose sight of the narrator's views on the social ambitions' (p. 114) of Becky Sharpe. As a signal or pointer, the title is, says Iser, 'explicitly ironic' (p. 117) and therefore establishes the perspective of the narrator which can then interact with the perspective of the character. This interaction then 'spurs the reader on to build up the syntheses which eventually individualize the aesthetic object' (p. 118). But the irony of 'Arcadian Simplicity' is not explicit in the sense that it announces itself before interpretation begins: it will be ironic only in the light of an interpretation – a specification of the author's purpose – already assumed. In the light of another interpretation of another specification of Thackeray's purpose, it will not be explicitly ironic at all, it will be explicitly something else, and the reader's 'building up' will follow a course other than the course described by Iser. Indeed the reader's building up begins with the characterization of 'Arcadian Simplicity' as ironic or as non-ironic or as anything at all. Again the textual segment that initiates the process of construction in Iser's sequence is itself a construction, and is not, at least in the way that Iser would claim, 'given'.

To this Iser might reply (and does reply in the *Diacritics* interview) that whatever one makes of 'Arcadian Simplicity' the words are, after all, there and do constitute a determinate textual feature. ('In the Thackeray example, we have the given textual segments of chapter heading and chapter.') But this assumes that the words (these or any other) are 'pointable to' apart from some or other interpretive perspective. That is, it assumes that there is a level of observation, a place for a reader to stand, where 'Arcadian Simplicity' can be seen *before* it receives an interpretation. But even to see it as a chapter heading is already to have assigned it an interpretation according to a system of intelligibility in which chapter headings are things that it is possible to see; and, moreover, the assigning of that interpretation is not something one does *after* seeing; it is the shape of seeing, and if seeing does not have this (interpretive) shape, it will have some other. Perception is never innocent of assumptions and the assumptions within which it occurs will be responsible for the contours of what is perceived. The conclusion is the one I have reached before: there can be no category of the 'given' if by given one means what is there before interpretation begins. (And if Iser doesn't mean that, it is hard to see what he does mean.)

It is a conclusion that must be extended to the larger theory that stands behind Iser's pronouncements on merely literary matters, the theory by which the world itself is 'given' in a way that the world of literary (read fictional) works are not. It is only if the world – or 'reality' – is itself a determinate object, an object without gaps that can be grasped immediately, an object that can be perceived rather than read, that *in*determinacy can be specified as a special feature of literary experience. Once, however, that move is made, it brings with it a set of interrelated assumptions: the assumption that looking at real objects is different from *imag*ining objects in a poem or novel; the assumption that in the one activity the viewer simply and passively takes in an already formed reality, while in the other he must participate in the construction of a reality; the assumption that knowledge of real people is more direct and immediate than knowledge of characters or lyric speakers: and, finally, the assumption that these two kinds of experience come to us in two kinds of language, one that requires only that we check its structure against the already constituted structure it reproduces or describes, and the other that requires us to produce the objects, events and persons to which it (in a curious, even mysterious, literary way) refers.

Underlying these assumptions, of course, is the familiar distinction between the determinate or given and the indeterminate or supplied: and they fall by the same reasoning which makes that distinction finally untenable: what must be supplied in literary experience must *also* be supplied in the 'real life' experience to which it is, point for point, opposed. Consider, for example, Iser's characterization of the difference between 'dyadic interaction' (that is, conversation between two people) as it is presented in the novels of Ivy Compton-Burnett and as it occurs in everyday life. In Compton-Burnett, Iser asserts, 'the pragmatically oriented speech act of everyday dialogue is . . . replaced by the imponderability out of which speech arises' (p. 193). By this Iser intends a contrast between fictional dialogue and a 'face-to-face situation' in which 'the partners in dyadic interaction can ask each other questions in order to ascertain how far their views have controlled contingency, or their images have bridged the gap of inexperienceability of one another's experience' (p. 166). That is in face-to-face dialogue communication is facilitated by the presence of a real object (the other person) which acts as an empirical check on the turns and twists of the conversation. Conversation is thus a particular instance of the general constraint on ordinary (as opposed to fictional) language: 'it presupposes reference to a given object [which] in turn demands a continuous individualization of the developing speech act so that utterance may gain its intended precision' (p. 184). The absence of this constraint in Compton-Burnett's novels is indicated by the fact that, despite the characters' willingness to ask each other questions 'in order to ensure that they have grasped what has been said', 'the various speech acts do not serve to promote understanding as regards facts and intentions, but instead they uncover more and more implications arising from every utterance' (p. 193). As the dialogue unfolds, the partners grow further and further apart as each response to the question 'what do you mean?' is received as evidence of a meaning to which the other will not admit, and in the end, 'the characters' images of each other become more and more monstrous' (p. 193). The dialogue is thus 'endless' (i.e. not ended by a clear and unambiguous achievement of understanding) and it is endless because, 'in Hilary Corke's words, the dialogue is "not a transcript of what he or she would have said in 'real life' but rather of what would have been said plus what would have been implied but not spoken plus what would have been understood though not implied".'

One's response to this can only be, as opposed to what? That is, however accurate this is as an account of conversation in Compton-Burnett, it is a perfectly accurate account of conversation in everyday life. Iser and Corke seem to believe that in everyday life we are in the position of being able to attend to what has been said independently of what is implied or of what is understood because it goes without saying. That is, they think that the pragmatic conditions of face-to-face discourse serve to fix the meanings of words, whereas in fictional discourse meanings are the products of a structure of assumptions and hypotheses, a structure which we, as readers, build. But in fact, it is just such a structure that is responsible for the shape meanings have in everyday life and even for the shape of the 'pragmatic conditions' in the context of which those meanings are received. Consider as an illustration a cartoon that appeared not long ago in the *New Yorker*. It shows a man seated in a chair, staring morosely at a television set. Above him stands a woman, presumably his wife, and she is obviously speaking to him with some force and conviction. The caption reads 'You look sorry, you act sorry, you say you're sorry, but you're not sorry.' So much for the ensured precision of face-to-face dyadic interaction! What the woman is able to hear depends on her assumption of the kind of man her husband is; she constructs an image of him (has been constructing it for a long time) and that image controls her sense of his intentions and produces what is for her the obvious literal meaning of his utterance and also of his facial expression and physical gesture. (What that literal meaning is, we aren't told, but it might be something like. 'O.K. I'm sorry, now leave me alone.') Moreover it is that image that defines for her the 'pragmatic conditions' of the interaction, the 'real life' situation as she sees it, no doubt in opposition to the situation as it is seen by him. At one point Iser says 'we must distinguish between perception and ideation as two different means of access to the world' (p. 137). But, as this example shows, that is precisely the distinction we cannot make because perception itself *is* an act of ideation, if by ideation we mean the inferring of a world from a set of assumptions (antecedently held) about what it must be like. To put it another way, mediated access to the world is the only access we ever have; in face-to-face situations or in the act of reading of a novel, the properties of objects, person and situations emerge as a consequence of acts of construction that follow (and because they follow they are not, in any simple sense, free) from a prestruc-tured understanding of the shapes any meaningful item could possibly have. What this means is that we know 'real people' no more directly than we know the characters in a novel; that 'real life' objects are no less 'ideated' than fictional objects; that ordinary language is no more in touch with an unmediated reality than the language of literature.

The obvious objection to this line of reasoning is that it flies in the fact of differences we all feel. As Iser puts it in the *Diacritics* inter-view (p. 72):

> My interpretation of the world may well be as much a product of linguistic acts as my interpretation of a literary text, but I maintain that there are substantial differences between the things being interpreted. First, the real world is perceivable through the senses, whereas the literary text is perceivable only through the imagination – unless one believes that reading the words sunset, music, silk, wine and scent is the same as seeing, hearing, touching, tasting, and smelling the real things. Secondly, all known experience suggests that the real world (uninterpreted) lives and functions independently of the individual observer, whereas the literary text does not. Thirdly, our contact with the

real world has immediate physical or social consequences, whereas our contact with the literary text need not, and indeed rarely does have any such consequence. [p. 72]

One should note first of all that in making his argument Iser is continually shifting his terms in order to make his different points. In the first sentence the literary text is itself an object, a part of the world, as indeed it must be if the directions or 'schemata' or 'textual segments' are to occupy the position of 'given' in relation to what must be supplied. But in the second sentence the literary text is suddenly not perceivable through the senses and is thus as far as one can tell no longer an object at all. I suppose that what Iser means is that things, persons and events to which a literary text refers are not perceivable through the senses, but that the literary text itself is. The text and the world, then, are both 'things', but they are different things and therefore they are interpreted differently. But this is to assume precisely what is in dispute, the objectivity of either the text or the world. The issue is not whether there are differences between them (or more properly between the material world and the world in the text) but whether those differences are equivalent to the distinction between what is given and what is supplied: and it is my contention that they are not, and that rather than being different objects of interpretation the world and the world of the text are different interpreted – that is, made – objects. To put it another way, one can agree with Iser that reading about sunsets, wine and silk is not the same as seeing, tasting and touching them without agreeing that seeing, touching, and tasting are natural rather than conventional activities. What can be seen will be a function of the categories of vision that already inform perception and those categories will be social and conventional and not imposed upon us by an independent world. One can see a hand raised in a classroom as a hand raised in a classroom only because one is already implicated in, and acting as an extending agent of, a conventional system of purposes, goals, understood practices, etc.; if one didn't see it as a hand raised in a classroom, one would see it as something else, and that something else would similarly be pick-outable only within some set of conventional categories or other; and even if one had recourse to a supposedly neutral vocabulary and described the action in terms of angles, movements, tendons, joints, etc., that description would itself be possible only under a *theory* of movement, ligatures, etc., and therefore would be descriptive only of what the theory (that is, the interpretation) prestipulates as available for description. Again the point is not that seeing (or tasting or touching) something is the same as reading about it, but that the two activities are alike conventional and mediated, and, therefore, whatever differences they might be said to have, they would not be differences between an activity that was in touch with (and therefore constrained by) the 'real world' and one that was not.

Does this mean, then, that everything, even the objects, events and persons of everyday life, is indeterminate? The question is an inevitable one in the context of the task Iser's theory sets for itself, the *control* of arbitrary (a word he uses often) subjectivities by fixed or determinate points of reference. He sees this as a problem peculiar to the reading of literature, since in the 'reading' of the world our 'individual dispositions' are constrained by its objects. But if the world and the objects in it are no less the product of human invention than the world of literary experience, the brakes are off everywhere and communication – ordinary and literary – would seem to be deprived of its ground. However, the conclusion I would draw from my argument is exactly the reverse. The brakes are *on* everywhere because in order for them to be off readers would have to be in a position to specify significance in a random or irresponsible way; but it is just the point of my examples – literary and non-literary – that there could be no such position because perception (and reading is an instance of perception) always occurs within a set of assumptions that preconstrains what could possibly be perceived (or heard, or tasted or touched). It is only if it were possible to perceive independently of assumptions, of interpretive categories, that irresponsible or arbitrary perception would be a danger. If perception is always conventional – prestructured by categories (like the classroom or some notion of genre) that are public and communal rather than individual and unique – then perception can never be arbitrary, and the project, Iser's project, of explaining how arbitrariness or subjectivity is to be controlled loses its urgency.

For the same reason, the question 'is everything then indeterminate' loses its force because it would make just as much sense to say that everything is determinate. Indeterminacy in Iser's theory refers to 'the subjectivist element of reading' (p. 24), that which is supplied by the 'individual observer' out of his private experience. What I have been saying is that there is no subjectivist element of reading, because the observer is never individual in the sense of unique or private, but is always the product of the categories of understanding that are his by virtue of his membership in a community of interpretation. It follows then that what that experience in turn produces is not open or free, but determinate, constrained by the possibilities that are built into a conventional system of intelligibility. Earlier, I concluded that the distinction between what is given and what is supplied won't hold up because everything is supplied, both the determinate and the indeterminate poles of the 'aesthetic object'; now I am arguing that the same distinction won't hold because everything is given. There is no paradox here. It is just that 'supplied' and 'given' will only make sense as fundamental categories of classification if the entities to which they refer are pure, if, at some level, we can speak meaningfully of a text that is simply there waiting for a reader who is, at least potentially, wholly free. But it is precisely that purity I have been calling into question by pointing out on the one hand that perception is always mediated (and therefore objects are never available directly), and on the other that perception is always conventional (and therefore readers are never free). In the absence of that purity one can say either that everything is determinate because nothing proceeds from an unfettered imagination, or that everything is indeterminate, because everything is produced by the activities of the reader (but by a reader who is, like what he produces, community property). The only thing that you can't say is that there is a distinction, at least insofar as it is an *absolute* distinction between a world that 'lives and functions independently' of interpretive activity and a world that is produced by interpretive activity.

This is not to say that such a distinction cannot be operative as a consequence of an overarching interpretive assumption. That is, if determinate and indeterminate (or given and supplied) are conventional categories *within* a system of intelligibility then those who are implicated in the system will 'see' in the sense of producing determinacies and indeterminacies, but everything they see will be at once constructed (as opposed to being simply 'found') and constrained (as opposed to being simply invented).

One sees this clearly in Iser's readings of Fielding and others, where the specification of 'textual segments' and 'blanks' is an interpretive gesture – grounded in an already assumed view of literary history and literary value – in relation to which the activities of individual readers are severely constrained. That is, Iser never gives any examples of readers going their own way (even in the modified sense allowed by his theory) because the reader he can imagine is always the creature of the machine he has already set in motion: in every analysis the reader is described as being 'guided', 'controlled', 'induced' and even 'jerked' (p. 130) and what he is guided or jerked by are textual elements that are themselves the product of interpretation. Again, there are two ways of seeing this, either as demonstrating that both text and reader are determinate, in that their respective shapes are in no sense free, or that both text and reader are indeterminate, in that the shape each has is the product of interpretive activity. In short, Iser's own analyses are continually pointing to the unavailability of the two contextual entities – the free-standing text and the free-standing reader – whose relationship he promises to describe.

A reader sympathetic to Iser might argue that he himself knows that his basic categories are conventional rather than natural. He does, after all, say at one point that 'pure perception is quite impossible' (p. 166). But when he says that, what he means is that perception is a compound of the object (purely perceived) *plus* the subjective perspective of the reader: otherwise he could not claim that 'textual segments' are given and determinate. In other words Iser doesn't take his own pronouncement seriously (if he did, he'd have to give up his theory), but nevertheless he receives the credit for having made it. Indeed this is a pattern in his work which has the effect of putting him on both sides of almost every issue. He criticizes theories 'which give the impression that texts automatically imprint themselves on the reader's mind' (p. 107) but his theory cannot get off the ground unless it claims exactly that for the set of directions that guide the reader's 'meaning assembly'. He argues that we are never able to experience one another directly (p. 165) but then he privileges face-to-face encounters as a form of communication that bridges 'the gap of inexperienceability' (p. 164). He claims to have rid himself of the subject/object dichotomy (p. 25), but he spends the entire book talking about their interaction, and acting as if the term 'inter-subjectivity' could hide the fact that the distinction between them remains as firm as ever. The theory is finally nothing more than a loosely constructed network of pasted together contradictions: push it hard at any point, and it immediately falls apart. Ask it a hard question – if one can argue about where the gaps are (or about whether or not there are any), how can they be distinguished from the givens? What authorizes the assumption that everyday life is characterized by continuity and determinacy? If gaps have increased in the nineteenth and twentieth centuries, and if literature is defined by the presence (strange word) of gaps, does this mean that literature is becoming more literary or that pre-nineteenth-century literature wasn't literature – and it can only respond by rehearsing its basic distinctions.

But the asking of hard questions is not something the theory encourages, and indeed its weaknesses from one point of view are its strengths from another. By defining his key terms in a number of ways, Iser provides himself in advance with a storehouse of defensive strategies. A theory that characterizes reality in one place as a set of determinate objects, and in another place as the product of 'thought systems', and in a third place as a heterogeneous flux will not be embarrassed by any question you might put to it. It is a marvelous machine whose very loose-jointedness makes it invulnerable to a frontal assault (including, no doubt, the assault I am now mounting). It is in fact not a theory at all, but a piece of literature that satisfies Iser's own criteria for an 'aesthetic object': it is full of gaps and the reader is invited to fill them in his own way. For that reason, no reader will ever feel threatened by the theory; no one will ever be afraid of Wolfgang Iser. Who could be anything but comfortable with someone who declares, in the first part of a sentence that 'I have endeavored to suspend my own tastes and my own beliefs', and concludes the same sentence by asserting 'that all our beliefs have theoretical presuppositions'? (*Diacritics* interview, pp. 73–74). The late Joan Weber once characterized Thomas Browne's ability to embrace contradictions cheerfully (like Tertullian he professed to believe things *because* they were impossible) by saying that he 'pulls the sting from pain'. Wolfgang Iser is the Thomas Browne of literary theory.

29 Wolfgang Iser

Talk like whales: a reply to Stanley Fish

> Why, Dr. Johnson, this is not so easy as you seem to think; for
> if you were to make little fishes talk, they would talk like
> WHALES.
>
> (Oliver Goldsmith, quoted in Boswell 1934: 231)

First things first: I must thank Stanley Fish for Part 1 of his article,
which is an admirable summary of my theory. He has a genuine
talent for précis-writing. Part II of his article, however, fails to display
a similar talent for commentary and judgement.

Let me begin by drawing attention to two statements, both of
which are contained in his opening paragraph:

> At a time when we are warned daily against the sirens of literary
> theory, Wolfgang Iser is notable because he does not appear on
> anyone's list. He is not included among those (Derrida, de Man,
> Bloom, Miller, Fish) who are thought of as subverting standards,
> values and the rule of common sense.
>
> (*Diacritics* 11(2) p. 2; see also this volume p. 407)

I should like to be interested to know on whose list Stanley Fish actually stands, but in the light of the arguments put forth in Part II, it
is a relief to note his awareness that others may accuse him of
subverting the rule of common sense.

> [Iser] is influential without being controversial, and at a moment
> when everyone is choosing up sides, he seems to be on no
> side at all or (it amounts to the same thing) on every side at
> once.
>
> (p. 407)

Well, I am sure that Professor Fish knows something of the history of literary theory, and that it is often characterized by misplaced distinctions and untenable oppositions. When intelligent men take sides, it is not necessarily the case that one group is right and the other wrong. A new framework of thought can embrace the rightness of both sides without seeking to reconcile the incompatible. I do not assume that all my predecessors (and contemporaries) in this field are incompetent, and if my theory appears to be 'influential without being controversial', perhaps this is because it includes *truths* from various sides. At least, I should like to think so.

In Part II of his article, Professor Fish mounts what he calls a 'frontal assault' on my distinction between determinacy and indeterminacy. The attack seems to me rather more like shadow boxing than a frontal assault, but I will do my best to parry the swipes and feints.

The argument begins by taking a statement out of its context and then distorting it:

> Each of these statements . . . is a version of the basic distinction . . . 'between a significance which is to be supplied, and a significance which has been supplied' [72] or, in other words between what is already given and what must be brought into being by interpretive activity.
>
> (p. 414)

His 'other words' are highly misleading, as is the statement that follows:

> He regards the world, or external reality, as itself determinate, something that is given rather than supplied.
>
> (p. 415)

Professor Fish's confusion is caused by the fact that he has telescoped three ideas into one. I draw a distinction between the given, the determinate, and the indeterminate. I maintain that the literary world differs from the real world because it is only accessible to the imagination, whereas the real world is also accessible to the senses and exists outside any description of it. The words of a text are given, the interpretation of the words is determinate, and the gaps between given elements and/or interpretations are the indeterminacies. The real world is given, our interpretation of the world is determinate, the gaps between given elements and/or our interpretations are the indeterminacies. The difference is that with the literary text, it is the interpretation of the words that produces the literary world – i.e. its real-ness, unlike that of the outside world, is not given.

Professor Fish handsomely proves my point without realizing it. After dissecting my Ivy Compton-Burnett example, he tries to draw a parallel with real life by referring to a cartoon in the *New Yorker* (I find it strange that he should take as his example another piece of fiction, but he appears to have difficulty with all kinds of distinctions):

> It shows a man seated in a chair, staring morosely at a television set. Above him stands a woman, presumably his wife, and she is obviously speaking to him with some force and conviction. The captions read, 'You look sorry, you act sorry, you say you're sorry, but you're not sorry.'
>
> (p. 419)

There then follows a piscine interpretation which offers us the actual thoughts of the wife and husband. Here we have a perfect illustration of the reading process at work, in all its stages, except that this particular piece of fiction offers a picture as well as words. What is given is the man seated and the woman standing, plus the captions. What is determinate is Professor Fish's view of the man as morose, the identification of the woman as his wife, the attributes of force and conviction. What is indeterminate is the link between the given elements (figures and captions) and between the two figures as interpretated by Professor Fish. It is he who has assembled the 'reality' of the cartoon (which is fiction) by way of its given elements and his ideations. If he were confronted with the two figures in person – i.e. in real life – he would supplement and possibly, in this case, even 'check' his interpretation by watching, listening, questioning etc. The fictional figures are dependent on him for their assembled significance, and he has no point of reference outside the fiction itself.

It is at this point that Professor Fish insists that 'perception itself is an act of ideation' (p. 420). He then defines ideation as the 'inferring of a world from a set of assumptions (antecedently held) about what it must be like' (p. 420). I would accept his definition, but I would not accept his implication that seeing the picture and captions *is* ideation. I could only do so if I knew that when Professor Fish had eye trouble he went to see his psychiatrist.

The next stage of the argument poses the same problem. Professor Fish magnanimously agrees that reading about sunsets, wine and silk is not the same as seeing, tasting and touching them, but he makes this concession 'without agreeing that seeing, touching and tasting are natural rather than conventional activities. What can be seen will be a function of the categories of vision that already inform perception, and those categories will be social and conventional and not imposed upon us by an independent world' (p. 421). I maintain that what can be seen will be there (unless the world is to be regarded as an hallucination), and it is the *interpretation* of what can be seen (i.e. *how* it is seen) that is a function of the various categories.

Before switching to the examples from literature that provide the focus for Professor Fish's objections, I must confess my bewilderment that he thinks interpretation a useful activity if, as he suggests, there are no givens to interpret: 'there can be no category of the "given" if by given one means what is there before interpretation begins' (p. 417). True, there is no unmediated given, but interpretation would be useless if it were not meant to open access to something we encounter. Interpretation is always informed by a set of assumptions or conventions, but these are also acted upon by what they intend to tackle. Hence the 'something' which is to be mediated exists prior to interpretation, acts as a constraint on interpretation, has repercussions on the anticipations operative in interpretation, and thus contributes to a hermeneutical process, the result of which is both a mediated given and a reshuffling of the initial assumptions. Professor Fish, however, creates a new hermeneutics by fusing interpretation and that which is to be interpreted into an indistinguishable whole, thus replacing the given by interpretation itself. Whenever I read Professor Fish I keep rubbing my eyes in order to make sure that I am not reading Bishop Berkeley.

Let us look at the two examples from literature to which Professor Fish takes exceptions. First the Allworthy example which he attacks. Here what is given is the name Allworthy. The next stage is the significance that the reader attaches to the name Allworthy, and whatever this may be (in most cases the idea that Allworthy must be a good man) will be determinate. The next 'given' may be, for instance, Blifil's piety. The link between the two factors is then indeterminate until the reader educes a determinate significance. And thus the process continues, with the reader supplying significances which are then altered by subsequent significances that have to be produced in order to bridge the gaps between (a) given elements and (b) his previous determinate interpretations.

As for external reality, yes, it is given, and no, it is not in itself determinate.

Professor Fish professes that 'there is no distinction between what the text gives and what the reader supplies; he supplies *everything*; the stars in a literary text are not fixed; they are just as variable as the lines that join them' (p. 416). The reader does not supply the name Allworthy. That is fixed. It is the qualities the reader attaches to the name that may vary, but so long as the reader attaches some determinate qualities to the name, and so long as the reader tries subsequently to link his original view of Allworthy to that gentleman's attitude towards Blifil, the distinction between determinacy and indeterminacy still holds good whether or not one agrees with my own version of interpretation of that relationship. Precisely the same argument applies to the next example of 'Arcadian Simplicity' in *Vanity Fair*. The term is given. The interpretation is made by the reader, and once made is determinate. Professor Fish anticipates this argument, and protests that 'this assumes that the words ... are "pointable to" apart from some or other interpretive perspective'. It is here that I believe he makes a major blunder, and to clarify it I must quote a later passage:

> Iser says 'we must distinguish between perception and ideation as two different means of access to the world' [237]. But ... that is precisely the distinction we cannot make because perception itself is an act of ideation.

> (p. 420)

This is like saying that because a man cannot help blinking when punched in the eye, it is impossible to distinguish between blinking and being punched. Of course it is impossible to perceive without ideating, but they are different activities. The words 'Arcadian Simplicity' are indeed pointable to – they are given. The moment I see them, I will supply them with a determinate significance, but this does not alter the fact that the term itself was given before I interpreted it.

This technique of distortion is made even clearer by the next stage of the 'assault': he correctly refers to my theory that 'the world itself is "given" in a way that the world of literary (read fictional) works are not'. However,

> It is only if the world – or 'reality' – is itself a determinate object, an object without gaps that can be grasped immediately, an object that can be perceived rather than read, that indeterminacy can be specified as a special feature of literary experience.
>
> (p. 418)

Once again Professor Fish pretends that I use 'given' and 'determinate' synonymously, but nowhere have I claimed this, nor have I claimed that indeterminacy is specific to literary experience and excluded from 'real' experience. I claim only that the world arising from the literary text (apart from the printed pages as a physical object) is accessible to the imagination but not the senses, whereas the outside world exists independently of the imagination, even though in perceiving it we cannot avoid also imagining it.

What follows is a list of assumptions attributed to me. They contain their fair share of distortions and I will comment on them individually:

1 The assumption 'that looking at real objects is different from *imagining* objects in a poem or novel'. (p. 418). Yes, it is.
2 The assumption 'that in the one activity the viewer simply and passively takes in an already formed reality, while in the other he must participate in the construction of a reality' (p. 418).

   I do not suggest that the viewer 'simply and passively' takes in an 'already formed reality'. I merely claim that that reality exists outside himself. It is 'given', though he himself must endow it with its determinacy. The reality of the novel as a created world is not 'given'.
3 The assumption 'that knowledge of real people is more direct and immediate than knowledge of characters or lyric speakers' (p. 418)

   I am suspicious of the word 'knowledge', but I would subscribe to the view that communication with real people is more direct and immediate than communication with fictional characters.
4 The assumption that 'these two kinds of experience come to us in two kinds of languages, one that requires only that we check its structure against the already constituted structure it reproduces or describes, and the other that requires us to produce the objects, events and persons to which . . . it refers' (p. 418). 'Only that we

check . . . ' – the exclusivity is Professor Fish's invention, not mine, and check in order to do what? My argument is that the literary description has no reference outside itself, whereas the documentary description has. This does not mean that the documentary description can be absolutely verified – it merely means that its reality is referable. 'Already constituted structure' is another piece of word juggling, since I am sure Professor Fish would include interpretation as part of the constitution, whereas I do not.

There follows Fish's recurring non sequitur:

> Underlying these assumptions, of course, is the familiar distinction between the determinate or given and the indeterminate or supplied . . .

(Here, of course, I reject totally the synonymity Professor Fish imposes on the terms.)

> . . . and they fall by the same reasoning which makes this distinction finally untenable: what must be supplied in literary experience must *also* be supplied in the 'real life' experience to which it is, point for point, opposed.

> (p. 418)

It appears that there is no difference between the determinate and the indeterminate, because there is a parallel between the literary and the real experience. Perhaps *Diacritics* readers can make more sense of this than I can, but the non-argument certainly raises points worth pursuing. I have never claimed that the two experiences are 'point for point' opposed and indeed the parallel between the two experiences is one I have acknowledged time and time again as far as the process of interpretation is concerned: the reader or observer tries to make something determinate out of something indeterminate. The distinction stands.

The argument continues with what seems to me a remarkable denial of subjectivism in reading:

> What I have been saying is that there is no subjectivist element of reading, because the observer is never individual in the sense of unique or private, but is always the product of the categories of understanding that are his by virtue of his membership in a community of interpretation.

> (pp. 422–3)

It is quite true that membership of the community helps to prevent arbitrary ideation, but if there is no subjectivist element in reading, how on earth does Professor Fish account for different interpretations of one and the same text? (The answer to that question is that he doesn't.)

> Earlier, I concluded that the distinction between what is given and what is supplied won't hold up because everything is supplied, both the determinate and indeterminate poles of the 'aesthetic object' . . .

(I am delighted to see that Professor Fish now draws a distinction between determinacy and indeterminacy.

> . . . now I am arguing that the same distinction won't hold because everything is given. There is no paradox here.
>
> (p. 423)

Well, paradoxes are not to be resolved by announcing that they have been resolved. And Professor Fish's attempt to justify his claim is not entirely persuasive. The argument runs that the categories of 'supplied' and 'given' only make sense if the entities they refer to are 'pure' (which they are not) and so:

> In the absence of that purity one can say either that everything is determinate, because nothing proceeds from an unfettered imagination, or that everything is indeterminate, because everything is produced by the activities of the reader . . .

(What was that about Iser being on no side or on every side?)

> . . . The only thing that you can't say is that there is a distinction, at least insofar as it is an *absolute* distinction between a world that 'lives and functions independently' of interpretive activity and a world that is produced by interpretive activity.
>
> (p. 423)

I will settle for a distinction, as opposed to an *'absolute'* distinction, along the lines I have already laid down.

We now come to the charge of dilettantism:

> A reader sympathetic to Iser might argue that he himself knows that his basic categories are conventional rather than natural. He does, after all, say at one point that 'pure perception is quite

impossible' [166]. But when he says that, what he means is that perception is a compound of the object (purely perceived) plus the subjective perspective of the reader; otherwise he could not claim that 'textual segments' are given and determinate. In other words Iser doesn't take his own pronouncement seriously (if he did, he'd have to give up his theory).

(p. 424)

I do take my pronouncements seriously, but I do not think I shall have to give up my theory. I stand by my statement that pure perception is impossible, and I accept Professor Fish's explanation of my words apart from the slyly interpolated parenthesis. The object is not purely perceived, but it is *there*. And because it is there it exerts some control on what we can do with it. Professor Fish would argue that because it is never perceived in an unmediated manner, it can offer no guidance to us. I disagree. The textual segments are not given in their determinacy, but given *and* subsequently determined. In the one instance, we have the given words or segments (e.g. Arcadian Simplicity), in the other we have determinate interpretations of the words or segments. Both are or become 'objects', but in neither instance do I claim that there is any purity of perception.

The piscine technique of putting words in my mouth and then arguing against them is continued right to the end of the 'assault'. I can only assure readers that I have never assumed that 'everyday life is characterized by continuity and determinacy', and I have never 'defined' literature 'by the presence . . . of gaps'.

In his conclusion, Stanley Fish attributes to me the ability Joan Weber attributed to Thomas Browne – namely, 'to embrace contradictions cheerfully (like Tertullian he professed to believe things *because* they were impossible) by saying that he "pulls the sting from pain". Wolfgang Iser is the Thomas Browne of literary theory' (p. 425).

After what I can only regard as an unjustified assault, I confess I feel more like Tom Brown than Thomas Browne. But that, of course, leads to the disturbing conclusion that Stanley Fish may have become the Flashman of literary theory.

The study of readers' meanings

EDITOR'S INTRODUCTION

Where Fish and Iser battle over the moment of the text–reader interaction, others have explored the area outside this interaction and argued that it is omnipresent in readers' responses. Although Fish introduces the concept of an 'interpretive community' (1980), making meanings in common, he does not really extend this idea beyond the confines of the classroom or vague notions of the 'academy'. A German theorist working parallel to Iser, Hans Robert Jauss (discussed by Palmer, this volume pp. 438–47), attempts to move outside the text–reader interaction by invoking an 'horizon of expectations' (Jauss 1982 p. 79), but this consists largely of a knowledge of the conventions of previous writing that the reader may (or may not) have encountered. However, as soon as literary theorists started to introduce the reader into their arguments in a serious way, empirical study of readers' meanings became an absolute necessity. As Palmer shows, theories of readership in the 1980s and 1990s therefore become inextricably entangled with difficult questions of method in order to address (a) what texts 'do' to readers; (b) how this is affected by readers' situation or context; and (c) how this is affected by more general 'cultural forces'.

The extract from Ien Ang's *Watching Dallas* (1984) stresses that the TV series *Dallas* is a specific audio-visual text which invites a diversity of readings. At the same time as inviting these readings *Dallas* also allows for a feeling of pleasure in their production. Ang argues that this pleasure is often derived from a simultaneous proximity and distance from the programme which is felt by the reader. The world of *Dallas* is unrealistic and seems far away; to interact with the text of *Dallas* is therefore to 'escape' from one's own world (albeit for a relatively short space of time). But the world of *Dallas* also contains recognizable elements such as the dilemmas of the characters; interaction with the text in this instance implies an incorporation of features of the readers' own lives into the reading. The text–reader interaction in *Dallas* can therefore be said to take place at some point between 'fiction' and 'reality', between the text and the reader.

It is also worth noting the method by which Ang is able to reach her conclusions. At a time when journalists in Europe were citing *Dallas* as an example of American cultural imperialism, Ang decided to investigate some of the reasons for Dutch fans' pleasure in a so thoroughly American arte-fact. She placed a small ad in a Dutch women's magazine inviting *Dallas* fans to write to her and state what they liked about the programme. The forty-two replies which Ang received (parts of which are quoted in the extract) make up the 'empirical' or 'ethnographic' data in the study. Although *Watching Dallas* is by no means envisaged as a full-scale rigorous sociological survey of readership – nor are its findings to be considered as the final, definitive word on what *Dallas* means – Ang reveals some hitherto neglected mechanisms to be at work in the text–reader interaction.

Janice Radway's methodology is not dissimilar to that of Ang, although it is carried out on a slightly larger scale. Radway was informed by a publishing associate of a bookstore employee in the Mid-West of the United States who regularly advised a cohort of sixty to seventy-five faithful customers on what romances to buy and which to avoid. Having made contact with the employee (whom she names Dot Evans), Radway gained access to the customers (residents of the pseudonymous town, Smithton) to be studied as an 'interpretive community'. The study was effected primarily by means of an analysis of the customers' reading material (nomi-nated favourite romances and Dot's recommendations), an evaluation of the customers' sociological situation (to begin with, why was the romance reading cohort made up exclusively of women?) and an investigation of reading habits. Radway asked the women to fill in questionnaires which addressed such topics as why they read and what were, for them, the most important ingredients of a romance novel.

In the extract (this volume pp. 448–65), Radway explains how the reading habits of the Smithton women are connected to their daily routine, as well as their education, social role and class position. These reading habits are to be understood in two senses: the women pick particular loca-tions and times of the day or week to do their reading; they also have specific habits of reading the romances, for example enjoying uninterrupted reads which enable them to swiftly reach the denouement of the narrative. Like Ang, Radway finds that the fictionality of the texts is sufficient to offer 'escape' (physically, in terms of the uninterrupted space required for the act of reading, and mentally, in the world depicted, which in most ways is separate from everyday routine). She also finds that the women incorpo-rate aspects of their daily life and social position into the text–reader interaction, identifying with the heroine, for example. Often, this is based not on straightforward similarities between the world depicted in the novels and the women's real world, but on the *desires* they harbour for their own social situation. The mechanisms of pleasure, therefore, are again identified in the complex interaction of what the text offers and what the reader brings.

Importantly, for Radway and Ang, seemingly uncomplicated activities such as reading a generic text, offer the opportunity for the exercise of the reader's pre-existing attitudes, values and experiences. This points once more to the communal imperatives anchoring meaning in communications.

Further reading   Emmanuel 1992; Purdie 1992; Ang 1991; Ang 1996; Radway 1988; Fiske 1990 pp. 62–83; Livingstone 1991; Cobley 1994; Morley 1992; Liebes and Katz 1993; Shepherd 1989; Phelps 1990; Eco 1979 pp. 175–199.

30 Jerry Palmer

The act of reading and the reader

It has become a basic axiom of recent theory that narrative has only a potential existence until it is realised in the act of delivery to an audience. Narrative consists of an interaction between a text and its audience; recognising this principle leads to a question: to what extent is the audience's response produced by the text and to what extent do the audience's responses define what the text is? Put in other terms: does a text have a meaning, immanent to it, or does it have as many meanings as are attached to it by different audiences?

At one limit of possible answers lies the assertion of authoritative distinctions between valid and non-valid responses to a text (e.g. Hirsch 1967); at the other the view implied by Douglas' judgement that a joke is not a joke unless it is *permitted* by its audience as well as perceived (Douglas 1968; cf. J. Palmer 1991). Viewed from within this dichotomy, differences between schools of interpretation – which assert apparently incompatible criteria for the validity of interpretation – are *relatively* unimportant, since all have in common the desire to demonstrate its possibility and importance; opposed to them is the belief in a plurality of meaning (W.B. Michaels 1980). Answers which are formulated in terms of some interaction between audience and text largely disregard the first alternative, since it is based upon the supposition that audiences must subordinate themselves to the structure of the text. Studies of interaction with which we are here concerned fall largely into two categories: those according to which texts produce active collaboration from their potential audience in the realisation of their structures; and those according to which meanings are attached to texts by actual audiences – rare are the studies which deal with both.

It is convenient to begin with the first category, often referred to as 'reception aesthetics'.

In this tradition the real reader is distinguished from the 'implied reader'. The real reader has a distinctive biography and a physical existence separate from the text; the implied reader on the other hand is the embodiment of

> all those predispositions necessary for a literary work to exercise its effect – predispositions laid down not by an empirical outside reality, but by the text itself. Consequently the implied reader as a concept has his roots firmly implanted in the structure of the text; he is a construct and in no way to be identified with any reader.
>
> (Iser 1978 p. 34)

However, we should not imagine that the real reader is irrelevant to the act of reading: without the real reader's beliefs and dispositions no communication would be possible, since there would be nothing to communicate with, as the reader would be a blank space. That is to say, Iser's focus is on the act of reading itself, not the reader (real or implied), and this act is situated between the text and its actualisation by a real reader (Iser 1980b). Thus the text is always a 'virtuality': 'fictional language provides instructions for the building of a situation and so for the production of an imaginary object' (Iser 1978 p. 64). For example, the opening words of Clavell's (1981) *Noble House* are:

Prologue

11.45

His name was Ian Dunrose and in torrential rain he drove his old MG sports car cautiously around the corner . . .

These words invite a series of speculations on the part of the reader: if this is the prologue, what are the main events? Why is the precise time important? Dunross has an old sports car and drives it cautiously: are these things related to his personality, or just to the force of circumstances? We probably also judge that this person is a central character rather than peripheral, since he is introduced in this way: the opening 'his' normally suggests reference to someone previously identified, but here it does not; the implication of status is clear. Obviously he is on his way somewhere: where? Why is he going anywhere at 11.45pm in torrential rain? etc., etc. (Compare Eagleton's analysis of the opening sentences of Updike's *Couples* (Eagleton 1983 pp. 74.).)

The activity of reading typically follows this pattern: at any point in the text the reader has a certain knowledge of what is past, and uses this as the basis of a set of expectations about what is to come. That set of expectations is also a set of retrospections, since the movement forwards through the text is always at the same time the reconstruction of the pathways that have led to the current state of affairs; the past of the text is whatever has led to the construction of the set of expectations with which the reader confronts the future of the text.

> This whole process represents the fulfilment of the potential, unexpressed reality of the text, but is to be seen only as a framework for a great variety of means by which the virtual dimension may be brought into being.
>
> (Iser 1980a p. 54)

We must therefore fill in the gaps left by the text itself, make connections, for the text always demands completion by the reader.

On the second page of *Noble House* we read that Dunross takes an elevator to a penthouse over an office block. On entering he says

> 'Evening, tai-pan' . . . with cold formality.

The text continues with a brief description of the man to whom he is speaking, who

> had ruled Struan's for eleven years. 'Drink?' He waved a hand at the Dom Perignon . . .

The phrase 'cold formality' gives added meaning to the word 'ruled': it implies some level of enmity between the two men, and the autocratic implications of 'ruled' perhaps help to explain it. Similarly with the gesture: we may impute the 'lordly' wave of the hand and the fact that he doesn't offer to pour the drink to the same feature of their relationship; or we may write it off as the result of long acquaintance, or the manners of the rich. Whichever way we read the words we make a connection, across the space of the text, between 'cold formality' and the later phrases. Note that not only does 'cold formality' inflect our reading of the subsequent words, but also 'ruled' and the gesture give us retrospection on the earlier phrase.

Do they imply that the dislike is shared? And this opens up a prospect for the forthcoming sentences, which we may well scan for indications of mutual enmity. In Iser's words:

> These gaps have a different effect on the process of anticipation and retrospection, and thus on the gestalt of the virtual dimension, for they may be filled in different ways. For this reason, one text is capable of several different realisations ... it [is] always the process of anticipation and retrospection that leads to the formation of the virtual dimension.
>
> (Iser 1980a pp. 55f.)

An extended example of this approach is to be found in Jauss (1974). Traditionally, one fundamental distinction between literary texts has turned on the relationship between the hero and the world in which he (and occasionally she) moves: the hero is either better, worse or of equal stature to this world (which implicitly includes the reader). This schema is to be found in Aristotle, and an influential recent version is in Frye (1971) (see J. Palmer 1990 ch. 7 for details). Jauss reworks this schema in terms of different forms of implied reader, or – as he calls it – different 'levels of identification' between hero and audience. That is to say, the existence of the hero has traditionally been thought in terms of a relationship between hero, action and 'the world'; it should be thought as the relationship hero–reader, through the concept of identification. Specifically, the nature of this relationship varies with the historical circumstances of the reader.

We should note that the historical differences between conditions of reception in Jauss are very broadly drawn, and coincide roughly with traditional divisions between one period of history and another. Those studies which start from meanings attached to texts by actual audiences make finer distinctions between different acts of reception of texts. The usual method is to select one or several audiences which have some distinctive feature(s) and to study the meanings they attach to some text or texts.

Liebes and Katz (1986) studied the range of meanings found in *Dallas* by a series of ethnically distinct audiences. They showed an episode of the serial to groups of viewers who were collected by asking a couple to invite some friends to a viewing and discussion in their home; this was to create as close an analogue as possible to the 'natural' viewing situation (it was easily established that discussion of the serial was normal in ordinary everyday life). The ethnic groups from which viewers were chosen were: second-generation Americans in the Los Angeles area; second-generation Israeli kibbutzniks; recent immigrants to Israel from the USSR; established immigrants to Israel from Morocco; and Israeli Arabs. While the choice of ethnic groups was clearly dictated by the researchers' location, they argue that the range of ethnicity is sufficiently large to give meaningful contrasts. Discussions – led by a researcher – were recorded and analysed for the presence or absence of recurrent themes, which could then be correlated with the ethnic origin of the discussants. Consistent correlations were taken to indicate that different ethnic groups saw different meanings in the text.

The themes which were observed were these:

1 The extent to which statements reflected the belief that *Dallas* referred directly to some recognisable feature of the real social world; at one extreme statements would indicate that the speaker accepted an unproblematic relationship between the text and the real world ('referential' statements); at the other they would be based upon an appreciation of its status as fiction ('critical' statements). For example: 'JR is a rich egotist' vs. 'JR is well-acted'.
2 Where statements were referential, they were distinguished by theme:
   (2a) motivations for action
   (2b) kinship and its norms
   (2c) moral dilemmas
   (2d) business relations
3 Referential statements were further distinguished by the degree to which they referred directly to some aspect of the real world ('realistic' statements) or to which they alluded to it 'painfully'; for example, 'wealth like JR's makes people do such-and-such' vs. 'If I was in JR's shoes, I would . . . '.
4 The grammatical person in which statements were made, which is taken to indicate whether discussants identify *Dallas* as referring to themselves and the group with which they identified, or to some other group.
5 The extent to which statements were normative, or judgemental, as against objective and descriptive.

When these themes are distributed by ethnic origin of discussant, the resulting distribution is taken to indicate differences in meaning

	Americans	Moroccans	Arabs	USSR	Kibbutzniks
Critical	27%	10%	11%	37%	28%
Referential	72%	90%	88%	62%	72%
Total: n = 100%	293	264	167	251	187
Approx ratio	2.5:1	9:1	8:1	2:1	2.5:1

Figure 30.1

attributed to the text. For example, the distinction referential/critical gives the distribution shown in Figure 30.1

This is typical of the results obtained: while all discussants are more likely to make referential statements than critical, it is clear that Arabs and Moroccans are far more likely to make them. This dispro-portion indicates a difference in attributed meaning, the difference being that Arabs or Moroccans are less able or willing to discuss the programme as 'only fiction' than the other groups; or are more inter-ested in discussing it in terms based on its assumed reference to some feature of the real world. The distribution of other themes revealed that:

1 All groups except Arabs gave prime consideration to questions of motivation; Arabs focused on kinship. Only Americans talked about business relations to any appreciable extent.
2 Americans and kibbutzniks were significantly more likely to make playful statements.
3 Arabs made significantly more comparisons between *Dallas* and their own communities than other groups.
4 All groups were more likely to make value-free, descriptive state-ments about the programme, in the ratio of 9:1, except the Arabs who made such statements in the ratio of 1.5:1; in other words, Arabs were far more likely to evaluate the programme (in terms of its real-world implications).

What general conclusions does this analysis permit? The authors combine the various measures we have seen into an index of distance from/involvement in the programme, and conclude that Americans and kibbutzniks are least involved in it, and that Arabs are by far the most involved. They offer two hypothetical explanations for this.

1 They argue that Arab culture is more based on the extended family than western culture, and that in Arab society the extended family is the real locus of both wealth and power; this is also true of *Dallas*.
2 They argue that *Dallas* represents western modernity, which is a challenge – both an opportunity and a threat – to the Arab way of life, indeed to 'traditional' societies in general.

What can such a study be taken to indicate about the relationship between texts and audiences?

Firstly, if its method is reliable, it shows that different audiences do indeed attach different meanings to texts (not that there was much doubt about that in the first place). Such doubts as attach to its method are twofold. We have already seen the difficulties involved in accurate coding of segments of fictional texts into categories and units of meaning; although non-fictional statements do indeed create less difficulties in categorisation – since their meanings are arguably less dependent upon a holistic context (i.e. an entire narrative) than are fictional meanings – unitisation is no less problematic. Moreover, in this study the meaning perceived in the text is assumed by fiat to be identical with the meaning that is attached to it in subsequent discussion. We shall see shortly that this assumption is problematic.

Secondly, the variation in meanings has been shown to correlate with ethnic or cultural difference; although the division between the discussant groups is based on ethnicity, the significant correlations appear to indicate cultural distinctions: crudely speaking, the 'westernised' discussants have relatively homogeneous responses compared with the 'non-' or 'less-westernised' groups. If we compare this conclusion with the approach favoured by 'reception aesthetics', we see that the 'reader in the text' is by no means identifiable with any particular 'real reader'. Implied readers are either universal in that they are no more than properties of the text (e.g. Todorov 1970), or only localised by the most generalised historical processes (Jauss 1974). The real readers studied by Liebes and Katz (1986) are highly sociologically specific.

Thirdly, we should note that there is a distinct methodological link between the discussion-based format of the study and the concept of the real reader as outlined here. In Liebes and Katz's study, the intrinsic meanings that *Dallas* may have are not systematically related to the meanings that are attached to it by viewers. Indeed, this separation is what permits the clear sociological conclusion that the study reaches, for if *Dallas* had some immanent meaning, that was *ex hypothesi* related to viewers' responses, then it would be difficult to distinguish between those meanings attached by viewers that derived from their sociology, and those that derived from the programme. For example, the conclusion about Arab viewers and the extended family: if *Dallas* systematically represents the family in this light, why do other viewers not perceive it? Clearly because their sociology does not predispose them to. But in that case, in what sense can we say that this view of the family is 'in' the text? Yet this is what Liebes and Katz assert of the Arab response to it, that the Arab response is not something randomly attached by the meeting of Arab culture and some western text, but that it arises in an interaction with a text which has this immanent meaning. In general, this difficulty seems to arise from the pursuit of the posi-tivist method, with its clear insistence upon factual observability as the only valid basis of evidence. The clearest statement of this link is to be found in Silbermann:

> the artistic life . . . is characterised by *the experience of art*. It is this meeting – resulting from conflict or contract – between the producer and the consumer, these social processes and these social actions, which concretise and assume a definite shape. Around them the art groups assemble; they alone, *in accordance with the methods of empirical sociology*, may and can, as sociolog-ical facts, be the centre and starting-point of observation and research.
>
> (Silbermann 1968 p. 583, emphasis added)

One of the rare studies which deals with both implied and real readers is Radway's (1984) *Reading the Romance*. The details of this investigation are sufficiently interesting to demand extended treat-ment elsewhere (J. Palmer 1990 ch. 11); here we are concerned with method. Radway got access to a group of women readers of romantic fiction who frequented the same bookshop, and was able to inter-view them, at length, and to administer a questionnaire based upon their responses to the earlier interview. The material covered here refers to readers' motives for reading and to the qualities they ascribe to both the texts they read and the act of reading itself. Here the method is not essentially different from Liebes and Katz's, since it consists of analysing a set of self-reported attitudes to narrative, albeit not quantitatively.

In crude outline, the interview material reveals that readers find in romances a form of 'emotional nurturance', both in the texts themselves and in the act of reading them. Radway then argues that in order to pursue the investigation further, what is needed is an analysis of the characteristics of the texts which the readers themselves nominate as particularly satisfying. That is to say, the readers themselves nominate texts and also describe why such texts are the source of satisfaction; the descriptions all centre on the form of the interaction between heroine and hero. By comparing what readers say about this set of texts with the texts themselves, Radway is able to construct a model of them which both conforms to what readers say and to an analysis of immanent features of the text (the method she uses here is closely akin to that used by Wright and analysed in J. Palmer 1990 ch. 2). In outline, what readers nominate as a good romance is based upon a set of psychological characteristics attributed to 'good' and 'bad' characters, and a narrative structure which distributes these characteristics clearly between characters who are the object of readers' empathy and those who are not. In other words, there is a clear link between what readers see in a text and the types of textual feature which structural analysis would look for in them.

It is important to note what Radway has achieved here. By constructing a textual analysis based upon readers' responses, she is able to demonstrate two points: firstly, that the meanings described by readers are not attributed at random to texts, that they derive from an interaction between text and reader; secondly, that the analysis of textuality advanced by the critic is firmly based in what readers themselves have seen in the text. In a further stage of the analysis she is able to construct a speculative model of the elements of our culture which are responsible for women seeking the forms of satisfaction that they do seek in such texts; the model in question is a feminist analysis of female gender roles in a patriarchal society. In so doing she has dealt with various problematic areas in earlier audience and response-oriented research.

In Iser and in Jauss, no attempt was made to ascertain the actual responses of real readers: response was a product of textual structures

and typical predispositions based upon broadly conceived characteristics of historically defined audiences. In empirical studies such
as Liebes and Katz, audience response is held to be whatever emerges
in subsequent discussion and only connected in the loosest of ways
with any textual structure; meanings thus appear to be attributed
randomly to texts. In Radway, these two types of process are brought
together and the interaction between them is firmly demonstrated by
the explicit linkage between textual structure and empirically
observed response; this, in turn, is placed in the context of cultural
forces – ideology, in short – that shape readers' responses even if
they are not aware of them.[1]

NOTE

1 For a recent brief review of literature on TV audiences which stresses these
   themes, see Gray (1987).

31 Janice A. Radway

Reading the romance

The reading habits and preferences of the Smithton women are complexly tied to their daily routines, which are themselves a function of education, social role, and class position. Most Smithton readers are married mothers of children, living in single-family homes in a sprawling suburb of a central midwestern state's second largest city (population 850,000 in 1970).[1] Its surrounding cornfields notwithstanding, Smithton itself is an urbanized area. Its 1970 population, which was close to 112,000 inhabitants, represented a 70 percent increase over that recorded by the 1960 census. The community is essentially a 'bedroom' community in that roughly 90 percent of those employed in 1970 worked outside Smithton itself. Although this has changed slightly in recent years with the building of the mall in which Dot herself works, the city is still largely residential and dominated by single-family homes, which account for 90 to 95 percent of the housing stock.

Dot and her family live on the fringe of one of Smithton's new housing developments in a large, split-level home. When I last visited Smithton, Dot, her husband, Dan, her eldest daughter, Kit, and her mother were living in the house, which is decorated with Dot's needlework and crafts, projects she enjoyed when her children were young. Dot's other two children, Dawn, who is nineteen and married, and Joe, who is twenty-one, do not live with the family. Dot herself was forty-eight years old at the time of the study. Dan, a journeyman plumber, seems both bemused by Dot's complete absorption in romances and proud of her success at the bookstore. Although he occasionally reads thrillers and some nonfiction, he spends his leisure time with fellow union members or working about the house.

Although she is now a self-confident and capable woman, Dot believes she was once very different. She claims that she has changed substantially in recent years, a change she attributes to her reading and her work with people in the bookstore. When asked how she first began reading romances, she responded that it was really at her doctor's instigation. Although he did not suggest reading specifically, he advised her about fifteen years ago that she needed to find an enjoyable leisure activity to which she could devote at least an hour a day. He was concerned about her physical and mental exhaustion, apparently brought on by her conscientious and diligent efforts to care for her husband, three small children, and her home. When he asked her what she did for herself all day and she could list *only* the tasks she performed for others, he insisted that she learn to spend some time on herself if she did not want to land in a hospital. Remembering that she loved to read as a child, she decided to try again. Thus began her interest in romance fiction. Dot read many kinds of books at first, but she soon began to concentrate on romances for reasons she cannot now explain. Her reading became so chronic that when she discovered that she could not rely on a single shop to provide all of the latest releases by her favorite authors, she found it necessary to check four different bookstores to get all of the romances she wanted. Most of her customers commented that before they discovered Dot they did the same thing. Some still attend garage sales and flea markets religiously to find out-of-print books by authors whose more recent books they have enjoyed.

All of the Smithton readers who answered the questionnaire were female. Dot reported that although she suspects some of the men who buy romances 'for their wives' are in fact buying them for themselves, all of the people she regularly advises are women. While the few houses that have conducted market-research surveys will not give out exact figures, officials at Harlequin, Silhouette, and Fawcett have all indicated separately that the majority of romance readers are married women between the ages of twenty-five and fifty. Fred Kerner, Harlequin's vice-president for publishing, for instance, recently reported to Barbara Brotman, of the *Chicago Tribune*, that 'Harlequin readers are overwhelmingly women of whom 49 percent work at least part-time. They range in age from 24 to 29, have average family incomes of $15,000–20,000 and have high school diplomas but haven't completed college' (Brotman 1980 p. B1). Harlequin will reveal little else about its audience, but a company executive did tell Margaret Jensen that the Harlequin reading population matches the profile of the 'North American English-speaking female population' in age, family income, employment status, and geographical location (M. Jensen 1980 p. 289). For example, he said that 22 percent of the female population and Harlequin readers are between the ages of twenty-five and thirty-four. Carol Reo, publicity director for Silhouette Romances, has also revealed that the romance audience is almost entirely female, but indicates that 65 percent of Silhouette's potential market is under the age of forty and that 45 percent attended college (quoted in Brotman 1980 p. B1). If these sketchy details are accurate, the Smithton readers may be more representative of the Silhouette audience than they are of Harlequin's (see also Mann 1974). Unfortunately, the lack of detailed information about the total American audience for Harlequins as well as for other kinds of romances makes it exceedingly difficult to judge the representivity of the Smithton group. Still, it appears evident that the Smithton readers are somewhat younger than either Jensen's Harlequin readers or the Mills and Boon audience.

The age differential may account for the fact that neither Dot nor many of her customers are Harlequin fans. Although Dot reviews Harlequins and slightly more than half of her customers (twenty-four) reported reading them, a full eighteen indicated that they *never* read a Harlequin romance. Moreover, only ten of Dot's customers indicated that Harlequins are among the kinds of romances they *most* like to read. The overwhelming preference of the group was for historicals, cited by twenty (48 percent) as their favorite subgenre within the romance category.[2] Because historicals typically include more explicit sex than the Harlequins and also tend to portray more independent and defiant heroines, we might expect that this subgenre would draw younger readers who are less offended by changing standards of gender behavior. This would seem to be corroborated by the fact that only two of the women who listed Harlequins as a favorite also listed historicals.

In addition, the Smithton group also seemed to like contemporary mystery romances and contemporary romances, which were cited by another twelve as being among their favorites. Silhouettes are contemporary romances and, like the historicals, are less conventional than the Harlequins. Not only is their sexual description more explicit but it is not unusual for them to include heroines with careers who expect to keep their jobs after marriage. The similarity between Smithton's tastes and the content of the Silhouettes may thus explain why both audiences are younger than that for the relatively staid Harlequins.

Despite the discrepancies in the various reports, romance reading apparently correlates strongly with the years of young adulthood and early middle age. This is further borne out in the present study by the Smithton women's responses to a question about when they first began to read romances. Although fifteen (36 percent) of the women reported that they began in adolescence between the ages of ten and nineteen, sixteen (38 percent) indicated that they picked up the habit between the ages of twenty and twenty-nine. Another ten (24 percent) adopted romance reading after age thirty.[3]

Thirty-two women (76 percent) in the Smithton group were married at the time of the survey, a proportion that compares almost exactly with the 75 percent of married women included in Jensen's group (Jensen 1980 pp. 290–291). An additional three (7 percent) of the Smithton women were single, while five (12 percent) were either widowed, separated, or divorced and not remarried.

Moreover, most of the women in the Smithton group were mothers with children *under* age eighteen (70 percent). Indeed, within the group, only five (12 percent) reported having no children at all. Nine (21 percent) of the Smithton women reported only one child, twelve (29 percent) claimed two children, eleven (27 percent) had three children, and three (7 percent) had four children. Interestingly enough, only five (12 percent) reported children under the age of five, while twenty-four of the women indicated that they had at least one child under age eighteen. Eleven (27 percent), however, reported that all of their children were over age eighteen. Fifteen (36 percent) reported children between ten and eighteen, and another fifteen (36 percent) had at least one child over age eighteen. The relatively advanced age of the Smithton readers' children is not surprising if one takes into account the age distribution of the women themselves and the fact that the mean age at first marriage within the group was 19.9 years.

Once again, the limited size of the sample and the lack of corroborating data from other sources suggest caution in the formation of hypotheses. Nonetheless, it appears that within the Smithton group romance reading correlates with motherhood and the care of children *other* than infants and toddlers.[4] This seems logical because the fact of the older children's attendance at school would allow the women greater time to read even as the children themselves continued to make heavy emotional demands on them for nurturance, advice, and attentive care. It will be seen later that it is precisely this emotional drain caused by a woman's duty to nurture and care for her children and husband that is addressed directly by romance reading at least within the minds of the women themselves.

Given the fact that fifteen (36 percent) of the Smithton readers reported children age ten and under, it should not be surprising to note that sixteen of the women (38 percent) reported that in the preceding week they were keeping house and/or caring for children on a full-time basis. Another nine (21 percent) were working part-time, while still another nine (21 percent) were holding down full-time jobs. In addition, two women failed to respond, two stated that they were retired, one listed herself as a student, and three indicated that they were currently unemployed and looking for work. These statistics seem to parallel those of the Mills and Boon study which found that 33 percent of the sample was represented by full-time housewives, while another 30 percent included housewives with full- or part-time jobs. Both studies suggest that romance reading is very often squeezed into busy daily schedules.

Although Fred Kerner's comment about the average $15,000–$20,000 income of the Harlequin audience is not very illuminating, neither is it at odds with the details reported by Dot's customers. Although four (10 percent) did not answer the question, eighteen (43 percent) in the group indicated a family income of somewhere between $15,000 and $24,999. Another fourteen (33 percent) claimed a joint income of $25,000 to $49,999, while four (10 percent) listed family earnings of over $50,000. The greater affluence of the Smithton group is probably accounted for by the fact that Dot's bookstore is located in one of the twelve most affluent counties in a state with 115. The median family income in Smithton, as reported by the 1970 United States census, was almost $11,000, which compares with the state median income of just slightly less than $9,000.

Before turning to the group's reading history and patterns, it should be noted that exactly half of the Smithton readers indicated that they had earned a high school diploma. Ten (24 percent) of the women reported completing less than three years of college; eight (19 percent) claimed at least a college degree or better. Only one person in the group indicated that she had not finished high school, while two failed to answer the question. Once again, as the Smithton readers appear to be more affluent than Harlequin readers, so also do they seem better educated; the Harlequin corporation claims that its readers are educated below even the statistical norm for the North American female population.

One final detail about the personal history of the Smithton women ought to be mentioned here: attendance at religious services was relatively high among Dot's customers. Although eight (19 percent) of the women indicated that they had not been to a service in the last two years, fifteen (36 percent) reported attendance 'once a week or more', while another eight (19 percent) indicated attendance 'once or a few times a month'. Another nine (21 percent) admitted going to services a few times a year, while two (5 percent) did not answer the question. The women reported membership in a wide variety of denominations. Eight (19 percent) of the women indicated that they were Methodists and eight (19 percent) checked 'Christian but non-denominational'. The next two groups most heavily represented in the sample were Catholics and Baptists, each with five (12 percent) of the Smithton women.

When the reading *histories* of these women are examined, it becomes clear that, for many of them, romance reading is simply a variation in a pattern of leisure activity they began early in life. Indeed, twenty-two of Dot's customers reported that they first began to read for pleasure before age ten. Another twelve (27 percent) adopted the habit between the ages of eleven and twenty. Only seven (17 percent) of the Smithton women indicated that they began pleasure reading after their teen years. These results parallel earlier findings about the adoption of the book habit. Phillip Ennis found in 1965, for instance, that of the 49 percent of the American population who were 'current readers', 34 percent consisted of those who started reading early in life and 15 percent consisted of those who began reading at an advanced age (cited in Yankelovich, Skelly and White 1978 p. 325).

When *current* reading habits are examined, however, it becomes clear that the women think that it is the romances that are especially necessary to their daily routine. Their intense reliance on these books suggests strongly that they help to fulfill deeply felt psychological needs. Indeed, one of the most striking findings to come out of the Smithton study was that thirty-seven (88 percent) of Dot's readers indicated that they read religiously every day. Only five of her regular customers claimed to read more sporadically. Twenty-two of the women, in fact, reported reading more than sixteen hours per week, and another ten (24 percent) claimed to read between eleven and fifteen hours weekly.[5] When asked to describe their typical reading pattern once they have begun a new romance, eleven (26 percent) selected the statement, 'I won't put it down until I've finished it unless it's absolutely necessary.' Thirty more indicated reading 'as much of it as I can until I'm interrupted or have something else to do.' None of Dot's customers reported a systematic reading pattern of 'a few pages a day until done', and only one admitted that she reads solely when she is in the mood. These figures suggest that the Smithton women become intensely involved in the stories they are reading and that once immersed in the romantic fantasy, Dot's customers do not like to return to reality without experiencing the resolution of the narrative.

This need to see the story and the emotions aroused by it resolved is so intense that many of the Smithton women have worked out an ingenious strategy to insure a regular and predictable arrival at the anticipated narrative conclusion. Although they categorize romances in several ways, one of the most basic distinctions they make is that between 'quick reads' and 'fat books'. Quick reads contain less than 200 pages and require no more than two hours of reading time. Harlequins, Silhouettes, and most Regencies are considered quick reads for occasions when they know they will not be able to 'make it through' a big book. If, for example, a woman has just finished one romance but still 'is not ready to quit', as one of my informants put it, she will 'grab a thin one' she knows she can finish before going to sleep. Fat books, on the other hand, tend to be saved for weekends or long evenings that promised to be uninterrupted, once again because the women dislike having to leave a story before it is concluded. This kind of uninterrupted reading is very highly valued within the Smithton group because it is associated with the pleasure of spending time alone.[6] A detailed exploration of the importance of this narrative and emotional resolution is in Radway (1984 ch. 4), where the structure of the romance story and its developing effect on the reader are considered in detail; let it be said here that the Smithton readers' strategies for avoiding disruption or discontinuity in the story betoken a profound need to arrive at the *ending* of the tale and thus to achieve or acquire the emotional gratification they already can anticipate.

Although their chronic reading of these books might sound unusual or idiosyncratic, the Yankelovich findings about romance reading, as noted before, indicate that romance readers are generally heavy consumers. Most, however, are probably not as obsessed as the Smithton readers seem to be. Unfortunately, the Yankelovich discovery that the average romance reader had read nine romances in the last six months does not tell us what proportion of the group read an even larger number of novels. Although 40 percent of the heavy readers (those who had read more than twenty-five books in the last six months) reported having read a romance, thus suggesting the possibility of a correlation between high levels of consumption and romance reading, the study gives no indication of how many of the romance readers actually read anywhere near the number the Smithton women report, which ranges from twenty-four to more than six hundred romances every six months (Yankelovich, Skelly and White 1978 pp. 141 and 144). I think it safe to say that the Smithton group's reliance on romances is not strictly comparable to that of the occasional reader. Rather, Dot's customers are women who spend a significant portion of every day participating vicariously in a fantasy world that they willingly admit bears little resemblance to the one they actually inhabit. Clearly, the experience must provide some form of required pleasure and reconstitution because it seems unlikely that so much time and money would be spent on an activity that functioned merely to fill otherwise unoccupied time.

The women confirmed this in their answers to a directed-response question about their reasons for reading romance fiction. When asked to rank in order the three most important motives for romance reading out of a list of eight, nineteen (45 percent) of the women listed 'simple relaxation' as the first choice. Another eight (19 percent) of the readers reported that they read romances 'because reading is just for me; it is my time.' Still another six (14 percent) said they read 'to learn about faraway places and times'; while five (12 percent) insisted that their primary reason is 'to escape my daily problems.' When these first choices are added to the second and third most important reasons for reading, the totals are distributed as in Table 31.1.

On the basis of these schematic answers alone I think it logical to conclude that romance is valued by the Smithton women because the experience itself is *different* from ordinary existence. Not only is it a relaxing release from the tension produced by daily problems and responsibilities, but it creates a time or space within which a

Table 31.1 Question: Which of the following best describes why you read romances?

a. To escape my daily problems	13
b. To learn about faraway places and times	19
c. For simple relaxation	33
d. Because I wish I had a romance like the heroine's	5
e. Because reading is just for me; it is my time	28
f. Because I like to read about the strong, virile heroes	4
g. Because reading is at least better than other forms of escape	5
h. Because romantic stories are never sad or depressing	10

woman can be entirely on her own, preoccupied with her personal needs, desires, and pleasure. It is also a means of transportation or escape to the exotic or, again, to that which is different.

It is important to point out here that the responses to the second questionnaire are different in important ways from the answers I received from the women in the face-to-face interviews and in the first survey. At the time of my initial visit in June 1980, our conversations about their reasons for romance reading were dominated by the words 'escape' and 'education'. Similarly, when asked by the first questionnaire to describe briefly what romances do 'better' than other books available today, of the thirty-one answering the undirected question, fourteen of the first respondents *volunteered* that they like romance fiction because it allows them to 'escape'. It should be noted that 'relaxation' was given only once as an answer, while no woman mentioned the idea of personal space.

Both answers *c* and *e* on the second form were given initially in the course of the interviews by two unusually articulate readers who elaborated more fully than most of the women on the meaning of the word 'escape'. They considered these two answers synonymous with it, but they also seemed to prefer the alternate responses because they did not so clearly imply a desire to avoid duties and responsibilities in the 'real' world. Although most of the other women settled for the word 'escape' on the first questionnaire, they also liked their sister readers' terms better. Once these were introduced in the group interviews, the other women agreed that romance reading functions best as relaxation and as a time for self-indulgence. Because the switch seemed to hint at feelings of guilt, I decided to add the more acceptable choices to the second survey. Although both answers *c* and *e* also imply movement away from something distasteful in the real present to a somehow more satisfying universe, a feature that appears to testify to romance reading's principal function as a therapeutic release and as a provider of vicarious pleasure, the fact of the women's preference for these two terms over their first spontaneous response suggests again that the women harbor complex feelings about the worth and propriety of romance reading.[7]

The women provided additional proof of their reliance on romance reading as a kind of tranquilizer or restorative agent in their responses to questions about preferred reading times and the habit of rereading favorite romances. When asked to choose from among seven statements the one that best described their reading pattern, twenty-four (57 percent) eschewed specification of a particular time of day in order to select the more general assertion, 'It's hard to say when I do most of my reading, since I read every chance I get.' Another fourteen claimed to read mostly in the evenings, usually because days were occupied by employment outside the home. In the case of either pattern, however, romances are not picked up idly as an old magazine might be merely to fill otherwise unoccupied time. Rather, romance reading is considered so enjoyable and beneficial by the women that they deliberately work it into busy schedules as often and as consistently as they can.

Rereading is not only a widely practiced habit among the Smithton women but tends to occur most frequently during times of stress or depression. Three-fourths of Dot's customers reported that they reread favorite books either 'sometimes' (twenty-one) or 'often' (eleven). They do so, they explained in the interviews, when they feel sad or unhappy because they know exactly how the chosen book will affect their state of mind. Peter Mann similarly discovered that 46 percent of Mills and Boon readers claimed to reread 'very often', while another 38 percent reported repeat reading 'now and then' (Mann 1974 p. 17). Unfortunately, he has provided no further information about why or when the women do so. Although it is possible that they may reread in order to savor the details of particular plots; it is clear that for the most part the Smithton women do not. For them, rereading is an activity engaged in expressly to lift the spirits. The following comment from one of the first questionnaires illustrates nicely the kind of correlation the Smithton women see between their daily needs and the effects of romance reading: 'Romances are not depressing and very seldom leave you feeling sad inside. When I read for enjoyment I want to be entertained and feel lifted out of my daily routine. And romances are the best type of reading for this effect. Romances also revive my usually optimistic outlook which often is very strained in day-to-day living.' Although all of Dot's customers know well that most romances end happily, when their own needs seem unusually pressing they often refuse even the relatively safe gamble of beginning a new romance. Instead, they turn to romance they have completed previously because they already know how its final resolution will affect them. Romance reading, it would seem, can be valued as much for the sameness of the response it evokes as for the variety of the adventures it promises.[8]

Interestingly enough, the Smithton readers hold contradictory opinions about the repetitious or formulaic quality of the fiction they read. On the one hand, they are reluctant to admit that the characters appearing in romances are similar. As Dot's daughter, Kit, explained when asked to describe a typical heroine in the historical romance, 'there isn't a typical one, they all have to be different or you'd be reading the same thing over and over.' Her sentiments were echoed frequently by her mother's customers, all of whom claim to value the variety and diversity of romance fiction.

On the other hand, these same women exhibit fairly rigid expectations about what is permissible in a romantic tale and express disappointment and outrage when those conventions are violated. In my first interview with Dot, she discussed a particular author who had submitted a historical novel to her publisher. Although the author explained repeatedly that the book was not a romance, the publisher insisted on packaging it with a standard romance cover in the hope of attracting the huge romance market. The author knew this would anger that audience and, as Dot remarked, 'she was not surprised when she got irate letters.' Clearly, romances may not deviate too significantly if regular readers are to be pleased. They expect and, indeed, rely upon certain events, characters, and progressions to provide the desired experience.

In all of their comments about the nature of the romance, the Smithton women placed heavy emphasis on the importance of *development* in the romance's portrayal of love. The following two definitions were echoed again and again in other remarks:

> Generally there are two people who come together for one reason or another, *grow to love each other* and *work together solving problems* along the way – united for a purpose. They are light

easy reading and always have a happy ending which makes one feel more light-hearted.

I think [a romance] is a man and woman meeting, the growing awareness, the culmination of the love – *whether it's going to jell or if it's going to fall apart* – but they [the heroine and the hero] have recognized that they have fallen in love [emphasis added].

The women usually articulated this insistence on process and development during discussions about the genre's characteristic preoccupation with what is typically termed 'a love–hate relationship'. Because the middle of every romantic narrative must create some form of conflict to keep the romantic pair apart until the proper moment, many authors settle for misunderstanding or distrust as the cause of the intermediary delay of the couple's happy union. Hero and heroine are shown to despise each other overtly, even though they are 'in love', primarily because each is jealous or suspicious of the other's motives and consequently fails to trust the other. Despite the frequency with which this pattern of conflict is suddenly explained away by the couple's mutual recognition that only misunderstanding is thwarting their relationship, the Smithton women are not convinced when a hero decides within two pages of the novel's conclusion that he has been mistaken about the heroine and that his apparent hatred is actually affection. Dot's customers dislike such 'about faces'; they prefer to see a hero and heroine gradually overcome distrust and suspicion and grow to love each other.

Although this depiction of love as a gradual process cannot be considered the defining feature of the genre for all of the Smithton women, slightly more than half (twenty-three) believe it one of the 'three most important ingredients' in the narrative. As might have been predicted, when responding to a request to rank order narrative features with respect to their importance to the genre, Dot's customers generally agreed that a happy ending is indispensable. Twenty-two of the women selected this as the essential ingredient in romance fiction out of a list of eleven choices, while a total of thirty-two listed it in first, second, or third place. The runner-up in the 'most important' category, however, was 'a slowly but consistently developing love between hero and heroine', placed by twenty-three of the women in first, second, or third place. Considered almost equally important by Dot's customers was the romance's inclusion of 'some detail about the heroine and the hero after they have finally

Table 31.2   Question: What are the three most important ingredients in a romance?

Response	First most important feature	Second most important feature	Third most important feature	Total who checked response in one of top three positions
a. A happy ending	22	4	6	32
b. Lots of scenes with explicit sexual description	0	0	0	0
c. Lots of details about faraway places and times	0	1	2	3
d. A long conflict between hero and heroine	2	1	1	4
e. Punishment of the villain	0	2	3	5
f. A slowly but consistently developing love between hero and heroine	8	9	6	23
g. A setting in a particular historical period	3	4	3	10
h. Lots of love scenes with some explicit sexual description	3	7	3	13
i. Lots of love scenes without explicit sexual description	0	3	1	4
j. Some detail about heroine and hero after they've gotten together	1	7	14	22
k. A very particular kind of hero and heroine	3	4	3	10

gotten together'.[9] Twenty-two of the women thought this one of the three most important ingredients in the genre. Table 31.2 summarizes the ranking responses of the Smithton women.

The obvious importance of the happy ending lends credence to the suggestion that romances are valued most for their ability to raise the spirits of the reader. They manage to do so, the rankings imply, by involving that reader vicariously in the gradual evolution of a loving relationship whose culmination she is later permitted to enjoy in the best romances through a description of the heroine's and hero's life together after their necessary union. When combined with the relative unimportance of detailed reports about sexual encounters, it seems clear that the Smithton readers are interested in the verbal working out of a romance, that is, in the reinterpretation of misunderstood actions and in declarations of mutual love rather than in the portrayal of sexual contact, through visual imagery.

Beatrice Faust (1980) has recently argued in *Women, Sex, and Pornography* that female sexuality is 'tactile, verbal, intimate, nurturant, process-oriented and somewhat inclined to monogamy', traits she attributes to biological predisposition and social reinforcement through culture (Faust 1980 p. 107). Although there are important problems with Faust's reliance on biology to account for female preferences in sexual encounters as well as with her assertion that such tastes characterize all women, her parallel claim that women are not excited by the kinds of visual displays and explicit description of physical contact that characterize male pornography is at least true of the Smithton readers. Dot and her customers are more interested in the affective responses of hero and heroine to each other than in a detailed account of their physical contact. Interestingly enough, the Smithton women also explained that they do not like explicit description because they prefer to imagine the scene in detail by themselves. Their wish to participate in the gradual growth of love and trust and to witness the way in which the heroine is eventually cared for by a man who also confesses that he 'needs' her suggests that the Smithton women do indeed want to see a woman attended to sexually in a tender, nurturant, and emotionally open way. It should be added that these preferences also hint at the existence of an equally powerful wish to see a man dependent upon a woman.

Although it will be impossible, then, to use this conclusion to bring a single, large picture into focus simply because there is no context-free, unmarked position from which to view the activity of romance reading in its entirety, I can perhaps use it to remind the reader of each of the snapshots provided herein, to juxtapose them rapidly in condensed space and time. Such a review will help underscore the semantic richness and ideological density of the actual process known as romantic reading and thus highlight once and for all the complicated nature of the connection between the romance and the culture that has given rise to it.

If we remember that texts are read and that reading itself is an activity carried on by real people in a preconstituted social context, it becomes possible to distinguish *analytically* between the meaning of the act and the meaning of the text as read. This analytic distinction then empowers us to question whether the significance of the act of reading itself might, under some conditions, contradict, undercut, or qualify the significance of producing a particular kind of story. When this methodological distinction is further complicated by an effort to render real readers' comprehension of each of the aspects of the activity as well as the covert significance and consequences underlying both, the possibilities for perceiving conflict and contradiction are increased even more. This is exactly what has resulted from this account of the reading preferences and behavior of Dorothy Evans and the Smithton women.

Ethnographic investigation, for instance, has led to the discovery that Dot and her customers see the act of reading as combative and compensatory. It is combative in the sense that it enables them to refuse the other-directed social role prescribed for them by their position within the institution of marriage. In picking up a book, as they have so eloquently told us, they refuse temporarily their family's otherwise constant demand that they attend to the wants of others even as they act deliberately to do something for their own private pleasure. Their activity is compensatory, then, in that it permits them to focus on themselves and to carve out a solitary space within an arena where their self-interest is usually identified with the interests of others and where they are defined as a public resource to be mined at will by the family. For them, romance reading addresses needs created in them but not met by patriarchal institutions and engendering practices.

It is striking to observe that this partial account of romance reading, which stresses its status as an oppositional or contestative act because the women use it to thwart common cultural expectations and to supply gratification ordinarily ruled out by the way the culture structures their lives, is not far removed from the account of folkloric practices elaborated recently by Luigi Lombardi-Satriani (1974 pp. 99–121) and José Limon (n.d. pp. 1–21). Although both are concerned only with folkloric behavior and the way indigenous folk performances contest the hegemonic imposition of bourgeois culture on such subordinate groups as 'workers, ... peasants, racial and cultural minorities, and women' (Limon n.d. p. 1), their definitions of contestation do not rule out entirely the sort of behavioral activity involving mass culture that I have discovered among the Smithton readers.

Lombardi-Satriani, for instance, argues that the folkloric cultures of subordinate groups may contest or oppose the dominant culture in two distinct ways. One the one hand, folklore may express overtly or metaphorically values that are different from or question those held by the dominant classes. On the other hand, opposition also can occur *because* a folkloric performance exists. Limon adds, however, that it is not the simple fact of a folkloric practice's existence that produces opposition: rather, opposition is effected when that performance 'counter-valuates'. What he means by counter-valuation is a process of inversion whereby the original socioeconomic limitations and devaluations of a subordinate group are first addressed by the folkloric performance and then transformed within or by it into something of value to the group. If the process is successful, Limon maintains, the performance contests by supplementation. In effect, it simultaneously acknowledges and meets the needs of the subordinate group, which, as the consequence of its subordination, are systematically ignored by the culture's practices and institutions.

When romance reading is examined, then as an activity that takes place within a specific social context, it becomes evident that this form of behavior both supplements and counter-valuates in Limon's sense. Romance reading supplements the avenues traditionally open to women for emotional gratification by supplying them vicariously with the attention and nurturance they do not get enough of in the round of day-to-day existence. It counter-valuates because the story opposes the female values of love and personal interaction to the male values of competition and public achievement and, at least in ideal romances, demonstrates the triumph of the former over the latter. Romance reading and writing might be seen therefore as a collectively elaborated female ritual through which women explore the consequences of their common social condition as the appendages of men and attempt to imagine a more perfect state where all the needs they so intensely feel and accept as given would be adequately addressed.

I must stress here, as I have throughout the book (Radway 1984), that this is *not* the only view of romance reading that might be taken. Women's domestic role in patriarchal culture, which is simultaneously addressed and counter-valuated in the imagination through a woman's encounter with romantic fiction, is left virtually intact by her leisure-time withdrawal. Although in restoring a woman's depleted sense of self romance reading may constitute tacit recognition that the current arrangement of the sexes is not ideal for her emotional well-being, it does nothing to alter a woman's social situation, itself very likely characterized by those dissatisfying patterns. In fact, this activity may very well obviate the need or desire to demand satisfaction in the real world because it can be so successfully met in fantasy.

NOTES

1. These and all other figures about Smithton were taken from the *Census of Population, 1970.* I have rounded off the numbers slightly to disguise the identity of Smithton.
2. Readers were instructed to identify the particular kind of romance they like to 'read the most' from a list of ten subgenres. The titles had been given to me by Dot during a lengthy discussion about the the different kinds of romances. Although I expected the women to check only one subgenre, almost all of them checked several as their favorites. The categories and totals follow: gothics, 6; contemporary mystery romances, 5; historicals 20; contemporary romances, 7; Harlequins, 10; Regencies, 4; family sagas, 1; plantation series, 3; spy thrillers, 0; transcendental romances, 0; other, 2.
3. It should be pointed out, however, that these findings could also indicate that romances were not heavily advertised or distributed when the majority of women in this sample were teenagers. Thus, the fact that so many have picked up the romance habit may be as much a function of the recent growth of the industry as of any particular need or predisposition on the part of the women at a particular stage in their life cycle. Still, as I will make clear in this and subsequent chapters, romances do address needs associated with the role of mothering for *this* particular group of readers.
4. Jensen also reports that all of the married women in her sample have children and that three-quarters have children still at home (1980 p. 291).
5. This compares with the eight-hour weekly average claimed by book readers who read fiction for leisure as reported in Yankelovich, Skelly and White (1978 p. 126).
6. Although the Smithton women also commented, as did Jensen's informants, on the ease with which 'light reading' like Harlequins and Silhouettes can be picked up and put down when other demands intervene, all of Dot's customers with whom I spoke expressed a preference for finishing a romance in one sitting. Jensen does not say whether her readers would have preferred to read in this way, although she does comment rather extensively on the fact that it is the material circumstances of their jobs as housewives and mothers that most often necessitate what she calls 'snatch' reading. She refers to an alternate pattern of reading several books, one after the other, as 'binge'. This is not exactly equivalent to the Smithton readers' practice with fat books, but some of them did mention engaging in such behavior as a special treat to themselves. See Jensen (1980 pp. 300–301 and 312–314).

7. The Smithton readers' patterns of explanation and justification is explored in more detail in Radway (1984 pp. 86–118).
8. For further discussion of this curious failure to trust that a new romance will end happily despite previous acquaintance with the genre see Radway (1984 pp. 186–208).
9. I included this choice on the final questionnaire because in many of the interviews the women had expressed a distaste for romances that end abruptly with the declaration of love between the principal characters.

32 Ien Ang

Dallas *between reality and fiction*

DALLAS AS TEXT

In reading the letters we encounter an avalanche of self-given 'reasons' why lovers of *Dallas* like watching the programme. The letter-writers extensively describe their viewing experiences and state what does and does not appeal to them.

> I find *Dallas* a super TV programme. For me it means relaxation twice a week, out of the daily rut. You may wonder why twice a week – well, that's because I watch it on Belgian TV too. You have to switch over, but you quickly pick it up again. I'm interested in the clothes, make-up and hair-dos too. Sometimes it's quite gripping too, for example in Miss Ellie's case. . . . And I think Ray Krebbs is wonderful. But I just think J.R. is a monster, a hypocrite, etc.
>
> (Letter 1)

> The reason I like watching it is that you can easily get really involved in their problems. Yet all the time you know it will all turn out all right again. In fact it's a flight from reality.
>
> (Letter 5)

> Why do I watch *Dallas* every Tuesday? Mainly because of Pamela and that wonderful love between her and Bobby. When I see those two I feel warmth radiating from them. I am happily married myself too and perhaps I see myself in Pamela. I find her very beautiful too (which I myself am not).
>
> (Letter 8)

First of all it's entertainment for me, part show, expensive clothes, beautiful horses, something I can just do with by the evening.

(Letter 11)

I think it's marvellous to project myself into *Dallas* and in my mind to give J.R. a good hiding when he's just pulled off yet another dirty trick, or admire Miss Ellie because she always tries to see the best in everyone or to bring it out in them.

(Letter 13)

I find *Dallas* marvellous, though it isn't an absolute 'must' for me. Reasons:
Everyone is so kind to one another (leaving aside J.R.) and they form a real family, being sociable, having their meals together, for example.
Witty dialogue.
Fast, characteristic of an American product.

(Letter 17)

My absorption in *Dallas* has to do with the fact that I follow everything coming from America. I have been there once – last year – and I started watching *Dallas* just to see the American city scene: those beautiful apartment blocks (especially the really beautiful one you see during the titles) and the cars.

(Letter 21)

I don't find everything entertaining. The farm doesn't interest me much. Now and then you get a whole episode with nothing but cowboys and cattle. I find that boring. I'm not keen on Westerns. Too macho. Like the episode when the Ewing men went hunting and were chased. Boring. After that it got better again, fortunately. . . . I like the pictures of the city too a lot. The office buildings in Dallas. The talks about oil. I really enjoy that.

(Letter 23; this letter is from a man)

I find the situations always so well chosen and excellently fitting together and everything runs so well from one thing into another. Then I find the milieu (a rich oil family, etc.) very well chosen.

(Letter 40, also from a man)

It is clear that there is not just one 'reason' for the pleasure of *Dallas*, which applies for everyone; each has his or her own more or less unique relationship to the programme. What appeals to us in such a television serial is connected with our individual life histories, with the social situation we are in, with the aesthetic and cultural preferences we have developed, and so on.

But though the ideas of each of the letter-writers are of course personal, they cannot be regarded as a direct expression of their 'motives' or 'reasons' for watching *Dallas*. They can at most be regarded as indications or symptoms of deeper psychological incentives and orientations. Furthermore, although these ideas can *appear* to be strictly personal for the letter-writers themselves, ultimately all these ideas are structured in a specific socio-cultural manner. And so we must take a look behind these ideas; we must subject them to a 'symptomatic reading' to be able to say something about the pleasure of *Dallas* that rises above the merely individual level.

It would be going too far to say that viewers are completely free to handle *Dallas* as they want, as the possibilities of experiencing pleasure in it are not infinite. *Dallas* itself, as an object of pleasure, sets its own limits on those possibilities. From the letter excerpts I have just quoted it emerges that the ideas expressed by these viewers contain many elements referring to what is to be seen in the programme – to its textual characteristics. This fact makes it necessary to go into the specific way in which *Dallas*, as a cultural object, is structured.

Dallas is a weekly television programme. A television programme consists of a series of electronic images and sounds which emerge from a television set. These images and sounds represent something: people talking, walking, drinking, high-rise apartment blocks, moving cars, and so on. From this standpoint a television programme can be looked on as a *text*: as a system of representation consisting of a specific combination of (visual and audible) signs. (For a foundation of this semiological approach to television programmes see e.g. Eco 1972 and Hall 1981.) The problem here, however, is that *Dallas* is a discontinuous text: it is a television serial consisting of a large number of episodes, each more or less forming a separate whole. Each episode can then in its turn be called a textual unit. For the sake of clarity I shall view the television serial *Dallas* as a whole as an incomplete, 'infinite' text. (see also Allen 1983.)

A text functions only if it is 'read'. Only in and through the practice of reading does the text have meaning (or several meanings) for the reader. In the confrontation between *Dallas* and its viewers the reading activity of the latter is therefore the connecting principle.

And this reading does not occur just anyhow. As David Morley says: 'The activity of "getting meaning" from [a] message is ... a problematic practice, however transparent and "natural" it may seem' (Morley 1980 p. 10). A reader has to know specific codes and conventions in order to be able to have any grasp of what a text is about. So it is not by any means a matter of course for viewers to know directly that in _Dallas_ they are dealing with a fictional text and not, for example, with a documentary. A great deal of cultural knowledge is necessary to be able to recognize a text as fiction. In _Dallas_ – as is the custom in all television serials – certain hints are given for this, such as the titles, presenting the actors one after another, the music, etc.

Any text employs certain rhetorical strategies to arouse the interest of the viewers, and obviously _Dallas_ succeeds in attracting the attention of millions of people with very varied social, cultural and psychological backgrounds, and maintaining their involvement in the programme. Very general and widespread structural characteristics of television programmes such as _Dallas_ contribute to this.

THE FUNCTION OF CHARACTERS

How do viewers get involved in a television serial like _Dallas_, and what does this involvement consist of? The Belgian media theoretician Jean-Marie Piemme (1975), in his book on the television serial genre, asserts that this involvement occurs because viewers are enabled to participate in the 'world' of the serial. This participation does not come of its own accord, but must be _produced_:

> If, in the serial ... participation can be brought about, this is certainly because this activity has psychological foundations, but it is also because these psychological foundations are confronted by a type of discourse allowing them to be activated. In other words, the structure of the discourse which sustains the serial produces the participation as well as the psychological attitude.
> (Piemme 1975 p. 176)

The structure of the text itself therefore plays an essential role in stimulating the involvement of viewers. More importantly still, according to Piemme, it is impossible to watch a television serial without some degree of personal involvement. 'To watch a serial', he states, 'is much more than seeing it: it is also involving oneself in it, letting oneself be held in suspense, sharing the feelings of the characters, discussing their psychological motivations and their conduct, deciding whether they are right or wrong, in other words living "their world" ' (ibid. p. 114). But what is there so particular about the textual structure of television serials that makes them able to effect such profound involvement?

In commonsense explanations of the attraction of television serials, textual structure and its effects are generally ignored. Often single elements of the story are held responsible for the popularity of a serial. Commentary in the press about *Dallas*, for example, shows a special preference for the striking role of the 'baddie' J.R. One of the letter-writers, however, mentions her preference for another *Dallas* character: 'Sue Ellen is definitely my favourite. She has a psychologically believable character. As she is, I am too to a lesser degree ("knocking one's head against a wall once too often") and I want to be (attractive). Identification, then' (Letter 17). But such identification with one character does not take place in a vacuum. One does not just recognize oneself in the ascribed characteristics of an isolated fictional character. That character occupies a specific position within the context of the narrative as a whole: only in relation to other characters in the narrative is her or his 'personality' brought out. In other words, identification with a character only becomes possible within the framework of the whole structure of the narrative.

Moreover, the involvement of the viewers cannot be described exclusively in terms of an imaginary identification with one or more characters. Several other aspects of the text contribute to this, such as the way in which the story is told, or the staging. This does not mean, however, that the characters play a subordinate role in the realization of participation. According to Piemme, in a television serial the characters even function as the pre-eminent narrative element which provides the point of impact for the involvement of viewers. But it is not so much the personalities ascribed to the characters in the story, as their formal narrative status that matters. In a fictional text like the television serial the characters are central. Through the characters the various elements of the text (situations, actions, locations, indications of time and so on) obtain a place and function in the plot. Because the viewer imagines the characters as active subjects, those elements are stripped of their arbitrariness and obtain meaning in the narrative. Furthermore, the 'lifelike' acting style ensures that the distance between actor and character is minimalized, so that the illusion is created that we are dealing with a 'real person'. The character therefore appears for the viewer as a person existing independently of the narrative situations shown in the serial. The character becomes a person appearing to lead an autonomous life outside the function of the serial; she or he becomes a person of flesh and blood, one of us. The popular press regularly plays on this illusion: the names of actors and actresses and those of the characters are often used interchangeably or merged – Larry 'J.R.' Hagman.

Being able to imagine the characters as 'real people' thus forms a necessary precondition for the involvement of viewers and is an anchor for the pleasure of *Dallas.* This theoretical assertion is reflected in the letters. When the letter-writers comment on the characters, it is almost always in the same way as we talk about people in daily life: in terms of character traits. The characters are not so much judged for their position in the *Dallas* narrative, as for *how they are.*

That at least is the case for the letter-writers who like *Dallas.* Those who dislike *Dallas* appear to keep a little more distant from the characters. Some of them even criticize their 'unreal' nature.

> One of them (his name escapes me) is always the bastard with his sneaky ideas and tricks, the other son is the goody together with his wife, J.R.'s wife (found the name now) is always 'sloshed' and going off alone to her room.
>
> (Letter 32)

> When they can't think up any more problems they send Digger after Miss Ellie and change Sue Ellen around a bit again, while J.R. (over the top) is well away with Sue Ellen's sister.
>
> (Letter 36)

> I find the characters appearing in the serial very caricatured. . . . J.R. with his crazy ideas: always the same teeth-gritting. He is also a very caricatured figure, that is obvious. Oh, how bad he is. It's really laid on thick. I find his wife the most lifelike figure in the serial. I think because she was in such a difficult position the writers had most chances with her. What I really can't stand though is the facial expression she has on. Has on, I can't call it anything else. It looks as though her head is cast in plastic.
>
> (Letter 41)

What is striking in these reactions is not only a rejection of the 'personalities' of the *Dallas* people, but also an indignation over their constructedness. Those who like *Dallas*, on the other hand, write much more sympathetically about them. In their descriptions a much greater emotional involvement emerges in the characters as people, even when they find them unsympathetic. As one fan of *Dallas* writes:

> Actually they are all a bit stupid. And oversensational. Affected and genuinely American. . . . And yet . . . the Ewings go though a lot more than I do. They seem to have a richer emotional life. Everyone knows them in Dallas. Sometimes they run into trouble, but they have a beautiful house and anything else they might want.
>
> (Letter 21)

The personalities of the characters are for some fans apparently so important that they have spontaneously included a whole list of characterizations and criticisms in their letters. They make clear to us how central the characters are in their viewing experience.

> I don't know whether it's what you want but I'll write what I myself think of the characters too.
> Miss Ellie: a nice woman.
> Jock: mean, doesn't know himself exactly what he wants, I think.
> Bobby: someone who has respect everywhere and for everyone (except for J.R. but that's understandable).
> J.R.: Just a bastard. I personally can't stand him but I must say he plays his role well.
> Pamela: a nice girl (I find her a woman of character; she can be nice, but nasty too).
> Sue Ellen: has had bad luck with J.R., but she makes up for it by being a flirt. I don't like her much. And she's too sharp-tongued.
> Lucy: she has rather too high an opinion of herself, other wise she's quite nice (she's made up too old).
> I don't know so much about the rest who take part in *Dallas* so I won't write about them. If you need what I've said here about these characters then I hope you can use it. If not tear it up.
>
> (Letter 3)

> Now I'll describe the main characters a little, perhaps that might be useful for you too. Here we go then.

Jock: a well-meaning duffer, rather surly and hard-headed, a very haughty man.

Miss Ellie: very nice, sensitive, understanding, courageous, in other words a real mother.

J.R.: very egotistic, hard as nails, keen on power, but a man with very little heart.

Sue Ellen: just *fantastic*, tremendous how that woman acts, the movements of her mouth, hands, etc. That woman really enters into her role, looking for love, snobbish, in short a real woman.

Pamela: a Barbie doll with no feelings, comes over as false and unsympathetic (a waxen robot).

Bobby: ditto.

Lucy: likeable, naïve, a real adolescent.

(Letter 12)

On the characters: Sue Ellen is definitely my favourite. She has a psychologically believable character. ... (Her friend, Dusty, really loves her and for that reason, although the cowboy business in the serial irritates me and so he does too a bit, I do like him as far as I can judge.)

Miss Ellie is all right too. She looks good, always knows the right thing to do (conciliatory and firm) within the family and her breast cancer gave her some depth.

Lucy has guts, but is a wicked little sod too.

The others don't offer much as characters, I believe. Pamela pouts, and is to sweet. I have absolutely nothing to say about Jock and Bobby; J.R. is really incredible, so mean.

(Letter 17)

What is interesting in these extracts is not so much the content of the character descriptions (although the difference in sympathies in itself is worth some attention), but the fact that 'genuineness' forms the basis for evaluation. The more 'genuine' a character appears to be, the more he or she is valued. But what is even more remarkable is that even for the severe critics 'genuineness' is the criterion by which they judge the characters. The only difference is that the severe critics tend to see them as 'unreal', whereas among the fans the opposite is the case. Characters who are 'caricatures' or 'improbable' are not esteemed, characters who are 'lifelike' or 'psychologically believable' are. Also, casually dropped remarks from fans quoted above ('I must say he plays his role well', 'she's made up too old' and 'tremendous how that woman acts, the movements of her mouth, hands, etc.') make clear that these letter-writers are very well aware that they are only dealing with fictional 'real people'. Such remarks indicate that these viewers would like that fictional element eliminated as far as possible. In their eyes actor and character should merge:

> then I find that all the actors and actresses act very well. So well even that, for example, I really find J.R. a bastard, or Sue Ellen a frustrated lady.
>
> (Letter 18)

> Because in my opinion they have chosen awfully good actors. I mean suitable for the role they are playing. The whole Ewing family is played so well that they are really human. Sometimes you get a film or a play and you think: God, if I really had to do that, I'd react quite differently. Then it seems so unreal. But usually *Dallas* could really happen, and the actors and actresses make it credible.
>
> (Letter 20)

> The people taking part in it act terribly well.
>
> (Letter 4)

The effect of 'genuineness' is then the most important thing these viewers expect. Only when they experience the fiction of the serial as 'genuine' can they feel involved in it. They have to be able to believe that the characters constructed in the text are 'real people' whom they can find pleasant or unpleasant, with whom they can feel affinity or otherwise, and so on. It could be said that such involvement is a necessary condition for the pleasure of *Dallas*.

BETWEEN REALITY AND FICTION

Let us summarize what has been said above. Many letter-writers contend that the pleasure of *Dallas* comes from the 'lifelike' character of the serial. If we subject their statements to closer analysis, then it appears that what is experienced as 'real' indicates above all a certain structure of feeling which is aroused by the programme: the tragic structure of feeling. In this many letter-writers who like *Dallas* seem to recognize themselves, and therefore experience it as 'real'.

And precisely this recognition arouses pleasure: 'I myself enjoy *Dallas* and the tears start to flow when anything tragic happens (in nearly every episode then)' (Letter 14).

The realism of *Dallas* is therefore produced by the construction of a *psychological* reality, and is not related to its (illusory) fit to an externally perceptible (social) reality. It could even be said that in *Dallas* an 'inner realism' is combined with an 'external unrealism'. The external manifestation of the fictional world of *Dallas* does also contribute to pleasure, not because of its reality value though, but because of its stylization:

> a bit of a show, expensive clothes, beautiful horses.
>
> (Letter 11)

> the serial is very relaxing to watch: beautiful people, a carefree life, restful surroundings.
>
> (Letter 19)

> I also pay attention to the clothes, make-up and hair-dos.
>
> (Letter 1)

> Then it's nice to see the clothes of the *Dallas* women.
>
> (Letter 9)

> There are a few minor details(!) which make the serial attractive, such as the splendid house and the beautiful landscape.
>
> (Letter 2)

> I started watching *Dallas* just to see the American city scene: the beautiful apartment blocks (especially the really beautiful ones you see during the titles) and the cars.
>
> (Letter 21)

It is probably the glamorous *mise-en-scène* of *Dallas* referred to in these letter extracts that is responsible for the fact that viewers are well aware they are watching a fictional world. The illusion of reality is therefore not total. Moreover, the fictional world is not uncritically accepted either. Various letter-writers show quite explicitly that they are aware that *Dallas* is a textual construction.

> You have to keep in mind the reality of life, and there's reality in it too the way it is in real life. . . . Although now and then I do find things a bit over the top.
>
> (Letter 6)

The good thing about it, I think, is that lots of things happen in it taken from life, so to speak. Such as ... Sue Ellen with her marital problems, though I do find that in the longer run that it is a bit overdone, she makes a game out of it. I think the serial writers do that deliberately, because lots of men find it terrific to watch her. And would even like to help her. Oh well. Those gallant Don Juans.

(Letter 10)

If they (the writers) write Pamela (or Bobby) out of the serial it will be over for me. The good relationship between those two is my reason for watching. But then, I still believe in 'true love'.

(Letter 8)

All these remarks suggest a distance between the 'real' and the fictional world. And precisely because the letter-writers are aware of this, it appears, they can indulge in the excessive emotions aroused in *Dallas*.

After a serial like that of poverty and misery, where spiritual character is concerned, because financially nothing is lacking, I often think with relief, now I can come back to my own world and I'm very happy in it. To have seen all those worries gives me a nice feeling – you're looking for it, you're bringing it on yourself.

(Letter 10)

Yes, it's actually ordinary daily problems that occur in it mainly and that you recognize. And then it's so marvellous that they solve them better than you've solved your own problems. Perhaps for me it's relativizing my own problems and troubles or just escaping them.

(Letter 4)

'Escape.' This word definitely sounds familiar. It is a term with a negative charge: it is generally not viewed as a sign of strength or courage if people seek refuge in a non-existent fantasy world. It is regarded as a lack of 'sense of reality'. Furthermore, the term often comes up in public discourses over mass entertainment: it is their supposed 'escapist' character that so often leads to a negative judgement of popular entertainment forms.[1] But precisely the fact that this view is so current should warn us to be cautious when we encounter it in the letters. What is the term 'escape' actually referring to, what does it mean for the letter-writers themselves? The term is misleading, because it presupposes a strict division between reality and fantasy, between 'sense of reality' and 'flight from reality'. But is it not rather the case that there is interaction between the two? One of the letter-writers formulates it as follows:

> The reason I like watching it is that it's nice to get dizzy on their problems. And you know all along that everything will turn out all right. In fact it's a flight from reality. I myself am a realistic person and I know that reality is different. Sometimes too I really enjoy having a good old cry with them. And why not? In this way my other bottled-up emotions find an outlet.
>
> (Letter 5)

'And you know all along that everything will turn out all right.' This is a key sentence, clearly defining the nature of the 'flight'. The 'flight' into a fictional fantasy world is not so much a denial of reality as playing with it. A game that enables one to place the limits of the fictional and the real under discussion, to make them fluid. And in that game an imaginary participation in the fictional world is experienced as pleasurable:

> I really like watching it, and especially Pamela and Bobby because it comes over (in the film) as real affection, although it's only a film.
>
> (Letter 6)

> I try to find more and more in the various characters. After each shocking event I try to imagine what they'll do. . . . In future there will be more sex in the serial. That is one aspect of a further illustration of the characters. But there are many more. It would be good too if the actors' thoughts were put in.
>
> (Letter 7)

> I find it's marvellous to project myself into *Dallas* and in my mind to give J.R. a good hiding when he's just pulled off yet another dirty trick, or admire Miss Ellie because she always tries to see the best in everyone or to bring it out in them. Also, I find it awfully nice to imagine myself in that world, such as: 'What would I do if Sue Ellen said that me me?' Or to see myself running around in a big city like Dallas.
>
> (Letter 13)

Thus, whatever there is to be said about the pleasure of *Dallas*, the field of tension between the fictional and the real seems to play an important part in it. Or, as a more theoretically minded letter-writer put it: 'It is easier and loads more pleasurable to dash away a tear because Ma Dallas has cancer – because she's only acting – than because of whatever annoying things are in your own life, and at least you have got rid of that tear' (Letter 22). A constant to and fro movement between identification with and distancing from the fictional world as constructed in the text therefore characterizes the involvement of the letter-writers who like *Dallas*. But one question still remains unanswered. How does Dallas succeed in producing those tears, that 'dizziness'? In other words, how does *Dallas* construct the tragic structure of feeling which is recognized by these viewers?

NOTE

1 For a fundamental critique of the way in which the concept of 'escape' is used in mass communications theory see Piemme (1978 ch. 4).

Glossary

Note: It is advisable to use this glossary for shorthand reference only. In virtually every case, the terminology used by different theorists can really be understood fully only within the shifting contexts of the whole of their work. Thus, after most short definitions in this glossary there appears the name of the writer with whom the term is associated in this volume.

accent Socially specific intonation, emphasis or stress on an utterance which can adjust its bearing from one situation to another (Vološinov).

algorithm Any systematic mathematical procedure but, in post-structuralism, Saussure's diagram of signified over signifier (Sd/Sr or s/s) that Lacan inverts (Lacan).

argument Part of the sign triad including **rheme** and **dicent**. It is the kind of sign which partakes of logic or reasoning (Peirce).

Berkeley, George (1685–1753) Irish-born British philosopher.

Bloomfield, Leonard (1887–1949) American linguist.

Chomsky, Noam (b. 1928) American linguist.

code This term sometimes refers to the kind of notation used to transmit any message (e.g. letters, numbers, heiroglyphics); sometimes it refers to the master system which generates a potentially infinite number of messages. Because the term is used in so many diverse ways (even within an individual theorist's *oeuvre*), it is advisable to refer only to its context of use on each occasion.

concretization Derived from Roman Ingarden, this term is used to describe the process by which the reader fills out the gaps in a text. The reader concretizes a text such as 'The man' by providing attributes such as hair colour, height, skin colour, age, etc. (Iser). See also **determinacy** and **indeterminacy**.

connotation Derived from Hjelmslev, the 'second-order meaning', or supplementing of a sign by associations from 'culture' (Barthes). See also **denotation**.

constative statement, constative Those individual utterances, the sole purpose of which seems to be to describe (Austin). See also **performative statement, locution, illocution, perlocution, empty speech** and **full speech**.

content Term introduced by Hjelmslev. The 'content plane' is the domain of Saussure's 'signified' (Barthes). See also **expression**.

deixis, deictic A linguistic phenomenon or category which refers only to context rather than any other general semantic features.

denotation Derived from Hjelmslev, the order of meaning in a sign where an object is indicated (theoretically) irrespective of cultural associations (Barthes). See also **connotation**.

determinacy The presented aspects of texts which do not require the extensive gap-filling action of **concretization** by readers (Iser).

diachrony (**diachronic**) Evolution through time. A diachronic linguistics is one which studies changes in languages (Saussure). See also **synchrony**.

diacritical An adjective to describe the difference from other signs that gives an individual sign **value** (Saussure).

dicent Sign which forms a triad with **rheme** and **argument**. This sign relates to its **interpretant** as a logical fact (Peirce).

Différance The phenomenon whereby 'meaning' in a signifying chain takes place not only because it *differs from*, but also because it *defers to*, other parts of the chain (Derrida).

discourse Like **code**, this term has numerous possible meanings within communication theory. In general, it is used in this volume as a synonym for 'instance(s) of parole'. Because the term is used in so many diverse ways (even within an individual theorist's *oeuvre*), it is advisable to refer only to its context of use on each occasion. (See MacCabe 1979 and Macdonell 1986).

empty speech The kind of speech which occurs most frequently in everyday discourse but also in the preliminary stages of the psychoanalytic situation. It is a speech which describes and operates with a naïve faith in its ability to refer. It seems to correspond to Austin's **constative** (Lacan; Borch-Jacobsen).

expression Term introduced by Hjelmslev. The 'expression' plane is the domain of Saussure's 'signifier' (Barthes).

field The range and the type of social activity in which speech participants are engaged (Halliday).

field/reverse field see **shot/reverse shot**

firstness The realm of pure feeling, untrammelled by any relations whatsoever (Peirce).

full speech The kind of speech which might occur in the later stages of the psychoanalytic situation. When analysands begin to recognize that the power of their speech to refer is illusory and that speech is a non-referential performance, they are partaking of 'full speech'.

This seems to correspond to Austin's **performative** (Lacan; Borch-Jacobsen).

Gram   see *différance*

ground   There are two general schools of thought in Peirce studies with regard to this term. For some, 'ground' represents the general grounds or habits of thought within which signs can be conceived to stand for something else; for others, 'ground' is the more specific respects in which a sign can stand for some other thing – by resemblance, physical connection or convention (Peirce).

Hegel, G. W. F. (1770–1831)   German philosopher.

icon   A sign which relates to its **object** by some character in itself or resemblance (Peirce).

ideational   This function represents the speaker's potential to encode the world around him/her, language and things that are already encoded. It is a part of **semantics** (Halliday; see also Kress and van Leeuwen). See also **linguistic system, interpersonal** and **textual**.

illocution, illocutionary   An utterance that performs or executes an act (Austin). See also **performative statement, constative statement, locution, perlocution, empty speech** and **full speech**.

indeterminacy   The non-presented features of texts which allow for interpretation and **concretization** by the reader (Iser).

index   A sign which relates to its **object** by a causal physical connection (Peirce).

interpersonal   This is the function in which the speaker *does* something as e.g. questioner/informer, or as the inhabitant of other communicative roles associated with the **situation** or language in general. It is part of **semantics** (Halliday). See also **linguistic system, ideational** and **textual**.

interpretant   A relation in a triad with **representamen** (sign) and **object**. It is often described as a sign in the mind but this is only one possible manifestation. It is, more accurately, the 'further sign' ('significate effect') that results from the link between representamen and object. If a photographer of a group picture indicates that the person at the front must move back and the subsequent movement causes all those behind that person to topple like dominoes, this is analogous to the production of interpretants. Interpretant, therefore, should in no way be equated with interpreter (Peirce).

Kant, Immanuel (1724–1804)   German philosopher.

langage   The general phenomenon of speech (Saussure).

langue   Language as a *system* of differences (Saussure).

legisign   The kind of **representamen** that has the capacity to embody a general law; only legisigns can give rise to symbols (Peirce).

linguistic system   The organization of language but particularly that area which is concerned with **semantics** (Halliday). See also **ideational, interpersonal** and **textual**.

locution, locutionary An utterance or part of an utterance which 'describes'. It will, at the same time, have an illocutionary and perlocutionary force (Austin). See also **constative statement, performative statement, illocution, perlocution, empty speech** and **full speech**.

Logos, **logocentric** Logos refers to the supposed rational power of the word to explain the world; logocentric designates any tendency which depends upon such a conception (Derrida).

meaning Derived from Grice, this refers to the 'intention' of a speaker to have some 'effect' on his or her listener(s). But this must also be combined with proper conventions which can realize the intended meaning (Searle).

metaphysics This term refers to that branch of philosophy which is concerned with first principles. These principles include the theory of *being* (ontology) and the theory of *knowledge* (epistemology). As such, then, metaphysics embraces the theory of signification.

mise-en-scène The literal translation of this film theory term is 'staging an event'. It refers to all those things that appear in front of the camera to be filmed and how they are specially arranged for the camera.

mode The channel of communication (e.g. speech or writing, as well as other choices) adopted in a specific **situation** (Halliday).

morpheme The smallest syntactic unit.

object This is one term in a triad with **interpretant** and **representamen**. It is that to which the representamen refers and is generally understood to have two existences. Firstly, the Immediate Object is a concept engendered by the representamen and corresponds to Saussure's 'signified'. Secondly, the Dynamic Object exists without the intervention of the representamen; the representamen can only hint at it and eventually bring it to the attention of the mind (Peirce).

paradigm, paradigmatic The relationship of substitution between units in a syntagm (Saussure).

parole An individual act of speech (Saussure).

performative statement, performative Those utterances which, palpably, *perform* an action whilst, as an apparent adjunct, describing. The sentence "I name this ship Queen Elizabeth", in the right circumstances, is an example of a performative (Austin). See also **constative statement, locution, illocution, perlocution, empty speech** and **full speech**.

perlocution, perlocutionary The 'effect' of an utterance or part of an utterance on a listener. A constative statement such as "I've had sixteen double whiskies tonight", may produce in listeners the perlocutions of 'disgust', 'fear', 'contempt', 'camaraderie'; etc. (Austin). See also **constative statement, performative statement, locution, illocution, empty speech** and **full speech**.

Phone, **phonic, phonologism** *Phone* refers specifically to sound (e.g. the spoken sign as opposed to the written one); any tendency which privileges sound over writing (or other forms of signification) falls prey to phonologism (Derrida).

positivism   Philosophical tradition whose roots are usually found in seven-teenth- and eighteenth-century British empiricism. Its main postulate is that only that which is available to observation can provide the first terms for any inquiry into the world.

pragmaticism   A term introduced by Peirce in the 1900s to distinguish his philosophical position from that of contemporary **pragmatism** in the United States.

Pragmatism   Philosophical position based on the theory of 'truth'. Associated with American philosophers, John Dewey (1859–1952), William James (1842–1910) and, initially, Peirce.

pragmatics   All those conditions, including the positions of language users, which contribute to the shaping of utterances. Not to be confused with **pragmatism** or **pragmaticism**.

propositions   The common 'content' (objects, predicates) which might occur in utterances with different meanings (Searle).

qualisign   A **representamen** that is made up of a quality (Peirce)

referee   The item to which reference is made in an instance of *parole*/discourse. The 'I' in an instance of parole is a referee because it is a linguistic category with no fixed definition or general signified (Benveniste).

referent   Derived from Ogden and Richards (1985; originally 1923), this term is commonly used in communication theory to designate the thing in the real world to which signs refer. This consists of both available things (the real chair one is sitting on while one produces the sign) and unavailable things (e.g. Napoleon; "in which case there may be a long list of sign-situations appearing in between the act and its referent: word – historian – contemporary record – eye-witness" [Ogden and Richards 1985 p. 11]). Because of the philosophical problems involved, one needs to be careful when invoking the concept of the referent (cf. **object**).

register (text variety)   Often defined as the kind of speech appropriate to a particular occupation, Halliday understands register generally as 'the meaning potential that is accessible in a given social context' (Halliday).

representamen/sign   This is always to be conceived as part of the triad which includes **object** and **interpretant**. The representamen is a First which does not exist independently but is always standing for some-thing else (Peirce).

rheme   A sign which has a qualitative possibility for its **interpretant** (Peirce).

rules   Searle identifies two very general kinds that are applicable to speech-act theory. The first are those that regulate a pre-existing activity (e.g. etiquette – to regulate interpersonal relationships). The second are constitutive rules (e.g. the rules of football *provide the grounds* for the game to take place). Illocutionary acts are found to be bound to constitutive rules (Searle).

Sapir, Edward (1884–1939) American linguist. Along with his pupil, **Whorf**, he put forth the hypothesis that language determines how we think and that the distinctions which are allowed for in one language do not appear in another.

secondness The realm of the most fundamental relations and oppositions (Peirce).

semantic(s) Meaning; the study of how linguistic signs denote.

'shifter' (Jakobson) see **deixis**.

shot/countershot see **shot/reverse shot**

shot/reverse shot (shot/countershot; field/reverse field) In audio-visual narration, the camera's alternating placement in the representation of two persons/objects. A common example is two characters having a conversation in a film: the camera will show a frontal view of one person speaking; when the other person speaks the shot will change and this time he or she will be shown from the front. Sometimes, the 'frontal' shot is not direct: it may be to one side or contain part of the 'non-frontal' interlocutor's body (e.g. an 'over the shoulder shot'). The 'constructedness' of the shot/reverse shot dynamic is nowhere more blatant than in TV interviews of politicians where 'the nods' of assent from the interlocutor are usually shot *after* the politician has departed and then, subsequently, edited into the broadcast interview.

signified The mental concept which is engendered by the material substance (signifier) of a sign (Saussure).

signifier The material substance that makes up one part of a sign; e.g. throat vibrations in a verbal sign, ink on paper in a written sign (Saussure).

sinsign A sign where something existent in the world makes up the **representamen** (Peirce).

situation The 'environment in which the text comes to life' (Halliday). See **field**, **tenor** and **mode**.

social structure This includes, in general terms, the general social context in which a **situation** might occur; the patterns of familial relationships in which speakers have been embedded; and class or caste relationships (Halliday).

suture Psychoanalytic term derived from Miller which was imported into film theory in the 1970s. It refers to the way in which subjects attempt to efface/lessen/eradicate the split between themselves and language. Spectatorship becomes a part of this process because 'mainstream' narrative film contains mechanisms which are analogous to the subject–language dilemma and 'solve' it in an imaginary way (Heath).

symbol A sign which relates to its **object** as a result of convention or habit – this conventional relation is maintained by the **interpretant** (Peirce).

synchrony (synchronic)   A static cross-section of a current state of affairs. The study of language as a functioning system (Saussure). See also **diachrony**.

syntagm, syntagmatic   A combination of units with an underlying logic (Saussure). See also **paradigm**.

syntax, syntactic   The rules (and study) of word combinations or sentence structure.

tenor   The set of role relationships among participants in a speech **situation** (Halliday).

text   Actualized meaning potential. The content of a linguistic interaction within an operational context (Halliday; cf. **theme**). Note: 'text' – not Halliday's usage of the term – is also the general designation in communication theory for *any* complex signification either linguistic or audio-visual (conversations, radio programmes, novels, painting, comics, films; etc.).

textual   The function which represents the speaker's ability to produce a **text**. It is the function of introducing a text into a given **situation** and is part of the general area of **semantics** (Halliday). See also **linguistic system**, **ideational** and **interpersonal**.

theme   The socially accented significance of a whole utterance according to the historical situation (Vološinov; cf. **text**).

thirdness   The realm of rules and generality (Peirce).

trace   In consonance with the Saussurean concept of **value**, trace refers to the way in which the play of differences in *langue*, dictates that there is never one stable, present identity for a participant in this play. There are only ever the traces of the other participants' differences (Derrida).

value   As opposed to having an individual identity, a sign gains its ability to signify as a result of its existence as one member in a system of differences between signs (Saussure).

Whorf, Benjamin Lee (1897–1941)   American linguist. See also **Sapir**.

Bibliography

Allen, R. C. (1983) 'On reading soaps: a primer', in E. A. Kaplan, (ed.) *Regarding Television*, Los Angeles: American Film Institute.

Allen, R. C. (1987) 'Reader-oriented criticism and television', in R. C. Allen (ed.) *Channels of Discourse*, London: Routledge.

Andrejčin, L. (1938) *Kategorie znaczniowe konjugacji bulgarskiej*, Cracow.

Ang, I. (1984) *Watching Dallas: Soap Opera and the Melodramatic Imagination*, London: Methuen.

Ang, I. (1991) *Desperately Seeking the Audience*, London: Routledge.

Ang, I. (1996) *Living Room Wars: Rethinking Media Audiences for a Postmodern World*, London: Routledge.

Appadurai, A. (1990) 'Disjuncture and difference in the global cultural economy', in M. Featherstone (ed.) *Global Culture: Nationalism, Globalization and Modernity*, London, Newbury Park, CA and New Delhi: Sage.

Arrivé, M. (1992) *Linguistics and Psychoanalysis: Freud, Saussure, Hjelmslev, Lacan and Others*, trans. J. Leader, Amsterdam: John Benjamins.

Austin, J. L. (1980) *How to Do Things with Words*, Oxford: Oxford University Press.

Baker, C. D. and Freebody, P. (1989) *Children's First Schoolbooks: Introductions to the Culture of Literacy*, Oxford: Blackwell.

Baker, C. D. and Luke, A. (eds) (1991) *Towards a Critical Sociology of Reading Pedagogy*, Amsterdam: John Benjamins.

Bakhtin, M. (1971) 'Discourse typology in prose', in L. Matejka and K. Pomorska (eds) *Readings in Russian Poetics*, Boston: Massachusetts Institute of Technology Press.

Bakhtin, M. (1973) *Problems of Dostoevsky's Poetics*, trans. R. W. Rotsel, New York: Ardis.

Bakhtin, M. (1984) *Rabelais and his World*, Bloomington: Indiana University Press.

Barthes, R. (1970) 'L'ancienne rhétorique' *Communications*, 16.

Barthes, R. (1973a) *Mythologies*, London: Paladin.

Barthes, R. (1973b) *Elements of Semiology*, New York: Hill & Wang.

Barthes, R. (1974) *S/Z*, Oxford: Blackwell.

Barthes, R. (1977) *Image-Music-Text*, Glasgow: Fontana.

Belsey, C. (1980) *Critical Practice*, London: Methuen.

Beniger, J. R. (1988) 'Information and communication: the new convergence', *Communication Research* 15 (2) 198–218.

Bennett, T. (1979) *Formalism and Marxism*, London: Methuen.

Benveniste, É. (1939a) 'The nature of the linguistic sign', *Problems* 45.

Benveniste, É. (1939b) 'The levels of linguistic analysis', *Problems* 302.

Benveniste, É. (1956) 'The nature of pronouns', *Problems*.

Benveniste, É. (1971) *Problems in General Linguistics*, trans. M. E. Meek, Coral Gables: University of Miami Press.

Benvenuto, B. and Kennedy, R. (1986) *The Works of Jacques Lacan: An Introduction*, London: Free Association.

Berger, P. L. and Luckmann, T. (1966) *The Social Construction of Reality: A Treatise in the Sociology of Knowledge*, Harmondsworth: Penguin.

Bernstein, B. (1971) *Class, Codes and Control* vol. 1, London: Routledge & Kegan Paul.

Bernstein, B. (ed.) (1973) *Class, Codes and Control* vol. 2, London: Routledge & Kegan Paul.

Bernstein, B. (1975) *Class, Codes and Control* vol. 3, London: Routledge & Kegan Paul.

Blakemore, D. (1992) *Understanding Utterances: An Introduction to Pragmatics*, Oxford: Blackwell.

Blanchot, M. (1947) 'Le règne animal de l'espirt', *Critique* 18.

Blanchot, M. (1949) *La Part du feu*, Paris: Gallimard.

Blanchot, M. (1981) 'La littérature et le droit à la mort', *De Kafka à Kafka*, Paris: Gallimard.

Bloomfield, L. (1933) *Language*, New York: Holt, Rinehart & Winston.

Bloomfield, L. (1946) 'Algonquian', in *Linguistic Structures of Native America*, New York: Viking Fund Publications in Anthropology.

Boas, F. (1947) *Kwakiutl Grammar*, Philadelphia, PA: American Philosophical Society.

Bogoraz, V. (1922) 'Chukchee', in *Handbook of Native American Indian Languages II*, 639–903.

Booth, W. C. (1978) *A Rhetoric of Irony*, Chicago: Chicago University Press.

Borch-Jacobsen, M. (1991) *Lacan the Absolute Master*, Stanford, CA: Stanford University Press.

Boswell, J. (1934) *Life of Johnson*, ed. G. B. Hill, revised and enlarged edn by L. F. Powell, Oxford: Oxford University Press.

Bourdieu, P. (1977) 'The economics of linguistic exchanges', *Social Sciences Information*, 16 645–668.

Bourdieu, P. and Passeron, J. C. (1977) *Reproduction in Education, Society and Culture*, trans. R. Nice, London: Sage.

Branigan, E. (1992) *Narrative Comprehension and Film*, London: Routledge.

Brecht, B. (1964) *Brecht on Theatre: The Development of an Aesthetic*, London: Methuen.

Brent, J. (1993) *Charles Sanders Peirce: A Life*, Bloomington: Indiana University Press.

Britton, A. (1979) 'The ideology of *Screen*', *Movie*, 26 2–28.

Brotman, B. (1980) 'Ah, romance! Harlequin has an affair for its readers', *Chicago Tribune* (2 June) B1.

Brunsdon, C. and Morley, D. (1978) *Everyday Television:* Nationwide, London: British Film Institute.

Bühler, K. (1934) *Sprach theorie*, Jena.

Burks, A. W. (1949) 'Icon, index, and symbol', *Philosophy and Phenomenological Research* 9 673–689.

Carnap, R. (1937) *Logical Syntax of Language*, New York: Harcourt Brace.

Chomsky, N. (1957) *Syntactic Structures*, The Hague: Mouton.

Cicourel, A. V.(1969) 'Generative semantics and the structure of social inter-action', in *International Days of Sociolinguistics*.

Clark, K. and Holquist, M. (1984) *Mikhail Bakhtin*, Cambridge, MA: Belknap Press.

Clavell, J. (1981) *Noble House*, London: Coronet.

Cobley, P. (1994) 'Throwing out the baby: populism and active audience theory', *Media, Culture and Society* 16 677–687.

Cobley, P. (forthcoming) *Semiotics for Beginners*, Cambridge: Icon Books.

Cohan, S. and Shires, L. M. (1988) *Telling Stories: A Theoretical Analysis of Narrative Fiction*, London: Routledge.

Colapietro, V. M. (1989) *Peirce's Approach to the Self: A Semiotic Perspective on Human Subjectivity*, Albany: SUNY Press.

Conklin, H. C. (1955) 'Hanunóo color categories', *Southwestern Journal of Anthropology* II 339–344.

Coward, R. and Ellis, J. (1977) *Language and Materialism: Developments in Semiology and the Theory of the Subject*, London: Routledge & Kegan Paul.

Culler, J. (1975) *Structuralist Poetics: Structuralism, Linguistics and the Study of Literature*, London: Routledge & Kegan Paul.

Culler, J. (1976) *Saussure*, Glasgow: Fontana.

Culler, J. (1981) *The Pursuit of Signs: Semiotics, Literature, Deconstruction*, London: Routledge & Kegan Paul.

Davis, N. Z. (1987) *Society and Culture in Early Modern France*, 2nd edn., Cambridge: Polity Press.

de Castell, S. C. and Luke, A. (1986) 'Models of literacy in North American schools: social and historical conditions and consequences', in S. C. de Castell, A. Luke and K. Egan (eds) *Literacy, Society and Schooling*, Cambridge: Cambridge University Press.

de Lauretis, T. (1984) *Alice Doesn't: Feminism, Semiotics, Cinema*, London: Macmillan.

Dentith, S. (ed.) (1995) *Bakhtinian Thought: An Introductory Reader*, London: Routledge.

Derrida, J. (1967) *De la grammatologie*, Paris: Editions de Minuit.

Derrida, J. (1972) 'Structure, sign and play in the discourse of the human sciences', in R. Macksey and E. Donato (eds) *The Structuralist Controversy*, Baltimore, MD and London: Johns Hopkins University Press.

Derrida, J. (1973) *Speech and Phenomena*, Evanston, IL: Northwestern University Press.

Derrida, J. (1976) *Of Grammatology*, Baltimore, MD and London: Johns Hopkins University Press.

Derrida, J. (1977) 'Limited, Inc. abc', *Glyph*, 2 162–254.

Derrida, J. (1982) *Margins of Philosophy*, Brighton: Harvester.

Derrida, J. (1987) *The Post Card: From Socrates to Freud and Beyond*, trans. A. Bass, Chicago: University of Chicago Press.

Derrida, J. (1991) 'Talking Liberties', Channel 4 television.

Descombes, V. (1983) *Grammaire d'objets en tous genres*, Paris: Minuit.

Dews, P. (1987) *Logics of Disintegration: Post-Structuralist Thought and the Claims of Critical Theory*, London: Verso.

Doane, M. A. (1987) *The Desire to Desire: The Woman's Film of the 1940s*, London: Macmillan.

Donald, J. (1990) 'Review of Fiske, *Television Culture*, and Allen, *Channels of Discourse*,' *Screen*, 31 (3) 113–119.

Dostoevskij, F. M. (1906) *Polnoe sobranie sočinenij F. M. Dostoevskogo* [The Complete Works of F. M. Dostoevskij] vol. IX.

Douglas, M. (1968) 'The social control of cognition', *Man* 3 361–376.

Douglas, M. (1972) 'Speech, class and Basil Bernstein', *The Listener* 2241 (9 March).

Dunant, S. (ed.) (1994) *The War of the Words: The Political Correctness Debate*, London: Virago.

Dundes, D. (1968) 'Introduction', in V. Propp *Morphology of the Folktale*, Austin: University of Texas Press.

During, S. (1993) 'Introduction', in During (ed.) *The Cultural Studies Reader*, London: Routledge.

Dyer, R. (1979) *Stars*, London: British Film Institute.

Eagleton, T. (1983) *Literary Theory: An Introduction*, Oxford: Blackwell.

Easthope, A. (1982) 'The Trajectory of *Screen*, 1971–1979', in F. Barker, P. Hulme, M. Iversen and D. Loxley (eds) *The Politics of Theory*, Colchester: University of Essex.

Easthope, A. (1983) *Poetry as Discourse*, London: Methuen.

Easthope, A. (1988) *British Post-Structuralism Since 1968*, London: Routledge.

Easthope, A. (1991) *Literary into Cultural Studies*, London: Routledge.

Eco, U. (1972) 'Towards a semiotic inquiry into the television message', *Working Papers in Cultural Studies* 2.

Eco, U. (1976) *A Theory of Semiotics*, Bloomington: Indiana University Press.

Eco, U. (1979) *The Role of the Reader: Explorations in the Semiotics of Texts*, Bloomington and London: Indiana University Press.

Eco, U. (1986) *Travels in Hyper-reality*, London: Picador.

Ehrlich, V. (1990) *Russian Formalism: History and Doctrine*, The Hague: Mouton.

Ellis, J. M. (1989) *Against Deconstruction*, Princeton, NJ: Princeton University Press.

Emmanuel, S. (1992) 'Ien Ang, *Watching Dallas*', in M. Barker, and A. Beezer, (eds) *Reading into Cultural Studies*, London: Routledge.

Fairclough, N. (1989) *Language and Power*, Harlow: Longman.

Fairclough, N. (1992) *Discourse and Social Change*, Oxford: Polity.

Faust, B. (1980) *Women, Sex and Pornography: A Controversial and Unique Study*, New York: Macmillan.

Ferguson, C. A. (1971) *Language Structure and Language Use*, Stanford, CA: Stanford University Press.

Firth, J. R. (1957) *Papers in Linguistics 1934–1951*, London: Oxford University Press.

Fish, S. (1980) *Is There a Text in this Class? The Authority of Interpretive Communities*, Cambridge, MA: Harvard University Press.

Fish, S. (1981) 'Why no one's afraid of Wolfgang Iser', *Diacritics* 11 (March) 2–13.

Fish, S. (1994) *There's No Such Thing as Free Speech: And It's a Good Thing, Too*, New York: Oxford University Press.

Fishman, J. A. (1968) 'The sociology of language', in J. A. Fishman (ed.) *Readings in the Sociology of Language*, The Hague: Mouton.

Fiske, J. (1990) *Television Culture*, London: Routledge.

Fiske, J. (1991) *Introduction to Communication Studies*, 2nd edn, London: Routledge.

Forrester, J. (1990) *The Seductions of Psychoanalysis: Freud, Lacan and Derrida*, Cambridge: Cambridge University Press.

Foucault, M. (1977) *Language, Counter-memory, Practice*, Oxford: Blackwell.

Foucault, M. (1979) *Discipline and Punish*, New York: Harper.

Foucault, M. (1988) *Technologies of the Self*, London: Tavistock.

Freud, S. (1962) *Two Short Accounts of Psychoanalysis*, Harmondsworth: Penguin.

Freund, E. (1987) *The Return of the Reader: Reader–Response Criticism*, London: Methuen.

Frow, J. (1984) 'Spectatorship', *Australian Journal of Communication* 5/6 21–38.

Frye, N. (1971) *The Anatomy of Criticism*, Princeton, NJ: Princeton University Press.

Galan, F. W. (1985) *Historic Structures: The Prague School Project, 1928–1946*, Austin: University of Texas Press.

Gallie, W. B. (1952) *Peirce and Pragmatism*, Harmondsworth: Penguin.

Gardiner, A. H. (1940) *The Theory of Proper Names*, London: Oxford University Press.

Gibson, J. (1968) *The Senses Considered as Perceptual Systems*, London: Allen & Unwin.

Godel, R. (1957) *Les Sources manuscrites du cours de linguistique générale de F. de Saussure*, Geneva and Paris: Droz et Minard.

Goody, J. (1988) *The Interface between the Written and the Oral*, Cambridge: Cambridge University Press.

Graff, H. J. (ed.) (1981) *Literacy and Social Development in the West*, Cambridge: Cambridge University Press.

Gray, A. (1987) 'Reading the audience', *Screen* 28(3) 24–35.

Green, B. (1987) 'Gender, genre and writing pedagogy', in I. Reid, (ed.) *The Place of Genre in Learning: Current Debates*, Victoria: Centre for Studies in Literary Education, Deakin University.

Greenfield, C. (1984) 'Theories of the subject: rewritings and contestations', *Australian Journal of Communication* 5/6 39–51.

Gregory, M. (1967) 'Aspects of varieties differentiation', *Journal of Linguistics* 3.

Grice, H. P. (1968) 'Uterrer's meaning, sentence meaning and word meaning', *Foundations of Language* 4 225–242.

Grice, H. P. (1975) 'Logic and conversation', in P. Cole, and J. Morgan (eds) *Syntax and Semantics 3: Speech Acts*, New York: Academic Press.

Grice, P. (1957) 'Meaning', *Philosophical Review* July 377–388.

Grosz, E. (1990) *Jacques Lacan: A Feminist Introduction*, London: Routledge.

Gumperz, J. J. (1971) *Language in Social Groups*, Stanford, CA: Stanford University Press.

Haas, M. (1940) *Tunica*, New York: J. J. Augustin.

Hall, S. (1981) 'Encoding/decoding', in S. Hall, D. Hobson, A. Lowe and P. Willis (eds) *Culture, Media, Language*, London: Hutchinson .

Halliday, M. A. K. (1967) *Grammar, Society and the Noun*, London: H. K. Lewis.

Halliday, M. A. K. (1969) 'Functional diversity in language, as seen from a consideration of modality and mood in English', *Foundations of Language* 6.

Halliday, M. A. K. (1973) *Explorations in the Function of Language*, London: Edward Arnold.

Halliday, M. A. K. (1975) *Learning How to Mean: Explorations in the Development of Language*, London: Edward Arnold.

Halliday, M. A. K. (1976) *System and Function in Language*, ed. G. Kress, Oxford: Oxford University Press.

Halliday, M. A. K. (1978) *Language as Social Semiotic*, London: Edward Arnold.

Halliday, M. A. K. (1985) *Introduction to Functional Grammar*, London: Edward Arnold.

Halliday, M. A. K., McIntosh, A. and Strevens, P. (1964) *The Linguistic Sciences and Language Teaching*, London: Longman.

Halpern, A. M. (1946) 'Yuma', in H. Hoijer, (ed.) *Linguistic Structures of Native America*, New York: Viking Fund Publications in Anthropology.

Harland, R. (1987) *Superstructuralism: The Philosophy of Structuralism and Post-Structuralism*, London: Methuen.

Harland, R. (1993) *Beyond Superstructuralism: The Syntagmatic Side of Language*, London: Routledge.

Harris, R. (1987) *Reading Saussure: A Critical Commentary on the*, Cours de linguistique générale, London: Duckworth.

Hartley, J. (1988) *Understanding News*, London: Routledge.

Hasan, R. (1973) 'Code, register and social dialect', in B. Bernstein (ed.) *Class, Codes and Control* vol. 2, London: Routledge & Kegan Paul.

Hasan, R. (1987) 'Directions from structuralism', in N. Fabb, D. Attridge, A. Durant and C. MacCabe (eds) *The Linguistics of Writing: Arguments Between Language and Literature*, Manchester: Manchester University Press.

Hawkes, T. (1977) *Structuralism and Semiotics*, London: Methuen.

Heath, S. (1981) *Questions of Cinema*, London: Macmillan.

Heath, S. B. (1981) 'Towards an ethnohistory of writing in American education', in M. F. Whitman (ed.) *Variation in Writing: Functional and Linguistic-Cultural Differences*, Hillsdale, NJ: Erlbaum.

Heath, S. B. (1982) 'What no bedtime story means: narrative skills at home and school' *Language in Society*, 11 49–76.

Hebdige, D. (1979) *Subculture: The Meaning of Style*, London: Methuen.

Hill, T. (1958) 'Institutional linguistics', *Orbis* 7.

Hirsch, E. D. (1967) *Validity in Interpretation*, New Haven, CT: Yale University Press.

Hjelmslev, L. (1961) *Prolegomena to a Theory of Language*, Madison: University of Wisconsin Press.

Hodge, R. (1988) 'Halliday and the stylistics of creativity' in D. Birch, and M. O'Toole, (eds) *Functions of Style*, London: Pinter.

Hodge, R. and Kress, G. R. (1988) *Social Semiotics*, Oxford: Blackwell.

Holdaway, D. (1976) *Foundations of Literacy*, Sydney: Ashton-Scholastic.

Holdcroft, D. (1991) *Saussure: Signs, Systems and Arbitrariness*, Cambridge: Cambridge University Press.

Holquist, M. (1990) *Dialogism: Bakhtin and his World*, London: Routledge.

Holub, R. C. (1984) *Reception Theory: A Critical Introduction*, London: Methuen.

Hoopes, J. (ed.) (1991) *Peirce on Signs: Writings on Semiotic*, Chapel Hill, NC and London: University of North Carolina Press.

Huddleston, R. (1969) 'Some observations on tense and deixis', *Language*, 45 777–806.

Hughes, R. (1994) *Culture of Complaint: The Fraying of America*, London: Harvill.

Hunter, I. (1989) *Culture and Government: The Emergence of Literary Education*, London: Macmillan.

Husserl, E. (1913) *Logische untersuchungen*, 2nd edn, [Logical Investigations], New York: Humanities Press.

Husserl, E. (1931) *Ideas*, trans. W. R. Boyce, New York: Collier.

Husserl, E. (1970) *Logical Investigations* vols I and II, London: Routledge & Kegan Paul.

Iser, W. (1974) *The Implied Reader: Patterns of Communication in Prose Fiction from Bunyan to Beckett*, Baltimore, MD and London: Johns Hopkins University Press.

Iser, W. (1978) *The Act of Reading: A Theory of Aesthetic Response*, Baltimore, MD and London: Johns Hopkins University Press.

Iser, W. (1980a) 'The reading process', in J. P. Tompkins (ed.) *Reader–Response Criticism: From Formalism to Post-Structuralism*, Baltimore, MD and London: Johns Hopkins University Press.

Iser, W. (1980b) 'Interaction between text and reader', in S. R. Suleiman and I. Crossman (eds) *The Reader in the Text: Essays on Audience and Interpretation*, Princeton, NJ: Princeton University Press.

Iser, W. (1981) 'Talk like whales', *Diacritics* 11 (September) 82–87.

Iser, W. (1989) *Prospecting: From Reader Response to Literary Anthropology*, Baltimore, MD and London: Johns Hopkins University Press.

Itten, J. (1961) *Kunst der Farbe*, Ravensburg: Otto Mair.

Jakobson, R. (1942) 'The Paleosiberian languages', *American Anthropologist* 44 602–620.

Jakobson, R. (1953) 'Results of the Conference of Anthropologists and Linguists', *International Journal of American Linguists* 19(2) supplement.

Jakobson, R. (1960) 'Closing statement: linguistics and poetics', in T.A. Sebeok (ed.) *Style in Language*, Cambridge, MA: Harvard University Press.

Jakobson, R. (1963) *Essais de linguistique générale*, Paris: Editions de Minuit.

Jakobson, R. and Halle, M. (1957) *Fundamentals of Language*, The Hague: Mouton.

Jameson, F. (1972) *The Prison-House of Language: A Critical Account of Structuralism and Russian Formalism*, Princeton, NJ: Princeton University Press.

Jauss, H. R. (1974) 'Levels of identification of hero and audience', *New Literary History*, 5 283–317.

Jauss, H. R. (1982) *Toward an Aesthetic of Reception*, Minneapolis: University of Minnesota Press.

Jay, M. (1994) *Downcast Eyes: The Denigration of Vision in Twentieth Century French Thought*, Berkeley: University of California Press.

Jensen, K. B. (1995) *The Social Semiotics of Mass Communication*, London and New Delhi: Sage.

Jensen, M. (1980) 'Women and romantic fiction: a case study of Harlequin

Enterprises, romances, and readers', unpublished Ph.D dissertation, McMaster University, Hamilton, Ontario.

Jespersen, O. (1922) *Language: Its Nature, Development, and Origin*, London: Allen & Unwin.

Katz, D. and Katz, R. (1960) *Handbuch der Psychologie* vol. 2, Basel: Schwabe.

Kojève, A. (1947) *Introduction à la lecture de Hegel*, Paris: Gallimard.

Kojève, A. (1969) *Introduction to the Reading of Hegel*, partial trans. J. H. Nichols jr, New York and London: Basic Books.

Krejnovič, E. A. (1934) 'Nivxskij (giljackij) jazyk', in *Jazyki i pis 'mennost' naradov Severa* Pt 3, Leningrad: Institut Naradov Severa.

Kress, G. R. (1985) *Linguistic Processes in Sociocultural Practice*, Geelong: Deakin University.

Kress, G. R. (1994) Learning to Write, 2nd edn, London: Routledge

Kress, G. R. (1996) 'Writing and learning to write' in D. Olson and N. Torrance (eds) *Handbook of New Developments in Education*, Oxford: Blackwell.

Kress, G. R. and Knapp, P. (1992) 'Genre in a social theory of language', *English in Education* (June) 4–15.

Kress, G. R. and van Leeuwen, T. (1992a) 'Trampling all over our unspoiled spot', *Southern Review* 25 (1) 27–38.

Kress, G. R. and van Leeuwen, T. (1992b) 'Structures of visual representation', *Journal of Literary Semantics* XXI (2) 91–117 .

Kroker, A. and Cook, D. (1986) *The Postmodern Scene: Excremental Culture and Hyper-Aesthetics*, New York: St Martins.

Labov, W. (1972) 'The logic of nonstandard English', in P. P. Giglioli (ed.) *Language and Social Context*, Harmondsworth: Penguin.

Lacan, J. (1961) 'L'identification', unpublished MS, 20 December.

Lacan, J. (1970) 'Radiophonie', *Scilicet* 2/3.

Lacan, J. (1975) *Le Séminaire xx: Encore*, Paris: Seuil.

Lacan, J. (1977) *Écrits: A Selection*, London: Tavistock.

Lacan, J. (1981) *Le Séminaire III: Les psychoses*, Paris: Seuil.

Lacan, J. (1988) *The Seminar of Jacques Lacan: Book II. The Ego in Freud's Theory and in the Technique of Psychoanalysis, 1954–55*, trans. S. Tomaselli, New York: Norton.

Lamb, S. M. (1971) 'Linguistic and cognitive networks', in P. Garvin (ed.) *Cognition: A Multiple View*, New York: Spartan Books.

Lamb, S. M. (1974) 'Discussion', in H. Parret (ed.) *Discussing Language*, The Hague: Mouton.

Lapsley, R. and Westlake, M. (1988) *Film Theory: An Introduction*, Manchester: Manchester University Press.

Larrucia, V. (1975) 'Little Red Riding Hood's metacommentary: paradoxical injunction, semiotics and behaviour', *Modern Language Notes*, 90 517–534.

Leader, D. (1995) *Lacan for Beginners*, Cambridge: Icon Books.

Lemaire, A. (1977) *Jacques Lacan*, London: Routledge.

Lemke, J. L. (1995) *Textual Politics: Discourse and Social Dynamics*, London and Bristol, PA: Taylor & Francis.

Lévi-Strauss, C. (1977) *Structural Anthropology 1*, Harmondsworth: Penguin.

Lévi-Strauss, C. (1978) 'Structure and form: reflections on a work by Vladimir Propp', in *Structural Anthropology 2*, Harmondsworth: Penguin.

Lévi-Strauss, C. (1987) *The View from Afar*, Harmondsworth: Penguin.

Liebes, T. and Katz, E. (1986) 'Patterns of involvement in television fiction', *European Journal of Communication*, 1 151–171.

Liebes, T. and Katz, E. (1993) *The Export of Meaning: Cross-Cultural Readings of Dallas*, 2nd edn, Oxford: Polity.

Limon, J. (n.d.) 'Folklore and the Mexican in the United States: A Marxist cultural perspective', unpublished paper.

Linksz, A. (1952) *Physiology of the Eye Vol. 2*, New York: Grune & Stratton.

Livingstone, S. M. (1991) 'Audience reception: the role of the viewer in retelling romantic drama', in J. Curran and M. Gurevitch (eds) *Mass Media and Society*, London: Edward Arnold.

Lodge, D. (1981) '*Middlemarch*, and the idea of the classic realist text', in A. Kettle (ed.) *The Nineteenth Century Novel: Critical Essays and Documents*, 2nd edn, London: Heinemann.

Lombardi-Satriani, L. (1974) 'Folklore as culture of contestation', *Journal of the Folklore Institute* 11 (June–August) 92–122.

Lorimer (n.d.) *The Burushaski Language*, British Library.

Lucid, D. P. (1988) *Soviet Semiotics: An Anthology*, Baltimore, MD and London: Johns Hopkins University Press.

Luke, A. (1988) *Literacy, Textbooks and Ideology: Post-war Literacy Instruction and the Myth of Dick and Jane*, London: Falmer Press.

Lull, J. (1990) *Inside Family Viewing: Ethnographic Research on Television's Audience*, London: Routledge.

Lunt, H. G. (1952) *Grammar of the Macedonian Literary Language*, Skopje: DTZavno Knigoizdatelstvo.

Lyons, J. (1977) *Semantics*, vol. 2, Cambridge: Cambridge University Press.

Lyons, J. (1981) *Language, Meaning and Context*, London: Fontana.

MacCabe, C. (1974) 'Realism and the cinema: notes on some Brechtian theses', *Screen*, 15 (2) 7–27.

MacCabe, C. (1977) 'Theory and film: principles of realism and pleasure', *Screen*, 17 (3) 46–61.

MacCabe, C. (1978) *James Joyce and the Revolution of the Word*, London: Macmillan.

MacCabe, C. (1979) 'On discourse', *Economy and Society*, 8 (4) 279–307.

Macdonell, D. (1986) *Theories of Discourse: An Introduction*, Oxford: Blackwell.

McDonnell, K. and Robins, K. (1980) 'Marxist cultural theory: the Althusserian smokescreen', in S. Clarke, T. Lovell, K. McDonnell, K. Robins and V. J. Seidler, *One-Dimensional Marxism: Althusser and the Politics of Culture*, London: Allison & Busby.

McHoul, A. W. (1991) 'readingS', in C. D. Baker and A. Luke (eds) *Towards a Critical Sociology of Reading Pedagogy*, Amsterdam: John Benjamins.

McQuail, D. and Windahl, S. (1993) *Communication Models for the Study of Mass Communication*, Harlow: Longman.

Macey, D. (1988) *Lacan in Contexts*, London: Verso.

Macksey, R. and Donato, E. (1972) *The Structuralist Controversy: The Languages of Criticism and the Sciences of Man*, Baltimore, MD and London: Johns Hopkins University Press.

Maerz, A. and Paul, R. (1953) *A Dictionary of Color*, New York: Crowell.

Malinowski, B. (1923) 'The problem of meaning in primitive languages', supplement 1 to C. K. Ogden and I. A. Richards (eds) *The Meaning of Meaning*, London: Kegan Paul.

Malinowski, B. (1935) *Coral Gardens and their Magic* 2, London: Allen & Unwin.

Mann, P. H. (1974) *A New Survey: The Facts about Romantic Fiction*, London: Mills & Boon.

Marcus, L. (1991) 'Taking a good look: Laura Mulvey's visual and other pleasures', *New Formations*, 15 (Winter).

Marr, N. Ja. (1926) *Po ètapam jafetskoj teorii* [Through the Japhetic Theory] (publisher not given).

Mayne, J. (1993) *Cinema and Spectatorship*, London: Routledge.

Mehan, H. (1979) *Learning Lessons*, Cambridge, MA: Harvard University Press.

Melrose, R. (1993) 'Jacques Derrida and the quest for a linguistics of indeterminacy', *Journal of Literary Semantics*, XXII (2) 124–164.

Merquior, J. G. (1986) *From Prague to Paris: A Critique of Structuralist and Post-Structuralist Thought*, London: Verso.

Metz, C. (1974) *Language and Cinema*, The Hague: Mouton.

Mey, J. L. (1993) *Pragmatics: An Introduction*, Oxford: Blackwell.

Michaels, S. (1981) 'Sharing time: children's narrative and differential access to literacy', *Language in Society*, 10 423–442.

Michaels, W. B. (1980) 'The interpreter's self: Peirce on the cartesian subject', in J. P. Tompkins (ed.) *Reader–Response Criticism: From Formalism to Post-Structuralism*, Baltimore, MD and London: Johns Hopkins University Press.

Miller, J. -A. (1966) 'La suture', *Cahiers pour l'analyse* (1) 37–49.

Miller, J.-A. (1977/8) 'Suture', *Screen*, 18 (4) 24–34.

Miller, P., Nemoianu, A. and DeJong, J. (1986) 'Early reading at home: its practice and meanings in a working-class community', in B. B. Schiefellin and P. Gilmore (eds) *The Acquisition of Literacy: Ethnographic Perspectives*, Norwood, NJ: Ablex.

Milner, J. -C. (1978) *L'Amour de la langue*, Paris: Seuil.

Milner, J. -C. (1979) 'Réflexions sur l'arbitraire du signe', *Ornicar?* 5 (83).

Moi, T. (1985) *Sexual/Textual Politics*, London: Methuen.

Morin, E. (1956) *Le Cinéma ou l'homme imaginaire*, Paris.

Morley, D. (1980) *The, Nationwide Audience*, London: British Film Institute.

Morley, D. (1986) *Family Television*, London: Routledge.

Morley, D. (1992) *Television, Audiences and Cultural Studies*, London: Routledge.

Morris, C. (1946) *Signs, Language and Behavior*, New York; Prentice-Hall.

Morris, P. (1994) *The Bakhtin Reader: Selected Writings of Bakhtin, Medvedev, Voloshinov*, London: Edward Arnold.

Morson, G. S. and Emerson, C. (1989) 'Introduction: Rethinking Bakhtin', in Morson and Emerson (eds) *Rethinking Bakhtin: Extensions and Challenges*, Evanston, IL: Northwestern University Press.

Muecke, S. (1982) 'Available discourses on aborigines', *Theoretical Strategies*, Local Consumption Series 2/3.

Mulvey, L. (1975) 'Visual pleasure and narrative cinema', *Screen*, 16 (3) 6–18.

Mulvey, L. (1989) *Visual and Other Pleasures*, London: Macmillan.

Norris, C. (1982) *Deconstruction: Theory and Practice*, London: Methuen.

Norris, C. (1987) *Derrida*, London: Fontana.

Ogden, C. K. and Richards, I. A. (1985) *The Meaning of Meaning: A Study of the Influence of Language on Thought and the Science of Symbolism*, London and Boston, MA: Ark.

O'Leary, J. (1992) 'Dons block degree for philosopher', *The Times*, 25 March p. 4.

Palmer, F. R. (1990) *Semantics*, 2nd edn, Cambridge: Cambridge University Press.

Palmer, J. (1987) *The Logic of the Absurd: On Film and Television Comedy*, London: British Film Institute.

Palmer, J. (1990) *Potboilers: Methods, Concepts and Case Studies in Popular Fiction*, London: Routledge.

Palmer, J. (1994) *Taking Humour Seriously*, London: Routledge.

Pateman, T. (1983) 'How is understanding an advert possible?', in H. Davis and P. Walton, (eds) *Language, Image, Media*, Oxford: Blackwell.

Payne, M. (1993) *Reading Theory: An Introduction to Lacan, Derrida and Kristeva*, Oxford: Blackwell .

Pearce, L. (1994) *Reading Dialogics*, London: Edward Arnold.

Pêcheux, M. (1982) *Language, Semantics and Ideology*, London: Macmillan.

Peirce, C. S. (1931–58) *Collected Papers of Charles Sanders Peirce* 8 vols, ed. C. Hartshorne, P. Weiss and A. W. Burks, Cambridge, MA: Harvard University Press.

Peirce, C. S. (1955) 'Logic as semiotic: the theory of signs', in J. Buchler (ed.) *Philosophical Writings of Peirce*, New York: Dover.

Perlina, N. (1983) 'Bakhtin–Medvedev–Voloshinov: An apple of discourse', *University of Ottawa Quarterly*, 53 (1) 33–47.

Perrault, C. (1975) *Perrault's Complete Fairy Tales*, Harmondsworth: Penguin.

Petrey, S. (1990) *Speech Acts and Literary Theory*, London: Routledge.

Pharies, D. A. (1985) *Charles S. Peirce and the Linguistic Sign*, Amsterdam and Philadelphia, PA: John Benjamins.

Phelps, L. W. (1990) 'Audience and authorship: the disappearing boundary', in G. Kirsch and D. H. Roen (eds) *A Sense of Audience in Written Communication*, London and Newbury Park, CA: Sage.

Piemme, J.-M. (1975) *La Propagande inavoué*, Paris: Union Générale d'Editions.

Piemme, J. -M. (1978) *La Télévision comme on la parle*, Brussels: Labor.

Prieto, L. (1975) *Pertinence et pratique*, Paris: Minuit.

Propp, V. (1968) *Morphology of the Folktale*, Austin: University of Texas Press.

Purdie, S. (1992) 'Janice Radway, *Reading the Romance*', in M. Barker and A. Beezer (eds) *Reading into Cultural Studies*, London: Routledge.

Radway, J. (1984) *Reading the Romance: Women, Patriarchy and Popular Literature*, Chapel Hill: University of North Carolina Press.

Radway, J. (1988) 'Reception study: ethnography and the problems of dispersed audiences and nomadic subjects', *Cultural Studies*, 2 (3) 359–376.

Ramstedt, G. J. (n.d.) *A Korean Grammar*. (Further details unknown.)

Rauch, I. (1978) 'Distinguishing semiotics from linguistics and the position of language in both', in R. W. Bailey, I. Rauch and L. Matejka (eds) *The Sign: Semiotics Around the World*, Ann Arbor: Michigan Slavic Publications.

Rawls, J. (1955) 'Two concepts of rules', *Philosophical Review*.

Reid, T. B. W. (1956) 'Linguistics, structuralism, philology', *Archivum Linguisticum* 8.

Richards, B. (1994) *Disciplines of Delight: The Psychoanalysis of Popular Culture*, London: Free Association.

Russell, B. (1940) *An Inquiry into Meaning and Truth*, London: Allen & Unwin.

Sahlins, M. (1975) 'Colors and cultures', *Semiotica*, 15 (1) 1–22.

Salt, B. (1976) 'The early development of film form', *Film Form* 1 (Spring) 97–98.

Sartre, J.-P. (1967) *Words*, Harmondsworth: Penguin.

Saussure, F. de (1916) *Cours de linguistique générale*, Paris: Payot.

Saussure, F. de (1922) *Cours de linguistique générale*, 2nd edn, Paris: Payot.

Saussure, F. de. (1974) *Course in General Linguistics*, trans. W. Baskin, Glasgow: Fontana.

Schleifer, R. (1987) *A. J. Greimas and the Nature of Meaning: Linguistics, Semiotics and Discourse Theory*, London: Croom Helm.

Scribner, S. and Cole, M. (1981) *The Psychology of Literacy*, Cambridge, MA: Harvard University Press.

Searle, J. (1964) 'How to derive "ought" from "is"', *Philosophical Review* January.

Searle, J. (1969) *Speech Acts*, Cambridge: Cambridge University Press.

Searle, J. (1971) *The Campus War*, Harmondsworth: Penguin.

Searle, J. (1972) 'What is a speech act?', in P. P. Giglioli (ed.) *Language and Social Context*, Harmondsworth: Penguin.

Searle, J. (1977) 'Reiterating the differences: a reply to Derrida', *Glyph*, 1 198–208.

Searle, J. (1983a) *Intentionality*, Cambridge: Cambridge University Press.

Searle, J. (1983b) 'The world turned upside down', *New York Review of Books*, (27 October) 73–79.

Sebeok, T. A. (1972) *Perspectives in Zoosemiotics*, The Hague: Mouton.

Seiter, E., Borchers, H., Kreutzner, G. and Warth, E. -M. (1989) *Remote Control: Television, Audiences and Cultural Power*, London: Routledge.

Shepherd, D. (1989) 'Bakhtin and the reader', in K. Hirschkop and D. Shepherd (eds) *Bakhtin and Cultural Theory*, Manchester: Manchester University Press.

Sheriff, J. K. (1989) *The Fate of Meaning: Charles Peirce, Structuralism and Literature*, Princeton, NJ: Princeton University Press.

Sheriff, J. K. (1994) *Charles Peirce's Guess at the Riddle: Grounds for Human Significance*, Bloomington and Indianapolis: Indiana University Press.

Shklovsky, V. (1965) 'Sterne's *Tristram Shandy*,: stylistic commentary', in L. T. Lemon and M. J. Reis (eds) *Russian Formalist Criticism: Four Essays*, Lincoln, NB and London: University of Nebraska Press.

Silbermann, A. (1968) 'A definition of the sociology of art', *International Social Science Journal*, 20 (4) 567–588.

Silverman, D. and Torode, B. (1980) *The Material Word: Some Theories of Language and its Limits*, London: Routledge & Kegan Paul.

Silverman, K. (1983) *The Subject of Semiotics*, Oxford: Oxford University Press.

Silverstone, R. (1994) *Television and Everyday Life*, London: Routledge.

Simpson, D. (1990) 'New brooms at Fawlty Towers: Colin MacCabe and Cambridge English', in B. Robbins (ed.) *Intellectuals: Aesthetics, Politics, Academics*, Minneapolis: University of Minnesota Press.

Smith, B. H. (1978) *On the Margins of Discourse: The Relation of Literature to Language*, Chicago: University of Chicago Press.

Soriano, M. (1968) *Les Contes de Perrault*, Paris: Gallimard.

Spencer, J. and Gregory, M. J. (1964) 'An approach to the study of style', in N. E. Enkvist, J. Spencer and M. J. Gregory, *Linguistics and Style*, London: Oxford University Press.

Sperber, D. (1979) 'Claude Lévi-Strauss', in J. Sturrock (ed.) *Structuralism and Since*, Oxford: Oxford University Press.

Sperber, D. and Wilson, D. (1995) *Relevance: Communication and Cognition*, 2nd edn, Oxford: Blackwell.

Stam, R., Burgoyne, R. and Flitterman-Lewis, S. (1992) *New Vocabularies in Film Semiotics: Structuralism, Post-Structuralism and Beyond*, London: Routledge.

Sturrock, J. (1979a) 'Roland Barthes', in J. Sturrock (ed.) *Structuralism and Since*, Oxford: Oxford University Press.

Sturrock, J. (ed.) (1979b) *Structuralism and Since*, Oxford: Oxford University Press.

Sturrock, J. (1986) *Structuralism*, London: Paladin.

Suleiman, S. and Crosman, I. (eds) (1980) *The Reader in the Text: Essays on Audience and Interpretation*, Princeton, NJ: Princeton University Press.

Thibault, P. (1989) 'Genres, codes and pedagogy: towards a critical semiotic account', *Southern Review*, 21 (3) 338–362 .

Thomas, J. (1995) *Meaning in Interaction: An Introduction to Pragmatics*, Harlow: Longman.

Thorndike, E. L. and Lorge, I. (1962) *The Teacher's Word Book of 30, 000 Words*, New York: Columbia University Press.

Threadgold, T. (1987) 'The semiotics of Halliday, Vološinov and Eco', *American Journal of Semiotics*, 4 (3) 107–142.

Titunik, I. R. (1985) 'Bakhtin &/or Vološinov &/or Medvedev: Dialogue &/or doubletalk?', *Language and Literary Theory*, 5 535–564.

Titunik, I. R. (1987) 'Introduction', in V. N. Vološinov, *Freudianism: A Critical Sketch*, Bloomington: Indiana University Press.

Tobin, Y. (1990) *Semiotics and Linguistics*, Harlow: Longman.

Todorov, T. (1970) *Introduction à la littérature fantastique*, Paris: Seuil.

Todorov, T. (1984) *Mikhail Bakhtin: The Dialogical Principle*, Minneapolis: University of Minnesota Press.

Tompkins, J. P. (ed.) (1980) *Reader–Response Criticism: From Formalism to Post-Structuralism*, Baltimore, MD and London: Johns Hopkins University Press.

Turner, G. J. (1973) 'Social class and children's language of control at age five and age seven', in B. Bernstein (ed.) *Class, Codes and Control*, vol. 2, London: Routledge & Kegan Paul.

Ure, J. and Ellis, J. (1974) 'El registro en la lingüistica descriptiva y en la sociologia lingüistica', in O. Uribe-Villegas (ed.) *La sociolingüistica actual: algunos de sus problemas, planteamientos y soluciones*, Mexico: Universidad Nacional Autonoma de Mexico. Translated as 'Register in descriptive linguistics and linguistic sociology', in O. Uribe-Villegas (ed.) *Issues in Sociolinguistics*, Hague: Mouton.

Vickers, B. (1993) *Appropriating Shakespeare: Contemporary Critical Quarrels*, London and New Haven, CT: Yale University Press.

Vološinov, V. N. (1929) *Marksizm I filosofijajazyka*, Leningrad: Priboj.

Vološinov, V. N. (1973) *Marxism and the Philosophy of Language*, New York: Seminar Press.

Vološinov, V. N. (1987) *Freudianism: A Critical Sketch*, Bloomington: Indiana University Press.

Wagner, D. A., Messick, B. M. and Spratt, I. (1986) 'Studying literacy in Morocco', in B. B. Schiefellin and P. Gilmore (eds) *The Acquisition of Literacy: Ethnographic Perspectives*, Norwood, NJ: Ablex.

Walkerdine, V. (1981) 'Sex, power and pedagogy', *Screen Education*, 38 14–21.

Watzlawick, P. *et al.* (1968) *Pragmatics of Human Communication*, London: Faber & Faber.

Weber, S. (1976) 'Saussure and the apparition of language', *Modern Language Notes*, 91 913–938.

Weber, S. (1991) *Return to Freud*, Cambridge: Cambridge University Press.

Weedon, C., Tolson, A. and Mort, S. (1981) 'Theories of language and subjectivity', in S. Hall, D. Hobson, A. Lowe and P. Willis (eds) *Culture, Media, Language*, London: Hutchinson.

Wegener, P. (1885) *Untersuchen über die Grundfragen der Sprachlebens*, Halle.

Weitman, S. R. (1973) 'National flags' *Semiotica*, 8 (4) 328–367 .

Whorf, B. L. (1946) 'The Hopi language, Toreva dialect', in *Linguistic Structures of Native America*, New York: Viking Fund Publications in Anthropology.

Willemen, P. (1978) 'Notes on subjectivity: on reading Edward Branigan's "Subjectivity under siege"' *Screen*, 19 (1) 41–7.

Williams, L. (1984) 'When the woman looks' in M. A. Doane, P. Mellencamp and L. Williams (eds) *Re-vision*, Frederick, MD: American Film Institute.

Williams, R. (1977) *Marxism and Literature*, Oxford: Oxford University Press.

Williamson, J. (1978) *Decoding Advertisements: Ideology and Meaning in Advertising*, London: Marion Boyars.

Williamson, J. (1986) *Consuming Passions: the Dynamics of Popular Culture*, London: Marion Boyars.

Wittgenstein, L. (1953) *Philosophical Investigations*, Oxford: Oxford University Press.

Wollen, P. (1972) *Signs and Meaning in the Cinema*, 2nd edn., Bloomington: Indiana University Press.

Wright, W. (1975) *Six-Guns and Society*, Berkeley: University of California Press.

Yankelovich, Skelly and White. (1978) *The 1978 Consumer Research Study on Reading and Book Purchasing*, Darien, CT: The Book Industry Study Group.

Zelenin, D. K. (1930) 'Tabn slov a nurodov vostočnoj Evropy i severnoj Azii II' *Shornik Muzeja Antropologie i Etnografii 9*

Zeman, J. J. (1973) 'Peirce's theory of signs', in T. A. Sebeok (ed.) *A Perfusion of Signs*, Bloomington and London: Indiana University Press.

Zinsser, C. (1986) 'For the Bible tells me so: teaching children in a fundamentalist church' in B. B. Schiefellin and P. Gilmore (eds) *The Acquisition of Literacy: Ethnographic Perspectives*, Norwood, NJ: Ablex.

Index